THE OXFORD BOOK OF AMERICAN ESSAYS

CHOSEN BY

BRANDER MATTHEWS

Essay Index in Reprint

Core Collection Books, inc.
GREAT NECK, NEW YORK

First Published 1914
Reprinted 1978

International Standard Book Number
0-8486-3008-4

Library of Congress — Catalog Card No. 77-092511

PRINTED IN THE UNITED STATES OF AMERICA

CONTENTS

	PAGE
INTRODUCTION	V
THE EPHEMERA: AN EMBLEM OF HUMAN LIFE	1
Benjamin Franklin (1706-1790).	
THE WHISTLE	4
Benjamin Franklin (1706-1790).	
DIALOGUE BETWEEN FRANKLIN AND THE GOUT	7
Benjamin Franklin (1706-1790).	
CONSOLATION FOR THE OLD BACHELOR	15
Francis Hopkinson (1737-1791).	
JOHN BULL	21
Washington Irving (1783-1859).	
THE MUTABILITY OF LITERATURE	34
Washington Irving (1783-1859).	
KEAN'S ACTING	47
Richard Henry Dana (1787-1879).	
GIFTS	62
Ralph Waldo Emerson (1803-1882).	
USES OF GREAT MEN	67
Ralph Waldo Emerson (1803-1882).	
BUDS AND BIRD-VOICES	88
Nathaniel Hawthorne (1804-1864).	
THE PHILOSOPHY OF COMPOSITION	99
Edgar Allan Poe (1809-1849).	
BREAD AND THE NEWSPAPER	114
Oliver Wendell Holmes (1809-1894).	
WALKING	128
Henry David Thoreau (1817-1862).	
ON A CERTAIN CONDESCENSION IN FOREIGNERS	166
James Russell Lowell (1819-1891).	
PREFACE TO "LEAVES OF GRASS"	194
Walt Whitman (1819-1892).	

Contents

	PAGE
AMERICANISM IN LITERATURE	213
Thomas Wentworth Higginson (1823-1911).	
THACKERAY IN AMERICA	229
George William Curtis (1824-1892).	
OUR MARCH TO WASHINGTON	241
Theodore Winthrop (1828-1861).	
CALVIN (A Study of Character)	268
Charles Dudley Warner (1829-1900).	
FIVE AMERICAN CONTRIBUTIONS TO CIVILIZATION	280
Charles William Eliot (1834-)	
I TALK OF DREAMS	308
William Dean Howells (1837-).	
AN IDYL OF THE HONEY-BEE	331
John Burroughs (1837-).	
CUT-OFF COPPLES'S	351
Clarence King (1842-1901).	
THE THÉÂTRE FRANÇAIS	368
Henry James (1843-).	
THEOCRITUS ON CAPE COD	394
Hamilton Wright Mabie (1846-).	
COLONIALISM IN THE UNITED STATES	410
Henry Cabot Lodge (1850-).	
NEW YORK AFTER PARIS	440
William Crary Brownell (1851-).	
THE TYRANNY OF THINGS	467
Edward Sandford Martin (1856-).	
FREE TRADE VS. PROTECTION IN LITERATURE	475
Samuel McChord Crothers (1857-).	
DANTE AND THE BOWERY	480
Theodore Roosevelt (1858-).	
THE REVOLT OF THE UNFIT	489
Nicholas Murray Butler (1862-).	
ON TRANSLATING THE ODES OF HORACE	497
William Peterfield Trent (1862-).	

INTRODUCTION

THE customary antithesis between "American" literature and "English" literature is unfortunate and misleading in that it seems to exclude American authors from the noble roll of those who have contributed to the literature of our mother-tongue. Of course, when we consider it carefully we cannot fail to see that the literature of a language is one and indivisible and that the nativity or the domicile of those who make it matters nothing. Just as Alexandrian literature is Greek, so American literature is English; and as Theocritus demands inclusion in any account of Greek literature, so Thoreau cannot be omitted from any history of English literature as a whole. The works of Anthony Hamilton and Rousseau, Mme. de Staël and M. Maeterlinck are not more indisputably a part of the literature of the French language than the works of Franklin and Emerson, of Hawthorne and Poe are part of the literature of the English language. Theocritus may never have set foot on the soil of Greece, and Thoreau never adventured himself on the Atlantic to visit the island-home of his ancestors; yet the former expressed himself in Greek and the latter in English,—and how can either be neglected in any comprehensive survey of the literature of his own tongue?

None the less is it undeniable that there is in Franklin and Emerson, in Walt Whitman and Mark Twain, whatever their mastery of the idiom they inherited in common with Steele and Carlyle, with Browning and Lamb, an indefinable and intangible flavor which distinguishes the first group from the second. The men who have set down the feelings and the thoughts, the words and the deeds of the inhabitants of the United States have not quite the same outlook on life that we find in the men who have made a similar record in the British Isles. The social atmosphere is not the same on the opposite shores of the Western ocean; and the social organization is different in many particulars. For all that American literature is,—in the apt phrase of Mr. Howells,—"a condition of English literature," nevertheless it is also distinctively American. American writers are as loyal to the finer traditions of English literature as British writers are; they take an equal pride that they are also heirs of Chaucer and Dryden and subjects of King Shakspere; yet they cannot help having the note of their own nationality.

Green, when he came to the Fourth of July, 1776, declared that thereafter the history of the English-speaking people flowed in two currents; and it is equally obvious that the stream of English literature has now two channels. The younger and the smaller is American—and what can we call the older and the ampler except British? A century ago there were published collections entitled the *British Poets,* the *British Novelists,* and the *British Essayists;* and the adjective was probably then chosen to indicate that these gatherings included the work of Scotch and Irish writers. Whatever the reason, the choice was happy; and the same adjective would serve to indicate now that the selections excluded the work of American writers. The British branch of English literature is the richer and the more various; yet the American branch has its own richness and its own variety, even if these qualities have revealed themselves only in the past hundred years.

It may be noted also that although American literature has not been adorned by so great a galaxy of brilliant names

Introduction

as illumined British literature in the nineteenth century, it has had the good fortune to possess more authors of cosmopolitan fame than can be found in the German literature of the past hundred years, in the Italian, or in the Spanish. A forgotten American essayist once asserted that "foreign nations are a contemporaneous posterity," and even if this smart saying is not to be taken too literally, it has its significance. There is therefore food for thought in the fact that at least half a dozen, not to say half a score, of American authors have won wide popularity outside the limits of their own language,—a statement which could not be made of as many German or Italian or Spanish authors of the nineteenth century. From the death of Goethe to the arrival of the playwrights of the present generation, perhaps Heine is the sole German writer either of prose or of verse who has established his reputation broadly among the readers of other tongues than his own. And not more than one or two Spanish or Italian authors have been received even by their fellow Latins, as warmly as the French and the Germans have welcomed Cooper and Poe, Emerson and Mark Twain.

It is to present typical and characteristic examples of the American contribution to English literature in the essay-form that this volume has been prepared. Perhaps the term "essay-form" is not happily chosen since the charm of the essay lies in the fact that it is not formal, that it may be whimsical in its point of departure, and capricious in its ramblings after it has got itself under way. Even the Essay is itself a chameleon, changing color while we study it. There is little in common between Locke's austere *Essay on the Human Understanding* and Lamb's fantastic and frolicsome essay on *Roast Pig*. He would be bold indeed who should take compass and chain to measure off the precise territory of the Essay and to mark with scientific exactness the boundaries which separate it from the Address on the one side and from the Letter on the other.

"Some (there are) that turn over all books and are equally searching in all papers," said Ben Jonson; "that write out of what they presently find or meet, without choice. . . . Such are all the Essayists, ever their master Montaigne." Bacon and Emerson followed in the footsteps of Montaigne, and present us with the results of their browsings among books and of their own dispersed meditations. In their hands the essay lacks cohesion and unity; it is essentially discursive. Montaigne never stuck to his text, when he had one; and the paragraphs of any of Emerson's essays might be shuffled without increasing their fortuitous discontinuity.

After Montaigne and Bacon came Steele and Addison, in whose hands the essay broadened its scope and took on a new aspect. The eighteenth century essay is so various that it may be accepted as the forerunner of the nineteenth century magazine, with its character-sketches and its brief tales, its literary and dramatic criticism, its obituary commemorations and its serial stories—for what but a serial story is the succession of papers devoted to the sayings and doings of Sir Roger? It was a new departure, although the writers of the *Tatler* and of the *Spectator* had profited by the *Conversations* of Walton and by the *Characters* of La Bruyère, by the epistles of Horace and by the comedies of Molière. (Has it ever been pointed out that the method of Steele and Addison in depicting Sir Roger is curiously akin to the method of Molière in presenting M. Jourdain?)

The delightful form of poetry which we call by a French name, *vers de société*, (although it has flourished more abundantly in English literature than in French) and which

Mr. Austin Dobson, one of its supreme masters, prefers to call by Cowper's term, "familiar verse," may be accepted as the metrical equivalent of the prose essay as this was developed and expanded by the English writers of the eighteenth century. And as the familiar verse of our language is ampler and richer than that of any other tongue, so also is the familiar essay. Indeed, the essay is one of the most characteristic expressions of the quality of our race. In its ease and its lightness and its variety, it is almost unthinkable in German; and even in French it is far less frequent than in English and far less assiduously cultivated.

As Emerson trod in the footsteps of Bacon so Washington Irving walked in the trail blazed by Steele and Addison and Goldsmith; and Franklin earlier, although his essays are in fact only letters, had revealed his possession of the special quality the essay demands,—the playful wisdom of a man of the world who is also a man of letters. Indeed, Dr. Franklin was far better fitted to shine as an essayist than his more ponderous contemporary, Dr. Johnson; certainly Franklin would never have "made little fishes talk like whales." And in the nineteenth century the American branch of English literature has had a group of essayists less numerous than that which adorned the British branch, but not less interesting or less important to their own people.

Among these American essayists we may find all sorts and conditions of writers,—poets adventuring themselves in prose, novelists eschewing story-telling, statesmen turning for a moment to matters of less weight, men of science and men of affairs chatting about themselves and airing their opinions at large. In their hands, as in the hands of their British contemporaries, the essay remains infinitely various, refusing to conform to any single type, and insisting on being itself and on expressing its author. We find in the best of these American essayists the familiar style and the everyday vocabulary, the apparent simplicity and the seeming absence of effort, the horror of pedantry and the scorn of affectation, which are the abiding characteristics of the true essay. We find also the flavor of good talk, of the sprightly conversation that may sparkle in front of a wood fire and that often vanishes with the curling blue smoke.

It is the bounden duty of every maker of an anthology to set forth the principles that have guided him in the choice of the examples he is proffering to the public. The present editor has excluded purely literary criticism, as not quite falling within the boundaries of the essay, properly so-called. Then he has avoided all set orations, although he has not hesitated to include more than one paper originally prepared to be read aloud by its writer, because these examples seemed to him to fall within the boundaries of the essay. (Nearly all of Emerson's essays, it may be noted, had been lectures in an early stage of their existence.) Furthermore he has omitted all fiction, strictly to be so termed, although he would gladly have welcomed an apologue like Mark Twain's "Traveling with a Reformer," which is essentially an essay despite its use of dialogue. He has included also Franklin's "Dialogue with the Gout," which is instinct with the true spirit of the essay; and he has accepted as essays Franklin's "Ephemera" and "The Whistle," although they were both of them letters to the same lady. As the essay flowers out of leisure and out of culture, and as there has been in the United States no long background of easy tranquillity, there is in the American branch of English literature a relative deficiency in certain of the lighter forms of the essay more abundantly represented in the British branch; and therefore the less frequent examples of these lighter forms have here been companioned by graver discussions, never grave enough, however, to be described as disquisitions. Finally, every selection is presented entire, except that Dana's paper on Kean's acting has been shorn of a needless preparatory note.

BRANDER MATTHEWS.

THE EPHEMERA: AN EMBLEM OF HUMAN LIFE

TO MADAME BRILLON, OF PASSY

Benjamin Franklin

You may remember, my dear friend, that when we lately spent that happy day in the delightful garden and sweet society of the Moulin Joly, I stopped a little in one of our walks, and stayed some time behind the company. We had been shown numberless skeletons of a kind of little fly, called an ephemera, whose successive generations, we were told, were bred and expired within the day. I happened to see a living company of them on a leaf, who appeared to be engaged in conversation. You know I understand all the inferior animal tongues. My too great application to the study of them is the best excuse I can give for the little progress I have made in your charming language. I listened through curiosity to the discourse of these little creatures; but as they, in their national vivacity, spoke three or four together, I could make but little of their conversation. I found, however, by some broken expressions that I heard now and then, they were disputing warmly on the merit of two foreign musicians, one a *cousin,* the other a *moscheto;* in which dispute they spent their time, seemingly as regardless of the shortness of life as if they had been sure of living a month. Happy people! thought I; you are certainly under a wise, just, and mild government, since you have no public grievances to complain of, nor any subject of contention but the perfections and imperfections of foreign music. I turned my head from them to an old gray-headed one, who was single on another leaf, and talking to himself. Being amused with his soliloquy, I put it down in writing, in hopes it will likewise amuse her to whom I am so much indebted for the most pleasing of all amusements, her delicious company and heavenly harmony.

"It was," said he, "the opinion of learned philosophers of our race, who lived and flourished long before my time, that this vast world, the Moulin Joly, could not itself subsist more than eighteen hours; and I think there was some foundation for that opinion, since, by the apparent motion of the great luminary that gives life to all nature, and which in my time has evidently declined considerably towards the ocean at the end of our earth, it must then finish its course, be extinguished in the waters that surround us, and leave the world in cold and darkness, necessarily producing universal death and destruction. I have lived seven of those hours, a great age, being no less than four hundred and twenty minutes of time. How very few of us continue so long! I have seen generations born, flourish, and expire. My present friends are the children and grandchildren of the friends of my youth, who are now, alas, no more! And I must soon follow them; for, by the course of nature, though still in health, I cannot expect to live above seven or eight minutes longer. What now avails all my toil and labor in amassing honey-dew on this leaf, which I cannot live to enjoy! What the political struggles I have been engaged in for the good of my compatriot inhabitants of this bush, or my philosophical studies for the benefit of our race in general! for in politics what can laws do without morals? Our present race of ephemeræ will in a course of minutes become corrupt,

The Ephemera: An Emblem of Human Life

like those of other and older bushes, and consequently as wretched. And in philosophy how small our progress! Alas! art is long, and life is short! My friends would comfort me with the idea of a name they say I shall leave behind me; and they tell me I have lived long enough to nature and to glory. But what will fame be to an ephemera who no longer exists? And what will become of all history in the eighteenth hour, when the world itself, even the whole Moulin Joly, shall come to its end and be buried in universal ruin?"

To me, after all my eager pursuits, no solid pleasures now remain, but the reflection of a long life spent in meaning well, the sensible conversation of a few good lady ephemeræ, and now and then a kind smile and a tune from the ever amiable *Brillante*.

THE WHISTLE

TO MADAME BRILLON

Benjamin Franklin

I RECEIVED my dear friend's two letters, one for Wednesday and one for Saturday. This is again Wednesday. I do not deserve one for to-day, because I have not answered the former. But, indolent as I am, and averse to writing, the fear of having no more of your pleasing epistles, if I do not contribute to the correspondence, obliges me to take up my pen; and as Mr. B. has kindly sent me word that he sets out to-morrow to see you, instead of spending this Wednesday evening, as I have done its namesakes, in your delightful company, I sit down to spend it in thinking of you, in writing to you, and in reading over and over again your letters.

I am charmed with your description of Paradise, and with your plan of living there; and I approve much of your conclusion, that, in the meantime, we should draw all the good we can from this world. In my opinion we might all draw more good from it than we do, and suffer less evil, if we would take care not to give too much for *whistles*. For to me it seems that most of the unhappy people we meet with are become so by neglect of that caution.

You ask what I mean? You love stories, and will excuse my telling one of myself.

When I was a child of seven years old, my friends, on a holiday, filled my pocket with coppers. I went directly to a shop where they sold toys for children; and being

The Whistle

charmed with the sound of a *whistle,* that I met by the way in the hands of another boy, I voluntarily offered and gave all my money for one. I then came home, and went whistling all over the house, much pleased with my *whistle,* but disturbing all the family. My brothers, and sisters, and cousins, understanding the bargain I had made, told me I had given four times as much for it as it was worth; put me in mind what good things I might have bought with the rest of the money; and laughed at me so much for my folly, that I cried with vexation; and the reflection gave me more chagrin than the *whistle* gave me pleasure.

This, however, was afterwards of use to me, the impression continuing on my mind; so that often, when I was tempted to buy some unnecessary thing, I said to myself, *Don't give too much for the whistle;* and I saved my money.

As I grew up, came into the world, and observed the actions of men, I thought I met with many, very many, who *gave too much for the whistle.*

When I saw one too ambitious of court favor, sacrificing his time in attendance on levees, his repose, his liberty, his virtue, and perhaps his friends, to attain it, I have said to myself, *This man gives too much for his whistle.*

When I saw another fond of popularity, constantly employing himself in political bustles, neglecting his own affairs, and ruining them by that neglect, *He pays, indeed,* said I, *too much for his whistle.*

If I knew a miser, who gave up every kind of comfortable living, all the pleasure of doing good to others, all the esteem of his fellow-citizens, and the joys of benevolent friendship, for the sake of accumulating wealth, *Poor man,* said I, *you pay too much for your whistle.*

When I met with a man of pleasure, sacrificing every laudable improvement of the mind, or of his fortune, to mere corporeal sensations, and ruining his health in their pursuit, *Mistaken man,* said I, *you are providing pain for yourself, instead of pleasure; you give too much for your whistle.*

If I see one fond of appearance, or fine clothes, fine houses, fine furniture, fine equipages, all above his fortune, for which he contracts debts, and ends his career in a prison, *Alas!* say I, *he has paid dear, very dear, for his whistle.*

When I see a beautiful sweet-tempered girl married to an ill-natured brute of a husband, *What a pity,* say I, *that she should pay so much for a whistle!*

In short, I conceive that great part of the miseries of mankind are brought upon them by the false estimates they have made of the value of things, and by their *giving too much for their whistles.*

Yet I ought to have charity for these unhappy people, when I consider that, with all this wisdom of which I am boasting, there are certain things in the world so tempting, for example, the apples of King John, which happily are not to be bought; for if they were put to sale by auction, I might very easily be led to ruin myself in the purchase, and find that I had once more given too much for the *whistle.*

Adieu, my dear friend, and believe me ever yours very sincerely and with unalterable affection.

DIALOGUE BETWEEN FRANKLIN AND THE GOUT

Midnight, 22 October, 1780.

FRANKLIN. Eh! Oh! eh! What have I done to merit these cruel sufferings?

GOUT. Many things; you have ate and drank too freely, and too much indulged those legs of yours in their indolence.

FRANKLIN. Who is it that accuses me?

GOUT. It is I, even I, the Gout.

FRANKLIN. What! my enemy in person?

GOUT. No, not your enemy.

FRANKLIN. I repeat it, my enemy; for you would not only torment my body to death, but ruin my good name; you reproach me as a glutton and a tippler; now all the world, that knows me, will allow that I am neither the one nor the other.

GOUT. The world may think as it pleases; it is always very complaisant to itself, and sometimes to its friends; but I very well know that the quantity of meat and drink proper for a man, who takes a reasonable degree of exercise, would be too much for another, who never takes any.

FRANKLIN. I take—eh! oh!—as much exercise—eh!— as I can, Madam Gout. You know my sedentary state, and on that account, it would seem, Madam Gout, as if you might spare me a little, seeing it is not altogether my own fault.

GOUT. Not a jot; your rhetoric and your politeness are thrown away; your apology avails nothing. If your situation in life is a sedentary one, your amusements, your recreation, at least, should be active. You ought to walk or ride; or, if the weather prevents that, play at billiards. But let us examine your course of life. While the mornings are long, and you have leisure to go abroad, what do you do? Why, instead of gaining an appetite for breakfast, by salutary exercise, you amuse yourself with books, pamphlets, or newspapers, which commonly are not worth the reading. Yet you eat an inordinate breakfast, four dishes of tea, with cream, and one or two buttered toasts, with slices of hung beef, which I fancy are not things the most easily digested. Immediately afterwards you sit down to write at your desk, or converse with persons who apply to you on business. Thus the time passes till one, without any kind of bodily exercise. But all this I could pardon, in regard, as you say, to your sedentary condition. But what is your practice after dinner? Walking in the beautiful gardens of those friends with whom you have dined would be the choice of men of sense; yours is to be fixed down to chess, where you are found engaged for two or three hours! This is your perpetual recreation, which is the least eligible of any for a sedentary man, because, instead of accelerating the motion of the fluids, the rigid attention it requires helps to retard the circulation and obstruct internal secretions. Wrapt in the speculations of this wretched game, you destroy your constitution. What can be expected from such a course of living, but a body replete with stagnant humors, ready to fall prey to all kinds of dangerous maladies, if I, the Gout, did not occasionally bring you relief by agitating those humors, and so purifying or dissipating them? If it was in some nook or alley in Paris, deprived of walks, that you played awhile at chess after dinner, this might be excusable; but the same taste prevails with you in Passy, Auteuil, Montmartre, or

Dialogue Between Franklin and the Gout

Sanoy, places where there are the finest gardens and walks, a pure air, beautiful women, and most agreeable and instructive conversation; all which you might enjoy by frequenting the walks. But these are rejected for this abominable game of chess. Fie, then, Mr. Franklin! But amidst my instructions, I had almost forgot to administer my wholesome corrections; so take that twinge,—and that.

FRANKLIN. Oh! eh! oh! Ohhh! As much instruction as you please, Madam Gout, and as many reproaches; but pray, Madam, a truce with your corrections!

GOUT. No, Sir, no,—I will not abate a particle of what is so much for your good,—therefore——

FRANKLIN. Oh! ehhh!—It is not fair to say I take no exercise, when I do very often, going out to dine and returning in my carriage.

GOUT. That, of all imaginable exercises, is the most slight and insignificant, if you allude to the motion of a carriage suspended on springs. By observing the degree of heat obtained by different kinds of motion, we may form an estimate of the quantity of exercise given by each. Thus, for example, if you turn out to walk in winter with cold feet, in an hour's time you will be in a glow all over; ride on horseback, the same effect will scarcely be perceived by four hours' round trotting; but if you loll in a carriage, such as you have mentioned, you may travel all day and gladly enter the last inn to warm your feet by a fire. Flatter yourself then no longer, that half an hour's airing in your carriage deserves the name of exercise. Providence has appointed few to roll in carriages, while he has given to all a pair of legs, which are machines infinitely more commodious and serviceable. Be grateful, then, and make a proper use of yours. Would you know how they forward the circulation of your fluids, in the very action of transporting you from place to place; observe when you walk, that all your weight is alternately thrown from one leg to the other; this occasions a great pressure on the vessels of the foot, and repels their contents; when relieved, by the weight being thrown on the other foot, the vessels of the first are allowed to replenish, and, by a return of this weight, this repulsion again succeeds; thus accelerating the circulation of the blood. The heat produced in any given time depends on the degree of this acceleration; the fluids are shaken, the humors attenuated, the secretions facilitated, and all goes well; the cheeks are ruddy, and health is established. Behold your fair friend at Auteuil; a lady who received from bounteous nature more really useful science than half a dozen such pretenders to philosophy as you have been able to extract from all your books. When she honors you with a visit, it is on foot. She walks all hours of the day, and leaves indolence, and its concomitant maladies, to be endured by her horses. In this, see at once the preservative of her health and personal charms. But when you go to Auteuil, you must have your carriage, though it is no farther from Passy to Auteuil than from Auteuil to Passy.

FRANKLIN. Your reasonings grow very tiresome.

GOUT. I stand corrected. I will be silent and continue my office; take that, and that.

FRANKLIN. Oh! Ohh! Talk on, I pray you.

GOUT. No, no; I have a good number of twinges for you to-night, and you may be sure of some more to-morrow.

FRANKLIN. What, with such a fever! I shall go distracted. Oh! eh! Can no one bear it for me?

GOUT. Ask that of your horses; they have served you faithfully.

FRANKLIN. How can you so cruelly sport with my torments?

GOUT. Sport! I am very serious. I have here a list of offenses against your own health distinctly written, and can justify every stroke inflicted on you.

FRANKLIN. Read it then.

GOUT. It is too long a detail; but I will briefly mention some particulars.

FRANKLIN. Proceed. I am all attention.

GOUT. Do you remember how often you have promised yourself, the following morning, a walk in the grove of Boulogne, in the garden de la Muette, or in your own garden, and have violated your promise, alleging, at one time, it was too cold, at another too warm, too windy, too moist, or what else you pleased; when in truth it was too nothing, but your insuperable love of ease?

FRANKLIN. That I confess may have happened occasionally, probably ten times in a year.

GOUT. Your confession is very far short of the truth; the gross amount is one hundred and ninety-nine times.

FRANKLIN. Is it possible?

GOUT. So possible, that it is fact; you may rely on the accuracy of my statement. You know M. Brillon's gardens, and what fine walks they contain; you know the handsome flight of an hundred steps, which lead from the terrace above to the lawn below. You have been in the practice of visiting this amiable family twice a week, after dinner, and it is a maxim of your own, that "a man may take as much exercise in walking a mile, up and down stairs, as in ten on level ground." What an opportunity was here for you to have had exercise in both these ways! Did you embrace it, and how often?

FRANKLIN. I cannot immediately answer that question.

GOUT. I will do it for you; not once.

FRANKLIN. Not once?

Gout. Even so. During the summer you went there at six o'clock. You found the charming lady, with her lovely children and friends, eager to walk with you, and entertain you with their agreeable conversation; and what has been your choice? Why, to sit on the terrace, satisfy yourself with the fine prospect, and passing your eye over the beauties of the garden below, without taking one step to descend and walk about in them. On the contrary, you call for tea and the chess-board; and lo! you are occupied in your seat till nine o'clock, and that besides two hours' play after dinner; and then, instead of walking home, which would have bestirred you a little, you step into your carriage. How absurd to suppose that all this carelessness can be reconcilable with health, without my interposition!

Franklin. I am convinced now of the justness of Poor Richard's remark, that "Our debts and our sins are always greater than we think for."

Gout. So it is. You philosophers are sages in your maxims, and fools in your conduct.

Franklin. But do you charge among my crimes, that I return in a carriage from M. Brillon's?

Gout. Certainly; for, having been seated all the while, you cannot object the fatigue of the day, and cannot want therefore the relief of a carriage.

Franklin. What then would you have me do with my carriage?

Gout. Burn it if you choose; you would at least get heat out of it once in this way; or, if you dislike that proposal, here's another for you; observe the poor peasants, who work in the vineyards and grounds about the villages of Passy, Auteuil, Chaillot, etc.; you may find every day among these deserving creatures, four or five old men and women, bent and perhaps crippled by weight of years, and too long and too great labor. After a most fatiguing day, these people have to trudge a mile or two to their smoky huts. Order your coachman to set them down. This is an act that will be good for your soul; and, at the same time, after your visit to the Brillons, if you return on foot, that will be good for your body.

FRANKLIN. Ah! how tiresome you are!

GOUT. Well, then, to my office; it should not be forgotten that I am your physician. There.

FRANKLIN. Ohhh! what a devil of a physician!

GOUT. How ungrateful you are to say so! Is it not I who, in the character of your physician, have saved you from the palsy, dropsy, and apoplexy? one or other of which would have done for you long ago, but for me.

FRANKLIN. I submit, and thank you for the past, but entreat the discontinuance of your visits for the future; for, in my mind, one had better die than be cured so dolefully. Permit me just to hint, that I have also not been unfriendly to *you*. I never feed physician or quack of any kind, to enter the list against you; if then you do not leave me to my repose, it may be said you are ungrateful too.

GOUT. I can scarcely acknowledge that as any objection. As to quacks, I despise them; they may kill you indeed, but cannot injure me. And, as to regular physicians, they are at last convinced that the gout, in such a subject as you are, is no disease, but a remedy; and wherefore cure a remedy?—but to our business,—there.

FRANKLIN. Oh! oh!—for Heaven's sake leave me! and I promise faithfully never more to play at chess, but to take exercise daily, and live temperately.

GOUT. I know you too well. You promise fair; but, after a few months of good health, you will return to your old habits; your fine promises will be forgotten like the forms of the last year's clouds. Let us then finish the account, and I will go. But I leave you with an assurance of visiting you again at a proper time and place; for my object is your good, and you are sensible now that I am your *real friend*.

CONSOLATION FOR THE OLD BACHELOR

Francis Hopkinson

Mr. Aitken: Your Old Bachelor having pathetically represented the miseries of his solitary situation, severely reproaching himself for having neglected to marry in his younger days, I would fain alleviate his distress, by showing that it is possible he might have been as unhappy—even in the honorable state of matrimony.

I am a shoemaker in this city, and by my industry and attention have been enabled to maintain my wife and a daughter, now six years old, in comfort and respect; and to lay by a little at the year's end, against a rainy day.

My good wife had long teased me to take her to New York, in order to visit Mrs. Snip, the lady of an eminent taylor in that city, and her cousin; from whom she had received many pressing invitations.

This jaunt had been the daily subject of discussion at breakfast, dinner, and supper for a month before the time fixed upon for putting it in execution. As our daughter Jenny could by no means be left at home, many and great were the preparations to equip Miss and her Mamma for this important journey; and yet, as my wife assured me, there was nothing provided but what was *absolutely necessary,* and which we could not possibly do without. My purse sweat at every pore.

At last, the long-expected day arrived, preceded by a very restless night. For, as my wife could not sleep for thinking on the approaching jaunt, neither would she suffer me to repose in quiet. If I happened through wearisomeness to fall into a slumber, she immediately roused me by some unseasonable question or remark: frequently asking if I was sure the apprentice had greased the chair-wheels, and seen that the harness was clean and in good order; often observing how surprised her cousin *Snip* would be to see us; and as often wondering how poor dear Miss *Jenny* would bear the fatigue of the journey. Thus past the night in delightful discourse, if that can with propriety be called a discourse, wherein my wife was the only speaker—my replies never exceeding the monosyllables *yes* or *no,* murmured between sleeping and waking.

No sooner was it fair daylight, but up started my notable wife, and soon roused the whole family. The little trunk was stuffed with baggage, even to bursting, and tied behind the chair, and the chair-box was crammed with trumpery which *we could not possibly do without.* Miss *Jenny* was drest, and breakfast devoured in haste: the old negro wench was called in, and the charge of the house committed to her care; and the two apprentices and the hired maid received many wholesome cautions and instructions for their conduct during our absence, all which they most liberally promised to observe; whilst I attended, with infinite patience, the adjustment of these preliminaries.

At length, however, we set off, and, turning the first corner, lost sight of our habitation, with great regret on my part, and no less joy on the part of Miss *Jenny* and her Mamma.

When we got to Poole's Bridge, there happened to be a great concourse of wagons, carts, &c., so that we could not pass for some time—Miss *Jenny* frightened—my wife very impatient and uneasy—wondered I did not call out to those impudent fellows to make way for us; observing that I had not the spirit of a louse. Having got through this difficulty, we proceeded without obstruction—my wife in good-humor again—Miss *Jenny* in high spirits. At *Kensington* fresh troubles arise. "Bless me, Miss *Jenny*," says my wife, "where is the bandbox?" "I don't know, Mamma; the last time I saw it, it was on the table in your room." What's to be done? The bandbox is left behind—it contains Miss *Jenny's* new wire-cap—there is no possibility of doing without it—as well no New York as no wire-cap—there is no alternative, we must e'en go back for it. Teased and mortified as I was, my good wife administered consolation by observing, "That it was my business to see that everything was put into the chair that ought to be, but there was no depending upon me for anything; and that she plainly saw I undertook this journey with an ill-will, merely because she had set her heart upon it." Silent patience was my only remedy. An hour and a half restored to us this essential requisite—the wire-cap—and brought us back to the place where we first missed it.

After innumerable difficulties and unparalleled dangers, occasioned by ruts, stumps, and tremendous bridges, we arrived at Neshamony ferry: but how to cross it was the question. My wife protested that neither she nor *Jenny* would go over in the boat with the horse. I assured her that there was not the least danger; that the horse was as quiet as a dog, and that I would hold him by the bridle all the way. These assurances had little weight: the most forcible argument was that she must go that way or not at all, for there was no other boat to be had. Thus persuaded, she ventured in—the flies were troublesome—the horse kicked—my wife in panics—Miss *Jenny* in tears. *Ditto* at *Trenton-ferry*.

As we started pretty early, and as the days were long, we reached Trenton by two o'clock. Here we dined. My wife found fault with everything; and whilst she disposed of what I thought a tolerable hearty meal, declared there was nothing fit to eat. Matters, however, would have gone on pretty well, but Miss *Jenny* began to cry with the toothache—sad lamentations over Miss *Jenny*—all my fault because I had not made the glazier replace a broken pane in her chamber window. N. B. I had been twice for him, and he promised to come, but was not so good as his word.

After dinner we again entered upon our journey—my wife in good-humor—Miss *Jenny's* toothache much easier—various chat—I acknowledge everything my wife says for fear of discomposing her. We arrive in good time at Princetown. My wife and daughter admire the College. We refresh ourselves with tea, and go to bed early, in order to be up by times for the next day's expedition.

In the morning we set off again in tolerable good-humor, and proceeded happily as far as *Rocky-hill*. Here my wife's fears and terrors returned with great force. I drove as carefully as possible; but coming to a place where one of the wheels must unavoidably go over the point of a small rock, my wife, in a great fright, seized hold of one of the reins, which happening to be the wrong one, she pulled the horse so as to force the wheel higher up the rock than it would otherwise have gone, and overset the chair. We were all tumbled hickledy-pickledy, into the road—Miss *Jenny's* face all bloody—the woods echo to her cries—my wife in a fainting-fit—and I in great misery; secretly and most devoutly wishing cousin *Snip* at the devil. Matters begin to mend—my wife recovers—Miss *Jenny* has only received a slight scratch on one of her cheeks—the horse stands quite still, and none of the harness broke. Matters grew worse again; the twine with which the bandbox was tied had broke in the fall, and the aforesaid wire-cap lay soaking in a nasty mudpuddle—grievous lamentations over the wire-cap—all my fault because I did not tie it better—

no remedy—no wire-caps to be bought at *Rocky-hill*. At night my wife discovered a small bruise on her hip—was apprehensive it might mortify—did not know but the bone might be broken or splintered—many instances of mortifications occasioned by small injuries.

After passing unhurt over the imminent dangers of *Passayack* and *Hackensack* rivers, and the yet more tremendous horrors of *Pawlas-hook* ferry, we arrived, at the close of the third day, at cousin *Snip's* in the city of New York.

Here we sojourned a tedious week; my wife spent as much money as would have maintained my family for a month at home, in purchasing a hundred useless articles *which we could not possibly do without;* and every night when we went to bed fatigued me with encomiums on her cousin *Snip;* leading to a history of the former grandeur of her family, and concluding with insinuations that I did not treat her with the attention and respect I ought.

On the seventh day my wife and cousin *Snip* had a pretty warm altercation respecting the comparative elegancies and advantages of New York and Philadelphia. The dispute ran high, and many aggravating words past between the two advocates. The next morning my wife declared that my business would not admit of a longer absence from home —and so after much ceremonious complaisance—in which my wife was by no means exceeded by her very polite cousin—we left the famous city of New York; and I with heart-felt satisfaction looked forward to the happy period of our safe arrival in Water-street, Philadelphia.

But this blessing was not to be obtained without much vexation and trouble. But lest I should seem tedious I shall not recount the adventures of our return—how we were caught in a thunderstorm—how our horse failed, by which we were benighted three miles from our stage—how my wife's panics returned—how Miss *Jenny* howled, and how very miserable I was made. Suffice it to say, that, after many distressing disasters, we arrived at the door of our own habitation in Water-street.

No sooner had we entered the house than we were informed that one of my apprentices had run away with the hired-maid, nobody knew where; the old negro had got drunk, fallen into the fire, and burnt out one of her eyes; and our best china-bowl was broken.

My good wife contrived, with her usual ingenuity, to throw the blame of all these misfortunes upon me. As this was a consolation to which I had been long accustomed in all untoward cases, I had recourse to my usual remedy, viz., silent patience. After sincerely praying that I might never more see cousin *Snip,* I sat industriously down to my trade, in order to retrieve my manifold losses.

This is only a miniature picture of the married state, which I present to your *Old Bachelor,* in hopes it may abate his choler, and reconcile him to a single life. But, if this opiate should not be sufficient to give him some ease, I may, perhaps, send him a stronger dose hereafter.

JOHN BULL

Washington Irving

"An old song, made by an aged old pate,
  Of an old worshipful gentleman who had a great estate,
  That kept a brave old house at a bountiful rate,
  And an old porter to relieve the poor at his gate.
  With an old study fill'd full of learned old books,
  With an old reverend chaplain, you might know him by his looks,
  With an old buttery hatch worn quite off the hooks,
  And an old kitchen that maintained half-a-dozen old cooks.
              Like an old courtier, etc."
                              —Old Song.

There is no species of humor in which the English more excel, than that which consists in caricaturing and giving ludicrous appellations, or nicknames. In this way they have whimsically designated, not merely individuals, but nations; and, in their fondness for pushing a joke, they have not spared even themselves. One would think that, in personifying itself, a nation would be apt to picture something grand, heroic and imposing, but it is characteristic of the peculiar humor of the English, and of their love for what is blunt, comic, and familiar, that they have embodied their national oddities in the figure of a sturdy, corpulent old fellow, with a three-cornered hat, red waistcoat, leather breeches, and stout oaken cudgel. Thus they have taken a singular delight in exhibiting their most private foibles in a laughable point of view; and have been so successful in their delineations, that there is scarcely a being in actual existence more absolutely present to the public mind than that eccentric personage, John Bull.

Perhaps the continual contemplation of the character thus drawn of them has contributed to fix it upon the nation; and thus to give reality to what at first may have been painted in a great measure from the imagination. Men are apt to acquire peculiarities that are continually ascribed to them. The common orders of English seem wonderfully captivated with the *beau ideal* which they have formed of John Bull, and endeavor to act up to the broad caricature that is perpetually before their eyes. Unluckily, they sometimes make their boasted Bull-ism an apology for their prejudice or grossness; and this I have especially noticed among those truly homebred and genuine sons of the soil who have never migrated beyond the sound of Bow-bells. If one of these should be a little uncouth in speech, and apt to utter impertinent truths, he confesses that he is a real John Bull, and always speaks his mind. If he now and then flies into an unreasonable burst of passion about trifles, he observes, that John Bull is a choleric old blade, but then his passion is over in a moment, and he bears no malice. If he betrays a coarseness of taste, and an insensibility to foreign refinements, he thanks heaven for his ignorance—he is a plain John Bull, and has no relish for frippery and nicknacks. His very proneness to be gulled by strangers, and to pay extravagantly for absurdities, is excused under the plea of munificence—for John is always more generous than wise.

Thus, under the name of John Bull, he will contrive to argue every fault into a merit, and will frankly convict himself of being the honestest fellow in existence.

However little, therefore, the character may have suited in the first instance, it has gradually adapted itself to the nation, or rather they have adapted themselves to each other; and a stranger who wishes to study English peculiarities, may gather much valuable information from the innumerable portraits of John Bull, as exhibited in the windows of the caricature-shops. Still, however, he is one of those fertile humorists, that are continually throwing out new portraits, and presenting different aspects from different points of view; and, often as he has been described, I cannot resist the temptation to give a slight sketch of him, such as he has met my eye.

John Bull, to all appearance, is a plain downright matter-of-fact fellow, with much less of poetry about him than rich prose. There is little of romance in his nature, but a vast deal of strong natural feeling. He excels in humor more than in wit; is jolly rather than gay; melancholy rather than morose; can easily be moved to a sudden tear, or surprised into a broad laugh; but he loathes sentiment, and has no turn for light pleasantry. He is a boon companion, if you allow him to have his humor, and to talk about himself; and he will stand by a friend in a quarrel, with life and purse, however soundly he may be cudgeled.

In this last respect, to tell the truth, he has a propensity to be somewhat too ready. He is a busy-minded personage, who thinks not merely for himself and family, but for all the country round, and is most generously disposed to be everybody's champion. He is continually volunteering his services to settle his neighbors' affairs, and takes it in great dudgeon if they engage in any matter of consequence without asking his advice; though he seldom engages in any friendly office of the kind without finishing by getting into a squabble with all parties, and then railing bitterly at their ingratitude. He unluckily took lessons in his youth in the noble science of defense, and having accomplished himself in the use of his limbs and his weapons, and become a perfect master at boxing and cudgel-play, he has had a troublesome life of it ever since. He cannot hear of a quarrel between the most distant of his neighbors, but he begins incontinently to fumble with the head of his cudgel, and consider whether his interest or honor does not require that he should meddle in the broil. Indeed he has extended his relations of pride and policy so completely over the whole country, that no event can take place, without infringing some of his finely-spun rights and dignities. Couched in his little domain, with these filaments stretching forth in every direction, he is like some choleric, bottle-bellied old spider, who has woven his web over a whole chamber, so that a fly cannot buzz, nor a breeze blow, without startling his repose, and causing him to sally forth wrathfully from his den.

Though really a good-hearted, good-tempered old fellow at bottom, yet he is singularly fond of being in the midst of contention. It is one of his peculiarities, however, that he only relishes the beginning of an affray; he always goes into a fight with alacrity, but comes out of it grumbling even when victorious; and though no one fights with more obstinacy to carry a contested point, yet, when the battle is over, and he comes to the reconciliation, he is so much taken up with the mere shaking of hands, that he is apt to let his antagonist pocket all that they have been quarreling about. It is not, therefore, fighting that he ought so much to be on his guard against, as making friends. It is difficult to cudgel him out of a farthing; but put him in a good humor, and you may bargain him out of all the money in his pocket. He is like a stout ship, which will weather the roughest storm uninjured, but roll its masts overboard in the succeeding calm.

He is a little fond of playing the magnifico abroad; of pulling out a long purse; flinging his money bravely about at boxing matches, horse races, cock fights, and carrying a high head among "gentlemen of the fancy:" but immediately after one of these fits of extravagance, he will be taken with violent qualms of economy; stop short at the most trivial expenditure; talk desperately of being ruined and brought upon the parish; and, in such moods, will not pay the smallest tradesman's bill, without violent altercation. He is in fact the most punctual and discontented paymaster in the world; drawing his coin out of his breeches pocket with infinite reluctance; paying to the uttermost farthing, but accompanying every guinea with a growl.

With all his talk of economy, however, he is a bountiful provider, and a hospitable housekeeper. His economy is of a whimsical kind, its chief object being to devise how he may afford to be extravagant; for he will begrudge himself a beefsteak and pint of port one day, that he may roast an ox whole, broach a hogshead of ale, and treat all his neighbors on the next.

His domestic establishment is enormously expensive: not so much from any great outward parade, as from the great consumption of solid beef and pudding; the vast number of followers he feeds and clothes; and his singular disposition to pay hugely for small services. He is a most kind and indulgent master, and, provided his servants humor his peculiarities, flatter his vanity a little now and then, and do not peculate grossly on him before his face, they may manage him to perfection. Everything that lives on him seems to thrive and grow fat. His house-servants are well paid, and pampered, and have little to do. His horses are sleek and lazy, and prance slowly before his state carriage; and his house-dogs sleep quietly about the door, and will hardly bark at a housebreaker.

His family mansion is an old castellated manor-house, gray with age, and of a most venerable, though weatherbeaten appearance. It has been built upon no regular plan, but is a vast accumulation of parts, erected in various tastes and ages. The center bears evident traces of

Saxon architecture, and is as solid as ponderous stone and old English oak can make it. Like all the relics of that style, it is full of obscure passages, intricate mazes, and dusky chambers; and though these have been partially lighted up in modern days, yet there are many places where you must still grope in the dark. Additions have been made to the original edifice from time to time, and great alterations have taken place; towers and battlements have been erected during wars and tumults: wings built in time of peace; and out-houses, lodges, and offices, run up according to the whim or convenience of different generations, until it has become one of the most spacious, rambling tenements imaginable. An entire wing is taken up with the family chapel, a reverend pile, that must have been exceedingly sumptuous, and, indeed, in spite of having been altered and simplified at various periods, has still a look of solemn religious pomp. Its walls within are stored with the monuments of John's ancestors; and it is snugly fitted up with soft cushions and well-lined chairs, where such of his family as are inclined to church services, may doze comfortably in the discharge of their duties.

To keep up this chapel has cost John much money; but he is stanch in his religion, and piqued in his zeal, from the circumstance that many dissenting chapels have been erected in his vicinity, and several of his neighbors, with whom he has had quarrels, are strong papists.

To do the duties of the chapel he maintains, at a large expense, a pious and portly family chaplain. He is a most learned and decorous personage, and a truly well-bred Christian, who always backs the old gentleman in his opinions, winks discreetly at his little peccadilloes, rebukes the children when refractory, and is of great use in exhorting the tenants to read their Bibles, say their prayers, and, above all, to pay their rents punctually, and without grumbling.

The family apartments are in a very antiquated taste, somewhat heavy, and often inconvenient, but full of the solemn magnificence of former times; fitted up with rich, though faded tapestry, unwieldy furniture, and loads of massy gorgeous old plate. The vast fireplaces, ample kitchens, extensive cellars, and sumptuous banqueting halls, all speak of the roaring hospitality of days of yore, of which the modern festivity at the manor-house is but a shadow. There are, however, complete suites of rooms apparently deserted and time-worn; and towers and turrets that are tottering to decay; so that in high winds there is danger of their tumbling about the ears of the household.

John has frequently been advised to have the old edifice thoroughly overhauled; and to have some of the useless parts pulled down, and the others strengthened with their materials; but the old gentleman always grows testy on this subject. He swears the house is an excellent house—that it is tight and weather proof, and not to be shaken by tempests—that it has stood for several hundred years, and, therefore, is not likely to tumble down now—that as to its being inconvenient, his family is accustomed to the inconveniences, and would not be comfortable without them—that as to its unwieldy size and irregular construction, these result from its being the growth of centuries, and being improved by the wisdom of every generation—that an old family, like his, requires a large house to dwell in; new, upstart families may live in modern cottages and snug boxes; but an old English family should inhabit an old English manor-house. If you point out any part of the building as superfluous, he insists that it is material to the strength or decoration of the rest, and the harmony of the whole; and swears that the parts are so built into each other, that if you pull down one, you run the risk of having the whole about your ears.

The secret of the matter is, that John has a great disposition to protect and patronize. He thinks it indispensable to the dignity of an ancient and honorable family, to be bounteous in its appointments, and to be eaten up by dependents; and so, partly from pride, and partly from kind-heartedness, he makes it a rule always to give shelter and maintenance to his superannuated servants.

The consequence is, that, like many other venerable family establishments, his manor is encumbered by old retainers whom he cannot turn off, and an old style which he cannot lay down. His mansion is like a great hospital of invalids, and, with all its magnitude, is not a whit too large for its inhabitants. Not a nook or corner but is of use in housing some useless personage. Groups of veteran beefeaters, gouty pensioners, and retired heroes of the buttery and the larder, are seen lolling about its walls, crawling over its lawns, dozing under its trees, or sunning themselves upon the benches at its doors. Every office and outhouse is garrisoned by these supernumeraries and their families; for they are amazingly prolific, and when they die off, are sure to leave John a legacy of hungry mouths to be provided for. A mattock cannot be struck against the most mouldering tumble-down tower, but out pops, from some cranny or loop-hole, the gray pate of some superannuated hanger-on, who has lived at John's expense all his life, and makes the most grievous outcry at their pulling down the roof from over the head of a worn-out servant of the family. This is an appeal that John's honest heart never can withstand; so that a man, who has faithfully eaten his beef and pudding all his life, is sure to be rewarded with a pipe and tankard in his old days.

A great part of his park, also, is turned into paddocks,

John Bull

where his broken-down chargers are turned loose to graze undisturbed for the remainder of their existence—a worthy example of grateful recollection, which if some of his neighbors were to imitate, would not be to their discredit. Indeed, it is one of his great pleasures to point out these old steeds to his visitors, to dwell on their good qualities, extol their past services, and boast, with some little vainglory, of the perilous adventures and hardy exploits through which they have carried him.

He is given, however, to indulge his veneration for family usages, and family encumbrances, to a whimsical extent. His manor is infested by gangs of gipsies; yet he will not suffer them to be driven off, because they have infested the place time out of mind, and been regular poachers upon every generation of the family. He will scarcely permit a dry branch to be lopped from the great trees that surround the house, lest it should molest the rooks, that have bred there for centuries. Owls have taken possession of the dovecote; but they are hereditary owls, and must not be disturbed. Swallows have nearly choked up every chimney with their nests; martins build in every frieze and cornice; crows flutter about the towers, and perch on every weathercock; and old gray-headed rats may be seen in every quarter of the house, running in and out of their holes undauntedly in broad daylight. In short, John has such a reverence for everything that has been long in the family, that he will not hear even of abuses being reformed, because they are good old family abuses.

All those whims and habits have concurred woefully to drain the old gentleman's purse; and as he prides himself on punctuality in money matters, and wishes to maintain his credit in the neighborhood, they have caused him great perplexity in meeting his engagements. This, too, has been increased by the altercations and heart-burnings which are continually taking place in his family. His children have been brought up to different callings, and are of different ways of thinking; and as they have always been allowed to speak their minds freely, they do not fail to exercise the privilege most clamorously in the present posture of his affairs. Some stand up for the honor of the race, and are clear that the old establishment should be kept up in all its state, whatever may be the cost; others, who are more prudent and considerate, entreat the old gentleman to retrench his expenses, and to put his whole system of housekeeping on a more moderate footing. He has, indeed, at times, seemed inclined to listen to their opinions, but their wholesome advice has been completely defeated by the obstreperous conduct of one of his sons. This is a noisy, rattle-pated fellow, of rather low habits, who neglects his business to frequent ale-houses—is the orator of village clubs, and a complete oracle among the poorest of his father's tenants. No sooner does he hear any of his brothers mention reform or retrenchment, than up he jumps, takes the words out of their mouths, and roars out for an overturn. When his tongue is once going nothing can stop it. He rants about the room; hectors the old man about his spendthrift practices; ridicules his tastes and pursuits; insists that he shall turn the old servants out of doors; give the broken-down horses to the hounds; send the fat chaplain packing, and take a field-preacher in his place— nay, that the whole family mansion shall be leveled with the ground, and a plain one of brick and mortar built in its place. He rails at every social entertainment and family festivity, and skulks away growling to the ale-house whenever an equipage drives up to the door. Though constantly complaining of the emptiness of his purse, yet he scruples not to spend all his pocket-money in these tavern convocations, and even runs up scores for the liquor over which he preaches about his father's extravagance.

It may readily be imagined how little such thwarting agrees with the old cavalier's fiery temperament. He has become so irritable, from repeated crossings, that the mere mention of retrenchment or reform is a signal for a brawl between him and the tavern oracle. As the latter is too sturdy and refractory for paternal discipline, having grown out of all fear of the cudgel, they have frequent scenes of wordy warfare, which at times run so high, that John is fain to call in the aid of his son Tom, an officer who has served abroad, but is at present living at home, on half-pay. This last is sure to stand by the old gentleman, right or wrong; likes nothing so much as a racketing, roystering life; and is ready at a wink or nod, to out saber, and flourish it over the orator's head, if he dares to array himself against paternal authority.

These family dissensions, as usual, have got abroad, and are rare food for scandal in John's neighborhood. People begin to look wise, and shake their heads, whenever his affairs are mentioned. They all "hope that matters are not so bad with him as represented; but when a man's own children begin to rail at his extravagance, things must be badly managed. They understand he is mortgaged over head and ears, and is continually dabbling with money lenders. He is certainly an open-handed old gentleman, but they fear he has lived too fast; indeed, they never knew any good come of this fondness for hunting, racing, reveling and prize-fighting. In short, Mr. Bull's estate is a very fine one, and has been in the family a long time; but, for all that, they have known many finer estates come to the hammer."

What is worst of all, is the effect which these pecuniary embarrassments and domestic feuds have had on the poor man himself. Instead of that jolly round corporation, and smug rosy face, which he used to present, he has of late become as shriveled and shrunk as a frost-bitten apple. His scarlet gold-laced waistcoat, which bellied out so bravely in those prosperous days when he sailed before the wind, now hangs loosely about him like a mainsail in a calm. His leather breeches are all in folds and wrinkles, and apparently have much ado to hold up the boots that yawn on both sides of his once sturdy legs.

Instead of strutting about as formerly, with his three-cornered hat on one side; flourishing his cudgel, and bringing it down every moment with a hearty thump upon the ground; looking everyone sturdily in the face, and trolling out a stave of a catch or a drinking song; he now goes about whistling thoughtfully to himself, with his head drooping down, his cudgel tucked under his arm, and his hands thrust to the bottom of his breeches pockets, which are evidently empty.

Such is the plight of honest John Bull at present; yet for all this the old fellow's spirit is as tall and as gallant as ever. If you drop the least expression of sympathy or concern, he takes fire in an instant; swears that he is the richest and stoutest fellow in the country; talks of laying out large sums to adorn his house or buy another estate; and with a valiant swagger and grasping of his cudgel, longs exceedingly to have another bout at quarter-staff.

Though there may be something rather whimsical in all this, yet I confess I cannot look upon John's situation without strong feelings of interest. With all his odd humors and obstinate prejudices, he is a sterling-hearted old blade. He may not be so wonderfully fine a fellow as he thinks himself, but he is at least twice as good as his neighbors represent him. His virtues are all his own; all plain, homebred, and unaffected. His very faults smack of the raciness of his good qualities. His extravagance savors of his generosity; his quarrelsomeness of his courage; his credulity of his open faith; his vanity of his pride; and his bluntness of his sincerity. They are all the redundancies of a rich and liberal character. He is like his own oak, rough without, but sound and solid within; whose bark abounds with excrescences in proportion to the growth and grandeur of the timber; and whose branches make a fearful groaning and murmuring in the least storm, from their very magnitude and luxuriance. There is something, too, in the appearance of his old family mansion that is extremely poetical and picturesque; and, as long as it can be rendered comfortably habitable, I should almost tremble to see it meddled with, during the present conflict of tastes and opinions. Some of his advisers are no doubt good architects, that might be of service; but many, I fear, are mere levelers, who, when they had once got to work with their mattocks on this venerable edifice, would never stop until they had brought it to the ground, and perhaps buried themselves among the ruins. All that I wish is, that John's present troubles may teach him more prudence in future. That he may cease to distress his mind about other people's affairs; that he may give up the fruitless attempt to promote the good of his neighbors, and the peace and happiness of the world, by dint of the cudgel; that he may remain quietly at home; gradually get his house into repair; cultivate his rich estate according to his fancy; husband his income—if he thinks proper; bring his unruly children into order—if he can; renew the jovial scenes of ancient prosperity; and long enjoy, on his paternal lands, a green, an honorable, and a merry old age.

THE MUTABILITY OF LITERATURE

A COLLOQUY IN WESTMINSTER ABBEY

Washington Irving

> "I know that all beneath the moon decays,
> And what by mortals in this world is brought,
> In time's great period shall return to nought.
> I know that all the muse's heavenly lays,
> With toil of sprite which are so dearly bought,
> As idle sounds, of few or none are sought,
> That there is nothing lighter than mere praise."
> —Drummond of Hawthornden.

There are certain half-dreaming moods of mind, in which we naturally steal away from noise and glare, and seek some quiet haunt, where we may indulge our reveries and build our air castles undisturbed. In such a mood I was loitering about the old gray cloisters of Westminster Abbey, enjoying that luxury of wandering thought which one is apt to dignify with the name of reflection; when suddenly an interruption of madcap boys from Westminster School, playing at football, broke in upon the monastic stillness of the place, making the vaulted passages and mouldering tombs echo with their merriment. I sought to take refuge from their noise by penetrating still deeper into the solitudes of the pile, and applied to one of the vergers for admission to the library. He conducted me through a portal rich with the crumbling sculpture of former ages, which opened upon a gloomy passage leading to the chapter-house and the chamber in which doomsday book is deposited. Just within the passage is a small door on the left.

THE MUTABILITY OF LITERATURE

To this the verger applied a key; it was double locked, and opened with some difficulty, as if seldom used. We now ascended a dark narrow staircase, and, passing through a second door, entered the library.

I found myself in a lofty antique hall, the roof supported by massive joists of old English oak. It was soberly lighted by a row of Gothic windows at a considerable height from the floor, and which apparently opened upon the roofs of the cloisters. An ancient picture of some reverend dignitary of the church in his robes hung over the fireplace. Around the hall and in a small gallery were the books, arranged in carved oaken cases. They consisted principally of old polemical writers, and were much more worn by time than use. In the center of the library was a solitary table with two or three books on it, an inkstand without ink, and a few pens parched by long disuse. The place seemed fitted for quiet study and profound meditation. It was buried deep among the massive walls of the abbey, and shut up from the tumult of the world. I could only hear now and then the shouts of the school-boys faintly swelling from the cloisters, and the sound of a bell tolling for prayers, echoing soberly along the roofs of the abbey. By degrees the shouts of merriment grew fainter and fainter, and at length died away; the bell ceased to toll, and a profound silence reigned through the dusky hall.

I had taken down a little thick quarto, curiously bound in parchment, with brass clasps, and seated myself at the table in a venerable elbow-chair. Instead of reading, however, I was beguiled by the solemn monastic air, and lifeless quiet of the place, into a train of musing. As I looked around upon the old volumes in their mouldering covers, thus ranged on the shelves, and apparently never disturbed in their repose, I could not but consider the library a kind of literary catacomb, where authors, like mummies, are piously entombed, and left to blacken and moulder in dusty oblivion.

How much, thought I, has each of these volumes, now thrust aside with such indifference, cost some aching head! how many weary days! how many sleepless nights! How have their authors buried themselves in the solitude of cells and cloisters; shut themselves up from the face of man, and the still more blessed face of nature; and devoted themselves to painful research and intense reflection! And all for what? to occupy an inch of dusty shelf—to have the title of their works read now and then in a future age, by some drowsy churchman or casual straggler like myself; and in another age to be lost, even to remembrance. Such is the amount of this boasted immortality. A mere temporary rumor, a local sound; like the tone of that bell which has just tolled among these towers, filling the ear for a moment—lingering transiently in echo—and then passing away like a thing that was not.

While I sat half murmuring, half meditating these unprofitable speculations with my head resting on my hand, I was thrumming with the other hand upon the quarto, until I accidentally loosened the clasps; when, to my utter astonishment, the little book gave two or three yawns, like one awaking from a deep sleep; then a husky hem; and at length began to talk. At first its voice was very hoarse and broken, being much troubled by a cobweb which some studious spider had woven across it; and having probably contracted a cold from long exposure to the chills and damps of the abbey. In a short time, however, it became more distinct, and I soon found it an exceedingly fluent conversable little tome. Its language, to be sure, was rather quaint and obsolete, and its pronunciation, what, in the present day, would be deemed barbarous; but I shall en-

The Mutability of Literature

deavor, as far as I am able, to render it in modern parlance.

It began with railings about the neglect of the world—about merit being suffered to languish in obscurity, and other such commonplace topics of literary repining, and complained bitterly that it had not been opened for more than two centuries; that the dean only looked now and then into the library, sometimes took down a volume or two, trifled with them for a few moments, and then returned them to their shelves. "What a plague do they mean," said the little quarto, which I began to perceive was somewhat choleric, "what a plague do they mean by keeping several thousand volumes of us shut up here, and watched by a set of old vergers, like so many beauties in a harem, merely to be looked at now and then by the dean? Books were written to give pleasure and to be enjoyed; and I would have a rule passed that the dean should pay each of us a visit at least once a year; or if he is not equal to the task, let them once in a while turn loose the whole school of Westminster among us, that at any rate we may now and then have an airing."

"Softly, my worthy friend," replied I, "you are not aware how much better you are off than most books of your generation. By being stored away in this ancient library, you are like the treasured remains of those saints and monarchs, which lie enshrined in the adjoining chapels; while the remains of your contemporary mortals, left to the ordinary course of nature, have long since returned to dust."

"Sir," said the little tome, ruffling his leaves and looking big, "I was written for all the world, not for the bookworms of an abbey. I was intended to circulate from hand to hand, like other great contemporary works; but here have I been clasped up for more than two centuries, and might have silently fallen a prey to these worms that are playing the very vengeance with my intestines, if you had not by chance given me an opportunity of uttering a few last words before I go to pieces."

"My good friend," rejoined I, "had you been left to the circulation of which you speak, you would long ere this have been no more. To judge from your physiognomy, you are now well stricken in years: very few of your contemporaries can be at present in existence; and those few owe their longevity to being immured like yourself in old libraries; which, suffer me to add, instead of likening to harems, you might more properly and gratefully have compared to those infirmaries attached to religious establishments, for the benefit of the old and decrepit, and where, by quiet fostering and no employment, they often endure to an amazingly good-for-nothing old age. You talk of your contemporaries as if in circulation—where do we meet with their works? what do we hear of Robert Groteste, of Lincoln? No one could have toiled harder than he for immortality. He is said to have written nearly two hundred volumes. He built, as it were, a pyramid of books to perpetuate his name: but, alas! the pyramid has long since fallen, and only a few fragments are scattered in various libraries, where they are scarcely disturbed even by the antiquarian. What do we hear of Giraldus Cambrensis, the historian, antiquary, philosopher, theologian, and poet? He declined two bishoprics, that he might shut himself up and write for posterity; but posterity never inquires after his labors. What of Henry of Huntingdon, who, besides a learned history of England, wrote a treatise on the contempt of the world, which the world has revenged by forgetting him? What is quoted of Joseph of Exeter, styled the miracle of his age in classical composition? Of his three great heroic poems one is lost forever, excepting a mere fragment; the others are known only to a few of the

The Mutability of Literature

curious in literature; and as to his love verses and epigrams, they have entirely disappeared. What is in current use of John Wallis, the Franciscan, who acquired the name of the tree of life? Of William of Malmsbury;—of Simeon of Durham;—of Benedict of Peterborough;—of John Hanvill of St. Albans;—of——"

"Prithee, friend," cried the quarto, in a testy tone, "how old do you think me? You are talking of authors that lived long before my time, and wrote either in Latin or French, so that they in a manner expatriated themselves, and deserved to be forgotten;[1] but I, sir, was ushered into the world from the press of the renowned Wynkyn de Worde. I was written in my own native tongue, at a time when the language had become fixed; and indeed I was considered a model of pure and elegant English."

(I should observe that these remarks were couched in such intolerably antiquated terms, that I have had infinite difficulty in rendering them into modern phraseology.)

"I cry your mercy," said I, "for mistaking your age; but it matters little: almost all the writers of your time have likewise passed into forgetfulness; and De Worde's publications are mere literary rarities among book-collectors. The purity and stability of language, too, on which you found your claims to perpetuity, have been the fallacious dependence of authors of every age, even back to the times of the worthy Robert of Gloucester, who wrote his history in rhymes of mongrel Saxon.[2] Even now many

[1] "In Latin and French hath many soueraine wittes had great delyte to endite, and have many noble thinges fulfilde, but certes there ben some that speaken their poisye in French, of which speche the Frenchmen have as good a fantasye as we have in hearying of Frenchmen's Englishe."—*Chaucer's Testament of Love.*

[2] "Holinshed, in his Chronicle, observes, 'afterwards, also, by deligent travell of Geffry Chaucer and of John Gowre, in the time of Richard the Second, and after them of John Scogan and John Lydgate, monke of Berrie, our said toong was brought to an

talk of Spenser's 'well of pure English undefiled,' as if the language ever sprang from a well or fountain-head, and was not rather a mere confluence of various tongues, perpetually subject to changes and intermixtures. It is this which has made English literature so extremely mutable, and the reputation built upon it so fleeting. Unless thought can be committed to something more permanent and unchangeable than such a medium, even thought must share the fate of everything else, and fall into decay. This should serve as a check upon the vanity and exultation of the most popular writer. He finds the language in which he has embarked his fame gradually altering, and subject to the dilapidations of time and the caprice of fashion. He looks back and beholds the early authors of his country, once the favorites of their day, supplanted by modern writers. A few short ages have covered them with obscurity, and their merits can only be relished by the quaint taste of the bookworm. And such, he anticipates, will be the fate of his own work, which, however it may be admired in its day, and held up as a model of purity, will in the course of years grow antiquated and obsolete; until it shall become almost as unintelligible in its native land as an Egyptian obelisk, or one of those Runic inscriptions said to exist in the deserts of Tartary. I declare," added I, with some emotion, " when I contemplate a modern library, filled with new works, in all the bravery of rich gilding and binding, I feel disposed to sit down and weep; like the good Xerxes, when he surveyed his army, pranked out in all the splendor of military array, and reflected that in one hundred years not one of them would be in existence!"

excellent passe, notwithstanding that it never came unto the type of perfection until the time of Queen Elizabeth, wherein John Jewell, Bishop of Sarum, John Fox, and sundrie learned and excellent writers, have fully accomplished the ornature of the same, to their great praise and immortal commendation.'"

THE MUTABILITY OF LITERATURE

"Ah," said the little quarto, with a heavy sigh, "I see how it is; these modern scribblers have superseded all the good old authors. I suppose nothing is read now-a-days but Sir Philip Sydney's *Arcadia,* Sackville's stately plays, and Mirror for Magistrates, or the fine-spun euphuisms of the 'unparalleled John Lyly.'"

"There you are again mistaken," said I; "the writers whom you suppose in vogue, because they happened to be so when you were last in circulation, have long since had their day. Sir Philip Sydney's *Arcadia,* the immortality of which was so fondly predicted by his admirers,[1] and which, in truth, is full of noble thoughts, delicate images, and graceful turns of language, is now scarcely ever mentioned. Sackville has strutted into obscurity; and even Lyly, though his writings were once the delight of a court, and apparently perpetuated by a proverb, is now scarcely known even by name. A whole crowd of authors who wrote and wrangled at the time, have likewise gone down, with all their writings and their controversies. Wave after wave of succeeding literature has rolled over them, until they are buried so deep, that it is only now and then that some industrious diver after fragments of antiquity brings up a specimen for the gratification of the curious.

"For my part," I continued, "I consider this mutability of language a wise precaution of Providence for the benefit of the world at large, and of authors in particular. To reason from analogy, we daily behold the varied and beau-

---

[1] "Live ever sweete booke; the simple image of his gentle witt, and the golden-pillar of his noble courage; and ever notify unto the world that thy writer was the secretary of eloquence, the breath of the muses, the honey-bee of the daintyest flowers of witt and arte, the pith of morale and intellectual virtues, the arme of Bellona in the field, the tonge of Suada in the chamber, the sprite of Practise in esse, and the paragon of excellency in print."—*Harvey, Pierce's Supererogation.*

tiful tribes of vegetables springing up, flourishing, adorning the fields for a short time, and then fading into dust, to make way for their successors. Were not this the case, the fecundity of nature would be a grievance instead of a blessing. The earth would groan with rank and excessive vegetation, and its surface become a tangled wilderness. In like manner the works of genius and learning decline, and make way for subsequent productions. Language gradually varies, and with it fade away the writings of authors who have flourished their allotted time; otherwise, the creative powers of genius would overstock the world, and the mind would be completely bewildered in the endless mazes of literature. Formerly there were some restraints on this excessive multiplication. Works had to be transcribed by hand, which was a slow and laborious operation; they were written either on parchment, which was expensive, so that one work was often erased to make way for another; or on papyrus, which was fragile and extremely perishable. Authorship was a limited and unprofitable craft, pursued chiefly by monks in the leisure and solitude of their cloisters. The accumulation of manuscripts was slow and costly, and confined almost entirely to monasteries. To these circumstances it may, in some measure, be owing that we have not been inundated by the intellect of antiquity; that the fountains of thought have not been broken up, and modern genius drowned in the deluge. But the inventions of paper and the press have put an end to all these restraints. They have made everyone a writer, and enabled every mind to pour itself into print, and diffuse itself over the whole intellectual world. The consequences are alarming. The stream of literature has swollen into a torrent—augmented into a river—expanded into a sea. A few centuries since, five or six hundred manuscripts constituted a great library; but what would you say to libraries such as actually exist, containing three or four hundred thousand volumes; legions of authors at the same time busy; and the press going on with fearfully increasing activity, to double and quadruple the number? Unless some unforeseen mortality should break out among the progeny of the muse, now that she has become so prolific, I tremble for posterity. I fear the mere fluctuation of language will not be sufficient. Criticism may do much. It increases with the increase of literature, and resembles one of those salutary checks on population spoken of by economists. All possible encouragement, therefore, should be given to the growth of critics, good or bad. But I fear all will be in vain; let criticism do what it may, writers will write, printers will print, and the world will inevitably be overstocked with good books. It will soon be the employment of a lifetime merely to learn their names. Many a man of passable information, at the present day, reads scarcely anything but reviews; and before long a man of erudition will be little better than a mere walking catalogue."

" My very good sir," said the little quarto, yawning most drearily in my face, " excuse my interrupting you, but I perceive you are rather given to prose. I would ask the fate of an author who was making some noise just as I left the world. His reputation, however, was considered quite temporary. The learned shook their heads at him, for he was a poor half-educated varlet, that knew little of Latin, and nothing of Greek, and had been obliged to run the country for deer-stealing. I think his name was Shakspeare. I presume he soon sunk into oblivion."

" On the contrary," said I, " it is owing to that very man that the literature of his period has experienced a duration beyond the ordinary term of English literature. There rise authors now and then, who seem proof against the mutability of language, because they have rooted themselves in the unchanging principles of human nature. They are like gigantic trees that we sometimes see on the banks of a stream; which, by their vast and deep roots, penetrating through the mere surface, and laying hold on the very foundations of the earth, preserve the soil around them from being swept away by the ever-flowing current, and hold up many a neighboring plant, and perhaps worthless weed, to perpetuity. Such is the case with Shakspeare, whom we behold defying the encroachments of time, retaining in modern use the language and literature of his day, and giving duration to many an indifferent author, merely from having flourished in his vicinity. But even he, I grieve to say, is gradually assuming the tint of age, and his whole form is overrun by a profusion of commentators, who, like clambering vines and creepers, almost bury the noble plant that upholds them."

Here the little quarto began to heave his sides and chuckle, until at length he broke out in a plethoric fit of laughter that had well nigh choked him, by reason of his excessive corpulency. "Mighty well!" cried he, as soon as he could recover breath, "mighty well! and so you would persuade me that the literature of an age is to be perpetuated by a vagabond deer-stealer! by a man without learning; by a poet, forsooth—a poet!" And here he wheezed forth another fit of laughter.

I confess that I felt somewhat nettled at this rudeness, which, however, I pardoned on account of his having flourished in a less polished age. I determined, nevertheless, not to give up my point.

"Yes," resumed I, positively, "a poet; for of all writers he has the best chance for immortality. Others may write from the head, but he writes from the heart, and the heart will always understand him. He is the faithful portrayer of nature, whose features are always the same and always interesting. Prose writers are voluminous and unwieldy; their pages are crowded with commonplaces, and their thoughts expanded into tediousness. But with the true poet everything is terse, touching, or brilliant. He gives the choicest thoughts in the choicest language. He illustrates them by everything that he sees most striking in nature and art. He enriches them by pictures of human life, such as it is passing before him. His writings, therefore, contain the spirit, the aroma, if I may use the phrase, of the age in which he lives. They are caskets which inclose within a small compass the wealth of the language—its family jewels, which are thus transmitted in a portable form to posterity. The setting may occasionally be antiquated, and require now and then to be renewed, as in the case of Chaucer; but the brilliancy and intrinsic value of the gems continue unaltered. Cast a look back over the long reach of literary history. What vast valleys of dullness, filled with monkish legends and academical controversies! what bogs of theological speculations! what dreary wastes of metaphysics! Here and there only do we behold the heaven-illuminated bards, elevated like beacons on their widely-separate heights, to transmit the pure light of poetical intelligence from age to age." [1]

I was just about to launch forth into eulogiums upon the

[1] " Thorow earth and waters deepe,
   The pen by skill doth passe:
And featly nyps the worldes abuse,
   And shoes us in a glasse,
The vertu and the vice
   Of every wight alyve;
The honey comb that bee doth make
   Is not so sweet in hyve,
As are the golden leves
   That drop from poet's head!
Which doth surmount our common talke
   As farre as dross doth lead."
—*Churchyard.*

poets of the day, when the sudden opening of the door caused me to turn my head. It was the verger, who came to inform me that it was time to close the library. I sought to have a parting word with the quarto, but the worthy little tome was silent; the clasps were closed: and it looked perfectly unconscious of all that had passed. I have been to the library two or three times since, and have endeavored to draw it into further conversation, but in vain; and whether all this rambling colloquy actually took place, or whether it was another of those odd day-dreams to which I am subject, I have never to this moment been able to discover.

KEAN'S ACTING

Richard Henry Dana

"For, doubtless, that indeed according to art is most eloquent, which turns and approaches nearest to nature, from whence it came."
—Milton.

"*Professed diversions!* cannot these escape?
. . . . .
We ransack tombs for *pastime;* from the dust
Call up the sleeping hero; bid him tread
The scene for our amusement: How like Gods
We sit; and, wrapt in immortality,
Shed generous tears on wretches born to die;
Their fate deploring, to forget *our own!*"
—Young.

I had scarcely thought of the theater for some years, when Kean arrived in this country; and it was more from curiosity than from any other motive, that I went to see, for the first time, the great actor of the age. I was soon lost to the recollection of being in a theater, or looking upon a great display of the "mimic art." The simplicity, earnestness, and sincerity of his acting made me forgetful of the fiction, and bore me away with the power of reality and truth. If this be acting, said I, as I returned home, I may as well make the theater my school, and henceforward study nature at second hand.

How can I describe one who is almost as full of beauties as nature itself,—who grows upon us the more we become acquainted with him, and makes us sensible that the first time we saw him in any part, however much he may have moved us, we had but a partial apprehension of the many excellences of his acting? We cease to consider it as a mere amusement. It is an intellectual feast; and he who goes to it with a disposition and capacity to relish it, will receive from it more nourishment for his mind, than he would be likely to do in many other ways in twice the time. Our faculties are opened and enlivened by it; our reflections and recollections are of an elevated kind; and the voice which is sounding in our ears, long after we have left him, creates an inward harmony which is for our good.

Kean, in truth, stands very much in that relation to other players whom we have seen, that Shakspeare does to other dramatists. One player is called classical; another makes fine points here, and another there; Kean makes more fine points than all of them together; but in him these are only little prominences, showing their bright heads above a beautifully undulated surface. A continual change is going on in him, partaking of the nature of the varying scenes he is passing through, and the many thoughts and feelings which are shifting within him.

In a clear autumnal day we may see, here and there, a massed white cloud edged with a blazing brightness against a blue sky, and now and then a dark pine swinging its top in the wind, with the melancholy sound of the sea; but who can note the shifting and untiring play of the leaves of the wood, and their passing hues, when each seems a living thing full of sensations, and happy in its rich attire? A sound, too, of universal harmony is in our ears, and a wide-spread beauty before our eyes, which we cannot define; yet a joy is in our hearts. Our delight increases in these, day after day, the longer we give ourselves to them, till at last we become, as it were, a part of the existence without us. So it is with natural characters. They grow upon us imperceptibly, till we become bound up in them, we scarce know when or how. So, in its degree, it will fare with the actor who is deeply filled with nature, and is perpetually throwing off her beautiful evanescences. Instead of becoming tired of him, as we do, after a time, of others, he will go on giving something which will be new to the observing mind, and will keep the feelings alive, because their action will be natural. I have no doubt, that, excepting those who go to a play as children look into a showbox, to admire and exclaim at distorted figures, and raw, unharmonious colors, there is no man of a moderately warm temperament, and with a tolerable share of insight into human nature, who would not find his interest in Kean increasing with a study of him. It is very possible that the excitement would lessen, but there would be a quieter pleasure, instead of it, stealing upon him, as he became familiar with the character of the acting.

Taken within his range of characters, the versatility of his playing is striking. He seems not the same being, now representing Richard, and, again, Hamlet; but the two characters alone appear before you, and as distinct individuals who had never known or heard of each other. So does he become the character he is to represent, that we have sometimes thought it a reason why he was not universally better liked here, in Richard; and that because the player did not make himself a little more visible, he must needs bear a share of our dislike of the cruel king. And this may be still more the case, as his construction of the character, whether right or wrong, creates in us an unmixed dislike of Richard, till the anguish of his mind makes him the object of pity; from which time, to the close, all allow that he plays the part better than anyone has done before him.

In his highest-wrought passion, when the limbs and muscles are alive and quivering, and his gestures hurried and vehement, nothing appears ranted or overacted; because he makes us feel, that, with all this, there is something still within him struggling for utterance. The very breaking and harshness of his voice, in these parts, help to this impression, and make up, in a good degree, for this defect, if it be a defect here.

Though he is on the very verge of truth in his passionate parts, he does not fall into extravagance; but runs along the dizzy edge of the roaring and beating sea, with feet as sure as we walk our parlors. We feel that he is safe, for some preternatural spirit upholds him as it hurries him onward; and while all is uptorn and tossing in the whirl of the passions, we see that there is a power and order over the whole.

A man has feelings sometimes which can only be breathed out; there is no utterance for them in words. I had hardly written this when the terrible "Ha!" with which Kean makes Lear hail Cornwall and Regan as they enter in the fourth scene of the second act, came to my mind. That cry seemed at the time to take me up and sweep me along in its wild swell. No description in the world could give a tolerably clear notion of it;—it must be formed, as well as it may be, from what is here said of its effect.

Kean's playing is sometimes but the outbreaking of inarticulate sounds;—the throttled struggle of rage, and the choking of grief,—the broken laugh of extreme suffering, when the mind is ready to deliver itself over to an insane joy,—the utterance of over-full love, which cannot and would not speak in express words, and that of wildering grief, which blanks all the faculties of man.

No other player whom I have heard has attempted these, except now and then; and should anyone have made the trial in the various ways in which Kean gives them, probably he would have failed. Kean thrills us with them, as if they were wrung from him in his agony. They have not the appearance of study or artifice. The truth is, that the labor of a mind of his genius constitutes its existence and delight. It is not like the toil of ordinary men at their task-work. What shows effort in them comes from him with the freedom and force of nature.

Some object to the frequent use of such sounds, and to others they are quite shocking. But those who permit themselves to consider that there are really violent passions in man's nature, and that they utter themselves a little differently from our ordinary feelings, understand and feel their language as they speak to us in Kean. Probably no actor has conceived passion with the intenseness and life that he does. It seems to enter into him and possess him, as evil spirits possessed men of old. It is curious to observe how some, who have sat very contentedly, year after year, and called the face-making, which they have seen, expression, and the stage-stride, dignity, and the noisy declamation, and all the rhodomontade of acting, energy and passion, complain that Kean is apt to be extravagant; when in truth he seems to be little more than a simple personation of the feeling or passion to be expressed at the time.

It has been so common a saying, that Lear is the most difficult of characters to personate, that we had taken it for granted no man could play it so as to satisfy us. Perhaps it is the hardest to represent. Yet the part which has generally been supposed the most difficult, the insanity of Lear, is scarcely more so than that of the choleric old king. Inefficient rage is almost always ridiculous; and an old man, with a broken-down body and a mind falling in pieces from the violence of its uncontrolled passions, is in constant danger of exciting, along with our pity, a feeling of contempt. It is a chance matter to which we may be most moved. And this it is which makes the opening of *Lear* so difficult.

We may as well notice here the objection which some make to the abrupt violence with which Kean begins in Lear. If this be a fault, it is Shakspeare, and not Kean, who is to blame; for, no doubt, he has conceived it according to his author. Perhaps, however, the mistake lies in this case, where it does in most others, with those who put themselves into the seat of judgment to pass upon great men.

In most instances, Shakspeare has given us the gradual growth of a passion, with such little accompaniments as agree with it, and go to make up the whole man. In Lear, his object being to represent the beginning and course of insanity, he has properly enough gone but a little back of it, and introduced to us an old man of good feelings enough, but one who had lived without any true principle of conduct, and whose unruled passions had grown strong with age, and were ready, upon a disappointment, to make shipwreck of an intellect never strong. To bring this about, he begins with an abruptness rather unusual; and the old king rushes in before us, with his passions at their height, and tearing him like fiends.

Kean gives this as soon as the fitting occasion offers itself. Had he put more of melancholy and depression and less of rage into the character, we should have been much puzzled at his so suddenly going mad. It would have required the change to have been slower; and besides, his insanity must have been of another kind. It must have been monotonous and complaining, instead of continually varying; at one time full of grief, at another playful, and then wild as the winds that roared about him, and fiery and sharp as the lightning that shot by him. The truth with which he conceived this was not finer than his execution

of it. Not for a moment, in his utmost violence, did he
suffer the imbecility of the old man's anger to touch upon
the ludicrous, when nothing but the justest conception and
feeling of the character could have saved him from it.

It has been said that Lear is a study for one who would
make himself acquainted with the workings of an insane
mind. And it is hardly less true, that the acting of Kean
was an embodying of these workings. His eye, when his
senses are first forsaking him, giving an inquiring look at
what he saw, as if all before him was undergoing a strange
and bewildering change which confused his brain,—the
wandering, lost motions of his hands, which seemed feeling
for something familiar to them, on which they might take
hold and be assured of a safe reality,—the under monotone
of his voice, as if he was questioning his own being, and
what surrounded him,—the continuous, but slight, oscillat-
ing motion of the body,—all these expressed, with fearful
truth, the bewildered state of a mind fast unsettling, and
making vain and weak efforts to find its way back to its
wonted reason. There was a childish, feeble gladness in
the eye, and a half-piteous smile about the mouth at times,
which one could scarce look upon without tears. As the
derangement increased upon him, his eye lost its notice
of objects about him, wandering over things as if he saw
them not, and fastening upon the creatures of his crazed
brain. The helpless and delighted fondness with which
he clings to Edgar, as an insane brother, is another instance of the justness of Kean's conceptions. Nor does he
lose the air of insanity, even in the fine moralizing parts,
and where he inveighs against the corruptions of the world.
There is a madness even in his reason.

The violent and immediate changes of the passions in
Lear, so difficult to manage without jarring upon us, are
given by Kean with a spirit and with a fitness to nature

which we had hardly thought possible. These are equally well done both before and after the loss of reason. The most difficult scene, in this respect, is the last interview between Lear and his daughters, Goneril and Regan,—(and how wonderfully does Kean carry it through!)—the scene which ends with the horrid shout and cry with which he runs out mad from their presence, as if the very brain had taken fire.

The last scene which we are allowed to have of Shakspeare's Lear, for the simply pathetic, was played by Kean with unmatched power. We sink down helpless under the oppressive grief. It lies like a dead weight upon our hearts. We are denied even the relief of tears; and are thankful for the shudder that seizes us when he kneels to his daughter in the deploring weakness of his crazed grief.

It is lamentable that Kean should not be allowed to show his unequaled powers in the last scene of Lear, as Shakspeare wrote it; and that this mighty work of genius should be profaned by the miserable, mawkish sort of by-play of Edgar's and Cordelia's loves. Nothing can surpass the impertinence of the man who made the change, but the folly of those who sanctioned it.

When I began, I had no other intention than that of giving a few general impressions made upon me by Kean's acting; but, falling accidentally upon his Lear, I have been led, unawares, into particulars. It is only to take these as some of the instances of his powers in Lear, and then to think of him as not inferior in his other characters, and some notion may be formed of the effect of Kean's playing upon those who understand and like him. Neither this, nor anything I might add, would be likely to reach his great and various powers.

If it could be said of anyone, it might be said of Kean

that he does not fall behind his author, but stands forward, the living representative of the character he has drawn. When he is not playing in Shakspeare, he fills up where his author is wanting; and when in Shakspeare, he gives not only what is set down, but whatever the situation and circumstances attendant upon the being he personates would naturally call forth. He seems, at the time, to have possessed himself of Shakspeare's imagination, and to have given it body and form. Read any scene in Shakspeare,—for instance, the last of *Lear* that is played,—and see how few words are there set down, and then remember how Kean fills out with varied and multiplied expression and circumstances, and the truth of this remark will be obvious enough. There are few men, I believe, let them have studied the plays of Shakspeare ever so attentively, who can see Kean in them without confessing that he has helped them to a truer and fuller conception of the author, notwithstanding what their own labors had done for them.

It is not easy to say in what character Kean plays best. He so fits himself to each in turn, that if the effect he produces at one time is less than at another, it is because of some inferiority in stage-effect in the character. Othello is probably the character best adapted to stage-effect, and Kean has an uninterrupted power over us in playing it. When he commands, we are awed; when his face is sensitive with love and love thrills in his soft tones, all that our imaginations had pictured to us is realized. His jealousy, his hate, his fixed purposes, are terrific and deadly; and the groans wrung from him in his grief have the pathos and anguish of Esau's, when he stood before his old, blind father, and sent up "an exceeding bitter cry."

Again, in Richard, how does he hurry forward to his object, sweeping away all between him and it! The world and its affairs are nothing to him, till he gains his end. He is all life, and action, and haste,—he fills every part of the stage, and seems to do all that is done.

I have before said that his voice is harsh and breaking in his high tones, in his rage, but that this defect is of little consequence in such places. Nor is it well suited to the more declamatory parts. This, again, is scarce worth considering; for how very little is there of mere declamation in good English plays! But it is one of the finest voices in the world for all the passions and feelings which can be uttered in the middle and lower tones. In Lear,—

> "If you have poison for me, I will drink it."

And again,—

> "You do me wrong to take me out o' the grave.
> Thou art a soul in bliss."

Why should I cite passages? Can any man open upon the scene in which these are contained, without Kean's piteous looks and tones being present to him? And does not the mere remembrance of them, as he reads, bring tears into his eyes? Yet, once more, in Othello,—

> "Had it pleased Heaven
> To try me with affliction," &c.

In the passage beginning with

> "O, now for ever
> Farewell the tranquil mind,"—

there was "a mysterious confluence of sounds" passing off into infinite distance, and every thought and feeling within him seemed traveling with them.

How graceful he is in Othello! It is not a practiced educated grace, but the "unbought grace" of his genius uttering itself in its beauty and grandeur in the movement of the outward man. When he says to Iago so touchingly, "Leave me, leave me, Iago," and, turning from him, walks to the back of the stage, raising his hands, and bringing them down upon his head, with clasped fingers, and stands thus with his back to us, there is a grace and majesty in his figure which we look on with admiration.

Talking of these things in Kean is something like reading the *Beauties of Shakspeare;* for he is as true in the subordinate as in the great parts. But he must be content to share with other men of genius, and think himself fortunate if one in a hundred sees his lesser beauties, and marks the truth and delicacy of his under-playing. For instance, when he has no share in the action going on, he is not busy in putting himself into attitudes to draw attention, but stands or sits in a simple posture, like one with an engaged mind. His countenance, too, is in a state of ordinary repose, with but a slight, general expression of the character of his thoughts; for this is all the face shows, when the mind is taken up in silence with its own reflections. It does not assume marked or violent expressions, as in soliloquy. When a man gives utterance to his thoughts, though alone, the charmed rest of the body is broken; he speaks in his gestures too, and the countenance is put into a sympathizing action.

I was first struck with this in his Hamlet; for the deep and quiet interest, so marked in Hamlet, made the justness of Kean's playing, in this respect, the more obvious. And since then, I have observed him attentively, and have found the same true acting in his other characters.

This right conception of situation and its general effect seems to require almost as much genius as his conceptions of his characters, and, indeed, may be considered as one with them. He deserves praise for it; for there is so much of the subtilty of nature in it, if one may so speak, that while a few are able, with his help, to put themselves into the situation, and perceive the justness of his acting in it, the rest, both those who like him upon the whole, as well as those who profess to see little in him, will be apt to let it pass by without observing it.

Like most men, however, Kean receives a partial reward, at least, for his sacrifice of the praise of the many to what he feels to be the truth. For when he passes from the state of natural repose, even into that of gentle motion and ordinary discourse, he is immediately filled with a spirit and life, which he makes everyone feel who is not armor-proof against him. This helps to the sparkling brightness and warmth of his playing, the grand secret of which, like that of colors in a picture, lies in a just contrast. We can all speculate concerning the general rules upon this; but when the man of genius gives us their results, how few are there who can trace them out with an observant eye, or look with a discerning satisfaction upon the great whole. Perhaps this very beauty in Kean has helped to an opinion, which, no doubt, is true, that he is, at times, too sharp and abrupt. I well remember, while once looking at a picture in which the shadow of a mountain fell, in strong outline, upon a part of a stream, I overheard some quite sensible people expressing their wonder that the artist should have made the water of two colors, seeing it was all one and the same thing.

Instances of Kean's keeping of situations were striking in the opening of the trial scene in *The Iron Chest,* and in *Hamlet,* when the father's ghost tells the story of his death.

The composure to which he is bent up, in the former, must be present with all who saw him. And, though from the immediate purpose, shall I pass by the startling and appalling change, when madness seized upon his brain, with the swiftness and power of a fanged monster? Wonderfully as this last part was played, we cannot well imagine how much the previous calm, and the suddenness of the unlooked-for change from it, added to the terror of the scene. The temple stood fixed on its foundations; the earthquake shook it, and it was a heap. Is this one of Kean's violent contrasts?

While Kean listened, in Hamlet, to the father's story, the entire man was absorbed in deep attention, mingled with a tempered awe. His posture was simple, with a slight inclination forward. The spirit was the spirit of his father, whom he had loved and reverenced, and who was to that moment ever present in his thoughts. The first superstitious terror at meeting him had passed off. The account of his father's appearance given him by Horatio and the watch, and his having followed him some distance, had, in a degree, familiarized him to the sight, and he stood before us in the stillness of one who was to hear, then or never, what was to be told, but without that eager reaching forward which other players give, and which would be right, perhaps, in any character but that of Hamlet, who connects the past and what is to come with the present, and mingles reflection with his immediate feelings, however deep.

As an instance of Kean's familiar, and, if I may be allowed to term, domestic acting, the first scene in the fourth act of his Sir Giles Overreach may be taken. His manner at meeting Lovell and through the conversation with him, the way in which he turns his chair and leans upon it, were as easy and natural as they could have been in real life, had Sir Giles been actually existing, and engaged at that moment in conversation in Lovell's room.

It is in these things, scarcely less than in the more prominent parts of his playing, that Kean shows himself the great actor. He must always make a deep impression; but to suppose the world at large capable of a right estimate of his different powers, would be forming a judgment against every-day proof. The gradual manner in which the character of his playing has opened upon me satisfies me, that in acting, as in everything else, however deep may be the first effect of genius upon us, we come slowly, and through study, to a perception of its minute beauties and delicate characteristics. After all, the greater part of men seldom get beyond the first general impression.

As there must needs go a *modicum* of fault-finding along with commendation, it may be well to remark, that Kean plays his hands too much at times, and moves about the dress over his breast and neck too frequently in his hurried and impatient passages, and that he does not always adhere with sufficient accuracy to the received readings of Shakspeare, and that the effect would be greater, upon the whole, were he to be more sparing of sudden changes from violent voice and gesticulation to a low conversation-tone and subdued manner.

His frequent use of these in Sir Giles Overreach is with good effect, for Sir Giles is playing his part; so, too, in Lear, for Lear's passions are gusty and shifting; but, in the main, it is a kind of playing too marked and striking to bear so frequent repetition, and had better sometimes be spared, where, considered alone, it might be properly enough used, for the sake of bringing it in at some other place with greater effect.

It is well to speak of these defects, for though the little faults of genius, in themselves considered, but slightly affect those who can enter into its true character, yet such are made impatient at the thought, that an opportunity is given those to carp who know not how to commend.

Though I have taken up a good deal of room, I must end

without speaking of many things which occur to me. Some will be of the opinion that I have already said enough. Thinking of Kean as I do, I could not honestly have said less; for I hold it to be a low and wicked thing to keep back from merit of any kind its due,—and, with Steele, that "there is something wonderful in the narrowness of those minds which can be pleased, and be barren of bounty to those who please them."

Although the self-important, out of self-concern, give praise sparingly, and the mean measure theirs by their likings or dislikings of a man, and the good even are often slow to allow the talents of the faulty their due, lest they bring the evil to repute; yet it is the wiser as well as the honester course, not to disparage an excellence because it neighbors upon a fault, nor to take away from another what is his of right, with a view to our own name, nor to rest our character for discernment upon the promptings of an unkind heart. Where God has not feared to bestow great powers, we may not fear giving them their due; nor need we be parsimonious of commendation, as if there were but a certain quantity for distribution, and our liberality would be to our loss; nor should we hold it safe to detract from another's merit, as if we could always keep the world blind, lest we live to see him whom we disparaged, praised, and whom we hated, loved.

Whatever be his failings, give every man a full and ready commendation for that in which he excels; it will do good to our own hearts, while it cheers his. Nor will it bring our judgment into question with the discerning; for enthusiasm for what is great does not argue such an unhappy want of discrimination as that measured and cold approval, which is bestowed alike upon men of mediocrity and upon those of gifted minds.

GIFTS

Ralph Waldo Emerson

"Gifts of one who loved me,—
'Twas high time they came;
When he ceased to love me,
Time they stopped for shame."

It is said that the world is in a state of bankruptcy, that the world owes the world more than the world can pay, and ought to go into chancery, and be sold. I do not think this general insolvency, which involves in some sort all the population, to be the reason of the difficulty experienced at Christmas and New Year, and other times, in bestowing gifts; since it is always so pleasant to be generous, though very vexatious to pay debts. But the impediment lies in the choosing. If, at any time, it comes into my head that a present is due from me to somebody, I am puzzled what to give until the opportunity is gone. Flowers and fruits are always fit presents; flowers, because they are a proud assertion that a ray of beauty outvalues all the utilities of the world. These gay natures contrast with the somewhat stern countenance of ordinary nature; they are like music heard out of a workhouse. Nature does not cocker us: we are children, not pets: she is not fond: everything is dealt to us without fear or favor, after severe universal laws. Yet these delicate flowers look like the frolic and interference of love and beauty. Men used to tell us that we love flattery, even though we are not deceived by it, because it shows that we are of importance enough to be courted.

Something like that pleasure the flowers give us: what am I to whom these sweet hints are addressed? Fruits are acceptable gifts because they are the flower of commodities, and admit of fantastic values being attached to them. If a man should send to me to come a hundred miles to visit him, and should set before me a basket of fine summer fruit, I should think there was some proportion between the labor and the reward.

For common gifts, necessity makes pertinences and beauty every day, and one is glad when an imperative leaves him no option, since if the man at the door have no shoes, you have not to consider whether you could procure him a paint-box. And as it is always pleasing to see a man eat bread, or drink water, in the house or out of doors, so it is always a great satisfaction to supply these first wants. Necessity does everything well. In our condition of universal dependence, it seems heroic to let the petitioner be the judge of his necessity, and to give all that is asked, though at great inconvenience. If it be a fantastic desire, it is better to leave to others the office of punishing him. I can think of many parts I should prefer playing to that of the Furies. Next to things of necessity, the rule for a gift which one of my friends prescribed is, that we might convey to some person that which properly belonged to his character, and was easily associated with him in thought. But our tokens of compliment and love are for the most part barbarous. Rings and other jewels are not gifts, but apologies for gifts. The only gift is a portion of thyself. Thou must bleed for me. Therefore the poet brings his poem; the shepherd, his lamb; the farmer, corn; the miner, a gem; the sailor, coral and shells; the painter, his picture; the girl, a handkerchief of her own sewing. This is right and pleasing, for it restores society in so far to the primary basis, when a man's biography is conveyed in his gift, and every man's wealth is an index of his merit. But it is a cold, lifeless business when you go to the shops to buy me something, which does not represent your life and talent, but a goldsmith's. This is fit for kings, and rich men who represent kings, and a false state of property, to make presents of gold and silver stuffs, as a kind of symbolical sin-offering, or payment of blackmail.

The law of benefits is a difficult channel, which requires careful sailing, or rude boats. It is not the office of a man to receive gifts. How dare you give them? We wish to be self-sustained. We do not quite forgive a giver. The hand that feeds us is in some danger of being bitten. We can receive anything from love, for that is a way of receiving it from ourselves; but not from anyone who assumes to bestow. We sometimes hate the meat which we eat, because there seems something of degrading dependence in living by it.

> "Brother, if Jove to thee a present make,
> Take heed that from his hands thou nothing take."

We ask the whole. Nothing less will content us. We arraign society if it do not give us besides earth, and fire, and water, opportunity, love, reverence, and objects of veneration.

He is a good man who can receive a gift well. We are either glad or sorry at a gift, and both emotions are unbecoming. Some violence, I think, is done, some degradation borne, when I rejoice or grieve at a gift. I am sorry when my independence is invaded, or when a gift comes from such as do not know my spirit, and so the act is not supported; and if the gift pleases me overmuch, then I should be ashamed that the donor should read my heart, and see that I love his commodity, and not him. The gift, to be true, must be the flowing of the giver unto me, correspondent to my flowing unto him. When the waters are at level, then my goods pass to him, and his to me. All his are mine, all mine his. I say to him, How can you give me this pot of oil, or this flagon of wine, when all your oil and wine is mine, which belief of mine this gift seems to deny? Hence the fitness of beautiful, not useful things for gifts. This giving is flat usurpation, and therefore when the beneficiary is ungrateful, as all beneficiaries hate all Timons, not at all considering the value of the gift, but looking back to the greater store it was taken from, I rather sympathize with the beneficiary than with the anger of my lord Timon. For, the expectation of gratitude is mean, and is continually punished by the total insensibility of the obliged person. It is a great happiness to get off without injury and heart-burning, from one who has had the ill-luck to be served by you. It is a very onerous business, this of being served, and the debtor naturally wishes to give you a slap. A golden text for these gentlemen is that which I so admire in the Buddhist, who never thanks, and who says, "Do not flatter your benefactors."

The reason for these discords I conceive to be that there is no commensurability between a man and any gift. You cannot give anything to a magnanimous person. After you have served him he at once puts you in debt by his magnanimity. The service a man renders his friend is trivial and selfish, compared with the service he knows his friend stood in readiness to yield him, alike before he had begun to serve his friend, and now also. Compared with that good-will I bear my friend, the benefit it is in my power to render him seems small. Besides, our action on each other, good as well as evil, is so incidental and at random, that we can seldom hear the acknowledgments of any person who would thank us for a benefit, without some shame and humiliation. We can rarely strike a direct stroke, but must be content with an oblique one; we seldom have the satisfaction of yielding a direct benefit, which is directly received. But rectitude scatters favors on every side without knowing it, and receives with wonder the thanks of all people.

I fear to breathe any treason against the majesty of love, which is the genius and god of gifts, and to whom we must not affect to prescribe. Let him give kingdoms or flower-leaves indifferently. There are persons from whom we always expect fairy-tokens; let us not cease to expect them. This is prerogative, and not to be limited by our municipal rules. For the rest, I like to see that we cannot be bought and sold. The best of hospitality and of generosity is also not in the will, but in fate. I find that I am not much to you; you do not need me; you do not feel me; then am I thrust out of doors, though you proffer me house and lands. No services are of any value, but only likeness. When I have attempted to join myself to others by services, it proved an intellectual trick,—no more. They eat your service like apples, and leave you out. But love them, and they feel you, and delight in you all the time.

USES OF GREAT MEN

Ralph Waldo Emerson

It is natural to believe in great men. If the companions of our childhood should turn out to be heroes, and their condition regal, it would not surprise us. All mythology opens with demigods, and the circumstance is high and poetic; that is, their genius is paramount. In the legends of the Gautama, the first men ate the earth, and found it deliciously sweet.

Nature seems to exist for the excellent. The world is upheld by the veracity of good men: they make the earth wholesome. They who lived with them found life glad and nutritious. Life is sweet and tolerable only in our belief in such society; and actually or ideally we manage to live with superiors. We call our children and our lands by their names. Their names are wrought into the verbs of language, their works and effigies are in our houses, and every circumstance of the day recalls an anecdote of them.

The search after the great is the dream of youth and the most serious occupation of manhood. We travel into foreign parts to find his works—if possible, to get a glimpse of him. But we are put off with fortune instead. You say the English are practical; the Germans are hospitable; in Valencia the climate is delicious; and in the hills of the Sacramento there is gold for the gathering. Yes, but I do not travel to find comfortable, rich, and hospitable people, or clear sky, or ingots that cost too much. But if there were any magnet that would point to the countries and houses where are the persons who are intrinsically rich and powerful, I would sell all, and buy it, and put myself on the road to-day.

The race goes with us on their credit. The knowledge that in the city is a man who invented the railroad raises the credit of all the citizens. But enormous populations, if they be beggars, are disgusting, like moving cheese, like hills of ants or of fleas—the more, the worse.

Our religion is the love and cherishing of these patrons. The gods of fable are the shining moments of great men. We run all our vessels into one mould. Our colossal theologies of Judaism, Christism, Buddhism, Mahometism, are the necessary and structural action of the human mind. The student of history is like a man going into a warehouse to buy cloths or carpets. He fancies he has a new article. If he go to the factory, he shall find that his new stuff still repeats the scrolls and rosettes which are found on the interior walls of the pyramids of Thebes. Our theism is the purification of the human mind. Man can paint, or make, or think nothing but man. He believes that the great material elements had their origin from his thought. And our philosophy finds one essence collected or distributed.

If now we proceed to inquire into the kinds of service we derive from others, let us be warned of the danger of modern studies, and begin low enough. We must not contend against love, or deny the substantial existence of other people. I know not what would happen to us. We have social strengths. Our affection towards others creates a sort of vantage or purchase which nothing will supply. I can do that by another which I cannot do alone. I can say to you what I cannot first say to myself. Other men are lenses through which we read our own minds. Each man seeks those of different quality from his own, and such as are good of their kind; that is, he seeks other men, and the *otherest*. The stronger the nature, the more it is reactive. Let us have the quality pure. A little genius let us leave alone. A main difference betwixt men is, whether they attend their own affair or not. Man is that noble endogenous plant which grows, like the palm, from within outward. His own affair, though impossible to others, he can open with celerity and in sport. It is easy to sugar to be sweet, and to nitre to be salt. We take a great deal of pains to waylay and entrap that which of itself will fall into our hands. I count him a great man who inhabits a higher sphere of thought, into which other men rise with labor and difficulty; he has but to open his eyes to see things in a true light, and in large relations; whilst they must make painful corrections, and keep a vigilant eye on many sources of error. His service to us is of like sort. It costs a beautiful person no exertion to paint her image on our eyes; yet how splendid is that benefit! It costs no more for a wise soul to convey his quality to other men. And everyone can do his best thing easiest. "*Peu de moyens, beaucoup d'effét.*" He is great who is what he is from nature, and who never reminds us of others.

But he must be related to us, and our life receive from him some promise of explanation. I cannot tell what I would know; but I have observed there are persons who, in their character and actions, answer questions which I have not skill to put. One man answers some questions which none of his contemporaries put, and is isolated. The past and passing religions and philosophies answer some other question. Certain men affect us as rich possibilities, but helpless to themselves and to their times,—the sport, perhaps, of some instinct that rules in the air,—they do not speak to our want. But the great are near; we know them at sight. They satisfy expectation, and fall into place. What is good is effective, generative; makes for itself room, food, and allies. A sound apple produces seed—a hybrid does not. Is a man in his place, he is constructive, fertile, magnetic, inundating armies with his purpose, which is thus executed. The river makes its own shores, and each legitimate idea makes its own channels and welcome—harvests for food, institutions for expression, weapons to fight with, and disciples to explain it. The true artist has the planet for his pedestal; the adventurer, after years of strife, has nothing broader than his own shoes.

Our common discourse respects two kinds of use or service from superior men. Direct giving is agreeable to the early belief of men; direct giving of material or metaphysical aid, as of health, eternal youth, fine senses, arts of healing, magical power, and prophecy. The boy believes there is a teacher who can sell him wisdom. Churches believe in imputed merit. But, in strictness, we are not much cognizant of direct serving. Man is endogenous, and education is his unfolding. The aid we have from others is mechanical, compared with the discoveries of nature in us. What is thus learned is delightful in the doing, and the effect remains. Right ethics are central, and go from the soul outward. Gift is contrary to the law of the universe. Serving others is serving us. I must absolve me to myself. "Mind thy affair," says the spirit; "coxcomb, would you meddle with the skies, or with other people?" Indirect service is left. Men have a pictorial or representative quality, and serve us in the intellect. Behmen and Swedenborg saw that things were representative. Men are also representative; first, of things, and secondly, of ideas.

As plants convert the minerals into food for animals, so each man converts some raw material in nature to human use. The inventors of fire, electricity, magnetism, iron, lead, glass, linen, silk, cotton; the makers of tools; the inventor of decimal notation; the geometer; the engineer; the musician, severally make an easy way for all through unknown and impossible confusions. Each man is, by secret liking, connected with some district of nature, whose agent and interpreter he is, as Linnæus, of plants; Huber, of bees; Fries, of lichens; Van Mons, of pears; Dalton, of atomic forms; Euclid, of lines; Newton, of fluxions.

A man is a center for nature, running out threads of relation through everything, fluid and solid, material and elemental. The earth rolls; every clod and stone comes to the meridian; so every organ, function, acid, crystal, grain of dust, has its relation to the brain. It waits long, but its turn comes. Each plant has its parasite, and each created thing its lover and poet. Justice has already been done to steam, to iron, to wood, to coal, to loadstone, to iodine, to corn and cotton; but how few materials are yet used by our arts! The mass of creatures and of qualities are still hid and expectant. It would seem as if each waited, like the enchanted princess in fairy tales, for a destined human deliverer. Each must be disenchanted, and walk forth to the day in human shape. In the history of discovery, the ripe and latent truth seems to have fashioned a brain for itself. A magnet must be made man, in some Gilbert, or Swedenborg, or Oersted, before the general mind can come to entertain its powers.

If we limit ourselves to the first advantages: a sober grace adheres to the mineral and botanic kingdoms, which in the highest moments comes up as the charm of nature, the glitter of the spar, the sureness of affinity, the veracity of angles. Light and darkness, heat and cold, hunger and food, sweet and sour, solid, liquid, and gas, circle us round in a wreath of pleasures, and, by their agreeable quarrel, beguile the day of life. The eye repeats every day the first eulogy on things—" He saw that they were good."

We know where to find them; and these performers are relished all the more after a little experience of the pretending races. We are entitled, also, to higher advantages. Something is wanting to science, until it has been humanized. The table of logarithms is one thing, and its vital play, in botany, music, optics, and architecture, another. There are advancements to numbers, anatomy, architecture, astronomy, little suspected at first, when, by union with intellect and will, they ascend into the life, and reappear in conversation, character, and politics.

But this comes later. We speak now only of our acquaintance with them in their own sphere, and the way in which they seem to fascinate and draw to them some genius who occupies himself with one thing all his life long. The possibility of interpretation lies in the identity of the observer with the observed. Each material thing has its celestial side; has its translation, through humanity, into the spiritual and necessary sphere, where it plays a part as indestructible as any other. And to these, their ends, all things continually ascend. The gases gather to the solid firmament; the chemic lump arrives at the plant, and grows; arrives at the quadruped, and walks; arrives at the man, and thinks. But also the constituency determines the vote of the representative. He is not only representative, but participant. Like can only be known by like. The reason why he knows about them is, that he is of them; he has just come out of nature, or from being a part of that thing. Animated chlorine knows of chlorine, and incarnate zinc, of zinc. Their quality makes his career; and he can variously publish their virtues, because they compose him. Man, made of the dust of the world, does not forget his origin; and all that is yet inanimate will one day speak and reason. Unpublished nature will have its whole secret told. Shall we say that quartz mountains will.

pulverize into innumerable Werners, Von Buchs, and Beaumonts; and the laboratory of the atmosphere holds in solution I know not what Berzeliuses and Davys?

Thus we sit by the fire, and take hold on the poles of the earth. This *quasi* omnipresence supplies the imbecility of our condition. In one of those celestial days, when heaven and earth meet and adorn each other, it seems a poverty that we can only spend it once: we wish for a thousand heads, a thousand bodies, that we might celebrate its immense beauty in many ways and places. Is this fancy? Well, in good faith, we are multiplied by our proxies. How easily we adopt their labors. Every ship that comes to America got its chart from Columbus. Every novel is a debtor to Homer. Every carpenter who shaves with a foreplane borrows the genius of a forgotten inventor. Life is girt all round with a zodiac of sciences, the contributions of men who have perished to add their point of light to our sky. Engineer, broker, jurist, physician, moralist, theologian, and every man, inasmuch as he has any science, is a definer and map-maker of the latitudes and longitudes of our condition. These road-makers on every hand enrich us. We must extend the area of life, and multiply our relations. We are as much gainers by finding a new property in the old earth as by acquiring a new planet.

We are too passive in the reception of these material or semi-material aids. We must not be sacks and stomachs. To ascend one step—we are better served through our sympathy. Activity is contagious. Looking where others look, and conversing with the same things, we catch the charm which lured them. Napoleon said, "You must not fight too often with one enemy, or you will teach him all your art of war." Talk much with any man of vigorous mind, and we acquire very fast the habit of looking at things in the same light, and, on each occurrence, we anticipate his thought.

Men are helpful through the intellect and the affections. Other help, I find a false appearance. If you affect to give me bread and fire, I perceive that I pay for it the full price, and at last it leaves me as it found me, neither better nor worse; but all mental and moral force is a positive good. It goes out from you, whether you will or not, and profits me whom you never thought of. I cannot even hear of personal vigor of any kind, great power of performance, without fresh resolution. We are emulous of all that man can do. Cecil's saying of Sir Walter Raleigh, " I know that he can toil terribly," is an electric touch. So are Clarendon's portraits—of Hampden: " who was of an industry and vigilance not to be tired out or wearied by the most laborious, and of parts not to be imposed on by the most subtle and sharp, and of a personal courage equal to his best parts;"—of Falkland: " who was so severe an adorer of truth that he could as easily have given himself leave to steal as to dissemble." We cannot read Plutarch without a tingling of the blood; and I accept the saying of the Chinese Mencius: " A sage is the instructor of a hundred ages. When the manners of Loo are heard of, the stupid become intelligent, and the wavering, determined."

This is the moral of biography; yet it is hard for departed men to touch the quick like our own companions, whose names may not last as long. What is he whom I never think of? whilst in every solitude are those who succor our genius, and stimulate us in wonderful manners. There is a power in love to divine another's destiny better than that other can, and, by heroic encouragements, hold him to his task. What has friendship so signal as its sublime attraction to whatever virtue is in us? We will never more think cheaply of ourselves, or of life. We are piqued to some purpose, and the industry of the diggers on the railroad will not again shame us.

Under this head, too, falls that homage, very pure, as I think, which all ranks pay to the hero of the day, from Coriolanus and Gracchus, down to Pitt, Lafayette, Wellington, Webster, Lamartine. Hear the shouts in the street! The people cannot see him enough. They delight in a man. Here is a head and a trunk! What a front! What eyes! Atlantean shoulders, and the whole carriage heroic, with equal inward force to guide the great machine! This pleasure of full expression to that which, in their private experience, is usually cramped and obstructed, runs, also, much higher, and is the secret of the reader's joy in literary genius. Nothing is kept back. There is fire enough to fuse the mountain of ore. Shakspeare's principal merit may be conveyed in saying that he, of all men, best understands the English language, and can say what he will. Yet these unchoked channels and floodgates of expression are only health or fortunate constitution. Shakspeare's name suggests other and purely intellectual benefits.

Senates and sovereigns have no compliment, with their medals, swords, and armorial coats, like the addressing to a human being thoughts out of a certain height, and presupposing his intelligence. This honor, which is possible in personal intercourse scarcely twice in a lifetime, genius perpetually pays; contented, if now and then, in a century, the proffer is accepted. The indicators of the values of matter are degraded to a sort of cooks and confectioners, on the appearance of the indicators of ideas. Genius is the naturalist or geographer of the supersensible regions, and draws their map; and, by acquainting us with new fields of activity, cools our affection for the old. These are at once accepted as the reality, of which the world we have conversed with is the show.

We go to the gymnasium and the swimming-school to see the power and beauty of the body; there is the like pleasure, and higher benefit, from witnessing intellectual feats of all kinds; as feats of memory, of mathematical combination, great power of abstraction, the transmutings of the imagination, even versatility and concentration, as these acts expose the invisible organs and members of the mind, which respond, member for member, to the parts of the body. For we thus enter a new gymnasium, and learn to choose men by their truest marks, taught, with Plato, "to choose those who can, without aid from the eyes or any other sense, proceed to truth and to being." Foremost among these activities are the summersaults, spells, and resurrections wrought by the imagination. When this wakes, a man seems to multiply ten times or a thousand times his force. It opens the delicious sense of indeterminate size, and inspires an audacious mental habit. We are as elastic as the gas of gunpowder, and a sentence in a book or a word dropped in conversation sets free our fancy, and instantly our heads are bathed with galaxies, and our feet tread the floor of the pit. And this benefit is real, because we are entitled to these enlargements, and, once having passed the bounds, shall never again be quite the miserable pedants we were.

The high functions of the intellect are so allied that some imaginative power usually appears in all eminent minds, even in arithmeticians of the first class, but especially in meditative men of an intuitive habit of thought. This class serve us, so that they have the perception of identity and the perception of reaction. The eyes of Plato, Shakspeare, Swedenborg, Goethe, never shut on either of these laws. The perception of these laws is a kind of meter of the mind. Little minds are little, through failure to see them.

Even these feasts have their surfeit. Our delight in

reason degenerates into idolatry of the herald. Especially when a mind of powerful method has instructed men, we find the examples of oppression. The dominion of Aristotle, the Ptolemaic astronomy, the credit of Luther, of Bacon, of Locke,—in religion, the history of hierarchies, of saints, and the sects which have taken the name of each founder,—are in point. Alas! every man is such a victim. The imbecility of men is always inviting the impudence of power. It is the delight of vulgar talent to dazzle and to blind the beholder. But true genius seeks to defend us from itself. True genius will not impoverish, but will liberate, and add new senses. If a wise man should appear in our village, he would create, in those who conversed with him, a new consciousness of wealth, by opening their eyes to unobserved advantages; he would establish a sense of immovable equality, calm us with assurances that we could not be cheated; as everyone would discern the checks and guaranties of condition. The rich would see their mistakes and poverty, the poor their escapes and their resources.

But nature brings all this about in due time. Rotation is her remedy. The soul is impatient of masters, and eager for change. Housekeepers say of a domestic who has been valuable, "She had lived with me long enough." We are tendencies, or rather symptoms, and none of us complete. We touch and go, and sip the foam of many lives. Rotation is the law of nature. When nature removes a great man, people explore the horizon for a successor; but none comes, and none will. His class is extinguished with him. In some other and quite different field, the next man will appear; not Jefferson, not Franklin, but now a great salesman; than a road-contractor; then a student of fishes; then a buffalo-hunting explorer, or a semi-savage Western general. Thus we make a stand against our rougher masters; but against the best there is a finer remedy. The power which they communicate is not theirs. When we are exalted by ideas, we do not owe this to Plato, but to the idea, to which, also, Plato was debtor.

I must not forget that we have a special debt to a single class. Life is a scale of degrees. Between rank and rank of our great men are wide intervals. Mankind have, in all ages, attached themselves to a few persons, who, either by the quality of that idea they embodied, or by the largeness of their reception, were entitled to the position of leaders and law-givers. These teach us the qualities of primary nature—admit us to the constitution of things. We swim, day by day, on a river of delusions, and are effectually amused with houses and towns in the air, of which the men about us are dupes. But life is a sincerity. In lucid intervals we say, "Let there be an entrance opened for me into realties; I have worn the fool's cap too long." We will know the meaning of our economies and politics. Give us the cipher, and, if persons and things are scores of a celestial music, let us read off the strains. We have been cheated of our reason; yet there have been sane men who enjoyed a rich and related existence. What they know they know for us. With each new mind, a new secret of nature transpires; nor can the Bible be closed until the last great man is born. These men correct the delirium of the animal spirits, make us considerate, and engage us to new aims and powers. The veneration of mankind selects these for the highest place. Witness the multitude of statues, pictures, and memorials which recall their genius in every city, village, house, and ship:

> "Ever their phantoms arise before us,
>   Our loftier brothers, but one in blood;
> At bed and table they lord it o'er us,
>   With looks of beauty, and words of good."

How to illustrate the distinctive benefit of ideas, the

service rendered by those who introduce moral truths into the general mind?—I am plagued, in all my living, with a perpetual tariff of prices. If I work in my garden and prune an apple-tree, I am well enough entertained, and could continue indefinitely in the like occupation. But it comes to mind that a day is gone, and I have got this precious nothing done. I go to Boston or New York, and run up and down on my affairs: they are sped, but so is the day. I am vexed by the recollection of this price I have paid for a trifling advantage. I remember the *peau d'âne,* on which whoso sat should have his desire, but a piece of the skin was gone for every wish. I go to a convention of philanthropists. Do what I can, I cannot keep my eyes off the clock. But if there should appear in the company some gentle soul who knows little of persons or parties, of Carolina or Cuba, but who announces a law that disposes these particulars, and so certifies me of the equity which checkmates every false player, bankrupts every self-seeker, and apprises me of my independence on any conditions of country, or time, or human body, that man liberates me; I forget the clock. I pass out of the sore relation to persons. I am healed of my hurts. I am made immortal by apprehending my possession of incorruptible goods. Here is great competition of rich and poor. We live in a market, where is only so much wheat, or wool, or land; and if I have so much more, every other must have so much less. I seem to have no good, without breach of good manners. Nobody is glad in the gladness of another, and our system is one of war, of an injurious superiority. Every child of the Saxon race is educated to wish to be first. It is our system; and a man comes to measure his greatness by the regrets, envies, and hatreds of his competitors. But in these new fields there is room: here are no self-esteems, no exclusions.

I admire great men of all classes, those who stand for facts and for thoughts; I like rough and smooth, "scourges of God" and "darlings of the human race." I like the first Cæsar; and Charles V, of Spain; and Charles XII, of Sweden; Richard Plantagenet; and Bonaparte, in France. I applaud a sufficient man, an officer equal to his office; captains, ministers, senators. I like a master standing firm on legs of iron, well-born, rich, handsome, eloquent, loaded with advantages, drawing all men by fascination into tributaries and supports of his power. Sword and staff, or talents sword-like or staff-like, carry on the work of the world. But I find him greater when he can abolish himself, and all heroes, by letting in this element of reason, irrespective of persons; this subtilizer, and irresistible upward force, into our thought, destroying individualism; the power so great that the potentate is nothing. Then he is a monarch who gives a constitution to his people; a pontiff who preaches the equality of souls, and releases his servants from their barbarous homages; an emperor who can spare his empire.

But I intended to specify, with a little minuteness, two or three points of service. Nature never spares the opium or nepenthe; but, wherever she mars her creature with some deformity or defect, lays her poppies plentifully on the bruise, and the sufferer goes joyfully through life, ignorant of the ruin, and incapable of seeing it, though all the world point their finger at it every day. The worthless and offensive members of society, whose existence is a social pest, invariably think themselves the most ill-used people alive, and never get over their astonishment at the ingratitude and selfishness of their contemporaries. Our globe discovers its hidden virtues, not only in heroes and archangels, but in gossips and nurses. Is it not a rare contrivance that lodged the due inertia in every creature, the conserving, resisting energy, the anger at being waked or changed? Altogether independent of the intellectual force in each is the pride of opinion, the security that we are right. Not the feeblest grandame, not a mowing idiot, but uses what spark of perception and faculty is left, to chuckle and triumph in his or her opinion over the absurdities of all the rest. Difference from me is the measure of absurdity. Not one has a misgiving of being wrong. Was it not a bright thought that made things cohere with this bitumen, fastest of cements? But, in the midst of this chuckle of self-gratulation, some figure goes by which Thersites too can love and admire. This is he that should marshal us the way we were going. There is no end to his aid. Without Plato, we should almost lose our faith in the possibility of a reasonable book. We seem to want but one, but we want one. We love to associate with heroic persons, since our receptivity is unlimited; and, with the great, our thoughts and manners easily become great. We are all wise in capacity, though so few in energy. There needs but one wise man in a company, and all are wise, so rapid is the contagion.

Great men are thus a collyrium to clear our eyes from egotism, and enable us to see other people and their works. But there are vices and follies incident to whole populations and ages. Men resemble their contemporaries, even more than their progenitors. It is observed in old couples, or in persons who have been housemates for a course of years, that they grow like; and if they should live long enough, we should not be able to know them apart. Nature abhors these complaisances, which threaten to melt the world into a lump, and hastens to break up such maudlin agglutinations. The like assimilation goes on between men of one town, of one sect, of one political party; and the ideas of the time are in the air, and infect all who breathe it.

Viewed from any high point, this city of New York, yonder city of London, the western civilization, would seem a bundle of insanities. We keep each other in countenance, and exasperate by emulation the frenzy of the time. The shield against the stingings of conscience is the universal practice, or our contemporaries. Again: it is very easy to be as wise and good as your companions. We learn of our contemporaries what they know, without effort, and almost through the pores of the skin. We catch it by sympathy, or as a wife arrives at the intellectual and moral elevations of her husband. But we stop where they stop. Very hardly can we take another step. The great, or such as hold of nature, and transcend fashions, by their fidelity to universal ideas, are saviors from these federal errors, and defend us from our contemporaries. They are the exceptions which we want, where all grows alike. A foreign greatness is the antidote for cabalism.

Thus we feed on genius, and refresh ourselves from too much conversation with our mates, and exult in the depth of nature in that direction in which he leads us. What indemnification is one great man for populations of pygmies! Every mother wishes one son a genius, though all the rest should be mediocre. But a new danger appears in the excess of influence of the great man. His attractions warp us from our place. We have become underlings and intellectual suicides. Ah! yonder in the horizon is our help: other great men, new qualities, counterweights and checks on each other. We cloy of the honey of each peculiar greatness. Every hero becomes a bore at last. Perhaps Voltaire was not bad-hearted, yet he said of the good Jesus, even, "I pray you, let me never hear that man's name again." They cry up the virtues of George Washington—"Damn George Washington!" is the poor Jacobin's whole speech and confutation. But it is human nature's indispensable defense. The centripetence augments the centrifugence. We balance one man with his opposite, and the health of the State depends on the see-saw.

There is, however, a speedy limit to the use of heroes. Every genius is defended from approach by quantities of unavailableness. They are very attractive, and seem at a distance our own; but we are hindered on all sides from approach. The more we are drawn, the more we are repelled. There is something not solid in the good that is done for us. The best discovery the discoverer makes for himself. It has something unreal for his companion, until he too has substantiated it. It seems as if the Deity dressed each soul which he sends into nature in certain virtues and powers not communicable to other men, and, sending it to perform one more turn through the circle of beings, wrote, "*Not transferable,*" and "*Good for this trip only,*" on these garments of the soul. There is somewhat deceptive about the intercourse of minds. The boundaries are invisible, but they are never crossed. There is such good will to impart, and such good will to receive, that each threatens to become the other; but the law of individuality collects its secret strength: you are you, and I am I, and so we remain.

For Nature wishes everything to remain itself; and whilst every individual strives to grow and exclude, and to exclude and grow, to the extremities of the universe, and to impose the law of its being on every other creature, Nature steadily aims to protect each against every other. Each is self-defended. Nothing is more marked than the power by which individuals are guarded from individuals, in a world where every benefactor becomes so easily a malefactor, only by continuation of his activity into places where it is not due; where children seem so much at the mercy of their foolish parents, and where almost all men are too social and interfering. We rightly speak of the guardian angels of children. How superior in their security from infusions of evil persons, from vulgarity and second thought! They shed their own abundant beauty on the objects they behold. Therefore, they are not at the mercy of such poor educators as we adults. If we huff and chide them, they soon come not to mind it, and get a self-reliance; and if we indulge them to folly, they learn the limitation elsewhere.

We need not fear excessive influence. A more generous trust is permitted. Serve the great. Stick at no humiliation. Grudge no office thou canst render. Be the limb of their body, the breath of their mouth. Compromise thy egotism. Who cares for that, so thou gain aught wider and nobler? Never mind the taunt of Boswellism: the devotion may easily be greater than the wretched pride which is guarding its own skirts. Be another—not thyself, but a Platonist; not a soul, but a Christian; not a naturalist, but a Cartesian; not a poet, but a Shaksperian. In vain; the wheels of tendency will not stop, nor will all the forces of inertia, fear, or of love itself, hold thee there. On, and forever onward! The microscope observes a monad or wheel-insect among the infusories circulating in water. Presently a dot appears on the animal, which enlarges to a slit, and it becomes two perfect animals. The ever-proceeding detachment appears not less in all thought, and in society. Children think they cannot live without their parents. But long before they are aware of it, the black dot has appeared, and the detachment taken place. Any accident will now reveal to them their independence.

But *great men*—the word is injurious. Is there caste? Is there fate? What becomes of the promise to virtue? The thoughtful youth laments the superfœtation of nature. " Generous and handsome," he says, " is your hero; but look at yonder poor Paddy, whose country is his wheelbarrow; look at his whole nation of Paddies." Why are the masses, from the dawn of history down, food for knives and powder? The idea dignifies a few leaders, who have sentiment, opinion, love, self-devotion; and they make war and death sacred; but what for the wretches whom they hire and kill? The cheapness of man is every day's tragedy. It is as real a loss that others should be low as that we should be low; for we must have society.

Is it a reply to these suggestions, to say society is a Pestalozzian school; all are teachers and pupils in turn. We are equally served by receiving and by imparting. Men who know the same things are not long the best company for each other. But bring to each an intelligent person of another experience, and it is as if you let off water from a lake, by cutting a lower basin. It seems a mechanical advantage, and great benefit it is to each speaker, as he can now paint out his thought to himself. We pass very fast, in our personal moods, from dignity to dependence. And if any appear never to assume the chair, but always to stand and serve, it is because we do not see the company in a sufficiently long period for the whole rotation of parts to come about. As to what we call the masses and common men—there are no common men. All men are at last of a size; and true art is only possible on the conviction that every talent has its apotheosis somewhere. Fair play, and an open field, and freshest laurels to all who have won them! But heaven reserves an equal scope for every creature. Each is uneasy until he has produced his private ray unto the concave sphere, and beheld his talent also in its last nobility and exaltation.

The heroes of the hour are relatively great—of a faster growth; or they are such, in whom, at the moment of success, a quality is ripe which is then in request. Other days will demand other qualities. Some rays escape the common observer, and want a finely adapted eye. Ask the great man if there be none greater. His companions are; and not the less great, but the more, that society cannot see them. Nature never sends a great man into the planet without confiding the secret to another soul.

One gracious fact emerges from these studies—that there is true ascension in our love. The reputations of the nineteenth century will one day be quoted to prove its barbarism. The genius of humanity is the real subject whose biography is written in our annals. We must infer much, and supply many chasms in the record. The history of the universe is symptomatic, and life is mnemonical. No man, in all the procession of famous men, is reason or illumination, or that essence we were looking for, but is an exhibition, in some quarter, of new possibilities. Could we one day complete the immense figure which these flagrant points compose! The study of many individuals leads us to an elemental region wherein the individual is lost, or wherein all touch by their summits. Thought and feeling, that break out there, cannot be impounded by any fence of personality. This is the key to the power of the greatest men—their spirit diffuses itself. A new quality of mind travels by night and by day, in concentric circles from its origin, and publishes itself by unknown methods; the union of all minds appears intimate; what gets admission to one cannot be kept out of any other; the smallest acquisition of truth or of energy, in any quarter, is so much good to the commonwealth of souls. If the disparities of talent and position vanish when the individuals are seen in the duration which is necessary to complete the career of each, even more swiftly the seeming injustice disappears when we ascend to the central identity of all the individuals, and know that they are made of the substance which ordaineth and doeth.

USES OF GREAT MEN

The genius of humanity is the right point of view of history. The qualities abide; the men who exhibit them have now more, now less, and pass away; the qualities remain on another brow. No experience is more familiar. Once you saw phœnixes: they are gone; the world is not therefore disenchanted. The vessels on which you read sacred emblems turn out to be common pottery; but the sense of the pictures is sacred, and you may still read them transferred to the walls of the world. For a time our teachers serve us personally, as meters or milestones of progress. Once they were angels of knowledge, and their figures touched the sky. Then we drew near, saw their means, culture, and limits; and they yielded their place to other geniuses. Happy, if a few names remain so high that we have not been able to read them nearer, and age and comparison have not robbed them of a ray. But, at last, we shall cease to look in men for completeness, and shall content ourselves with their social and delegated quality. All that respects the individual is temporary and prospective, like the individual himself, who is ascending out of his limits into a catholic existence. We have never come at the true and best benefit of any genius, so long as we believe him an original force. In the moment when he ceases to help us as a cause, he begins to help us more as an effect. Then he appears as an exponent of a vaster mind and will. The opaque self becomes transparent with the light of the First Cause.

Yet, within the limits of human education and agency, we may say great men exist that there may be greater men. The destiny of organized nature is amelioration, and who can tell its limits? It is for man to tame the chaos; on every side, whilst he lives, to scatter the seeds of science and of song, that climate, corn, animals, men, may be milder, and the germs of love and benefit may be multiplied.

BUDS AND BIRD-VOICES

Nathaniel Hawthorne

Balmy Spring—weeks later than we expected, and months later than we longed for her—comes at last to revive the moss on the roof and walls of our old mansion. She peeps brightly into my study window, inviting me to throw it open and create a summer atmosphere by the intermixture of her genial breath with the black and cheerless comfort of the stove. As the casement ascends, forth into infinite space fly the innumerable forms of thought or fancy that have kept me company in the retirement of this little chamber during the sluggish lapse of wintry weather—visions gay, grotesque and sad, pictures of real life tinted with nature's homely gray and russet, scenes in dreamland bedizened with rainbow-hues which faded before they were well laid on. All these may vanish now, and leave me to mold a fresh existence out of sunshine. Brooding Meditation may flap her dusky wings and take her owl-like flight, blinking amid the cheerfulness of noontide. Such companions befit the season of frosted window-panes and crackling fires, when the blast howls through the black-ash trees of our avenue, and the drifting snow-storm chokes up the wood paths and fills the highway from stone wall to stone wall. In the spring and summer time all somber thoughts should follow the winter northward with the somber and thoughtful crows. The old paradisiacal economy of life is again in force: we live, not to think nor to labor, but for the simple end of

Buds and Bird-Voices

being happy; nothing for the present hour is worthy of man's infinite capacity save to imbibe the warm smile of heaven and sympathize with the reviving earth.

The present Spring comes onward with fleeter footsteps because Winter lingered so unconscionably long that with her best diligence she can hardly retrieve half the allotted period of her reign. It is but a fortnight since I stood on the brink of our swollen river and beheld the accumulated ice of four frozen months go down the stream. Except in streaks here and there upon the hillsides, the whole visible universe was then covered with deep snow the nethermost layer of which had been deposited by an early December storm. It was a sight to make the beholder torpid, in the impossibility of imagining how this vast white napkin was to be removed from the face of the corpse-like world in less time than had been required to spread it there. But who can estimate the power of gentle influences, whether amid material desolation or the moral winter of man's heart? There have been no tempestuous rains—even no sultry days—but a constant breath of southern winds, with now a day of kindly sunshine, and now a no less kindly mist, or a soft descent of showers, in which a smile and a blessing seemed to have been steeped. The snow has vanished as if by magic; whatever heaps may be hidden in the woods and deep gorges of the hills, only two solitary specks remain in the landscape, and those I shall almost regret to miss when to-morrow I look for them in vain. Never before, methinks, has spring pressed so closely on the footsteps of retreating winter. Along the roadside the green blades of grass have sprouted on the very edge of the snowdrifts. The pastures and mowing fields have not yet assumed a general aspect of verdure, but neither have they the cheerless brown tint which they wear in later autumn, when vegetation has entirely ceased;

there is now a faint shadow of life, gradually brightening into the warm reality. Some tracts in a happy exposure—as, for instance, yonder southwestern slope of an orchard, in front of that old red farmhouse beyond the river—such patches of land already wear a beautiful and tender green to which no future luxuriance can add a charm. It looks unreal—a prophecy, a hope, a transitory effect of some peculiar light, which will vanish with the slightest motion of the eye. But beauty is never a delusion; not these verdant tracts but the dark and barren landscape all around them is a shadow and a dream. Each moment wins some portion of the earth from death to life; a sudden gleam of verdure brightens along the sunny slope of a bank which an instant ago was brown and bare. You look again, and, behold an apparition of green grass!

The trees in our orchard and elsewhere are as yet naked, but already appear full of life and vegetable blood. It seems as if by one magic touch they might instantaneously burst into full foliage, and that the wind which now sighs through their naked branches might make sudden music amid innumerable leaves. The moss-grown willow tree which for forty years past has overshadowed these western windows will be among the first to put on its green attire. There are some objections to the willow: it is not a dry and cleanly tree, and impresses the beholder with an association of sliminess. No trees, I think, are perfectly agreeable as companions unless they have glossy leaves, dry bark, and a firm and hard texture of trunk and branches. But the willow is almost the earliest to gladden us with the promise and reality of beauty in its graceful and delicate foliage, and the last to scatter its yellow, yet scarcely-withered, leaves upon the ground. All through the winter, too, its yellow twigs give it a sunny aspect which is not without a cheering influence even in the grayest and gloomiest day. Beneath a clouded sky it faithfully remembers the sunshine. Our old house would lose a charm were the willow to be cut down, with its golden crown over the snow-covered roof, and its heap of summer verdure.

The lilac shrubs under my study windows are likewise almost in leaf; in two or three days more I may put forth my hand and pluck the topmost bough in its freshest green. These lilacs are very aged, and have lost the luxuriant foliage of their prime. The heart or the judgment or the moral sense or the taste is dissatisfied with their present aspect. Old age is not venerable when it embodies itself in lilacs, rose-bushes, or any other ornamental shrubs; it seems as if such plants, as they grow only for beauty, ought to flourish only in immortal youth—or, at least, to die before their sad decrepitude. Trees of beauty are trees of paradise, and therefore not subject to decay by their original nature, though they have lost that precious birthright by being transplanted to an earthly soil. There is a kind of ludicrous unfitness in the idea of a time-stricken and grandfatherly lilac-bush. The analogy holds good in human life. Persons who can only be graceful and ornamental—who can give the world nothing but flowers— should die young, and never be seen with gray hair and wrinkles, any more than the flower-shrubs with mossy bark and blighted foliage, like the lilacs under my window. Not that beauty is worthy of less than immortality. No; the beautiful should live forever, and thence, perhaps, the sense of impropriety when we see it triumphed over by time. Apple trees, on the other hand, grow old without reproach. Let them live as long as they may, and contort themselves into whatever perversity of shape they please, and deck their withered limbs with a springtime gaudiness of pink-blossoms, still they are respectable, even if they afford us only an apple or two in a season. Those few apples—or, at all events, the remembrance of apples in bygone years—are the atonement which utilitarianism inexorably demands for the privilege of lengthened life. Human flower shrubs, if they will grow old on earth, should, besides their lovely blossoms, bear some kind of fruit that will satisfy earthly appetites, else neither man nor the decorum of nature will deem it fit that the moss should gather on them.

One of the first things that strikes the attention when the white sheet of winter is withdrawn is the neglect and disarray that lay hidden beneath it. Nature is not cleanly, according to our prejudices. The beauty of preceding years, now transformed to brown and blighted deformity, obstructs the brightening loveliness of the present hour. Our avenue is strewn with the whole crop of autumn's withered leaves. There are quantities of decayed branches which one tempest after another has flung down, black and rotten, and one or two with the ruin of a bird's nest clinging to them. In the garden are the dried bean-vines, the brown stalks of the asparagus-bed, and melancholy old cabbages which were frozen into the soil before their unthrifty cultivator could find time to gather them. How invariable throughout all the forms of life do we find these intermingled memorials of death! On the soil of thought and in the garden of the heart, as well as in the sensual world, lie withered leaves—the ideas and feelings that we have done with. There is no wind strong enough to sweep them away; infinite space will not garner them from our sight. What mean they? Why may we not be permitted to live and enjoy as if this were the first life and our own the primal enjoyment, instead of treading always on these dry bones and mouldering relics from the aged accumulation of which springs all that now appears so young and new? Sweet must have been the spring-time of Eden, when no earlier year had strewn its decay upon the virgin turf,

BUDS AND BIRD-VOICES

and no former experience had ripened into summer and faded into autumn in the hearts of its inhabitants! That was a world worth living in.—Oh, thou murmurer, it is out of the very wantonness of such a life that thou feignest these idle lamentations. There is no decay. Each human soul is the first created inhabitant of its own Eden.—We dwell in an old moss-covered mansion and tread in the worn footprints of the past and have a gray clergyman's ghost for our daily and nightly inmate, yet all these outward circumstances are made less than visionary by the renewing power of the spirit. Should the spirit ever lose this power—should the withered leaves and the rotten branches and the moss-covered house and the ghost of the gray past ever become its realities, and the verdure and the freshness merely its faint dream—then let it pray to be released from earth. It will need the air of heaven to revive its pristine energies.

What an unlooked for flight was this from our shadowy avenue of black-ash and balm-of-gilead trees into the infinite! Now we have our feet again upon the turf. Nowhere does the grass spring up so industriously as in this homely yard, along the base of the stone wall and in the sheltered nooks of the buildings, and especially around the southern door-step—a locality which seems particularly favorable to its growth, for it is already tall enough to bend over and wave in the wind. I observe that several weeds—and, most frequently, a plant that stains the fingers with its yellow juice—have survived and retained their freshness and sap throughout the winter. One knows not how they have deserved such an exception from the common lot of their race. They are now the patriarchs of the departed year, and may preach mortality to the present generation of flowers and weeds.

Among the delights of spring, how is it possible to forget

the birds? Even the crows were welcome, as the sable harbingers of a brighter and livelier race. They visited us before the snow was off, but seem mostly to have betaken themselves to remote depths of the woods, which they haunt all summer long. Many a time shall I disturb them there, and feel as if I had intruded among a company of silent worshipers as they sit in Sabbath stillness among the treetops. Their voices, when they speak, are in admirable accordance with the tranquil solitude of a summer afternoon, and, resounding so far above the head, their loud clamor increases the religious quiet of the scene instead of breaking it. A crow, however, has no real pretensions to religion, in spite of his gravity of mien and black attire; he is certainly a thief, and probably an infidel. The gulls are far more respectable, in a moral point of view. These denizens of sea-beaten rocks and haunters of the lonely beach come up our inland river at this season, and soar high overhead, flapping their broad wings in the upper sunshine. They are among the most picturesque of birds, because they so float and rest upon the air as to become almost stationary parts of the landscape. The imagination has time to grow acquainted with them; they have not flitted away in a moment. You go up among the clouds and greet these lofty-flighted gulls, and repose confidently with them upon the sustaining atmosphere. Ducks have their haunts along the solitary places of the river, and alight in flocks upon the broad bosom of the overflowed meadows. Their flight is too rapid and determined for the eye to catch enjoyment from it, although it never fails to stir up the heart with the sportsman's ineradicable instinct. They have now gone farther northward, but will visit us again in autumn.

The smaller birds—the little songsters of the woods, and those that haunt man's dwellings and claim human friendship by building their nests under the sheltering eaves or among the orchard trees—these require a touch more delicate and a gentler heart than mine to do them justice. Their outburst of melody is like a brook let loose from wintry chains. We need not deem it a too high and solemn word to call it a hymn of praise to the Creator, since Nature, who pictures the reviving year in so many sights of beauty, has expressed the sentiment of renewed life in no other sound save the notes of these blessed birds. Their music, however, just now seems to be incidental, and not the result of a set purpose. They are discussing the economy of life and love and the site and architecture of their summer residences, and have no time to sit on a twig and pour forth solemn hymns or overtures, operas, symphonies and waltzes. Anxious questions are asked, grave subjects are settled in quick and animated debate, and only by occasional accident, as from pure ecstasy, does a rich warble roll its tiny waves of golden sound through the atmosphere. Their little bodies are as busy as their voices; they are in a constant flutter and restlessness. Even when two or three retreat to a tree-top to hold council, they wag their tails and heads all the time with the irrepressible activity of their nature, which perhaps renders their brief span of life in reality as long as the patriarchal age of sluggish man. The blackbirds—three species of which consort together—are the noisiest of all our feathered citizens. Great companies of them—more than the famous "four-and-twenty" whom Mother Goose has immortalized—congregate in contiguous tree-tops and vociferate with all the clamor and confusion of a turbulent political meeting. Politics, certainly, must be the occasion of such tumultuous debates, but still, unlike all other politicians, they instill melody into their individual utterances and produce harmony as a general effect. Of all bird-voices, none are more sweet and cheerful to my ear than those of swallows in the dim, sun-streaked interior of a lofty barn; they address the heart with even a closer sympathy than Robin Redbreast. But, indeed, all these winged people that dwell in the vicinity of homesteads seem to partake of human nature and possess the germ, if not the development, of immortal souls. We hear them saying their melodious prayers at morning's blush and eventide. A little while ago, in the deep of night, there came the lively thrill of a bird's note from a neighboring tree—a real song such as greets the purple dawn or mingles with the yellow sunshine. What could the little bird mean by pouring it forth at midnight? Probably the music gushed out of the midst of a dream in which he fancied himself in paradise with his mate, but suddenly awoke on a cold, leafless bough with a New England mist penetrating through his feathers. That was a sad exchange of imagination for reality.

Insects are among the earliest births of spring. Multitudes, of I know not what species, appeared long ago on the surface of the snow. Clouds of them almost too minute for sight hover in a beam of sunshine, and vanish as if annihilated when they pass into the shade. A mosquito has already been heard to sound the small horror of his bugle-horn. Wasps infest the sunny windows of the house. A bee entered one of the chambers with a prophecy of flowers. Rare butterflies came before the snow was off, flaunting in the chill breeze, and looking forlorn and all astray in spite of the magnificence of their dark velvet cloaks with golden borders.

The fields and wood-paths have as yet few charms to entice the wanderer. In a walk the other day I found no violets nor anemones, nor anything in the likeness of a flower. It was worth while, however, to ascend our opposite hill for the sake of gaining a general idea of the advance of spring, which I had hitherto been studying in its minute developments. The river lay round me in a semicircle, overflowing all the meadows which give it its Indian name, and offering a noble breadth to sparkle in the sunbeams. Along the hither shore a row of trees stood up to their knees in water, and afar off, on the surface of the stream, tufts of bushes thrust up their heads, as it were, to breathe. The most striking objects were great solitary trees here and there with a mile-wide waste of water all around them. The curtailment of the trunk by its immersion in the river quite destroys the fair proportions of the tree, and thus makes us sensible of a regularity and propriety in the usual forms of nature. The flood of the present season, though it never amounts to a freshet on our quiet stream, has encroached farther upon the land than any previous one for at least a score of years. It has overflowed stone fences, and even rendered a portion of the highway navigable for boats. The waters, however, are now gradually subsiding; islands become annexed to the mainland, and other islands emerge like new creations from the watery waste. The scene supplies an admirable image of the receding of the Nile—except that there is no deposit of black slime—or of Noah's flood, only that there is a freshness and novelty in these recovered portions of the continent which give the impression of a world just made rather than of one so polluted that a deluge had been requisite to purify it. These upspringing islands are the greenest spots in the landscape; the first gleam of sunlight suffices to cover them with verdure.

Thank Providence for spring! The earth—and man himself, by sympathy with his birthplace—would be far other than we find them if life toiled wearily onward without this periodical infusion of the primal spirit. Will the world ever be so decayed that spring may not renew its greenness? Can man be so dismally age-stricken that no faintest sunshine of his youth may revisit him once a year? It is impossible. The moss on our time-worn mansion brightens into beauty, the good old pastor who once dwelt here renewed his prime, regained his boyhood, in the genial breezes of his ninetieth spring. Alas for the worn and heavy soul if, whether in youth or age, it have outlived its privilege of springtime sprightliness! From such a soul the world must hope no reformation of its evil—no sympathy with the lofty faith and gallant struggles of those who contend in its behalf. Summer works in the present and thinks not of the future; autumn is a rich conservative; winter has utterly lost its faith, and clings tremulously to the remembrance of what has been; but spring, with its outgushing life, is the true type of the movement.

THE PHILOSOPHY OF COMPOSITION

Edgar Allan Poe

Charles Dickens, in a note now lying before me, alluding to an examination I once made of the mechanism of *Barnaby Rudge,* says—" By the way, are you aware that Godwin wrote his *Caleb Williams* backwards? He first involved his hero in a web of difficulties, forming the second volume, and then, for the first, cast about him for some mode of accounting for what had been done."

I cannot think this the *precise* mode of procedure on the part of Godwin—and indeed what he himself acknowledges, is not altogether in accordance with Mr. Dickens' idea—but the author of *Caleb Williams* was too good an artist not to perceive the advantage derivable from at least a somewhat similar process. Nothing is more clear than that every plot, worth the name, must be elaborated to its *dénouement* before anything be attempted with the pen. It is only with the *dénouement* constantly in view that we can give a plot its indispensable air of consequence, or causation, by making the incidents, and especially the tone at all points, tend to the development of the intention.

There is a radical error, I think, in the usual mode of constructing a story. Either history affords a thesis—or one is suggested by an incident of the day—or, at best, the author sets himself to work in the combination of striking events to form merely the basis of his narrative—designing, generally, to fill in with description, dialogue, or autorial comment, whatever crevices of fact, or action, may, from page to page, render themselves apparent.

I prefer commencing with the consideration of an *effect*. Keeping originality *always* in view—for he is false to himself who ventures to dispense with so obvious and so easily attainable a source of interest—I say to myself, in the first place, " Of the innumerable effects, or impressions, of which the heart, the intellect, or (more generally) the soul is susceptible, what one shall I, on the present occasion, select?" Having chosen a novel, first, and secondly a vivid effect, I consider whether it can be best wrought by incident or tone—whether by ordinary incidents and peculiar tone, or the converse, or by peculiarity both of incident and tone—afterward looking about me (or rather within) for such combinations of event, or tone, as shall best aid me in the construction of the effect.

I have often thought how interesting a magazine paper might be written by any author who would—that is to say, who could—detail, step by step, the processes by which any one of his compositions attained its ultimate point of completion! Why such a paper has never been given to the world, I am much at a loss to say—but, perhaps, the autorial vanity has had more to do with the omission than any one other cause. Most writers—poets in especial—prefer having it understood that they compose by a species of fine frenzy—an ecstatic intuition—and would positively shudder at letting the public take a peep behind the scenes, at the elaborate and vacillating crudities of thought—at the true purposes seized only at the last moment—at the innumerable glimpses of idea that arrived not at the maturity of full view—at the fully matured fancies discarded in despair as unmanageable—at the cautious selections and rejections—at the painful erasures and interpolations—in a word, at the wheels and pinions—the tackle for scene-shifting—the step-ladders and demon-traps—the cock's feathers, the red paint and the black patches, which, in ninety-nine cases out of the hundred, constitute the properties of the literary *histrio*.

I am aware, on the other hand, that the case is by no means common, in which an author is at all in condition to retrace the steps by which his conclusions have been attained. In general, suggestions, having arisen pell-mell, are pursued and forgotten in a similar manner.

For my own part, I have neither sympathy with the repugnance alluded to, nor, at any time, the least difficulty in recalling to mind the progressive steps of any of my compositions; and, since the interest of an analysis, or reconstruction, such as I have considered a *desideratum,* is quite independent of any real or fancied interest in the thing analyzed, it will not be regarded as a breach of decorum on my part to show the *modus operandi* by which some one of my own works was put together. I select "The Raven," as the most generally known. It is my design to render it manifest that no one point in its composition is referable either to accident or intuition—that the work proceeded, step by step, to its completion with the precision and rigid consequence of a mathematical problem.

Let us dismiss, as irrelevant to the poem, *per se,* the circumstance—or say the necessity—which, in the first place, gave rise to the intention of composing *a* poem that should suit at once the popular and the critical taste.

We commence, then, with this intention.

The initial consideration was that of extent. If any literary work is too long to be read at one sitting, we must be content to dispense with the immensely important effect derivable from unity of impression—for, if two sittings be required, the affairs of the world interfere, and everything like totality is at once destroyed. But since, *ceteris paribus,* no poet can afford to dispense with *anything* that may advance his design, it but remains to be seen whether there is, in extent, any advantage to counterbalance the loss of unity which attends it. Here I say no, at once. What we term a long poem is, in fact, merely a succession of brief ones—that is to say, of brief poetical effects. It is needless to demonstrate that a poem is such, only inasmuch as it intensely excites, by elevating, the soul; and all intense excitements are, through a psychal necessity, brief. For this reason, at least one-half of the *Paradise Lost* is essentially prose—a succession of poetical excitements interspersed, *inevitably*, with corresponding depressions—the whole being deprived, through the extremeness of its length, of the vastly important artistic element, totality, or unity, of effect.

It appears evident, then, that there is a distinct limit, as regards length, to all works of literary art—the limit of a single sitting—and that, although in certain classes of prose composition, such as *Robinson Crusoe,* (demanding no unity,) this limit may be advantageously overpassed, it can never properly be overpassed in a poem. Within this limit, the extent of a poem may be made to bear mathematical relation to its merit—in other words, to the excitement or elevation—again in other words, to the degree of the true poetical effect which it is capable of inducing; for it is clear that the brevity must be in direct ratio of the intensity of the intended effect:—this, with one proviso—that a certain degree of duration is absolutely requisite for the production of any effect at all.

Holding in view these considerations, as well as that degree of excitement which I deemed not above the popular, while not below the critical, taste, I reached at once what I conceived the proper *length* for my intended poem—a length of about one hundred lines. It is, in fact, a hundred and eight.

My next thought concerned the choice of an impression, or effect, to be conveyed: and here I may as well observe that, throughout the construction, I kept steadily in view the design of rendering the work *universally* appreciable. I should be carried too far out of my immediate topic were I to demonstrate a point upon which I have repeatedly insisted, and which, with the poetical, stands not in the slightest need of demonstration—the point, I mean, that Beauty is the sole legitimate province of the poem. A few words, however, in elucidation of my real meaning, which some of my friends have evinced a disposition to misrepresent. That pleasure which is at once the most intense, the most elevating, and the most pure, is, I believe, found in the contemplation of the beautiful. When, indeed, men speak of Beauty, they mean, precisely, not a quality, as is supposed, but an effect—they refer, in short, just to that intense and pure elevation of *soul—not* of intellect, or of heart—upon which I have commented, and which is experienced in consequence of contemplating "the beautiful." Now I designate Beauty as the province of the poem, merely because it is an obvious rule of Art that effects should be made to spring from direct causes—that objects should be attained through means best adapted for their attainment—no one as yet having been weak enough to deny that the peculiar elevation alluded to is *most readily* attained in the poem. Now the object, Truth, or the satisfaction of the intellect, and the object Passion, or the excitement of the heart, are, although attainable, to a certain extent, in poetry, far more readily attainable in prose. Truth, in fact, demands a precision, and Passion, a *homeliness* (the truly passionate will comprehend me) which are absolutely antagonistic to that Beauty which, I maintain, is the excitement, or pleasurable elevation, of the soul. It by no means follows from anything here said, that passion, or even truth, may not be introduced, and even profitably introduced, into a poem—for they may serve in elucidation, or aid the general effect, as do discords in music, by contrast—but the true artist will always contrive, first, to tone them into proper subservience to the predominant aim, and, secondly, to enveil them, as far as possible, in that Beauty which is the atmosphere and the essence of the poem.

Regarding, then, Beauty as my province, my next question referred to the *tone* of its highest manifestation—and all experience has shown that this tone is one of *sadness*. Beauty of whatever kind, in its supreme development, invariably excites the sensitive soul to tears. Melancholy is thus the most legitimate of all the poetical tones.

The length, the province, and the tone, being thus determined, I betook myself to ordinary induction, with the view of obtaining some artistic piquancy which might serve me as a key-note in the construction of the poem—some pivot upon which the whole structure might turn. In carefully thinking over all the usual artistic effects—or more properly *points,* in the theatrical sense—I did not fail to perceive immediately that no one had been so universally employed as that of the *refrain.* The universality of its employment sufficed to assure me of its intrinsic value, and spared me the necessity of submitting it to analysis. I considered it, however, with regard to its susceptibility of improvement, and soon saw it to be in a primitive condition. As commonly used, the *refrain,* or burden, not only is limited to lyric verse, but depends for its impression upon the force of monotone—both in sound and thought. The pleasure is deduced solely from the sense of identity—of repetition. I resolved to diversify, and so vastly heighten, the effect, by adhering, in general, to the monotone of sound, while I continually varied that of thought: that is to say, I determined to produce continuously novel effects, by the variation *of the application* of the *refrain*—the *refrain* itself remaining, for the most part, unvaried.

These points being settled, I next bethought me of the *nature* of my *refrain*. Since its application was to be repeatedly varied, it was clear that the *refrain* itself must be brief, for there would have been an insurmountable difficulty in frequent variations of application in any sentence of length. In proportion to the brevity of the sentence, would, of course, be the facility of the variation. This led me at once to a single word as the best *refrain*.

The question now arose as to the *character* of the word. Having made up my mind to a *refrain,* the division of the poem into stanzas was, of course, a corollary: the *refrain* forming the close to each stanza. That such a close, to have force, must be sonorous and susceptible of protracted emphasis, admitted no doubt: and these considerations inevitably led me to the long *o* as the most sonorous vowel, in connection with *r* as the most producible consonant.

The sound of the *refrain* being thus determined, it became necessary to select a word embodying this sound, and at the same time in the fullest possible keeping with that melancholy which I had predetermined as the tone of the poem. In such a search it would have been absolutely impossible to overlook the word "Nevermore." In fact, it was the very first which presented itself.

The next *desideratum* was a pretext for the continuous use of the one word "nevermore." In observing the difficulty which I at once found in inventing a sufficiently plausible reason for its continuous repetition, I did not fail to perceive that this difficulty arose solely from the preassumption that the word was to be so continuously or monotonously spoken by *a human* being—I did not fail to perceive, in short, that the difficulty lay in the reconciliation of this monotony with the exercise of reason on the part of the creature repeating the word. Here, then, immediately arose the idea of a *non*-reasoning creature capable of speech; and, very naturally, a parrot, in the first instance, suggested itself, but was superseded forthwith by a Raven, as equally capable of speech, and infinitely more in keeping with the intended *tone*.

I had now gone so far as the conception of a Raven—the bird of ill omen—monotonously repeating the one word, "Nevermore," at the conclusion of each stanza, in a poem of melancholy tone, and in length about one hundred lines. Now, never losing sight of the object *supremeness,* or perfection, at all points, I asked myself—"Of all melancholy topics, what, according to the *universal* understanding of mankind, is the *most* melancholy?" Death—was the obvious reply. "And when," I said, "is this most melancholy of topics most poetical?" From what I have already explained at some length, the answer, here also, is obvious—"When it most closely allies itself to *Beauty:* the death, then, of a beautiful woman is, unquestionably, the most poetical topic in the world—and equally is it beyond doubt that the lips best suited for such topic are those of a bereaved lover."

I had now to combine the two ideas, of a lover lamenting his deceased mistress and a Raven continuously repeating the word "Nevermore"—I had to combine these, bearing in mind my design of varying, at every turn, the *application* of the word repeated; but the only intelligible mode of such combination is that of imagining the Raven employing the word in answer to the queries of the lover. And here it was that I saw at once the opportunity afforded for the effect on which I had been depending—that is to say, the effect of the *variation of application.* I saw that I could make the first query propounded by the lover—the first query to which the Raven should reply " Nevermore "—that I could make this first query a commonplace one—the second less so—the third still less, and so on—until at length the lover, startled from his original *nonchalance* by the melancholy character of the word itself—by its frequent repetition— and by a consideration of the ominous reputation of the fowl that uttered it—is at length excited to superstition, and wildly propounds queries of a far different character— queries whose solution he has passionately at heart—propounds them half in superstition and half in that species of despair which delights in self-torture—propounds them not altogether because he believes in the prophetic or demoniac character of the bird (which, reason assures him, is merely repeating a lesson learned by rote) but because he experiences a frenzied pleasure in so modeling his questions as to receive from the *expected* " Nevermore " the most delicious because the most intolerable of sorrow. Perceiving the opportunity thus afforded me—or, more strictly, thus forced upon me in the progress of the construction—I first established in mind the climax, or concluding query— that to which " Nevermore " should be in the last place an answer—that in reply to which this word " Nevermore " should involve the utmost conceivable amount of sorrow and despair.

Here then the poem may be said to have its beginning —at the end, where all works of art should begin—for it was here, at this point of my preconsiderations, that I first put pen to paper in the composition of the stanza:

" ' Prophet,' said I, ' thing of evil! prophet still if bird or devil!
By that heaven that bends above us—by that God we both adore,
Tell this soul with sorrow laden, if within the distant Aidenn,
It shall clasp a sainted maiden whom the angels name Lenore—
Clasp a rare and radiant maiden whom the angels name Lenore.'
      Quoth the raven ' Nevermore.' "

I composed this stanza, at this point, first that, by establishing the climax, I might the better vary and graduate, as regards seriousness and importance, the preceding queries of the lover—and, secondly, that I might definitely settle the rhythm, the meter, and the length and general arrangement of the stanza—as well as graduate the stanzas which were to precede, so that none of them might surpass this in rhythmical effect. Had I been able, in the subsequent composition, to construct more vigorous stanzas, I should, without scruple, have purposely enfeebled them, so as not to interfere with the climacteric effect.

And here I may as well say a few words of the versification. My first object (as usual) was originality. The extent to which this has been neglected, in versification, is one of the most unaccountable things in the world. Admitting that there is little possibility of variety in mere *rhythm,* it is still clear that the possible varieties of meter and stanza are absolutely infinite—and yet, *for centuries, no man, in verse, has ever done, or ever seemed to think of doing, an original thing.* The fact is, originality (unless in minds of very unusual force) is by no means a matter, as some suppose, of impulse or intuition. In general, to be found, it must be elaborately sought, and although a positive merit of the highest class, demands in its attainment less of invention than negation.

Of course, I pretend to no originality in either the rhythm or meter of the "Raven." The former is trochaic—the latter is octameter acatalectic, alternating with heptameter catalectic repeated in the *refrain* of the fifth verse, and terminating with tetrameter catalectic. Less pedantically—the feet employed throughout (trochees) consist of a long syllable followed by a short: the first line of the stanza consists of eight of these feet—the second of seven and a half (in effect two-thirds)—the third of eight—the fourth of seven and a half—the fifth the same—the sixth three and a half. Now, each of these lines, taken individually, has been employed before, and what originality the "Raven" has, is in their *combination into stanza;* nothing even remotely approaching this combination has ever been attempted. The effect of this originality of combination is aided by other unusual, and some altogether novel, effects, arising from an extension of the application of the principles of rhyme and alliteration.

The next point to be considered was the mode of bringing together the lover and the Raven—and the first branch of this consideration was the *locale*. For this the most natural suggestion might seem to be a forest, or the fields —but it has always appeared to me that a close *circumscription of space* is absolutely necessary to the effect of insulated incident:—it has the force of a frame to a picture. It has an indisputable moral power in keeping concentrated the attention, and, of course, must not be confounded with mere unity of place.

I determined, then, to place the lover in his chamber— in a chamber rendered sacred to him by memories of her who had frequented it. The room is represented as richly furnished—this in mere pursuance of the ideas I have already explained on the subject of Beauty, as the sole true poetical thesis.

The *locale* being thus determined, I had now to introduce the bird—and the thought of introducing him through the window, was inevitable. The idea of making the lover suppose, in the first instance, that the flapping of the wings of the bird against the shutter, is a "tapping" at the door, originated in a wish to increase, by prolonging, the reader's curiosity, and in a desire to admit the incidental effect arising from the lover's throwing open the door, finding all dark, and thence adopting the half-fancy that it was the spirit of his mistress that knocked.

I made the night tempestuous, first, to account for the Raven's seeking admission, and secondly, for the effect of contrast with the (physical) serenity within the chamber.

I made the bird alight on the bust of Pallas, also for the effect of contrast between the marble and the plumage—it being understood that the bust was absolutely *suggested* by the bird—the bust of *Pallas* being chosen, first, as most in keeping with the scholarship of the lover, and, secondly, for the sonorousness of the word, Pallas, itself.

About the middle of the poem, also, I have availed myself of the force of contrast, with a view of deepening the ultimate impression. For example, an air of the fantastic—approaching as nearly to the ludicrous as was admissible—is given to the Raven's entrance. He comes in " with many a flirt and flutter."

" Not the *least obeisance made he*—not a moment stopped or stayed he,
But with mien of lord or lady, perched above my chamber door."

In the two stanzas which follow, the design is more obviously carried out:—

" Then this ebony bird beguiling my sad fancy into smiling
By the *grave and stern decorum of the countenance it wore,*
'Though thy *crest be shorn and shaven* thou,' I said, 'art sure no craven,
Ghastly grim and ancient Raven wandering from the nightly shore—
Tell me what thy lordly name is on the Night's Plutonian shore!'
    Quoth the Raven 'Nevermore.'

" Much I marveled *this ungainly fowl* to hear discourse so plainly,
Though its answer little meaning—little relevancy bore;
For we cannot help agreeing that no living human being
Ever yet was blessed with seeing bird above his chamber door—
Bird or beast upon the sculptured bust above his chamber door,
    With such name as 'Nevermore.'"

The effect of the *dénouement* being thus provided for, I immediately drop the fantastic for a tone of the most profound seriousness:—this tone commencing in the stanza directly following the one last quoted, with the line,

"But the Raven, sitting lonely on that placid bust, spoke only," etc.

From this epoch the lover no longer jests—no longer sees anything even of the fantastic in the Raven's demeanor. He speaks of him as a "grim, ungainly, ghastly, gaunt, and ominous bird of yore," and feels the "fiery eyes" burning into his "bosom's core." This revolution of thought, or fancy, on the lover's part, is intended to induce a similar one on the part of the reader—to bring the mind into a proper frame for the *dénouement*—which is now brought about as rapidly and as *directly* as possible.

With the *dénouement* proper—with the Raven's reply, "Nevermore," to the lover's final demand if he shall meet his mistress in another world—the poem, in its obvious phase, that of a simple narrative, may be said to have its completion. So far, everything is within the limits of the accountable—of the real. A raven, having learned by rote the single word "Nevermore," and having escaped from the custody of its owner, is driven at midnight, through the violence of a storm, to seek admission at a window from which a light still gleams—the chamber-window of a student, occupied half in poring over a volume, half in dreaming of a beloved mistress deceased. The casement being thrown open at the fluttering of the bird's wings, the bird itself perches on the most convenient seat out of the immediate reach of the student, who, amused by the incident and the oddity of the visitor's demeanor, demands of it, in jest and without looking for a reply, its name. The raven addressed, answers with its customary word, "Nevermore"—a word which finds immediate echo in the melancholy heart of the student, who, giving utterance aloud to certain thoughts suggested by the occasion, is again startled by the fowl's repetition of "Nevermore." The student now guesses the state of the case, but is impelled, as I have before explained, by the human thirst for self-torture, and in part by superstition, to propound such queries to the bird as will bring him, the lover, the most of the luxury of sorrow, through the anticipated answer "Nevermore." With the indulgence, to the utmost extreme, of this self-torture, the narration, in what I have termed its first or obvious phase, has a natural termination, and so far there has been no overstepping of the limits of the real.

But in subjects so handled, however skillfully, or with however vivid an array of incident, there is always a certain hardness or nakedness, which repels the artistical eye. Two things are invariably required—first, some amount of complexity, or more properly, adaptation; and, secondly, some amount of suggestiveness—some undercurrent, however indefinite, of meaning. It is this latter, in especial, which imparts to a work of art so much of that *richness* (to borrow from colloquy a forcible term) which we are too fond of confounding with *the ideal*. It is the *excess* of the suggested meaning—it is the rendering this the upper instead of the under current of the theme—which turns into prose (and that of the very flattest kind) the so-called poetry of the so-called transcendentalists.

Holding these opinions, I added the two concluding stanzas of the poem—their suggestiveness being thus made to pervade all the narrative which has preceded them. The undercurrent of meaning is rendered first apparent in the lines—

"'Take thy beak from out *my heart,* and take thy form from off my door!'
    Quoth the Raven 'Nevermore!'"

It will be observed that the words, "from out my heart," involve the first metaphorical expression in the poem. They, with the answer, "Nevermore," dispose the mind to seek a moral in all that has been previously narrated. The reader begins now to regard the Raven as emblematical—but it is not until the very last line of the very last stanza, that the intention of making him emblematical of *Mournful and Never-ending Remembrance* is permitted distinctly to be seen:

" And the Raven, never flitting, still is sitting, still is sitting,
  On the pallid bust of Pallas just above my chamber door;
And his eyes have all the seeming of a demon's that is dreaming,
And the lamplight o'er him streaming throws his shadow on the floor;
And my soul *from out that shadow* that lies floating on the floor
  Shall be lifted—nevermore."

BREAD AND THE NEWSPAPER

Oliver Wendell Holmes

This is the new version of the *Panem et Circenses* of the Roman populace. It is our *ultimatum,* as that was theirs. They must have something to eat, and the circus-shows to look at. We must have something to eat, and the papers to read.

Everything else we can give up. If we are rich, we can lay down our carriages, stay away from Newport or Saratoga, and adjourn the trip to Europe *sine die.* If we live in a small way, there are at least new dresses and bonnets and every-day luxuries which we can dispense with. If the young Zouave of the family looks smart in his new uniform, its respectable head is content, though he himself grow seedy as a caraway-umbel late in the season. He will cheerfully calm the perturbed nap of his old beaver by patient brushing in place of buying a new one, if only the Lieutenant's jaunty cap is what it should be. We all take a pride in sharing the epidemic economy of the time. Only *bread and the newspaper* we must have, whatever else we do without.

How this war is simplifying our mode of being! We live on our emotions, as the sick man is said in the common speech to be nourished by his fever. Our ordinary mental food has become distasteful, and what would have been intellectual luxuries at other times, are now absolutely repulsive.

All this change in our manner of existence implies that

we have experienced some very profound impression, which will sooner or later betray itself in permanent effects on the minds and bodies of many among us. We cannot forget Corvisart's observation of the frequency with which diseases of the heart were noticed as the consequence of the terrible emotions produced by the scenes of the great French Revolution. Laennec tells the story of a convent, of which he was the medical director, where all the nuns were subjected to the severest penances and schooled in the most painful doctrines. They all became consumptive soon after their entrance, so that, in the course of his ten years' attendance, all the inmates died out two or three times, and were replaced by new ones. He does not hesitate to attribute the disease from which they suffered to those depressing moral influences to which they were subjected.

So far we have noticed little more than disturbances of the nervous system as a consequence of the war excitement in non-combatants. Take the first trifling example which comes to our recollection. A sad disaster to the Federal army was told the other day in the presence of two gentlemen and a lady. Both the gentlemen complained of a sudden feeling at the *epigastrium,* or, less learnedly, the pit of the stomach, changed color, and confessed to a slight tremor about the knees. The lady had a "*grande révolution,*" as French patients say,—went home, and kept her bed for the rest of the day. Perhaps the reader may smile at the mention of such trivial indispositions, but in more sensitive natures death itself follows in some cases from no more serious cause. An old gentleman fell senseless in fatal apoplexy, on hearing of Napoleon's return from Elba. One of our early friends, who recently died of the same complaint, was thought to have had his attack mainly in consequence of the excitements of the time.

We all know what the *war fever* is in our young men,—

what a devouring passion it becomes in those whom it assails. Patriotism is the fire of it, no doubt, but this is fed with fuel of all sorts. The love of adventure, the contagion of example, the fear of losing the chance of participating in the great events of the time, the desire of personal distinction, all help to produce those singular transformations which we often witness, turning the most peaceful of our youth into the most ardent of our soldiers. But something of the same fever in a different form reaches a good many non-combatants, who have no thought of losing a drop of precious blood belonging to themselves or their families. Some of the symptoms we shall mention are almost universal; they are as plain in the people we meet everywhere as the marks of an influenza, when that is prevailing.

The first is a nervous restlessness of a very peculiar character. Men cannot think, or write, or attend to their ordinary business. They stroll up and down the streets, or saunter out upon the public places. We confessed to an illustrious author that we laid down the volume of his work which we were reading when the war broke out. It was as interesting as a romance, but the romance of the past grew pale before the red light of the terrible present. Meeting the same author not long afterwards, he confessed that he had laid down his pen at the same time that we had closed his book. He could not write about the sixteenth century any more than we could read about it, while the nineteenth was in the very agony and bloody sweat of its great sacrifice.

Another most eminent scholar told us in all simplicity that he had fallen into such a state that he would read the same telegraphic dispatches over and over again in different papers, as if they were new, until he felt as if he were an idiot. Who did not do just the same thing, and does not often do it still, now that the first flush of the fever is over? Another person always goes through the side streets on his way for the noon *extra*,—he is so afraid somebody will meet him and *tell* the news he wishes to *read*, first on the bulletin-board, and then in the great capitals and leaded type of the newspaper.

When any startling piece of war-news comes, it keeps repeating itself in our minds in spite of all we can do. The same trains of thought go tramping round in circle through the brain, like the supernumeraries that make up the grand army of a stage-show. Now, if a thought goes round through the brain a thousand times in a day, it will have worn as deep a track as one which has passed through it once a week for twenty years. This accounts for the ages we seem to have lived since the twelfth of April last, and, to state it more generally, for that *ex post facto* operation of a great calamity, or any very powerful impression, which we once illustrated by the image of a stain spreading backwards from the leaf of life open before us through all those which we have already turned.

Blessed are those who can sleep quietly in times like these! Yet, not wholly blessed, either: for what is more painful than the awaking from peaceful unconsciousness to a sense that there is something wrong,—we cannot at first think what,—and then groping our way about through the twilight of our thoughts until we come full upon the misery, which, like some evil bird, seemed to have flown away, but which sits waiting for us on its perch by our pillow in the gray of the morning?

The converse of this is perhaps still more painful. Many have the feeling in their waking hours that the trouble they are aching with is, after all, only a dream,—if they will rub their eyes briskly enough and shake themselves, they will awake out of it, and find all their supposed grief is unreal. This attempt to cajole ourselves out of an ugly fact always reminds us of those unhappy flies who have been indulging in the dangerous sweets of the paper prepared for their especial use.

Watch one of them. He does not feel quite well,—at least, he suspects himself of indisposition. Nothing serious,—let us just rub our fore-feet together, as the enormous creature who provides for us rubs his hands, and all will be right. He rubs them with that peculiar twisting movement of his, and pauses for the effect. No! all is not quite right yet. Ah! it is our head that is not set on just as it ought to be. Let us settle *that* where it should be, and *then* we shall certainly be in good trim again. So he pulls his head about as an old lady adjusts her cap, and passes his fore-paw over it like a kitten washing herself.—Poor fellow! It is not a fancy, but a fact, that he has to deal with. If he could read the letters at the head of the sheet, he would see they were *Fly-Paper.*—So with us, when, in our waking misery, we try to think we dream! Perhaps very young persons may not understand this; as we grow older, our waking and dreaming life run more and more into each other.

Another symptom of our excited condition is seen in the breaking up of old habits. The newspaper is as imperious as a Russian Ukase; it will be had, and it will be read. To this all else must give place. If we must go out at unusual hours to get it, we shall go, in spite of after-dinner nap or evening somnolence. If it finds us in company, it will not stand on ceremony, but cuts short the compliment and the story by the divine right of its telegraphic dispatches.

War is a very old story, but it is a new one to this generation of Americans. Our own nearest relation in the ascending line remembers the Revolution well. How should she forget it? Did she not lose her doll, which was left behind, when she was carried out of Boston, about that time growing uncomfortable by reason of cannon-balls dropping in from the neighboring heights at all hours,—in token of which see the tower of Brattle Street Church at this very day? War in her memory means '76. As for the brush of 1812, "we did not think much about that"; and everybody knows that the Mexican business did not concern us much, except in its political relations. No! war is a new thing to all of us who are not in the last quarter of their century. We are learning many strange matters from our fresh experience. And besides, there are new conditions of existence which make war as it is with us very different from war as it has been.

The first and obvious difference consists in the fact that the whole nation is now penetrated by the ramifications of a network of iron nerves which flash sensation and volition backward and forward to and from towns and provinces as if they were organs and limbs of a single living body. The second is the vast system of iron muscles which, as it were, move the limbs of the mighty organism one upon another. What was the railroad-force which put the Sixth Regiment in Baltimore on the 19th of April but a contraction and extension of the arm of Massachusetts with a clenched fist full of bayonets at the end of it?

This perpetual intercommunication, joined to the power of instantaneous action, keeps us always alive with excitement. It is not a breathless courier who comes back with the report from an army we have lost sight of for a month, nor a single bulletin which tells us all we are to know for a week of some great engagement, but almost hourly paragraphs, laden with truth or falsehood as the case may be, making us restless always for the last fact or rumor they are telling. And so of the movements of our armies. To-night the stout lumbermen of Maine are encamped under their own fragrant pines. In a score or two of hours they are among the tobacco-fields and the slave-pens of Virginia. The war passion burned like scattered coals of fire in the households of Revolutionary times; now it rushes all through the land like a flame over the prairie. And this instant diffusion of every fact and feeling produces another singular effect in the equalizing and steadying of public opinion. We may not be able to see a month ahead of us; but as to what has passed a week afterwards it is as thoroughly talked out and judged as it would have been in a whole season before our national nervous system was organized.

> "As the wild tempest wakes the slumbering sea,
> Thou only teachest all that man can be!"

We indulged in the above apostrophe to War in a Phi Beta Kappa poem of long ago, which we liked better before we read Mr. Cutler's beautiful prolonged lyric delivered at the recent anniversary of that Society.

Oftentimes, in paroxysms of peace and good-will towards all mankind, we have felt twinges of conscience about the passage,—especially when one of our orators showed us that a ship of war costs as much to build and keep as a college, and that every port-hole we could stop would give us a new professor. Now we begin to think that there was some meaning in our poor couplet. War *has* taught us, as nothing else could, what we can be and are. It has exalted our manhood and our womanhood, and driven us all back upon our substantial human qualities, for a long time more or less kept out of sight by the spirit of commerce, the love of art, science, or literature, or other qualities not belonging to all of us as men and women.

It is at this very moment doing more to melt away the

petty social distinctions which keep generous souls apart from each other, than the preaching of the Beloved Disciple himself would do. We are finding out that not only "patriotism is eloquence," but that heroism is gentility. All ranks are wonderfully equalized under the fire of a masked battery. The plain artisan or the rough fireman, who faces the lead and iron like a man, is the truest representative we can show of the heroes of Crécy and Agincourt. And if one of our fine gentlemen puts off his straw-colored kids and stands by the other, shoulder to shoulder, or leads him on to the attack, he is as honorable in our eyes and in theirs as if he were ill-dressed and his hands were soiled with labor.

Even our poor "Brahmins,"—whom a critic in ground-glass spectacles (the same who grasps his statistics by the blade and strikes at his supposed antagonist with the handle) oddly confounds with the "bloated aristocracy," whereas they are very commonly pallid, undervitalized, shy, sensitive creatures, whose only birthright is an aptitude for learning,—even these poor New England Brahmins of ours, *subvirates* of an organizable base as they often are, count as full men, if their courage is big enough for the uniform which hangs so loosely about their slender figures.

A young man was drowned not very long ago in the river running under our windows. A few days afterwards a field-piece was dragged to the water's edge, and fired many times over the river. We asked a bystander, who looked like a fisherman, what that was for. It was to "break the gall," he said, and so bring the drowned person to the surface. A strange physiological fancy and a very odd *non sequitur;* but that is not our present point. A good many extraordinary objects do really come to the surface when the great guns of war shake the waters, as when they roared over Charleston harbor.

Treason came up, hideous, fit only to be huddled into its dishonorable grave. But the wrecks of precious virtues, which had been covered with the waves of prosperity, came up also. And all sorts of unexpected and unheard-of things, which had lain unseen during our national life of fourscore years, came up and are coming up daily, shaken from their bed by the concussions of the artillery bellowing around us.

It is a shame to own it, but there were persons otherwise respectable not unwilling to say that they believed the old valor of Revolutionary times had died out from among us. They talked about our own Northern people as the English in the last centuries used to talk about the French,—Goldsmith's old soldier, it may be remembered, called one Englishman good for five of them. As Napoleon spoke of the English, again, as a nation of shopkeepers, so these persons affected to consider the multitude of their countrymen as unwarlike artisans,—forgetting that Paul Revere taught himself the value of liberty in working upon gold, and Nathanael Greene fitted himself to shape armies in the labor of forging iron.

These persons have learned better now. The bravery of our free working-people was overlaid, but not smothered; sunken, but not drowned. The hands which had been busy conquering the elements had only to change their weapons and their adversaries, and they were as ready to conquer the masses of living force opposed to them as they had been to build towns, to dam rivers, to hunt whales, to harvest ice, to hammer brute matter into every shape civilization can ask for.

Another great fact came to the surface, and is coming up every day in new shapes,—that we are one people. It is easy to say that a man is a man in Maine or Minnesota, but not so easy to feel it, all through our bones and marrow. The camp is deprovincializing us very fast. Brave Winthrop, marching with the city *élégants,* seems to have been a little startled to find how wonderfully human were the hard-handed men of the Eighth Massachusetts. It takes all the nonsense out of everybody, or ought to do it, to see how fairly the real manhood of a country is distributed over its surface. And then, just as we are beginning to think our own soil has a monopoly of heroes as well as of cotton, up turns a regiment of gallant Irishmen, like the Sixty-ninth, to show us that continental provincialism is as bad as that of Coos County, New Hampshire, or of Broadway, New York.

Here, too, side by side in the same great camp, are half a dozen chaplains, representing half a dozen modes of religious belief. When the masked battery opens, does the "Baptist" Lieutenant believe in his heart that God takes better care of him than of his "Congregationalist" Colonel? Does any man really suppose, that, of a score of noble young fellows who have just laid down their lives for their country, the *Homoousians* are received to the mansions of bliss, and the *Homoiousians* translated from the battle-field to the abodes of everlasting woe? War not only teaches what man can be, but it teaches also what he must not be. He must not be a bigot and a fool in the presence of that day of judgment proclaimed by the trumpet which calls to battle, and where a man should have but two thoughts: to do his duty, and trust his Maker. Let our brave dead come back from the fields where they have fallen for law and liberty, and if you will follow them to their graves, you will find out what the Broad Church means; the narrow church is sparing of its exclusive formulæ over the coffins wrapped in the flag which the fallen heroes had defended! Very little comparatively do we hear at such times of the dogmas on which men differ; very much of the faith and trust in which all sincere Christians can agree. It is a noble lesson, and nothing less noisy than the voice of cannon can teach it so that it shall be heard over all the angry cries of theological disputants.

Now, too, we have a chance to test the sagacity of our friends, and to get at their principles of judgment. Perhaps most of us will agree that our faith in domestic prophets has been diminished by the experience of the last six months. We had the notable predictions attributed to the Secretary of State, which so unpleasantly refused to fulfill themselves. We were infested at one time with a set of ominous-looking seers, who shook their heads and muttered obscurely about some mighty preparations that were making to substitute the rule of the minority for that of the majority. Organizations were darkly hinted at; some thought our armories would be seized; and there are not wanting ancient women in the neighboring University town who consider that the country was saved by the intrepid band of students who stood guard, night after night, over the G. R. cannon and the pile of balls in the Cambridge Arsenal.

As a general rule, it is safe to say that the best prophecies are those which the sages *remember* after the event prophesied of has come to pass, and remind us that they have made long ago. Those who are rash enough to predict publicly beforehand commonly give us what they hope, or what they fear, or some conclusion from an abstraction of their own, or some guess founded on private information not half so good as what everybody gets who reads the papers,—*never* by any possibility a word that we can depend on, simply because there are cobwebs of contingency between every to-day and to-morrow that no field-glass can penetrate when fifty of them lie woven one over another. Prophesy as much as you like, but always *hedge*. Say that you think the rebels are weaker than is commonly supposed, but, on the other hand, that they may prove to be even stronger than is anticipated. Say what you like,—only don't be too peremptory and dogmatic; we *know* that wiser men than you have been notoriously deceived in their predictions in this very matter.

"Ibis et redibis nunquam in bello peribis."

Let that be your model; and remember, on peril of your reputation as a prophet, not to put a stop before or after the *nunquam*.

There are two or three facts connected with *time,* besides that already referred to, which strike us very forcibly in their relation to the great events passing around us. We spoke of the long period seeming to have elapsed since this war began. The buds were then swelling which held the leaves that are still green. It seems as old as Time himself. We cannot fail to observe how the mind brings together the scenes of to-day and those of the old Revolution. We shut up eighty years into each other like the joints of a pocket-telescope. When the young men from Middlesex dropped in Baltimore the other day, it seemed to bring Lexington and the other Nineteenth of April close to us. War has always been the mint in which the world's history has been coined, and now every day or week or month has a new medal for us. It was Warren that the first impression bore in the last great coinage; if it is Ellsworth now, the new face hardly seems fresher than the old. All battle-fields are alike in their main features. The young fellows who fell in our earlier struggle seemed like old men to us until within these few months; now we remember they were like these fiery youth we are cheering as they go to the fight; it seems as if the grass of our bloody hillside was crimsoned but yesterday, and the cannon-ball imbedded in the church-tower would feel warm, if we laid our hand upon it.

Nay, in this our quickened life we feel that all the battles from earliest time to our own day, where Right and Wrong have grappled, are but one great battle, varied with brief pauses or hasty bivouacs upon the field of conflict. The issues seem to vary, but it is always a right against a claim, and, however the struggle of the hour may go, a movement onward of the campaign, which uses defeat as well as victory to serve its mighty ends. The very implements of our warfare change less than we think. Our bullets and cannonballs have lengthened into bolts like those which whistled out of old arbalests. Our soldiers fight with weapons, such as are pictured on the walls of Theban tombs, wearing a newly invented head-gear as old as the days of the Pyramids.

Whatever miseries this war brings upon us, it is making us wiser, and, we trust, better. Wiser, for we are learning our weakness, our narrowness, our selfishness, our ignorance, in lessons of sorrow and shame. Better, because all that is noble in men and women is demanded by the time, and our people are rising to the standard the time calls for. For this is the question the hour is putting to each of us: Are you ready, if need be, to sacrifice all that you have and hope for in this world, that the generations to follow you may inherit a whole country whose natural conditions shall be peace, and not a broken province which must live under the perpetual threat, if not in the constant presence, of war and all that war brings with it? If we are all ready for this sacrifice, battles may be lost, but the campaign and its grand object must be won.

Heaven is very kind in its way of putting questions to mortals. We are not abruptly asked to give up all that we most care for, in view of the momentous issues before us.

Perhaps we shall never be asked to give up all, but we have already been called upon to part with much that is dear to us, and should be ready to yield the rest as it is called for. The time may come when even the cheap public print shall be a burden our means cannot support, and we can only listen in the square that was once the market-place to the voices of those who proclaim defeat or victory. Then there will be only our daily food left. When we have nothing to read and nothing to eat, it will be a favorable moment to offer a compromise. At present we have all that nature absolutely demands,—we can live on bread and the newspaper.

WALKING

Henry David Thoreau

I wish to speak a word for Nature, for absolute freedom and wildness, as contrasted with a freedom and culture merely civil,—to regard man as an inhabitant, or a part and parcel of Nature, rather than a member of society. I wish to make an extreme statement, if so I may make an emphatic one, for there are enough champions of civilization: the minister and the school-committee, and every one of you will take care of that.

I have met with but one or two persons in the course of my life who understood the art of Walking, that is, of taking walks,—who had a genius, so to speak, for *sauntering:* which word is beautifully derived from "idle people who roved about the country, in the Middle Ages, and asked charity, under pretense of going *à la Sainte Terre,*" to the Holy Land, till the children exclaimed, "There goes a *Sainte-Terrer,*" a Saunterer,—a Holy-Lander. They who never go to the Holy Land in their walks, as they pretend, are indeed mere idlers and vagabonds; but they who do go there are saunterers in the good sense, such as I mean. Some, however, would derive the word from *sans terre,* without land or a home, which, therefore, in the good sense, will mean, having no particular home, but equally at home everywhere. For this is the secret of successful sauntering. He who sits still in a house all the time may be the greatest vagrant of all; but the saunterer, in the good sense, is no more vagrant than the meandering river, which is all the while sedulously seeking the shortest course to the sea. But I prefer the first, which, indeed, is the most probable derivation. For every walk is a sort of crusade, preached by some Peter the Hermit in us, to go forth and reconquer this Holy Land from the hands of the Infidels.

It is true, we are but faint-hearted crusaders, even the walkers, nowadays, who undertake no persevering, never-ending enterprises. Our expeditions are but tours, and come round again at evening to the old hearth-side from which we set out. Half the walk is but retracing our steps. We should go forth on the shortest walk, perchance, in the spirit of undying adventure, never to return,—prepared to send back our embalmed hearts only as relics to our desolate kingdoms. If you are ready to leave father and mother, and brother and sister, and wife and child and friends, and never see them again,—if you have paid your debts, and made your will, and settled all your affairs, and are a free man, then you are ready for a walk.

To come down to my own experience, my companion and I, for I sometimes have a companion, take pleasure in fancying ourselves knights of a new, or rather an old, order,—not Equestrians or Chevaliers, not Ritters or riders, but Walkers, a still more ancient and honorable class, I trust. The chivalric and heroic spirit which once belonged to the Rider seems now to reside in, or perchance to have subsided into, the Walker,—not the Knight, but Walker Errant. He is a sort of fourth estate, outside of Church and State and People.

We have felt that we almost alone hereabouts practiced this noble art; though, to tell the truth, at least, if their own assertions are to be received, most of my townsmen would fain walk sometimes, as I do, but they cannot. No wealth can buy the requisite leisure, freedom, and independence, which are the capital in this profession. It comes only by the grace of God. It requires a direct dispensation from Heaven to become a walker. You must be born into the family of the Walkers. *Ambulator nascitur, non fit.* Some of my townsmen, it is true, can remember and have described to me some walks which they took ten years ago, in which they were so blessed as to lose themselves for half an hour in the woods; but I know very well that they have confined themselves to the highway ever since, whatever pretensions they may make to belong to this select class. No doubt they were elevated for a moment as by the reminiscence of a previous state of existence, when even they were foresters and outlaws.

> "When he came to grene wode,
>   In a mery mornynge,
>   There he herde the notes small
>   Of byrdes mery syngynge.
>
> "It is ferre gone, sayd Robyn,
>   That I was last here;
>   Me lyste a lytell for to shote
>   At the donne dere."

I think that I cannot preserve my health and spirits, unless I spend four hours a day at least,—and it is commonly more than that,—sauntering through the woods and over the hills and fields, absolutely free from all worldly engagements. You may safely say, A penny for your thoughts, or a thousand pounds. When sometimes I am reminded that the mechanics and shopkeepers stay in their shops not only all the forenoon, but all the afternoon too, sitting with crossed legs, so many of them,—as if the legs were made to sit upon, and not to stand or walk upon,—I think that they deserve some credit for not having all committed suicide long ago.

I, who cannot stay in my chamber for a single day without acquiring some rust, and when sometimes I have stolen forth for a walk at the eleventh hour of four o'clock in the afternoon, too late to redeem the day, when the shades of night were already beginning to be mingled with the daylight, have felt as if I had committed some sin to be atoned for,—I confess that I am astonished at the power of endurance, to say nothing of the moral insensibility, of my neighbors who confine themselves to shops and offices the whole day for weeks and months, ay, and years almost together. I know not what manner of stuff they are of,— sitting there now at three o'clock in the afternoon, as if it were three o'clock in the morning. Bonaparte may talk of the three-o'clock-in-the-morning courage, but it is nothing to the courage which can sit down cheerfully at this hour in the afternoon over against one's self whom you have known all the morning, to starve out a garrison to whom you are bound by such strong ties of sympathy. I wonder that about this time, or say between four and five o'clock in the afternoon, too late for the morning papers and too early for the evening ones, there is not a general explosion heard up and down the street, scattering a legion of antiquated and house-bred notions and whims to the four winds for an airing,—and so the evil cure itself.

How womankind, who are confined to the house still more than men, stand it I do not know; but I have ground to suspect that most of them do not *stand* it at all. When, early in a summer afternoon, we have been shaking the dust of the village from the skirts of our garments, making haste past those houses with purely Doric or Gothic fronts, which have such an air of repose about them, my companion whispers that probably about these times their occupants are all gone to bed. Then it is that I appreciate the beauty and the glory of architecture, which itself never turns in, but forever stands out and erect, keeping watch over the slumberers.

No doubt temperament, and, above all, age, have a good deal to do with it. As a man grows older, his ability to sit still and follow indoor occupations increases. He grows vespertinal in his habits as the evening of life approaches, till at last he comes forth only just before sundown, and gets all the walk that he requires in half an hour.

But the walking of which I speak has nothing in it akin to taking exercise, as it is called, as the sick take medicine at stated hours,—as the swinging of dumb-bells or chairs; but is itself the enterprise and adventure of the day. If you would get exercise, go in search of the springs of life. Think of a man's swinging dumb-bells for his health, when those springs are bubbling up in far-off pastures unsought by him!

Moreover, you must walk like a camel, which is said to be the only beast which ruminates when walking. When a traveler asked Wordsworth's servant to show him her master's study, she answered, "Here is his library, but his study is out of doors."

Living much out of doors, in the sun and wind, will no doubt produce a certain roughness of character,—will cause a thicker cuticle to grow over some of the finer qualities of our nature, as on the face and hands, or as severe manual labor robs the hands of some of their delicacy of touch. So staying in the house, on the other hand, may produce a softness and smoothness, not to say thinness of skin, accompanied by an increased sensibility to certain impressions. Perhaps we should be more susceptible to some influences important to our intellectual and moral growth, if the sun had shone and the wind blown on us a little less; and no doubt it is a nice matter to proportion rightly the thick and thin skin. But methinks that is a scurf that will fall off fast enough,—that the natural remedy is to be found in the proportion which the night bears to the day, the winter to the summer, thought to experience. There will be so much the more air and sunshine in our thoughts. The callous palms of the laborer are conversant with finer tissues of self-respect and heroism, whose touch thrills the heart, than the languid fingers of idleness. That is mere sentimentality that lies abed by day and thinks itself white, far from the tan and callus of experience.

When we walk, we naturally go to the fields and woods: what would become of us, if we walked only in a garden or a mall? Even some sects of philosophers have felt the necessity of importing the woods to themselves, since they did not go to the woods. " They planted groves and walks of Platanes," where they took *subdiales ambulationes* in porticos open to the air. Of course it is of no use to direct our steps to the woods, if they do not carry us thither. I am alarmed when it happens that I have walked a mile into the woods bodily, without getting there in spirit. In my afternoon walk I would fain forget all my morning occupations and my obligations to society. But it sometimes happens that I cannot easily shake off the village. The thought of some work will run in my head, and I am not where my body is,—I am out of my senses. In my walks I would fain return to my senses. What business have I in the woods, if I am thinking of something out of the woods? I suspect myself, and cannot help a shudder, when I find myself so implicated even in what are called good works,— for this may sometimes happen.

My vicinity affords many good walks; and though for so many years I have walked almost every day, and sometimes for several days together, I have not yet exhausted them. An absolutely new prospect is a great happiness, and I can still get this any afternoon. Two or three hours' walking will carry me to as strange a country as I expect ever to see. A single farmhouse which I had not seen before is sometimes as good as the dominions of the King of Dahomey. There is in fact a sort of harmony discoverable between the capabilities of the landscape within a circle of ten miles' radius, or the limits of an afternoon walk, and the threescore years and ten of human life. It will never become quite familiar to you.

Nowadays almost all man's improvements, so called, as the building of houses, and the cutting down of the forest and of all large trees, simply deform the landscape, and make it more and more tame and cheap. A people who would begin by burning the fences and let the forest stand! I saw the fences half consumed, their ends lost in the middle of the prairie, and some worldly miser with a surveyor looking after his bounds, while heaven had taken place around him, and he did not see the angels going to and fro, but was looking for an old post-hole in the midst of paradise. I looked again, and saw him standing in the middle of a boggy, stygian fen, surrounded by devils, and he had found his bounds without a doubt, three little stones, where a stake had been driven, and looking nearer, I saw that the Prince of Darkness was his surveyor.

I can easily walk ten, fifteen, twenty, any number of miles, commencing at my own door, without going by any house, without crossing a road except where the fox and the mink do: first along by the river, and then the brook, and then the meadow and the woodside. There are square miles in my vicinity which have no inhabitant. From many a hill I can see civilization and the abodes of man afar. The farmers and their works are scarcely more obvious than woodchucks and their burrows. Man and his affairs, church and state and school, trade and commerce, and manufactures and agriculture, even politics, the most alarming of them all,—I am pleased to see how little space they occupy in the landscape. Politics is but a narrow field, and that still narrower highway yonder leads to it. I sometimes direct the traveler thither. If you would go to the political world, follow the great road,—follow that marketman, keep his dust in your eyes, and it will lead you straight to it; for it, too, has its place merely, and does not occupy all space. I pass from it as from a bean-field into the forest, and it is forgotten. In one half-hour I can walk off to some portion of the earth's surface where a man does not stand from one year's end to another, and there, consequently, politics are not, for they are but as the cigar-smoke of a man.

The village is the place to which the roads tend, a sort of expansion of the highway, as a lake of a river. It is the body of which roads are the arms and legs,—a trivial or quadrivial place, the thoroughfare and ordinary of travelers. The word is from the Latin *villa,* which, together with *via,* a way, or more anciently *ved* and *vella,* Varro derives from *veho,* to carry, because the villa is the place to and from which things are carried. They who got their living by teaming were said *vellaturam facere.* Hence, too, apparently, the Latin word *vilis* and our vile; also *villain.* This suggests what kind of degeneracy villagers are liable to. They are wayworn by the travel that goes by and over them, without traveling themselves.

Some do not walk at all; others walk in the highways; a few walk across lots. Roads are made for horses and men of business. I do not travel in them much, comparatively, because I am not in a hurry to get to any tavern or grocery or livery-stable or depot to which they lead. I am a good horse to travel, but not from choice a roadster. The landscape-painter uses the figures of men to mark a road. He would not make that use of my figure. I walk out into a Nature such as the old prophets and poets, Menu, Moses, Homer, Chaucer, walked in. You may name it America, but it is not America: neither Americus Vespucius, nor Columbus, nor the rest were the discoverers of it. There is a truer account of it in mythology than in any history of America, so called, that I have seen.

However, there are a few old roads that may be trodden with profit, as if they led somewhere now that they are nearly discontinued. There is the Old Marlborough Road, which does not go to Marlborough now, methinks, unless that is Marlborough where it carries me. I am the bolder to speak of it here, because I presume that there are one or two such roads in every town.

THE OLD MARLBOROUGH ROAD.

>Where they once dug for money,
>But never found any;
>Where sometimes Martial Miles
>   Singly files,
>   And Elijah Wood,
>   I fear for no good:
>   No other man,
>   Save Elisha Dugan,—
>   O man of wild habits,
>   Partridges and rabbits,
>   Who hast no cares
>   Only to set snares,
>   Who liv'st all alone,
>   Close to the bone,
>   And where life is sweetest
>   Constantly eatest.
>When the spring stirs my blood
> With the instinct to travel,
> I can get enough gravel
>On the Old Marlborough Road.
>   Nobody repairs it,
>   For nobody wears it;
>   It is a living way,
>   As the Christians say.

Walking

Not many there be
  Who enter therein,
Only the guests of the
  Irishman Quin.
What is it, what is it,
  But a direction out there,
And the bare possibility
  Of going somewhere?
    Great guideboards of stone,
    But travelers noné;
    Cenotaphs of the towns
    Named on their crowns.
    It is worth going to see
    Where you *might* be.
    What king
    Did the thing,
    I am still wondering;
    Set up how or when,
    By what selectmen,
    Gourgas or Lee,
    Clark or Darby?
    They're a great endeavor
    To be something forever;
    Blank tablets of stone,
    Where a traveler might groan,
    And in one sentence
    Grave all that is known;
    Which another might read,
    In his extreme need.
    I know one or two
    Lines that would do,
    Literature that might stand
    All over the land,
    Which a man could remember
    Till next December,
    And read again in the spring,
    After the thawing.
If with fancy unfurled
  You leave your abode,
You may go round the world
  By the Old Marlborough Road.

At present, in this vicinity, the best part of the land is not private property; the landscape is not owned, and the walker enjoys comparative freedom. But possibly the day will come when it will be partitioned off into so-called pleasure-grounds, in which a few will take a narrow and exclusive pleasure only,—when fences shall be multiplied, and man-traps and other engines invented to confine men to the *public* road, and walking over the surface of God's earth shall be construed to mean trespassing on some gentleman's grounds. To enjoy a thing exclusively is commonly to exclude yourself from the true enjoyment of it. Let us improve our opportunities, then, before the evil days come.

What is it that makes it so hard sometimes to determine whither we will walk? I believe that there is a subtile magnetism in Nature, which, if we unconsciously yield to it, will direct us aright. It is not indifferent to us which way we walk. There is a right way; but we are very liable from heedlessness and stupidity to take the wrong one. We would fain take that walk, never yet taken by us through this actual world, which is perfectly symbolical of the path which we love to travel in the interior and ideal world; and sometimes, no doubt, we find it difficult to choose our direction, because it does not yet exist distinctly in our idea.

When I go out of the house for a walk, uncertain as yet whither I will bend my steps, and submit myself to my instinct to decide for me, I find, strange and whimsical as it may seem, that I finally and inevitably settle southwest, toward some particular wood or meadow or deserted pasture or hill in that direction. My needle is slow to settle,—varies a few degrees, and does not always point due southwest, it is true, and it has good authority for this variation, but it always settles between west and south-south-west. The future lies that way to me, and the earth seems more unexhausted and richer on that side. The outline which would bound my walks would be, not a circle, but a parabola, or rather like one of those cometary orbits which have been thought to be non-returning curves, in this case opening westward, in which my house occupies the place of the sun. I turn round and round irresolute sometimes for a quarter of an hour, until I decide, for a thousandth time, that I will walk into the southwest or west. Eastward I go only by force; but westward I go free. Thither no business leads me. It is hard for me to believe that I shall find fair landscapes or sufficient wildness and freedom behind the eastern horizon. I am not excited by the prospect of a walk thither; but I believe that the forest which I see in the western horizon stretches uninterruptedly toward the setting sun, and there are no towns nor cities in it of enough consequence to disturb me. Let me live where I will, on this side is the city, on that the wilderness, and ever I am leaving the city more and more, and withdrawing into the wilderness. I should not lay so much stress on this fact, if I did not believe that something like this is the prevailing tendency of my countrymen. I must walk toward Oregon, and not toward Europe. And that way the nation is moving, and I may say that mankind progress from east to west. Within a few years we have witnessed the phenomenon of a southeastward migration, in the settlement of Australia; but this affects us as a retrograde movement, and judging from the moral and physical character of the first generation of Australians, has not yet proved a successful experiment. The eastern Tartars think that there is nothing west beyond Thibet. "The world ends there," say they, "beyond there is nothing but a shoreless sea." It is unmitigated East where they live.

We go eastward to realize history and study the works of art and literature, retracing the steps of the race; we go westward as into the future, with a spirit of enterprise and adventure. The Atlantic is a Lethean stream, in our passage over which we have had an opportunity to forget the Old World and its institutions. If we do not succeed this time, there is perhaps one more chance for the race left before it arrives on the banks of the Styx; and that is in the Lethe of the Pacific, which is three times as wide.

I know not how significant it is, or how far it is an evidence of singularity, that an individual should thus consent in his pettiest walk with the general movement of the race; but I know that something akin to the migratory instinct in birds and quadrupeds,—which, in some instances, is known to have affected the squirrel tribe, impelling them to a general and mysterious movement, in which they were seen, say some, crossing the broadest rivers, each on its particular chip, with its tail raised for a sail, and bridging narrower streams with their dead,—that something like the *furor* which affects the domestic cattle in the spring, and which is referred to a worm in their tails,—affects both nations and individuals, either perennially or from time to time. Not a flock of wild geese cackles over our town, but it to some extent unsettles the value of real estate here, and, if I were a broker, I should probably take that disturbance into account.

> "Than longen folk to gon on pilgrimages,
> And palmeres for to seken strange strondes."

Every sunset which I witness inspires me with the desire to go to a West as distant and as fair as that into which the sun goes down. He appears to migrate westward daily, and tempt us to follow him. He is the Great Western Pioneer whom the nations follow. We dream all night of those mountain-ridges in the horizon, though they may be of vapor only, which were last gilded by his rays. The island of Atlantis, and the islands and gardens of the Hesperides, a sort of terrestrial paradise, appear to have been the Great West of the ancients, enveloped in mystery and poetry. Who has not seen in imagination, when looking into the sunset sky, the gardens of the Hesperides, and the foundation of all those fables?

Columbus felt the westward tendency more strongly than any before. He obeyed it, and found a New World for Castile and Leon. The herd of men in those days scented fresh pastures from afar.

> " And now the sun had stretched out all the hills,
> And now was dropped into the western bay;
> At last *he* rose, and twitched his mantle blue;
> To-morrow to fresh woods and pastures new."

Where on the globe can there be found an area of equal extent with that occupied by the bulk of our States, so fertile and so rich and varied in its productions, and at the same time so habitable by the European, as this is? Michaux, who knew but part of them, says that " the species of large trees are much more numerous in North America than in Europe; in the United States there are more than one hundred and forty species that exceed thirty feet in height; in France there are but thirty that attain this size." Later botanists more than confirm his observations. Humboldt came to America to realize his youthful dreams of a tropical vegetation, and he beheld it in its greatest perfection in the primitive forests of the Amazon, the most gigantic wilderness on the earth, which he has so eloquently described. The geographer Guyot, himself a European, goes farther,—farther than I am ready to follow him; yet not when he says,—" As the plant is made for the animal, as the vegetable world is made for the animal world, America is made for the man of the Old World. . . . The man of the Old World sets out upon his way. Leaving the highlands of Asia, he descends from station to station towards Europe. Each of his steps is marked by a new civilization superior to the preceding, by a greater power of development. Arrived at the Atlantic, he pauses on the shore of this unknown ocean, the bounds of which he knows not, and turns upon his footprints for an instant." When he has exhausted the rich soil of Europe, and reinvigorated himself, "then recommences his adventurous career westward as in the earliest ages." So far Guyot.

From this western impulse coming in contact with the barrier of the Atlantic sprang the commerce and enterprise of modern times. The younger Michaux, in his *Travels West of the Alleghanies in 1802,* says that the common inquiry in the newly settled West was, "'From what part of the world have you come?' As if these vast and fertile regions would naturally be the place of meeting and common country of all the inhabitants of the globe."

To use an obsolete Latin word, I might say, *Ex Oriente lux; ex Occidente* FRUX. From the East light; from the West fruit.

Sir Francis Head, an English traveler and a Governor-General of Canada, tells us that "in both the northern and southern hemispheres of the New World, Nature has not only outlined her works on a larger scale, but has painted the whole picture with brighter and more costly colors than she used in delineating and in beautifying the Old World. . . . The heavens of America appear infinitely higher, the sky is bluer, the air is fresher, the cold is intenser, the moon looks larger, the stars are brighter, the thunder is louder, the lightning is vivider, the wind is stronger, the rain is heavier, the mountains are higher, the rivers longer, the forests bigger, the plains broader." This statement will do at least to set against Buffon's account of this part of the world and its productions.

Linnæus said long ago, "Nescio quæ facies *læta, glabra* plantis Americanis: I know not what there is of joyous and smooth in the aspect of American plants;" and I think that in this country there are no, or at most very few, *Africanæ bestiæ,* African beasts, as the Romans called them, and that in this respect also it is peculiarly fitted for the habitation of man. We are told that within three miles of the center of the East-Indian city of Singapore, some of the inhabitants are annually carried off by tigers; but the traveler can lie down in the woods at night almost anywhere in North America without fear of wild beasts.

These are encouraging testimonies. If the moon looks larger here than in Europe, probably the sun looks larger also. If the heavens of America appear infinitely higher, and the stars brighter, I trust that these facts are symbolical of the height to which the philosophy and poetry and religion of her inhabitants may one day soar. At length, perchance, the immaterial heaven will appear as much higher to the American mind, and the intimations that star it as much brighter. For I believe that climate does thus react on man,—as there is something in the mountain-air that feeds the spirit and inspires. Will not man grow to greater perfection intellectually as well as physically under these influences? Or is it unimportant how many foggy days there are in his life? I trust that we shall be more imaginative, that our thoughts will be clearer, fresher, and more ethereal, as our sky,—our understanding more comprehensive and broader, like our plains,—our intellect generally on a grander scale, like our thunder and lightning, our rivers and mountains and forests,—and our hearts shall even correspond in breadth and depth and grandeur to our inland seas. Perchance there will appear to the traveler something, he knows not what, of *læta* and *glabra,* of joyous and serene, in our very faces. Else to what end does the world go on, and why was America discovered?

To Americans I hardly need to say,—

"Westward the star of empire takes its way."

As a true patriot, I should be ashamed to think that Adam in paradise was more favorably situated on the whole than the backwoodsman in this country.

Our sympathies in Massachusetts are not confined to New England; though we may be estranged from the South, we sympathize with the West. There is the home of the younger sons, as among the Scandinavians they took to the sea for their inheritance. It is too late to be studying Hebrew; it is more important to understand even the slang of to-day.

Some months ago I went to see a panorama of the Rhine. It was like a dream of the Middle Ages. I floated down its historic stream in something more than imagination, under bridges built by the Romans, and repaired by later heroes, past cities and castles whose very names were music to my ears, and each of which was the subject of a legend. There were Ehrenbreitstein and Rolandseck and Coblentz, which I knew only in history. They were ruins that interested me chiefly. There seemed to come up from its waters and its vine-clad hills and valleys a hushed music as of Crusaders departing for the Holy Land. I floated along under the spell of enchantment, as if I had been transported to an heroic age, and breathed an atmosphere of chivalry.

Soon after, I went to see a panorama of the Mississippi, and as I worked my way up the river in the light of to-day, and saw the steamboats wooding up, counted the rising cities, gazed on the fresh ruins of Nauvoo, beheld the Indians moving west across the stream, and, as before I had looked up the Moselle now looked up the Ohio and the Missouri, and heard the legends of Dubuque and of We-nona's Cliff,—still thinking more of the future than of the past or present,—I saw that this was a Rhine stream of a different kind; that the foundations of castles were yet to be laid, and the famous bridges were yet to be thrown over the river; and I felt that *this was the heroic age itself*, though we know it not, for the hero is commonly the simplest and obscurest of men.

The West of which I speak is but another name for the Wild; and what I have been preparing to say is, that in Wildness is the preservation of the World. Every tree sends its fibers forth in search of the Wild. The cities import it at any price. Men plow and sail for it. From the forest and wilderness come the tonics and barks which brace mankind. Our ancestors were savages. The story of Romulus and Remus being suckled by a wolf is not a meaningless fable. The founders of every State which has risen to eminence have drawn their nourishment and vigor from a similar wild source. It was because the children of the Empire were not suckled by the wolf that they were conquered and displaced by the children of the Northern forests who were.

I believe in the forest, and in the meadow, and in the night in which the corn grows. We require an infusion of hemlock-spruce or arbor-vitæ in our tea. There is a difference between eating and drinking for strength and from mere gluttony. The Hottentots eagerly devour the marrow of the koodoo and other antelopes raw, as a matter of course. Some of our Northern Indians eat raw the marrow of the Arctic reindeer, as well as various other parts, including the summits of the antlers, as long as they are soft. And herein, perchance, they have stolen a march on the cooks of Paris. They get what usually goes to feed the fire. This is probably better than stall-fed beef and slaughter-house pork to make a man of. Give me a wildness whose glance no civilization can endure,—as if we lived on the marrow of koodoos devoured raw.

There are some intervals which border the strain of the wood-thrush, to which I would migrate,—wild lands where no settler has squatted; to which, methinks, I am already acclimated.

The African hunter Cummings tells us that the skin of the eland, as well as that of most other antelopes just killed, emits the most delicious perfume of trees and grass. I would have every man so much like a wild antelope, so much a part and parcel of Nature, that his very person should thus sweetly advertise our senses of his presence, and remind us of those parts of Nature which he most haunts. I feel no disposition to be satirical, when the trapper's coat emits the odor of musquash even; it is a sweeter scent to me than that which commonly exhales from the merchant's or the scholar's garments. When I go into their wardrobes and handle their vestments, I am reminded of no grassy plains and flowery meads which they have frequented, but of dusty merchants' exchanges and libraries rather.

A tanned skin is something more than respectable, and perhaps olive is a fitter color than white for a man,—a denizen of the woods. "The pale white man!" I do not wonder that the African pitied him. Darwin the naturalist says, "A white man bathing by the side of a Tahitian was like a plant bleached by the gardener's art, compared with a fine, dark green one, growing vigorously in the open fields."

Ben Jonson exclaims,—

> "How near to good is what is fair!"

So I would say,—

> How near to good is what is *wild!*

Life consists with wildness. The most alive is the wildest. Not yet subdued to man, its presence refreshes him. One who pressed forward incessantly and never rested from his labors, who grew fast and made infinite demands on life, would always find himself in a new country or wilderness, and surrounded by the raw material of life. He would be climbing over the prostrate stems of primitive forest-trees.

Hope and the future for me are not in lawns and cultivated fields, not in towns and cities, but in the impervious and quaking swamps. When, formerly, I have analyzed my partiality for some farm which I had contemplated purchasing, I have frequently found that I was attracted solely by a few square rods of impermeable and unfathomable bog,—a natural sink in one corner of it. That was the jewel which dazzled me. I derive more of my subsistence from the swamps which surround my native town than from the cultivated gardens in the village. There are no richer parterres to my eyes than the dense beds of dwarf andromeda (*Cassandra calyculata*) which cover these tender places on the earth's surface. Botany cannot go farther than tell me the names of the shrubs which grow there,— the high-blueberry, panicled andromeda, lamb-kill, azalea, and rhodora,—all standing in the quaking sphagnum. I often think that I should like to have my house front on this mass of dull red bushes, omitting other flower pots and borders, transplanted spruce and trim box, even graveled walks,—to have this fertile spot under my windows, not a few imported barrow-fulls of soil only to cover the sand which was thrown out in digging the cellar. Why not put my house, my parlor, behind this plot, instead of behind that meager assemblage of curiosities, that poor apology for a Nature and Art, which I call my front-yard? It is an effort to clear up and make a decent appearance when the carpenter and mason have departed, though done as much for the passer-by as the dweller within. The most tasteful front-yard fence was never an agreeable object of study to me; the most elaborate ornaments, acorn-tops, or what not, soon wearied and disgusted me. Bring your sills up to the very edge of the swamp, then, (though it may not be the best place for a dry cellar,) so that there be no access on that side to citizens. Front-yards are not made to walk in, but, at most, through, and you could go in the back way.

Yes, though you may think me perverse, if it were proposed to me to dwell in the neighborhood of the most beautiful garden that ever human art contrived, or else of a Dismal swamp, I should certainly decide for the swamp. How vain, then, have been all your labors, citizens, for me!

My spirits infallibly rise in proportion to the outward dreariness. Give me the ocean, the desert, or the wilderness! In the desert, pure air and solitude compensate for want of moisture and fertility. The traveler Burton says of it,—"Your *morale* improves; you become frank and cordial, hospitable and single-minded. . . . In the desert, spirituous liquors excite only disgust. There is a keen enjoyment in a mere animal existence." They who have been traveling long on the steppes of Tartary say,—"On reëntering cultivated lands, the agitation, perplexity, and turmoil of civilization oppressed and suffocated us; the air seemed to fail us, and we felt every moment as if about to die of asphyxia." When I would recreate myself, I seek the darkest wood, the thickest and most interminable, and, to the citizen, most dismal swamp. I enter a swamp as a sacred place,—a *sanctum sanctorum.* There is the strength, the marrow of Nature. The wild-wood covers the virgin mold,—and the same soil is good for men and for trees. A man's health requires as many acres of meadow to his prospect as his farm does loads of muck. There are the strong meats on which he feeds. A town is saved, not more by the righteous men in it than by the woods and swamps that surround it. A township where one primitive forest waves above, while another primitive forest rots below,—such a town is fitted to raise not only corn and potatoes, but poets and philosophers for the coming ages. In such a soil grew Homer and Confucius and the rest, and out of such a wilderness comes the Reformer eating locusts and wild honey.

To preserve wild animals implies generally the creation of a forest for them to dwell in or resort to. So it is with man. A hundred years ago they sold bark in our streets peeled from our own woods. In the very aspect of those primitive and rugged trees, there was, methinks, a tanning principle which hardened and consolidated the fibers of men's thoughts. Ah! already I shudder for these comparatively degenerate days of my native village, when you cannot collect a load of bark of good thickness,—and we no longer produce tar and turpentine.

The civilized nations—Greece, Rome, England—have been sustained by the primitive forests which anciently rotted where they stand. They survive as long as the soil is not exhausted. Alas for human culture! little is to be expected of a nation, when the vegetable mould is exhausted, and it is compelled to make manure of the bones of its fathers. There the poet sustains himself merely by his own superfluous fat, and the philosopher comes down on his marrow-bones.

It is said to be the task of the American "to work the virgin soil," and that "agriculture here already assumes proportions unknown everywhere else." I think that the farmer displaces the Indian even because he redeems the meadow, and so makes himself stronger and in some respects more natural. I was surveying for a man the other day a single straight line one hundred and thirty-two rods long, through a swamp, at whose entrance might have been written the words which Dante read over the entrance to the infernal regions,—"Leave all hope, ye that enter,"— that is, of ever getting out again; where at one time I saw my employer actually up to his neck and swimming for his life in his property, though it was still winter. He had another similar swamp which I could not survey at all, because it was completely under water, and nevertheless, with regard to a third swamp, which I did *survey* from a distance, he remarked to me, true to his instincts, that he would not part with it for any consideration, on account of the mud which it contained. And that man intends to put a girdling ditch round the whole in the course of forty months, and so redeem it by the magic of his spade. I refer to him only as the type of a class.

The weapons with which we have gained our most important victories, which should be handed down as heirlooms from father to son, are not the sword and the lance, but the bushwhack, the turf-cutter, the spade, and the boghoe, rusted with the blood of many a meadow, and begrimed with the dust of many a hard-fought field. The very winds blew the Indian's cornfield into the meadow, and pointed out the way which he had not the skill to follow. He had no better implement with which to intrench himself in the land than a clam-shell. But the farmer is armed with plow and spade.

In literature it is only the wild that attracts us. Dullness is but another name for tameness. It is the uncivilized free and wild thinking in *Hamlet* and the *Iliad,* in all the scriptures and mythologies, not learned in the schools, that delights us. As the wild duck is more swift and beautiful than the tame, so is the wild—the mallard—

thought, which 'mid falling dews wings its way above the fens. A truly good book is something as natural, and as unexpectedly and unaccountably fair and perfect, as a wild flower discovered on the prairies of the West or in the jungles of the East. Genius is a light which makes the darkness visible, like the lightning's flash, which perchance shatters the temple of knowledge itself,—and not a taper lighted at the hearthstone of the race, which pales before the light of common day.

English literature, from the days of the minstrels to the Lake Poets,—Chaucer and Spenser and Milton, and even Shakespeare, included,—breathes no quite fresh and, in this sense, wild strain. It is an essentially tame and civilized literature, reflecting Greece and Rome. Her wilderness is a green wood,—her wild man a Robin Hood. There is plenty of genial love of Nature, but not so much of Nature herself. Her chronicles inform us when her wild animals, but not when the wild man in her, became extinct.

The science of Humboldt is one thing, poetry is another thing. The poet to-day, notwithstanding all the discoveries of science, and the accumulated learning of mankind, enjoys no advantage over Homer.

Where is the literature which gives expression to Nature? He would be a poet who could impress the winds and streams into his service, to speak for him; who nailed words to their primitive senses, as farmers drive down stakes in the spring, which the frost has heaved; who derived his words as often as he used them,—transplanted them to his page with earth adhering to their roots; whose words were so true and fresh and natural that they would appear to expand like the buds at the approach of spring, though they lay half-smothered between two musty leaves in a library, —ay, to bloom and bear fruit there, after their kind, annually, for the faithful reader, in sympathy with surrounding Nature.

I do not know of any poetry to quote which adequately expresses this yearning for the Wild. Approached from this side, the best poetry is tame. I do not know where to find in any literature, ancient or modern, any account which contents me of that Nature with which even I am acquainted. You will perceive that I demand something which no Augustan nor Elizabethan age, which no *culture,* in short, can give. Mythology comes nearer to it than anything. How much more fertile a Nature, at least, has Grecian mythology its root in than English literature! Mythology is the crop which the Old World bore before its soil was exhausted, before the fancy and imagination were affected with blight; and which it still bears, wherever its pristine vigor is unabated. All other literatures endure only as the elms which overshadow our houses; but this is like the great dragon-tree of the Western Isles, as old as mankind, and, whether that does or not, will endure as long; for the decay of other literatures makes the soil in which it thrives.

The West is preparing to add its fables to those of the East. The valleys of the Ganges, the Nile, and the Rhine, having yielded their crop, it remains to be seen what the valleys of the Amazon, the Plate, the Orinoco, the St. Lawrence, and the Mississippi will produce. Perchance, when, in the course of ages, American liberty has become a fiction of the past,—as it is to some extent a fiction of the present,—the poets of the world will be inspired by American mythology.

The wildest dreams of wild men, even, are not the less true, though they may not recommend themselves to the sense which is most common among Englishmen and Americans to-day. It is not every truth that recommends itself to the common sense. Nature has a place for the wild clematis as well as for the cabbage. Some expressions of truth are reminiscent,—others merely *sensible,* as the phrase is,—others prophetic. Some forms of disease, even, may prophesy forms of health. The geologist has discovered that the figures of serpents, griffins, flying dragons, and other fanciful embellishments of heraldry, have their prototypes in the forms of fossil species which were extinct before man was created, and hence " indicate a faint and shadowy knowledge of a previous state of organic existence." The Hindoos dreamed that the earth rested on an elephant, and the elephant on a tortoise, and the tortoise on a serpent; and though it may be an unimportant coincidence, it will not be out of place here to state, that a fossil tortoise has lately been discovered in Asia large enough to support an elephant. I confess that I am partial to these wild fancies, which transcend the order of time and development. They are the sublimest recreation of the intellect. The partridge loves peas, but not those that go with her into the pot.

In short, all good things are wild and free. There is something in a strain of music, whether produced by an instrument or by the human voice,—take the sound of a bugle in a summer night, for instance,—which by its wildness, to speak without satire, reminds me of the cries emitted by wild beasts in their native forests. It is so much of their wildness as I can understand. Give me for my friends and neighbors wild men, not tame ones. The wildness of the savage is but a faint symbol of the awful ferity with which good men and lovers meet.

I love even to see the domestic animals reassert their native rights,—any evidence that they have not wholly lost their original wild habits and vigor; as when my neighbor's cow breaks out of her pasture early in the spring and boldly swims the river, a cold, gray tide, twenty-five or thirty rods wide, swollen by the melted snow. It is the buffalo crossing the Mississippi. This exploit confers some dignity on the herd in my eyes,—already dignified. The seeds of instinct are preserved under the thick hides of cattle and horses, like seeds in the bowels of the earth, an indefinite period.

Any sportiveness in cattle is unexpected. I saw one day a herd of a dozen bullocks and cows running about and frisking in unwieldy sport, like huge rats, even like kittens. They shook their heads, raised their tails, and rushed up and down a hill, and I perceived by their horns, as well as by their activity, their relation to the deer tribe. But, alas! a sudden loud *Whoa!* would have damped their ardor at once, reduced them from venison to beef, and stiffened their sides and sinews like the locomotive. Who but the Evil One has cried, "Whoa!" to mankind? Indeed, the life of cattle, like that of many men, is but a sort of locomotiveness; they move a side at a time, and man, by his machinery, is meeting the horse and the ox half-way. Whatever part the whip has touched is thenceforth palsied. Who would ever think of a *side* of any of the supple cat tribe, as we speak of a *side* of beef?

I rejoice that horses and steers have to be broken before they can be made the slaves of men, and that men themselves have some wild oats still left to sow before they become submissive members of society. Undoubtedly, all men are not equally fit subjects for civilization; and because the majority, like dogs and sheep, are tame by inherited disposition, this is no reason why the others should have their natures broken that they may be reduced to the same level. Men are in the main alike, but they were made several in order that they might be various. If a low use is to be served, one man will do nearly or quite as well as another; if a high one, individual excellence is to be regarded. Any man can stop a hole to keep the wind away, but no other man could serve so rare a use as the author of this illustration did. Confucius says,—" The skins of the tiger and the leopard, when they are tanned, are as the skins of the dog and the sheep tanned." But it is not the part of a true culture to tame tigers, any more than it is to make sheep ferocious; and tanning their skins for shoes is not the best use to which they can be put.

When looking over a list of men's names in a foreign language, as of military officers, or of authors who have written on a particular subject, I am reminded once more that there is nothing in a name. The name Menschikoff, for instance, has nothing in it to my ears more human than a whisker, and it may belong to a rat. As the names of the Poles and Russians are to us, so are ours to them. It is as if they had been named by the child's rigmarole,—*Iery wiery ichery van, tittle-tol-tan.* I see in my mind a herd of wild creatures swarming over the earth, and to each the herdsman has affixed some barbarous sound in his own dialect. The names of men are of course as cheap and meaningless as *Bose* and *Tray*, the names of dogs.

Methinks it would be some advantage to philosophy, if men were named merely in the gross, as they are known. It would be necessary only to know the genus and perhaps the race or variety, to know the individual. We are not prepared to believe that every private soldier in a Roman army had a name of his own,—because we have not supposed that he had a character of his own. At present our only true names are nicknames. I knew a boy who, from his peculiar energy, was called "Buster" by his playmates, and this rightly supplanted his Christian name. Some travelers tell us that an Indian had no name given him at first, but earned it, and his name was his fame; and among some tribes he acquired a new name with every new exploit. It is pitiful when a man bears a name for convenience merely, who has earned neither name nor fame.

I will not allow mere names to make distinctions for me, but still see men in herds for all them. A familiar name cannot make a man less strange to me. It may be given to a savage who retains in secret his own wild title earned in the woods. We have a wild savage in us, and a savage name is perchance somewhere recorded as ours. I see that my neighbor, who bears the familiar epithet William, or Edwin, takes it off with his jacket. It does not adhere to him when asleep or in anger, or aroused by any passion or inspiration. I seem to hear pronounced by some of his kin at such a time his original wild name in some jaw-breaking or else melodious tongue.

Here is this vast, savage, howling mother of ours, Nature, lying all around, with such beauty, and such affection for her children, as the leopard; and yet we are so early weaned from her breast to society, to that culture which is exclusively an interaction of man on man,—a sort of breeding in and in, which produces at most a merely English nobility, a civilization destined to have a speedy limit.

In society, in the best institutions of men, it is easy to detect a certain precocity. When we should still be growing children, we are already little men. Give me a culture which imports much muck from the meadows, and deepens the soil,—not that which trusts to heating manures, and improved implements and modes of culture only!

Many a poor, sore-eyed student that I have heard of would grow faster, both intellectually and physically, if, instead of sitting up so very late, he honestly slumbered a fool's allowance.

There may be an excess even of informing light. Niepce, a Frenchman, discovered "actinism," that power in the sun's rays which produces a chemical effect,—that granite rocks, and stone structures, and statues of metal, "are all alike destructively acted upon during the hours of sunshine, and, but for provisions of Nature no less wonderful, would soon perish under the delicate touch of the most subtile of the agencies of the universe." But he observed that "those bodies which underwent this change during the daylight possessed the power of restoring themselves to their original conditions during the hours of night, when this excitement was no longer influencing them." Hence it has been inferred that "the hours of darkness are as necessary to the inorganic creation as we know night and sleep are to the organic kingdom." Not even does the moon shine every night, but gives place to darkness.

I would not have every man nor every part of a man cultivated, any more than I would have every acre of earth cultivated: part will be tillage, but the greater part will be meadow and forest, not only serving an immediate use, but preparing a mould against a distant future, by the annual decay of the vegetation which it supports.

There are other letters for the child to learn than those which Cadmus invented. The Spaniards have a good term to express this wild and dusky knowledge—*Gramática parda,* tawny grammar,—a kind of mother-wit derived from that same leopard to which I have referred.

We have heard of a Society for the Diffusion of Useful Knowledge. It is said that knowledge is power; and the like. Methinks there is equal need of a Society for the Diffusion of Useful Ignorance, what we will call Beautiful Knowledge, a knowledge useful in a higher sense: for what is most of our boasted so-called knowledge but a conceit that we know something, which robs us of the advantage of our actual ignorance? What we call knowledge is often our positive ignorance; ignorance our negative knowledge. By long years of patient industry and reading of the newspapers,—for what are the libraries of science but files of newspapers?—a man accumulates a myriad facts, lays them up in his memory, and then when in some spring of his life he saunters abroad into the Great Fields of thought, he, as it were, goes to grass like a horse, and leaves all his harness behind in the stable. I would say to the Society for the Diffusion of Useful Knowledge, sometimes,—Go to grass. You have eaten hay long enough. The spring has come with its green crop. The very cows are driven to their country pastures before the end of May; though I have heard of one unnatural farmer who kept his cow in the barn and fed her on hay all the year round. So, frequently, the Society for the Diffusion of Useful Knowledge treats its cattle.

A man's ignorance sometimes is not only useful, but beautiful,—while his knowledge, so called, is oftentimes worse than useless, besides being ugly. Which is the best man to deal with,—he who knows nothing about a subject, and, what is extremely rare, knows that he knows nothing, or he who really knows something about it, but thinks that he knows all?

My desire for knowledge is intermittent; but my desire to bathe my head in atmospheres unknown to my feet is perennial and constant. The highest that we can attain to is not Knowledge, but Sympathy with Intelligence. I do not know that this higher knowledge amounts to anything more definite than a novel and grand surprise on a sudden revelation of the insufficiency of all that we called Knowledge before,—a discovery that there are more things in heaven and earth than are dreamed of in our philosophy. It is the lighting up of the mist by the sun. Man cannot *know* in any higher sense than this, any more than he can look serenely and with impunity in the face of sun: Ὡς τὶ νοῶν, οὐ κεῖνον νοήσεις,—" You will not perceive that, as perceiving a particular thing," say the Chaldean Oracles.

There is something servile in the habit of seeking after a law which we may obey. We may study the laws of matter at and for our convenience, but a successful life knows no law. It is an unfortunate discovery certainly, that of a law which binds us where we did not know before that we were bound. Live free, child of the mist,—and with respect to knowledge we are all children of the mist. The man who takes the liberty to live is superior to all the laws, by virtue of his relation to the law-maker. " That is active duty," says the Vishnu Purana, " which is not for our bondage; that is knowledge which is for our liberation: all other duty is good only unto weariness; all other knowledge is only the cleverness of an artist."

It is remarkable how few events or crises there are in our histories; how little exercised we have been in our minds; how few experiences we have had. I would fain be assured that I am growing apace and rankly, though my very growth disturb this dull equanimity,—though it be with struggle through long, dark, muggy nights or seasons of gloom. It would be well, if all our lives were a divine tragedy even, instead of this trivial comedy or farce. Dante, Bunyan, and others, appear to have been exercised in their minds more than we: they were subjected to a kind of culture such as our district schools and colleges do not contemplate. Even Mahomet, though many may scream at his name, had a good deal more to live for, ay, and to die for, than they have commonly.

When, at rare intervals, some thought visits one, as perchance he is walking on a railroad, then indeed the cars go by without his hearing them. But soon, by some inexorable law, our life goes by and the cars return.

> "Gentle breeze, that wanderest unseen,
> And bendest the thistles round Loira of storms,
> Traveler of the windy glens,
> Why hast thou left my ear so soon?"

While almost all men feel an attraction drawing them to society, few are attracted strongly to Nature. In their relation to Nature men appear to me for the most part, notwithstanding their arts, lower than the animals. It is not often a beautiful relation, as in the case of the animals. How little appreciation of the beauty of the landscape there is among us! We have to be told that the Greeks called the world Κόσμος, Beauty, or Order, but we do not see clearly why they did so, and we esteem it at best only a curious philological fact.

For my part, I feel that with regard to Nature I live a sort of border life, on the confines of a world into which I make occasional and transional and transient forays only, and my patriotism and allegiance to the State into whose territories I seem to retreat are those of a moss-trooper. Unto a life which I call natural I would gladly follow even a will-o'-the-wisp through bogs and sloughs unimaginable, but no moon nor firefly has shown me the causeway to it. Nature is a personality so vast and universal that we have never seen one of her features. The walker in the familiar fields which stretch around my native town sometimes finds himself in another land than is described in their owners' deeds, as it were in some far-away field on the confines of the actual Concord, where her jurisdiction ceases, and the idea which the word Concord suggests ceases to be suggested. These farms which I have myself surveyed, these bounds which I have set up, appear dimly still as through a mist; but they have no chemistry to fix them; they fade from the surface of the glass; and the picture which the painter painted stands out dimly from beneath. The world with which we are commonly acquainted leaves no trace, and it will have no anniversary.

I took a walk on Spaulding's Farm the other afternoon. I saw the setting sun lighting up the opposite side of a stately pine wood. Its golden rays straggled into the aisles of the wood as into some noble hall. I was impressed as if some ancient and altogether admirable and shining family had settled there in that part of the land called Concord, unknown to me,—to whom the sun was servant,—who had not gone into society in the village,—who had not been called on. I saw their park, their pleasure-ground, beyond through the wood, in Spaulding's cranberry-meadow. The pines furnished them with gables as they grew. Their house was not obvious to vision; the trees grew through it. I do not know whether I heard the sounds of a suppressed hilarity or not. They seemed to recline on the sunbeams. They have sons and daughters. They are quite well. The farmer's cart-path, which leads directly through their hall, does not in the least put them out,—as the muddy bottom of a pool is sometimes seen through the reflected skies. They never heard of Spaulding, and do not know that he is their neighbor,—notwithstanding I heard him whistle as he drove his team through the house. Nothing can equal the serenity of their lives. Their coat of arms is simply a lichen. I saw it painted on the pines and oaks. Their attics were in the tops of the trees. They are of no politics. There was no noise of labor. I did not perceive that they were weaving or spinning. Yet I did detect, when the wind lulled and hearing was done away, the finest imaginable sweet musical hum,—as of a distant hive in May, which perchance was the sound of their thinking.

They had no idle thoughts, and no one without could see their work, for their industry was not as in knots and excrescences embayed.

But I find it difficult to remember them. They fade irrevocably out of my mind even now while I speak and endeavor to recall them, and recollect myself. It is only after a long and serious effort to recollect my best thoughts that I become again aware of their cohabitancy. If it were not for such families as this, I think I should move out of Concord.

We are accustomed to say in New England that few and fewer pigeons visit us every year. Our forests furnish no mast for them. So, it would seem, few and fewer thoughts visit each growing man from year to year, for the grove in our minds is laid waste,—sold to feed unnecessary fires of ambition, or sent to mill, and there is scarcely a twig left for them to perch on. They no longer build nor breed with us. In some more genial season, perchance, a faint shadow flits across the landscape of the mind, cast by the *wings* of some thought in its vernal or autumnal migration, but, looking up, we are unable to detect the substance of the thought itself. Our winged thoughts are turned to poultry. They no longer soar, and they attain only to a Shanghai and Cochin-China grandeur. Those *gra-a-ate thoughts,* those *gra-a-ate men* you hear of!

We hug the earth,—how rarely we mount! Methinks we might elevate ourselves a little more. We might climb a tree, at least. I found my account in climbing a tree once. It was a tall white pine, on the top of a hill; and though I got well pitched, I was well paid for it, for I discovered new mountains in the horizon which I had never seen before, —so much more of the earth and the heavens. I might have walked about the foot of the tree for threescore years and ten, and yet I certainly should never have seen them. But, above all, I discovered around me,—it was near the end of June,—on the ends of the topmost branches only, a few minute and delicate red cone-like blossoms, the fertile flower of the white pine looking heavenward. I carried straightway to the village the topmost spire, and showed it to stranger jurymen who walked the streets,—for it was court-week,—and to farmers and lumber-dealers and woodchoppers and hunters, and not one had ever seen the like before, but they wondered as at a star dropped down. Tell of ancient architects finishing their works on the tops of columns as perfectly as on the lower and more visible parts! Nature has from the first expanded the minute blossoms of the forest only toward the heavens, above men's heads and unobserved by them. We see only the flowers that are under our feet in the meadows. The pines have developed their delicate blossoms on the highest twigs of the wood every summer for ages, as well over the heads of Nature's red children as of her white ones; yet scarcely a farmer or hunter in the land has ever seen them.

Above all, we cannot afford not to live in the present. He is blessed over all mortals who loses no moment of the passing life in remembering the past. Unless our philosophy hears the cock crow in every barn-yard within our horizon, it is belated. That sound commonly reminds us that we are growing rusty and antique in our employments and habits of thought. His philosophy comes down to a more recent time than ours. There is something suggested by it that is a newer testament,—the gospel according to this moment. He has not fallen astern; he has got up early, and kept up early, and to be where he is to be in season, in the foremost rank of time. It is an expression of the health and soundness of Nature, a brag for all the world,—

healthiness as of a spring burst forth, a new fountain of the Muses, to celebrate this last instant of time. Where he lives no fugitive slave laws are passed. Who has not betrayed his master many times since last he heard that note?

The merit of this bird's strain is in its freedom from all plaintiveness. The singer can easily move us to tears or to laughter, but where is he who can excite in us a pure morning joy? When, in doleful dumps, breaking the awful stillness of our wooden sidewalk on a Sunday, or, perchance, a watcher in the house of mourning, I hear a cockerel crow far or near, I think to myself, " There is one of us well, at any rate,"—and with a sudden gush return to my senses.

We had a remarkable sunset one day last November. I was walking in a meadow, the source of a small brook, when the sun at last, just before setting, after a cold gray day, reached a clear stratum in the horizon, and the softest, brightest morning sunlight fell on the dry grass and on the stems of the trees in the opposite horizon, and on the leaves of the shrub-oaks on the hill-side, while our shadows stretched long over the meadow eastward, as if we were the only motes in its beams. It was such a light as we could not have imagined a moment before, and the air also was so warm and serene that nothing was wanting to make a paradise of that meadow. When we reflected that this was not a solitary phenomenon, never to happen again, but that it would happen forever and ever an infinite number of evenings, and cheer and reassure the latest child that walked there, it was more glorious still.

The sun sets on some retired meadow, where no house is visible, with all the glory and splendor that it lavishes on cities, and perchance, as it has never set before,—where there is but a solitary marsh-hawk to have his wings gilded by it, or only a musquash looks out from his cabin, and there is some little black-veined brook in the midst of the marsh, just beginning to meander, winding slowly round a decaying stump. We walked in so pure and bright a light, gilding the withered grass and leaves, so softly and serenely bright, I thought I had never bathed in such a golden flood, without a ripple or a murmur to it. The west side of every wood and rising ground gleamed like the boundary of Elysium, and the sun on our backs seemed like a gentle herdsman driving us home at evening.

So we saunter toward the Holy Land, till one day the sun shall shine more brightly than ever he has done, shall perchance shine into our minds and hearts, and light up our whole lives with a great awakening light, as warm and serene and golden as on a bank-side in autumn.

ON A CERTAIN CONDESCENSION IN FOREIGNERS *

James Russell Lowell

Walking one day toward the Village, as we used to call it in the good old days when almost every dweller in the town had been born in it, I was enjoying that delicious sense of disenthralment from the actual which the deepening twilight brings with it, giving as it does a sort of obscure novelty to things familiar. The coolness, the hush, broken only by the distant bleat of some belated goat, querulous to be disburdened of her milky load, the few faint stars, more guessed as yet than seen, the sense that the coming dark would so soon fold me in the secure privacy of its disguise, —all things combined in a result as near absolute peace as can be hoped for by a man who knows that there is a writ out against him in the hands of the printer's devil. For the moment, I was enjoying the blessed privilege of thinking without being called on to stand and deliver what I thought to the small public who are good enough to take any interest therein. I love old ways, and the path I was walking felt kindly to the feet it had known for almost fifty years. How many fleeting impressions it had shared with me! How many times I had lingered to study the shadows of the leaves mezzotinted upon the turf that edged it by the moon, of the bare boughs etched with a touch beyond Rembrandt by the same unconscious artist on the smooth page of snow! If I turned round, through dusky tree-gaps

* From the *Atlantic Monthly*, January, 1869.

came the first twinkle of evening lamps in the dear old homestead. On Corey's hill I could see these tiny pharoses of love and home and sweet domestic thoughts flash out one by one across the blackening salt-meadow between. How much has not kerosene added to the cheerfulness of our evening landscape! A pair of night-herons flapped heavily over me toward the hidden river. The war was ended. I might walk townward without that aching dread of bulletins that had darkened the July sunshine and twice made the scarlet leaves of October seem stained with blood. I remembered with a pang, half-proud, half-painful, how, so many years ago, I had walked over the same path and felt round my finger the soft pressure of a little hand that was one day to harden with faithful grip of saber. On how many paths, leading to how many homes where proud Memory does all she can to fill up the fireside gaps with shining shapes, must not men be walking in just such pensive mood as I? Ah, young heroes, safe in immortal youth as those of Homer, you at least carried your ideal hence untarnished! It is locked for you beyond moth or rust in the treasure-chamber of Death.

Is not a country, I thought, that has had such as they in it, that could give such as they a brave joy in dying for it, worth something, then? And as I felt more and more the soothing magic of evening's cool palm upon my temples, as my fancy came home from its revery, and my senses, with reawakened curiosity, ran to the front windows again from the viewless closet of abstraction, and felt a strange charm in finding the old tree and shabby fence still there under the travesty of falling night, nay, were conscious of an unsuspected newness in familiar stars and the fading outlines of hills my earliest horizon, I was conscious of an immortal soul, and could not but rejoice in the unwaning goodliness of the world into which I had been born without any merit of my own. I thought of dear Henry Vaughan's rainbow, "Still young and fine!" I remembered people who had to go over to the Alps to learn what the divine silence of snow was, who must run to Italy before they were conscious of the miracle wrought every day under their very noses by the sunset, who must call upon the Berkshire hills to teach them what a painter autumn was, while close at hand the Fresh Pond meadows made all oriels cheap with hues that showed as if a sunset-cloud had been wrecked among their maples. One might be worse off than even in America, I thought. There are some things so elastic that even the heavy roller of democracy cannot flatten them altogether down. The mind can weave itself warmly in the cocoon of its own thoughts and dwell a hermit anywhere. A country without traditions, without ennobling associations, a scramble of *parvenus,* with a horrible consciousness of shoddy running through politics, manners, art, literature, nay, religion itself? I confess, it did not seem so to me there in that illimitable quiet, that serene self-possession of nature, where Collins might have brooded his " Ode to Evening," or where those verses on Solitude in Dodsley's Collection, that Hawthorne liked so much, might have been composed. Traditions? Granting that we had none, all that is worth having in them is the common property of the soul,—an estate in gavelkind for all the sons of Adam,—and, moreover, if a man cannot stand on his two feet (the prime quality of whoever has left any tradition behind him), were it not better for him to be honest about it at once, and go down on all fours? And for associations, if one have not the wit to make them for himself out of native earth, no ready-made ones of other men will avail much. Lexington is none the worse to me for not being in Greece, nor Gettysburg that its name is not Marathon. "Blessed old fields," I was just exclaiming to myself, like one of Mrs. Radcliffe's heroes, " dear acres, innocently secure from history, which these eyes first beheld, may you be also those to which they shall at last slowly darken!" when I was interrupted by a voice which asked me in German whether I was the Herr Professor, Doctor, So-and-so? The " Doctor " was by brevet or vaticination, to make the grade easier to my pocket.

One feels so intimately assured that he is made up, in part, of shreds and leavings of the past, in part of the interpolations of other people, that an honest man would be slow in saying *yes* to such a question. But " my name is So-and-so " is a safe answer, and I gave it. While I had been romancing with myself, the street-lamps had been lighted, and it was under one of these detectives that have robbed the Old Road of its privilege of sanctuary after nightfall that I was ambushed by my foe. The inexorable villain had taken my description, it appears, that I might have the less chance to escape him. Dr. Holmes tells us that we change our substance, not every seven years, as was once believed, but with every breath we draw. Why had I not the wit to avail myself of the subterfuge, and, like Peter, to renounce my identity, especially, as in certain moods of mind, I have often more than doubted of it myself? When a man is, as it were, his own front-door, and is thus knocked at, why may he not assume the right of that sacred wood to make every house a castle, by denying himself to all visitations? I was truly not at home when the question was put to me, but had to recall myself from all out-of-doors, and to piece my self-consciousness hastily together as well as I could before I answered it.

I knew perfectly well what was coming. It is seldom that debtors or good Samaritans waylay people under gas-lamps in order to force money upon them, so far as I have seen or heard. I was also aware, from considerable experience, that every foreigner is persuaded that, by doing this country the favor of coming to it, he has laid every native thereof under an obligation, pecuniary or other, as the case may be, whose discharge he is entitled to on demand duly made in person or by letter. Too much learning (of this kind) had made me mad in the provincial sense of the word. I had begun life with the theory of giving something to every beggar that came along, though sure of never finding a native-born countryman among them. In a small way, I was resolved to emulate Hatem Tai's tent, with its three hundred and sixty-five entrances, one for every day in the year,—I know not whether he was astronomer enough to add another for leap-years. The beggars were a kind of German-silver aristocracy; not real plate, to be sure, but better than nothing. Where everybody was overworked, they supplied the comfortable equipoise of absolute leisure, so æsthetically needful. Besides, I was but too conscious of a vagrant fiber in myself, which too often thrilled me in my solitary walks with the temptation to wander on into infinite space, and by a single spasm of resolution to emancipate myself from the drudgery of prosaic serfdom to respectability and the regular course of things. This prompting has been at times my familiar demon, and I could not but feel a kind of respectful sympathy for men who had dared what I had only sketched out to myself as a splendid possibility. For seven years I helped maintain one heroic man on an imaginary journey to Portland,— as fine an example as I have ever known of hopeless loyalty to an ideal. I assisted another so long in a fruitless attempt to reach Mecklenburg-Schwerin, that at last we grinned in each other's faces when we met, like a couple of augurs. He was possessed by this harmless mania as some are by the North Pole, and I shall never forget his look of regretful compassion (as for one who was sacrificing his higher life to the fleshpots of Egypt) when I at last advised him somewhat strenuously to go to the D——, whither the road was so much traveled that he could not miss it. General Banks, in his noble zeal for the honor of his country, would confer on the Secretary of State the power of imprisoning, in case of war, all these seekers of the unattainable, thus by a stroke of the pen annihilating the single poetic element in our humdrum life. Alas! not everybody has the genius to be a Bobbin-Boy, or doubtless all these also would have chosen that more prosperous line of life! But moralists, sociologists, political economists, and taxes have slowly convinced me that my beggarly sympathies were a sin against society. Especially was the Buckle doctrine of averages (so flattering to our free-will) persuasive with me; for as there must be in every year a certain number who would bestow an alms on these abridged editions of the Wandering Jew, the withdrawal of my quota could make no possible difference, since some destined proxy must always step forward to fill my gap. Just so many misdirected letters every year and no more! Would it were as easy to reckon up the number of men on whose backs fate has written the wrong address, so that they arrive by mistake in Congress and other places where they do not belong! May not these wanderers of whom I speak have been sent into the world without any proper address at all? Where is our Dead-Letter Office for such? And if wiser social arrangements should furnish us with something of the sort, fancy (horrible thought!) how many a workingman's friend (a kind of industry in which the labor is light and the wages heavy) would be sent thither because not called for in the office where he at present lies!

But I am leaving my new acquaintance too long under the lamp-post. The same Gano .which had betrayed me to him revealed to me a well-set young man of about half my own age, as well dressed, so far as I could see, as I was, and with every natural qualification for getting his own livelihood as good, if not better, than my own. He had been reduced to the painful necessity of calling upon me by a series of crosses beginning with the Baden Revolution (for which, I own, he seemed rather young,—but perhaps he referred to a kind of revolution practiced every season at Baden-Baden), continued by repeated failures in business, for amounts which must convince me of his entire respectability, and ending with our Civil War. During the latter, he had served with distinction as a soldier, taking a main part in every important battle, with a rapid list of which he favored me, and no doubt would have admitted that, impartial as Jonathan Wild's great ancestor, he had been on both sides, had I baited him with a few hints of conservative opinions on a subject so distressing to a gentleman wishing to profit by one's sympathy and unhappily doubtful as to which way it might lean. For all these reasons, and, as he seemed to imply, for his merit in consenting to be born in Germany, he considered himself my natural creditor to the extent of five dollars, which he would handsomely consent to accept in greenbacks, though he preferred specie. The offer was certainly a generous one, and the claim presented with an assurance that carried conviction. But, unhappily, I had been led to remark a curious natural phenomenon. If I was ever weak enough to give anything to a petitioner of whatever nationality, it always rained decayed compatriots of his for a month after. *Post hoc ergo propter hoc* may not always be safe logic, but here I seemed to perceive a natural connection of cause and effect. Now, a few days before I had been so tickled with a paper (professedly written by a benevolent American clergyman) certifying that the bearer, a hard-working German, had long " sofered with rheumatic paints in his limps," that, after copying the passage into my note-book, I thought it but fair to pay a trifling *honorarium* to the author. I had pulled the string of the shower-bath! It had been running shipwrecked sailors for some time, but forthwith it began to pour Teutons, redolent of *lager-bier*. I could not help associating the apparition of my new friend with this series of otherwise unaccountable phenomena. I accordingly made up my mind to deny the debt, and modestly did so, pleading a native bias towards impecuniosity to the full as strong as his own. He took a high tone with me at once, such as an honest man would naturally take with a confessed repudiator. He even brought down his proud stomach so far as to join himself to me for the rest of my townward walk, that he might give me his views of the American people, and thus inclusively of myself.

I know not whether it is because I am pigeon-livered and lack gall, or whether it is from an overmastering sense of drollery, but I am apt to submit to such bastings with a patience which afterwards surprises me, being not without my share of warmth in the blood. Perhaps it is because I so often meet with young persons who know vastly more than I do, and especially with so many foreigners whose knowledge of this country is superior to my own. However it may be, I listened for some time with tolerable composure as my self-appointed lecturer gave me in detail his opinions of my country and its people. America, he informed me, was without arts, science, literature, culture, or any native hope of supplying them. We were a people wholly given to money-getting, and who, having got it, knew no other use for it than to hold it fast. I am fain to confess that I felt a sensible itching of the biceps, and that my fingers closed with such a grip as he had just informed me was one of the effects of our unhappy climate. But happening just then to be where I could avoid temptation by dodging down a by-street, I hastily left him to finish his diatribe to the lamp-post, which could stand it better than I. That young man will never know how near he came to being assaulted by a respectable gentleman of middle age, at the corner of Church Street. I have never felt quite satisfied that I did all my duty by him in not knocking him down. But perhaps he might have knocked *me* down, and then?

The capacity of indignation makes an essential part of the outfit of every honest man, but I am inclined to doubt whether he is a wise one who allows himself to act upon its first hints. It should be rather, I suspect, a *latent* heat in the blood, which makes itself felt in character, a steady reserve for the brain, warming the ovum of thought to life, rather than cooking it by a too hasty enthusiasm in reaching the boiling-point. As my pulse gradually fell back to its normal beat, I reflected that I had been uncomfortably near making a fool of myself,—a handy salve of euphuism for our vanity, though it does not always make a just allowance to Nature for her share in the business. What possible claim had my Teutonic friend to rob me of my composure? I am not, I think, specially thin-skinned as to other people's opinions of myself, having, as I conceive, later and fuller intelligence on that point than anybody else can give me. Life is continually weighing us in very sensitive scales, and telling every one of us precisely what his real weight is to the last grain of dust. Whoever at fifty does not rate himself quite as low as most of his acquaintance would be likely to put him, must be either a fool or a great man, and I humbly disclaim being either. But if I was not smarting in person from any scattering shot of my late companion's commination, why should I grow hot at any implication of my country therein? Surely *her* shoulders are broad enough, if yours or mine are not, to bear up under a considerable avalanche of this kind. It is the bit of truth in every slander, the hint of likeness in every caricature, that makes us smart. "Art thou *there*, old Truepenny?" How did your blade know its way so well to that one loose rivet in our armor? I wondered whether Americans were oversensitive in this respect, whether they were more touchy than other folks. On the whole, I thought we were not. Plutarch, who at least had studied philosophy, if he had not mastered it, could not stomach something Herodotus had said of Bœotia, and devoted an essay to showing up the delightful old traveler's malice and ill-breeding. French editors leave out of Montaigne's "Travels" some remarks of his about France, for reasons best known to themselves. Pachydermatous Deutschland, covered with trophies from every field of letters, still winces under that question which Père Bouhours put two centuries ago, *Si un Allemand peut être bel-esprit?* John Bull grew apoplectic with angry amazement at the audacious persiflage of Pückler-Muskau. To be sure, he was a prince,—but that was not all of it, for a chance phrase of gentle Hawthorne sent a spasm through all the journals of England. Then this tenderness is not peculiar to *us?* Console yourself, dear man and brother, whatever else you may be sure of, be sure at least of this, that you are dreadfully like other people. Human nature has a much greater genius for sameness than for originality, or the world would be at a sad pass shortly. The surprising thing is that men have such a taste for this somewhat musty flavor, that an Englishman, for example, should feel himself defrauded, nay, even outraged, when he comes over here and finds a people speaking what he admits to be something like English, and yet so very different from (or, as he would say, to) those he left at home. Nothing, I am sure, equals *my* thankfulness when I meet an Englishman who is *not* like every other, or, I may add, an American of the same odd turn.

Certainly it is no shame to a man that he should be as nice about his country as about his sweetheart, and who ever heard even the friendliest appreciation of that unexpressive she that did not seem to fall infinitely short? Yet it would hardly be wise to hold everyone an enemy who could not see her with our own enchanted eyes. It seems to be the common opinion of foreigners that Americans are *too* tender upon this point. Perhaps we are; and if so, there must be a reason for it. Have we had fair play? Could the eyes of what is called Good Society (though it is so seldom true either to the adjective or noun) look upon a nation of democrats with any chance of receiving an undistorted image? Were not those, moreover, who found in the old order of things an earthly paradise, paying them quarterly dividends for the wisdom of their ancestors, with the punctuality of the seasons, unconsciously bribed to misunderstand if not to misrepresent us? Whether at war or at peace, there we were, a standing menace to all earthly paradises of that kind, fatal underminers of the very credit on which the dividends were based, all the more hateful and terrible that our destructive agency was so insidious, working invisible in the elements, as it seemed, active while they slept, and coming upon them in the darkness like an armed man. *Could* Laius have the proper feelings of a father towards Œdipus, announced as his destined destroyer by infallible oracles, and felt to be such by every conscious fiber of his soul? For more than a century the Dutch were the laughing-stock of polite Europe. They were butter-firkins, swillers of beer and schnaps, and their *vrouws* from whom Holbein painted the all-but loveliest of Madonnas, Rembrandt the graceful girl who sits immortal on his knee in Dresden, and Rubens his abounding goddesses, were the synonymes of clumsy vulgarity. Even so late as Irving the ships of the greatest navigators in the world were represented as sailing equally well stern-foremost. That the aristocratic Venetians should have

> " Riveted with gigantic piles
> Thorough the center their new-catchëd miles,"

was heroic. But the far more marvelous achievement of the Dutch in the same kind was ludicrous even to republican Marvell. Meanwhile, during that very century of scorn, they were the best artists, sailors, merchants, bankers, printers, scholars, jurisconsults, and statesmen in Europe, and the genius of Motley has revealed them to us, earning a right to themselves by the most heroic struggle in human annals. But, alas! they were not merely simple burghers who had fairly made themselves High Mightinesses, and could treat on equal terms with anointed kings, but their commonwealth carried in its bosom the germs of democracy. They even unmuzzled, at least after dark, that dreadful mastiff, the Press, whose scent is, or ought to be, so keen for wolves in sheep's clothing and for certain other animals in lions' skins. They made fun of Sacred Majesty, and, what was worse, managed uncommonly well without it. In an age when periwigs made so large a part of the natural dignity of man, people with such a turn of mind were dangerous. How could they seem other than vulgar and hateful?

In the natural course of things we succeeded to this unenviable position of general butt. The Dutch had thriven under it pretty well, and there was hope that we could at least contrive to worry along. And we certainly did in a very redoubtable fashion. Perhaps we deserved some of the sarcasm more than our Dutch predecessors in office. We had nothing to boast of in arts or letters, and were given to bragging overmuch of our merely material prosperity, due quite as much to the virtue of our continent as to our own. There was some truth in Carlyle's sneer, after all. Till we had succeeded in some higher way than this, we had only the success of physical growth. Our greatness, like that of enormous Russia, was greatness on the map,—barbarian mass only; but had we gone down, like that other Atlantis, in some vast cataclysm, we should have covered but a pin's point on the chart of memory, compared with those ideal spaces occupied by tiny Attica and cramped England. At the same time, our critics somewhat too easily forgot that material must make ready the foundation for ideal triumphs, that the arts have no chance in poor countries. And it must be allowed that democracy stood for a great deal in our shortcoming. The *Edinburgh Review* never would have thought of asking, "Who reads a Russian book?" and England was satisfied with iron from Sweden without being impertinently inquisitive after her painters and statuaries. Was it that they expected too much from the mere miracle of Freedom? Is it not the highest art of a Republic to make men of flesh and blood, and not the marble ideals of such? It may be fairly doubted whether we have produced this higher type of man yet. Perhaps it is the collective, not the individual, humanity that is to have a chance of nobler development among us. We shall see. We have a vast amount of imported ignorance, and, still worse, of native ready-made knowledge, to digest before even the preliminaries of such a consummation can be arranged. We have got to learn that statesmanship is the most complicated of all arts, and to come back to the apprenticeship-system too hastily abandoned. At present, we trust a man with making constitutions on less proof of competence than we should demand before we gave him our shoe to patch. We have nearly reached the limit of the reaction from the old notion, which paid too much regard to birth and station as qualifications for office, and have touched the extreme point in the opposite direction, putting the highest of human functions up at auction to be bid for by any creature capable of going upright on two legs. In some places, we have arrived at a point at which civil society is no longer possible, and already another reaction has begun, not backwards to the old system, but towards fitness either from natural aptitude or special training. But will it always be safe to let evils work their own cure by becoming unendurable? Every one of them leaves its taint in the constitution of the body-politic, each in itself, perhaps, trifling, but all together powerful for evil.

But whatever we might do or leave undone, we were not genteel, and it was uncomfortable to be continually reminded that, though we should boast that we were the Great West till we were black in the face, it did not bring us an inch nearer to the world's West-End. That sacred inclosure of respectability was tabooed to us. The Holy Alliance did not inscribe us on its visiting-list. The Old World of wigs and orders and liveries would shop with us, but we must ring at the area-bell, and not venture to awaken the more august clamors of the knocker. Our manners, it must be granted, had none of those graces that stamp the caste of Vere de Vere, in whatever museum of British antiquities they may be hidden. In short, we were vulgar.

This was one of those horribly vague accusations, the victim of which has no defense. An umbrella is of no avail against a Scotch mist. It envelops you, it penetrates at every pore, it wets you through without seeming to wet you at all. Vulgarity is an eighth deadly sin, added to the list in these latter days, and worse than all the others put together, since it perils your salvation in *this* world,—far the more important of the two in the minds of most men.

It profits nothing to draw nice distinctions between essential and conventional, for the convention in this case *is* the essence, and you may break every command of the decalogue with perfect good-breeding, nay, if you are adroit, without losing caste. We, indeed, had it not to lose, for we had never gained it. "*How* am I vulgar?" asks the culprit, shudderingly. "Because thou art not like unto Us," answers Lucifer, Son of the Morning, and there is no more to be said. The god of this world may be a fallen angel, but he has us *there!* We were as clean,—so far as my observation goes, I think we were cleaner, morally and physically, than the English, and therefore, of course, than everybody else. But we did not pronounce the diphthong *ou* as they did, and we said *eether* and not *eyther*, following therein the fashion of our ancestors, who unhappily could bring over no English better than Shakespeare's; and we did not stammer as they had learned to do from the courtiers, who in this way flattered the Hanoverian king, a foreigner among the people he had come to reign over. Worse than all, we might have the noblest ideas and the finest sentiments in the world, but we vented them through that organ by which men are led rather than leaders, though some physiologists would persuade us that Nature furnishes her captains with a fine handle to their faces that Opportunity may get a good purchase on them for dragging them to the front.

This state of things was so painful that excellent people were not wanting who gave their whole genius to reproducing here the original Bull, whether by gaiters, the cut of their whiskers, by a factitious brutality in their tone, or by an accent that was forever tripping and falling flat over the tangled roots of our common tongue. Martyrs to a false ideal, it never occurred to them that nothing is more hateful to gods and men than a second-rate Englishman,

On a Certain Condescension in Foreigners 181

and for the very reason that this planet never produced a more splendid creature than the first-rate one, witness Shakespeare and the Indian Mutiny. If we could contrive to be not too unobtrusively our simple selves, we should be the most delightful of human beings, and the most original; whereas, when the plating of Anglicism rubs off, as it always will in points that come to much wear, we are liable to very unpleasing conjectures about the quality of the metal underneath. Perhaps one reason why the average Briton spreads himself here with such an easy air of superiority may be owing to the fact that he meets with so many bad imitations as to conclude himself the only real thing in a wilderness of shams. He fancies himself moving through an endless Bloomsbury, where his mere apparition confers honor as an avatar of the court-end of the universe. Not a Bull of them all but is persuaded he bears Europa upon his back. This is the sort of fellow whose patronage is so divertingly insufferable. Thank Heaven he is not the only specimen of cater-cousinship from the dear old Mother Island that is shown to us! Among genuine things, I know nothing more genuine than the better men whose limbs were made in England. So manly-tender, so brave, so true, so warranted to wear, they make us proud to feel that blood is thicker than water.

But it is not merely the Englishman; every European candidly admits in himself some right of primogeniture in respect of us, and pats this shaggy continent on the back with a lively sense of generous unbending. The German who plays the bass-viol has a well-founded contempt, which he is not always nice in concealing, for a country so few of whose children ever take that noble instrument between their knees. His cousin, the Ph.D. from Göttingen, cannot help despising a people who do not grow loud and red over Aryans and Turanians, and are indifferent about their descent from either. The Frenchman feels an easy mastery in speaking his mother tongue, and attributes it to some native superiority of parts that lifts him high above us barbarians of the West. The Italian *prima donna* sweeps a curtsy of careless pity to the over-facile pit which unsexes her with the *bravo!* innocently meant to show a familiarity with foreign usage. But all without exception make no secret of regarding us as the goose bound to deliver them a golden egg in return for *their* cackle. Such men as Agassiz, Guyot, and Goldwin Smith come with gifts in their hands; but since it is commonly European failures who bring hither their remarkable gifts and acquirements, this view of the case is sometimes just the least bit in the world provoking. To think what a delicious seclusion of contempt we enjoyed till California and our own ostentatious *parvenus,* flinging gold away in Europe that might have endowed libraries at home, gave us the ill repute of riches! What a shabby downfall from the Arcadia which the French officers of our Revolutionary War fancied they saw here through Rousseau-tinted spectacles! Something of Arcadia there really was, something of the Old Age; and that divine provincialism were cheaply repurchased could we have it back again in exchange for the tawdry upholstery that has taken its place.

For some reason or other, the European has rarely been able to see America except in caricature. Would the first Review of the world have printed the *niaiseries* of Mr. Maurice Sand as a picture of society in any civilized country? Mr. Sand, to be sure, has inherited nothing of his famous mother's literary outfit, except the pseudonyme. But since the conductors of the *Revue* could not have published his story because it was clever, they must have thought it valuable for its truth. As true as the last-century Englishman's picture of Jean Crapaud! We do not ask to be sprinkled with rosewater, but may perhaps fairly protest against being drenched with the rinsings of an unclean imagination. The next time the *Revue* allows such ill-bred persons to throw their slops out of its first-floor windows, let it honestly preface the discharge with a *gardez-l'eau!* that we may run from under in season. And Mr. Duvergier d'Hauranne, who knows how to be entertaining! I know *le Français est plutôt indiscret que confiant,* and the pen slides too easily when indiscretions will fetch so much a page; but should we not have been *tant-soit-peu* more cautious had we been writing about people on the other side of the Channel? But then it is a fact in the natural history of the American long familiar to Europeans, that he abhors privacy, knows not the meaning of reserve, lives in hotels because of their greater publicity, and is never so pleased as when his domestic affairs (if he may be said to have any) are paraded in the newspapers. Barnum, it is well known, represents perfectly the average national sentiment in this respect. However it be, we are not treated like other people, or perhaps I should say like people who are ever likely to be met with in society.

Is it in the climate? Either I have a false notion of European manners, or else the atmosphere affects them strangely when exported hither. Perhaps they suffer from the sea-voyage like some of the more delicate wines. During our Civil War an English gentleman of the highest description was kind enough to call upon me, mainly, as it seemed, to inform me how entirely he sympathized with the Confederates, and how sure he felt that we could never subdue them,—"they were the *gentlemen* of the country, you know." Another, the first greetings hardly over, asked me how I accounted for the universal meagerness of my countrymen. To a thinner man than I, or from a stouter man than he, the question *might* have been offensive. The

Marquis of Hartington[1] wore a secession badge at a public ball in New York. In a civilized country he might have been roughly handled; but here, where the *bienséances* are not so well understood, of course nobody minded it. A French traveler told me he had been a good deal in the British colonies, and had been astonished to see how soon the people became Americanized. He added, with delightful *bonhomie,* and as if he were sure it would charm me, that "they even began to talk through their noses, just like you!" I was naturally ravished with this testimony to the assimilating power of democracy, and could only reply that I hoped they would never adopt our democratic patent-method of seeming to settle one's honest debts, for they would find it paying through the nose in the long-run. I am a man of the New World, and do not know precisely the present fashion of May-Fair, but I have a kind of feeling that if an American (*mutato nomine, de te* is always frightfully possible) were to do this kind of thing under a European roof, it would induce some disagreeable reflections as to the ethical results of democracy. I read the other day in print the remark of a British tourist who had eaten large quantities of our salt, such as it is (I grant it has not the European savor), that the Americans were hospitable, no doubt, but that it was partly because they longed for foreign visitors to relieve the tedium of their dead-level existence, and partly from ostentation. What shall we do? Shall we close our doors? Not I, for one,

---

[1] One of Mr. Lincoln's neatest strokes of humor was his treatment of this gentleman when a laudable curiosity induced him to be presented to the President of the Broken Bubble. Mr. Lincoln persisted in calling him Mr. Partington. Surely the refinement of good-breeding could go no further. Giving the young man his real name (already notorious in the newspapers) would have made his visit an insult. Had Henri IV. done this, it would have been famous.

if I should so have forfeited the friendship of L. S., most lovable of men. He somehow seems to find us human, at least, and so did Clough, whose poetry will one of these days, perhaps, be found to have been the best utterance in verse of this generation.

The fine old Tory aversion of former times was not hard to bear. There was something even refreshing in it, as in a northeaster to a hardy temperament. When a British parson, traveling in Newfoundland while the slash of our separation was still raw, after prophesying a glorious future for an island that continued to dry its fish under the ægis of Saint George, glances disdainfully over his spectacles in parting at the U. S. A., and forebodes for them a " speedy relapse into barbarism," now that they have madly cut themselves off from the humanizing influences of Britain, I smile with barbarian self-conceit. But this kind of thing became by degrees an unpleasant anachronism. For meanwhile the young giant was growing, was beginning indeed to feel tight in his clothes, was obliged to let in a gore here and there in Texas, in California, in New Mexico, in Alaska, and had the scissors and needle and thread ready for Canada when the time came. His shadow loomed like a Brocken-specter over against Europe,—the shadow of what they were coming to, that was the unpleasant part of it. Even in such misty image as they had of him, it was painfully evident that his clothes were not of any cut hitherto fashionable, nor conceivable by a Bond Street tailor,—and this in an age, too, when everything depends upon clothes, when, if we do not keep up appearances, the seeming-solid frame of this universe, nay, your very God, would slump into himself, like a mockery king of snow, being nothing, after all, but a prevailing mode. From this moment the young giant assumed the respectable aspect of a phenomenon, to be got rid of if possible, but at any rate as legitimate a subject of human study as the glacial period or the silurian what-d'ye-call-ems. If the man of the primeval drift-heaps be so absorbingly interesting, why not the man of the drift that is just beginning, of the drift into whose irresistible current we are just being sucked whether we will or no? If I were in their place, I confess I should not be frightened. Man has survived so much, and contrived to be comfortable on this planet after surviving so much! I am something of a protestant in matters of government also, and am willing to get rid of vestments and ceremonies and to come down to bare benches, if only faith in God take the place of a general agreement to profess confidence in ritual and sham. Every mortal man of us holds stock in the only public debt that is absolutely sure of payment, and that is the debt of the Maker of this Universe to the Universe he has made. I have no notion of selling out my shares in a panic.

It was something to have advanced even to the dignity of a phenomenon, and yet I do not know that the relation of the individual American to the individual European was bettered by it; and that, after all, must adjust itself comfortably before there can be a right understanding between the two. We had been a desert, we became a museum. People came hither for scientific and not social ends. The very cockney could not complete his education without taking a vacant stare at us in passing. But the sociologists (I think they call themselves so) were the hardest to bear. There was no escape. I have even known a professor of this fearful science to come disguised in petticoats. We were cross-examined as a chemist cross-examines a new substance. Human? yes, all the elements are present, though abnormally combined. Civilized? Hm! that needs a stricter assay. No entomologist could take a more friendly interest in a strange bug. After a few such experiences,

I, for one, have felt as if I were merely one of those horrid things preserved in spirits (and very bad spirits, too) in a cabinet. I was not the fellow-being of these explorers: I was a curiosity; I was a *specimen*. Hath not an American organs, dimensions, senses, affections, passions even as a European hath? If you prick us, do we not bleed? If you tickle us, do we not laugh? I will not keep on with Shylock to his next question but one.

Till after our Civil War it never seemed to enter the head of any foreigner, especially of any Englishman, that an American had what could be called a country, except as a place to eat, sleep, and trade in. Then it seemed to strike them suddenly. "By Jove, you know, fellahs don't fight like that for a shop-till!" No, I rather think not. To Americans America is something more than a promise and an expectation. It has a past and traditions of its own. A descent from men who sacrificed everything and came hither, not to better their fortunes, but to plant their idea in virgin soil, should be a good pedigree. There was never colony save this that went forth, not to seek gold, but God. Is it not as well to have sprung from such as these as from some burly beggar who came over with Wilhelmus Conquestor, unless, indeed, a line grow better as it runs farther away from stalwart ancestors? And for our history, it is dry enough, no doubt, in the books, but, for all that, is of a kind that tells in the blood. I have admitted that Carlyle's sneer had a show of truth in it. But what does he himself, like a true Scot, admire in the Hohenzollerns? First of all, that they were *canny*, a thrifty, forehanded race. Next, that they made a good fight from generation to generation with the chaos around them. That is precisely the battle which the English race on this continent has been carrying doughtily on for two centuries and a half. Doughtily and silently, for you cannot hear in Europe "that crash, the death-song of the perfect tree," that has been going on here from sturdy father to sturdy son, and making this continent habitable for the weaker Old World breed that has swarmed to it during the last half-century. If ever men did a good stroke of work on this planet, it was the forefathers of those whom you are wondering whether it would not be prudent to acknowledge as far-off cousins. Alas, man of genius, to whom we owe so much, could you see nothing more than the burning of a foul chimney in that clash of Michael and Satan which flamed up under your very eyes?

Before our war we were to Europe but a huge mob of adventurers and shopkeepers. Leigh Hunt expressed it well enough when he said that he could never think of America without seeing a gigantic counter stretched all along the seaboard. Feudalism had by degrees made commerce, the great civilizer, contemptible. But a tradesman with sword on thigh and very prompt of stroke was not only redoubtable, he had become respectable also. Few people, I suspect, alluded twice to a needle in Sir John Hawkwood's presence, after that doughty fighter had exchanged it for a more dangerous tool of the same metal. Democracy had been hitherto only a ludicrous effort to reverse the laws of nature by thrusting Cleon into the place of Pericles. But a democracy that could fight for an abstraction, whose members held life and goods cheap compared with that larger life which we call country, was not merely unheard of, but portentous. It was the nightmare of the Old World taking upon itself flesh and blood, turning out to be substance and not dream. Since the Norman crusader clanged down upon the throne of the *porphyrogeniti,* carefully-draped appearances had never received such a shock, had never been so rudely called on to produce their titles to the empire of the world. Authority has had its periods not unlike those of geology, and at last comes Man claiming kingship in right of his mere manhood. The world of the Saurians might be in some respects more picturesque, but the march of events is inexorable, and it is bygone.

The young giant had certainly got out of long-clothes. He had become the *enfant terrible* of the human household. It was not and will not be easy for the world (especially for our British cousins) to look upon us as grown up. The youngest of nations, its people must also be young and to be treated accordingly, was the syllogism. Youth has its good qualities, as people feel who are losing it, but boyishness is another thing. We had been somewhat boyish as a nation, a little loud, a little pushing, a little braggart. But might it not partly have been because we felt that we had certain claims to respect that were not admitted? The war which established our position as a vigorous nationality has also sobered us. A nation, like a man, cannot look death in the eye for four years without some strange reflections, without arriving at some clearer consciousness of the stuff it is made of, without some great moral change. Such a change, or the beginning of it, no observant person can fail to see here. Our thought and our politics, our bearing as a people, are assuming a manlier tone. We have been compelled to see what was weak in democracy as well as what was strong. We have begun obscurely to recognize that things do not go of themselves, and that popular government is not in itself a panacea, is no better than any other form except as the virtue and wisdom of the people make it so, and that when men undertake to do their own kingship, they enter upon the dangers and responsibilities as well as the privileges of the function. Above all, it looks as if we were on the way to be persuaded that no government can be carried on by declamation. It is noticeable also that facility of communication has made the best English and French thought far more directly operative here than ever before. Without being Europeanized, our discussion of important questions in statesmanship, in political economy, in æsthetics, is taking a broader scope and a higher tone. It had certainly been provincial, one might almost say local, to a very unpleasant extent. Perhaps our experience in soldiership has taught us to value training more than we have been popularly wont. We may possibly come to the conclusion, one of these days, that self-made men may not be always equally skillful in the manufacture of wisdom, may not be divinely commissioned to fabricate the higher qualities of opinion on all possible topics of human interest.

So long as we continue to be the most common-schooled and the least cultivated people in the world, I suppose we must consent to endure this condescending manner of foreigners toward us. The more friendly they mean to be the more ludicrously prominent it becomes. They can never appreciate the immense amount of silent work that has been done here, making this continent slowly fit for the abode of man, and which will demonstrate itself, let us hope, in the character of the people. Outsiders can only be expected to judge a nation by the amount it has contributed to the civilization of the world; the amount, that is, that can be seen and handled. A great place in history can only be achieved by competitive examinations, nay, by a long course of them. How much new thought have we contributed to the common stock? Till that question can be triumphantly answered, or needs no answer, we must continue to be simply interesting as an experiment, to be studied as a problem, and not respected as an attained result or an accomplished solution. Perhaps, as I have hinted, their patronizing manner toward us is the fair result of their failing to see here anything more than a poor imitation, a plaster-cast of Europe. And are they not partly right? If the tone of the uncultivated American has too often the arrogance of the barbarian, is not that of the cultivated as often vulgarly apologetic? In the American they meet with is there the simplicity, the manliness, the absence of sham, the sincere human nature, the sensitiveness to duty and implied obligation, that in any way distinguishes us from what our orators call "the effete civilization of the Old World"? Is there a politician among us daring enough (except a Dana here and there) to risk his future on the chance of our keeping our word with the exactness of superstitious communities like England? Is it certain that we shall be ashamed of a bankruptcy of honor, if we can only keep the letter of our bond? I hope we shall be able to answer all these questions with a frank *yes*. At any rate, we would advise our visitors that we are not merely curious creatures, but belong to the family of man, and that, as individuals, we are not to be always subjected to the competitive examination above mentioned, even if we acknowledged their competence as an examining board. Above all, we beg them to remember that America is not to us, as to them, a mere object of external interest to be discussed and analyzed, but *in* us, part of our very marrow. Let them not suppose that we conceive of ourselves as exiles from the graces and amenities of an older date than we, though very much at home in a state of things not yet all it might be or should be, but which we mean to make so, and which we find both wholesome and pleasant for men (though perhaps not for *dilettanti*) to live in. "The full tide of human existence" may be felt here as keenly as Johnson felt it at Charing Cross, and in a larger sense. I know one person who is singular enough to think Cambridge the very best spot on the habitable globe. "Doubtless God *could* have made a better, but doubtless he never did."

It will take England a great while to get over her airs of patronage toward us, or even passably to conceal them. She cannot help confounding the people with the country, and regarding us as lusty juveniles. She has a conviction that whatever good there is in us is wholly English, when the truth is that we are worth nothing except so far as we have disinfected ourselves of Anglicism. She is especially condescending just now, and lavishes sugar-plums on us as if we had not outgrown them. I am no believer in sudden conversions, especially in sudden conversions to a favorable opinion of people who have just proved you to be mistaken in judgment and therefore unwise in policy. I never blamed her for not wishing well to democracy,—how should she?—but Alabamas are not wishes. Let her not be too hasty in believing Mr. Reverdy Johnson's pleasant words. Though there is no thoughtful man in America who would not consider a war with England the greatest of calamities, yet the feeling towards her here is very far from cordial, whatever our Minister may say in the effusion that comes after ample dining. Mr. Adams, with his famous " My Lord, this means war," perfectly represented his country. Justly or not, we have a feeling that we have been wronged, not merely insulted. The only sure way of bringing about a healthy relation between the two countries is for Englishmen to clear their minds of the notion that we are always to be treated as a kind of inferior and deported Englishman whose nature they perfectly understand, and whose back they accordingly stroke the wrong way of the fur with amazing perseverance. Let them learn to treat us naturally on our merits as human beings, as they would a German or a Frenchman, and not as if we were a kind of counterfeit Briton whose crime appeared in every shade of difference, and before long there would come that right feeling which we naturally call a good understanding. The common blood, and still more the common language, are fatal instruments of misapprehension. Let them give up *trying* to understand us, still more thinking that they do, and acting in various absurd ways as the necessary consequence, for they will never arrive at that devoutly-to-be-wished consummation, till they learn to look at us as we are and not as they suppose us to be. Dear old long-estranged mother-in-law, it is a great many years since we parted. Since 1660, when you married again, you have been a stepmother to us. Put on your spectacles, dear madam. Yes, we *have* grown, and changed likewise. You would not let us darken your doors, if you could help it. We know that perfectly well. But pray, when we look to be treated as men, don't shake that rattle in our faces, nor talk baby to us any longer.

> "Do, child, go to it grandam, child;
> Give grandam kingdom, and it grandam will
> Give it a plum, a cherry, and a fig!"

PREFACE TO "LEAVES OF GRASS"

1855

Walt Whitman

AMERICA does not repel the past, or what the past has produced under its forms, or amid other politics, or the idea of castes, or the old religions—accepts the lesson with calmness—is not impatient because the slough still sticks to opinions and manners in literature, while the life which served its requirements has passed into the new life of the new forms—perceives that the corpse is slowly borne from the eating and sleeping rooms of the house—perceives that it waits a little while in the door—that it was fittest for its days—that its action has descended to the stalwart and well-shaped heir who approaches—and that he shall be fittest for his days.

The Americans of all nations at any time upon the earth, have probably the fullest poetical nature. The United States themselves are essentially the greatest poem. In the history of the earth hitherto, the largest and most stirring appear tame and orderly to their ampler largeness and stir. Here at last is something in the doings of man that corresponds with the broadcast doings of the day and night. Here is action untied from strings, necessarily blind to particulars and details, magnificently moving in masses. Here is the hospitality which for ever indicates heroes. Here the performance, disdaining the trivial, unapproach'd in the tremendous audacity of its crowds and groupings, and the push of its perspective, spreads with crampless and flowing breadth, and showers its prolific and splendid extravagance. One sees it must indeed own the riches of the summer and winter, and need never be bankrupt while corn grows from the ground, or the orchards drop apples, or the bays contain fish, or men beget children upon women.

Other states indicate themselves in their deputies—but the genius of the United States is not best or most in its executives or legislatures, nor in its ambassadors or authors, or colleges or churches or parlors, nor even in its newspapers or inventors—but always most in the common people, south, north, west, east, in all its States, through all its mighty amplitude. The largeness of the nation, however, were monstrous without a corresponding largeness and generosity of the spirit of the citizen. Not swarming states, nor streets and steamships, nor prosperous business, nor farms, nor capital, nor learning, may suffice for the ideal of man—nor suffice the poet. No reminiscences may suffice either. A live nation can always cut a deep mark, and can have the best authority the cheapest—namely, from its own soul. This is the sum of the profitable uses of individuals or states, and of present action and grandeur, and of the subjects of poets. (As if it were necessary to trot back generation after generation to the eastern records! As if the beauty and sacredness of the demonstrable must fall behind that of the mythical! As if men do not make their mark out of any times! As if the opening of the western continent by discovery, and what has transpired in North and South America, were less than the small theater of the antique, or the aimless sleep-walking of the middle ages!) The pride of the United States leaves the wealth and finesse of the cities, and all returns of commerce and agriculture, and all the magnitude of geography or shows of exterior victory, to enjoy the sight and realization of full-sized men, or one full-sized man unconquerable and simple.

The American poets are to inclose old and new, for America is the race of races. The expression of the American poet is to be transcendent and new. It is to be indirect, and not direct or descriptive or epic. Its quality goes through these to much more. Let the age and wars of other nations be chanted, and their eras and characters be illustrated, and that finish the verse. Not so the great psalm of the republic. Here the theme is creative, and has vista. Whatever stagnates in the flat of custom or obedience or legislation, the great poet never stagnates. Obedience does not master him, he masters it. High up out of reach he stands, turning a concentrated light—he turns the pivot with his finger—he baffles the swiftest runners as he stands, and easily overtakes and envelopes them. The time straying toward infidelity and confections and persiflage he withholds by steady faith. Faith is the antiseptic of the soul—it pervades the common people and preserves them—they never give up believing and expecting and trusting. There is that indescribable freshness and unconsciousness about an illiterate person, that humbles and mocks the power of the noblest expressive genius. The poet sees for a certainty how one not a great artist may be just as sacred and perfect as the greatest artist.

The power to destroy or remould is freely used by the greatest poet, but seldom the power of attack. What is past is past. If he does not expose superior models, and prove himself by every step he takes, he is not what is wanted. The presence of the great poet conquers—not parleying, or struggling, or any prepared attempts. Now he has passed that way, see after him! There is not left any vestige of despair, or misanthropy, or cunning, or exclusiveness, or the ignominy of a nativity or color, or delusion of hell or the necessity of hell—and no man thenceforward shall be degraded for ignorance or weakness or sin. The greatest poet hardly knows pettiness or triviality. If he breathes into anything that was before thought small, it dilates with the grandeur and life of the universe. He is a seer—he is individual—he is complete in himself—the others are as good as he, only he sees it, and they do not. He is not one of the chorus—he does not stop for any regulation—he is the president of regulation. What the eyesight does to the rest, he does to the rest. Who knows the curious mystery of the eyesight? The other senses corroborate themselves, but this is removed from any proof but its own, and foreruns the identities of the spiritual world. A single glance of it mocks all the investigations of man, and all the instruments and books of the earth, and all reasoning. What is marvelous? what is unlikely? what is impossible or baseless or vague—after you have once just open'd the space of a peach-pit, and given audience to far and near, and to the sunset, and had all things enter with electric swiftness, softly and duly, without confusion or jostling or jam?

The land and sea, the animals, fishes and birds, the sky of heaven and the orbs, the forests, mountains and rivers, are not small themes—but folks expect of the poet to indicate more than the beauty and dignity which always attach to dumb real objects—they expect him to indicate the path between reality and their souls. Men and women perceive the beauty well enough—probably as well as he. The passionate tenacity of hunters, woodmen, early risers, cultivators of gardens and orchards and fields, the love of healthy women for the manly form, seafaring persons, drivers of horses, the passion for light and the open air, all is an old varied sign of the unfailing perception of beauty, and of a residence of the poetic in out-door people. They can never be assisted by poets to perceive—some may, but they never can. The poetic quality is not marshal'd in rhyme or uniformity, or abstract addresses to things, nor in melancholy complaints or good precepts, but is the life of these and much else, and is in the soul. The profit of rhyme is that it drops seeds of a sweeter and more luxuriant rhyme, and of uniformity that it conveys itself into its own roots in the ground out of sight. The rhyme and uniformity of perfect poems show the free growth of metrical laws, and bud from them as unerringly and loosely as lilacs and roses on a bush, and take shapes as compact as the shapes of chestnuts and oranges, and melons and pears, and shed the perfume impalpable to form. The fluency and ornaments of the finest poems or music or orations or recitations, are not independent but dependent. All beauty comes from beautiful blood and a beautiful brain. If the greatnesses are in conjunction in a man or woman, it is enough—the fact will prevail through the universe; but the gaggery and gilt of a million years will not prevail. Who troubles himself about his ornaments or fluency is lost. This is what you shall do: Love the earth and sun and the animals, despise riches, give alms to everyone that asks, stand up for the stupid and crazy, devote your income and labor to others, hate tyrants, argue not concerning God, have patience and indulgence toward the people, take off your hat to nothing known or unknown, or to any man or number of men—go freely with powerful uneducated persons, and with the young, and with the mothers of families—re-examine all you have been told in school or church or in any book, and dismiss whatever insults your own soul; and your very flesh shall be a great poem, and have the richest fluency, not only in its words, but in the silent lines of its lips and face, and between the lashes of your eyes, and in every motion and joint of your body. The poet shall not spend his time in unneeded work. He shall know that the ground is already plow'd and manured; others may not know it, but he shall. He shall go directly to the creation. His trust shall master the trust of everything he touches—and shall master all attachment.

The known universe has one complete lover, and that is the greatest poet. He consumes an eternal passion, and is indifferent which chance happens, and which possible contingency of fortune or misfortune, and persuades daily and hourly his delicious pay. What balks or breaks others is fuel for his burning progress to contact and amorous joy. Other proportions of the reception of pleasure dwindle to nothing to his proportions. All expected from heaven or from the highest, he is rapport with in the sight of the daybreak, or the scenes of the winter woods, or the presence of children playing, or with his arm round the neck of a man or woman. His love above all love has leisure and expanse—he leaves room ahead of himself. He is no irresolute or suspicious lover—he is sure—he scorns intervals. His experience and the showers and thrills are not for nothing. Nothing can jar him—suffering and darkness cannot—death and fear cannot. To him complaint and jealousy and envy are corpses buried and rotten in the earth—he saw them buried. The sea is not surer of the shore, or the shore of the sea, than he is of the fruition of his love, and of all perfection and beauty.

The fruition of beauty is no chance of miss or hit—it is as inevitable as life—it is exact and plumb as gravitation. From the eyesight proceeds another eyesight, and from the hearing proceeds another hearing, and from the voice proceeds another voice, eternally curious of the harmony of things with man. These understand the law of perfection in masses and floods—that it is profuse and impartial—that there is not a minute of the light or dark, nor an acre of the earth and sea, without it—nor any direction of the sky, nor any trade or employment, nor any turn of events. This is the reason that about the proper expression of beauty there is precision and balance. One part does not need to be thrust above another. The best singer is not the one who has the most lithe and powerful organ. The pleasure of poems is not in them that take the handsomest measure and sound.

Without effort, and without exposing in the least how it is done, the greatest poet brings the spirit of any or all events and passions and scenes and persons, some more and some less, to bear on your individual character as you hear or read. To do this well is to compete with the laws that pursue and follow Time. What is the purpose must surely be there, and the clew of it must be there—and the faintest indication is the indication of the best, and then becomes the clearest indication. Past and present and future are not disjoin'd but join'd. The greatest poet forms the consistence of what is to be, from what has been and is. He drags the dead out of their coffins and stands them again on their feet. He says to the past, Rise and walk before me that I may realize you. He learns the lesson—he places himself where the future becomes present. The greatest poet does not only dazzle his rays over character and scenes and passions—he finally ascends, and finishes all—he exhibits the pinnacles that no man can tell what they are for, or what is beyond—he glows a moment on the extremest verge. He is most wonderful in his last half-hidden smile or frown; by that flash of the moment of parting the one that sees it shall be encouraged or terrified afterward for many years. The greatest poet does not moralize or make applications of morals—he knows the soul. The soul has that measureless pride which consists in never acknowledging any lessons or deductions but its own. But it has sympathy as measureless as its pride, and the one balances the other, and neither can stretch too far while it stretches in company with the other. The inmost secrets of art sleep with the twain. The greatest poet has lain close betwixt both, and they are vital in his style and thoughts.

The art of art, the glory of expression and the sunshine of the light of letters, is simplicity. Nothing is better than simplicity—nothing can make up for excess, or for the lack of definiteness. To carry on the heave of impulse and pierce intellectual depths and give all subjects their articulations, are powers neither common nor very uncommon. But to speak in literature with the perfect rectitude and insouciance of the movements of animals, and the unimpeachableness of the sentiment of trees in the woods and grass by the roadside, is the flawless triumph of art. If you have look'd on him who has achiev'd it you have look'd on one of the masters of the artists of all nations and times. You shall not contemplate the flight of the gray gull over the bay, or the mettlesome action of the blood horse, or the tall leaning of sunflowers on their stalk, or the appearance of the sun journeying through heaven, or the appearance of the moon afterward, with any more satisfaction than you shall contemplate him. The great poet has less a mark'd style, and is more the channel of thoughts and things without increase or diminution, and is the free channel of himself. He swears to his art, I will not be meddlesome, I will not have in my writing any elegance, or effect, or originality, to hang in the way between me and the rest like curtains. I will have nothing hang in the way, not the richest curtains. What I tell I tell for precisely what it is. Let who may exalt or startle or fascinate or soothe, I will have purposes as health or heat or snow has, and be as regardless of observation. What I experience or portray shall go from my composition without a shred of my composition. You shall stand by my side and look in the mirror with me.

The old red blood and stainless gentility of great poets

will be proved by their unconstraint. A heroic person walks at his ease through and out of that custom or precedent or authority that suits him not. Of the traits of the brotherhood of first-class writers, savans, musicians, inventors and artists, nothing is finer than silent defiance advancing from new free forms. In the need of poems, philosophy, politics, mechanism, science, behavior, the craft of art, an appropriate native grand opera, shipcraft, or any craft, he is greatest for ever and ever who contributes the greatest original practical example. The cleanest expression is that which finds no sphere worthy of itself, and makes one.

The messages of great poems to each man and woman are, Come to us on equal terms, only then can you understand us. We are no better than you, what we inclose you inclose, what we enjoy you may enjoy. Did you suppose there could be only one Supreme? We affirm there can be unnumber'd Supremes, and that one does not countervail another any more than one eyesight countervails another—and that men can be good or grand only of the consciousness of their supremacy within them. What do you think is the grandeur of storms and dismemberments, and the deadliest battles and wrecks, and the wildest fury of the elements, and the power of the sea, and the motion of Nature, and the throes of human desires, and dignity and hate and love? It is that something in the soul which says, Rage on, whirl on, I tread master here and everywhere—Master of the spasms of the sky and of the shatter of the sea, Master of nature and passion and death, and of all terror and all pain.

The American bards shall be mark'd for generosity and affection, and for encouraging competitors. They shall be Kosmos, without monopoly or secrecy, glad to pass anything to anyone—hungry for equals night and day. They shall not be careful of riches and privilege—they shall be riches and privilege—they shall perceive who the most affluent man is. The most affluent man is he that confronts all the shows he sees by equivalents out of the stronger wealth of himself. The American bard shall delineate no class of persons, nor one or two out of the strata of interests, nor love most nor truth most, nor the soul most, nor the body most—and not be for the Eastern States more than the Western, or the Northern States more than the Southern.

Exact science and its practical movements are no checks on the greatest poet, but always his encouragement and support. The outset and remembrance are there—there the arms that lifted him first, and braced him best—there he returns after all his goings and comings. The sailor and traveler—the anatomist, chemist, astronomer, geologist, phrenologist, spiritualist, mathematician, historian, and lexicographer, are not poets, but they are the lawgivers of poets, and their construction underlies the structure of every perfect poem. No matter what rises or is utter'd, they sent the seed of the conception of it—of them and by them stand the visible proofs of souls. If there shall be love and content between the father and the son, and if the greatness of the son is the exuding of the greatness of the father, there shall be love between the poet and the man of demonstrable science. In the beauty of poems are henceforth the tuft and final applause of science.

Great is the faith of the flush of knowledge, and of the investigation of the depths of qualities and things. Cleaving and circling here swells the soul of the poet, yet is president of itself always. The depths are fathomless, and therefore calm. The innocence and nakedness are resumed—they are neither modest nor immodest. The whole theory of the supernatural, and all that was twined with it or educed out of it, departs as a dream. What has ever happen'd—what happens, and whatever may or shall happen, the vital laws inclose all. They are sufficient for any case and for all cases—none to be hurried or retarded—any special miracle of affairs or persons inadmissible in the vast clear scheme where every motion and every spear of grass, and the frames and spirits of men and women and all that concerns them, are unspeakably perfect miracles, all referring to all, and each distinct and in its place. It is also not consistent with the reality of the soul to admit that there is anything in the known universe more divine than men and women.

Men and women, and the earth and all upon it, are to be taken as they are, and the investigation of their past and present and future shall be unintermitted, and shall be done with perfect candor. Upon this basis philosophy speculates, ever looking towards the poet, ever regarding the eternal tendencies of all toward happiness, never inconsistent with what is clear to the senses and to the soul. For the eternal tendencies of all toward happiness make the only point of sane philosophy. Whatever comprehends less than that—whatever is less than the laws of light and of astronomical motion—or less than the laws that follow the thief, the liar, the glutton and the drunkard, through this life and doubtless afterward—or less than vast stretches of time, or the slow formation of density, or the patient upheaving of strata—is of no account. Whatever would put God in a poem or system of philosophy as contending against some being or influence, is also of no account. Sanity and ensemble characterize the great master—spoilt in one principle, all is spoilt. The great master has nothing to do with miracles. He sees health for himself in being one of the mass—he sees the hiatus in singular eminence. To the perfect shape comes common ground. To be under the general law is great, for that is to correspond with it. The master knows that he is unspeakably great, and that all are unspeakably great—that nothing, for instance, is greater than to conceive children, and bring them up well—that to *be* is just as great as to perceive or tell.

In the make of the great masters the idea of political liberty is indispensable. Liberty takes the adherence of heroes wherever man and woman exist—but never takes any adherence or welcome from the rest more than from poets. They are the voice and exposition of liberty. They out of ages are worthy the grand idea—to them it is confided, and they must sustain it. Nothing has precedence of it, and nothing can warp or degrade it.

As the attributes of the poets of the kosmos concenter in the real body, and in the pleasure of things, they possess the superiority of genuineness over all fiction and romance. As they emit themselves, facts are shower'd over with light —the daylight is lit with more volatile light—the deep between the setting and rising sun goes deeper many fold. Each precise object or condition or combination or process exhibits a beauty—the multiplication table its—old age its— the carpenter's trade its—the grand opera its—the huge-hull'd clean-shap'd New York clipper at sea under steam or full sail gleams with unmatch'd beauty—the American circles and large harmonies of government gleam with theirs —and the commonest definite intentions and actions with theirs. The poets of the kosmos advance through all interpositions and coverings and turmoils and stratagems to first principles. They are of use—they dissolve poverty from its need, and riches from its conceit. You large proprietor, they say, shall not realize or perceive more than anyone else. The owner of the library is not he who holds a legal title to it, having bought and paid for it. Anyone and everyone is owner of the library, (indeed he or she alone is owner,) who can read the same through all the varieties of tongues and subjects and styles, and in whom they enter with ease, and make supple and powerful and rich and large.

These American States, strong and healthy and accomplish'd, shall receive no pleasure from violations of natural models, and must not permit them. In paintings or mouldings or carvings in mineral or wood, or in the illustrations of books or newspapers, or in the patterns of woven stuffs, or anything to beautify rooms or furniture or costumes, or to put upon cornices or monuments, or on the prows or sterns of ships, or to put anywhere before the human eye indoors or out, that which distorts honest shapes, or which creates unearthly beings or places or contingencies, is a nuisance and revolt. Of the human form especially, it is so great it must never be made ridiculous. Of ornaments to a work nothing outre can be allow'd—but those ornaments can be allow'd that conform to the perfect facts of the open air, and that flow out of the nature of the work, and come irrepressibly from it, and are necessary to the completion of the work. Most works are most beautiful without ornament. Exaggerations will be revenged in human physiology. Clean and vigorous children are jetted and conceiv'd only in those communities where the models of natural forms are public every day. Great genius and the people of these States must never be demean'd to romances. As soon as histories are properly told, no more need of romances.

The great poets are to be known by the absence in them of tricks, and by the justification of perfect personal candor. All faults may be forgiven of him who has perfect candor. Henceforth let no man of us lie, for we have seen that openness wins the inner and outer world, and that there is no single exception, and that never since our earth gather'd itself in a mass have deceit or subterfuge or prevarication attracted its smallest particle or the faintest tinge of a shade—and that through the enveloping wealth and rank of a state, or the whole republic of states, a sneak or sly person shall be discover'd and despised—and that the soul has never once been fool'd and never can be fool'd—and thrift without the loving nod of the soul is only a fœtid puff—and there never grew up in any of the continents of the globe, nor upon any planet or satellite, nor in that condition which precedes the birth of babes, nor at any time during the changes of life, nor in any stretch of abeyance or action of vitality, nor in any process of formation or reformation anywhere, a being whose instinct hated the truth.

Extreme caution or prudence, the soundest organic health, large hope and comparison and fondness for women and children, large alimentiveness and destructiveness and causality, with a perfect sense of the oneness of nature, and the propriety of the same spirit applied to human affairs, are called up of the float of the brain of the world to be parts of the greatest poet from his birth out of his mother's womb, and from her birth out of her mother's. Caution seldom goes far enough. It has been thought that the prudent citizen was the citizen who applied himself to solid gains, and did well for himself and for his family, and completed a lawful life without debt or crime. The greatest poet sees and admits these economies as he sees the economies of food and sleep, but has higher notions of prudence than to think he gives much when he gives a few slight attentions at the latch of the gate. The premises of the prudence of life are not the hospitality of it, or the ripeness and harvest of it. Beyond the independence of a little sum laid aside for burial-money, and of a few clap-boards around and shingles overhead on a lot of American soil own'd, and the easy dollars that supply the year's plain clothing and meals, the melancholy prudence of the abandonment of such a great being as a man is, to the toss and pallor of years of money-making, with all their scorching days and icy nights, and all their stifling deceits and underhand dodgings, or infinitesimals of parlors, or shameless stuffing while others starve, and all the loss of the bloom and odor of the earth, and of the flowers and atmosphere, and of the sea, and of the true taste of the women and men you pass or have to do with in youth or middle age, and the issuing sickness and desperate revolt at the close of a life without elevation or naïveté, (even if you have achiev'd a secure 10,000 a year, or election to Congress or the Governorship,) and the ghastly chatter of a death without serenity or majesty, is the great fraud upon modern civilization and forethought, blotching the surface and system which civilization undeniably drafts, and moistening with tears the immense features it spreads and spreads with such velocity before the reach'd kisses of the soul.

Ever the right explanation remains to be made about prudence. The prudence of the mere wealth and respectability of the most esteem'd life appears too faint for the eye to observe at all, when little and large alike drop quietly aside at the thought of the prudence suitable for immortality. What is the wisdom that fills the thinness of a year, or seventy or eighty years—to the wisdom spaced out by ages, and coming back at a certain time with strong reinforcements and rich presents, and the clear faces of wedding-guests as far as you can look, in every direction, running gayly toward you? Only the soul is of itself—all else has reference to what ensues. All that a person does or thinks is of consequence. Nor can the push of charity or personal force ever be anything else than the profoundest reason, whether it brings argument to hand or no. No specification is necessary—to add or subtract or divide is in vain. Little or big, learn'd or unlearn'd, white or black, legal or illegal, sick or well, from the first inspiration down the windpipe to the last expiration out of it, all that a male or female does that is vigorous and benevolent and clean is so much sure profit to him or her in the unshakable order of the universe, and through the whole scope of it forever. The prudence of the greatest poet answers at last the craving and glut of the soul, puts off nothing, permits no let-up for its own case or any case, has no particular sabbath or judgment day, divides not the living from the dead, or the righteous from the unrighteous, is satisfied with the present, matches every thought or act by its correlative, and knows no possible forgiveness or deputed atonement.

The direct trial of him who would be the greatest poet is to-day. If he does not flood himself with the immediate age as with vast oceanic tides—if he be not himself the age transfigur'd, and if to him is not open'd the eternity which gives similitude to all periods and locations and processes, and animate and inanimate forms, and which is the bond of time, and rises up from its inconceivable vagueness and infiniteness in the swimming shapes of to-day, and is held by the ductile anchors of life, and makes the present spot the passage from what was to what shall be, and commits itself to the representation of this wave of an hour, and this one of the sixty beautiful children of the wave—let him merge in the general run, and wait his development.

Still the final test of poems, or any character or work, remains. The prescient poet projects himself centuries ahead, and judges performer or performance after the changes of time. Does it live through them? Does it still hold on untired? Will the same style, and the direction of genius to similar points, be satisfactory now? Have the marches of tens and hundreds and thousands of years made willing detours to the right hand and the left hand for his sake? Is he beloved long and long after he is buried? Does the young man think often of him? and the young woman think often of him? and do the middle-aged and the old think of him?

A great poem is for ages and ages in common, and for all degrees and complexions, and all departments and sects, and for a woman as much as a man, and a man as much as a woman. A great poem is no finish to a man or woman, but rather a beginning. Has anyone fancied he could sit at last under some due authority, and rest satisfied with explanations, and realize, and be content and full? To no such terminus does the greatest poet bring—he brings neither cessation nor shelter'd fatness and ease. The touch of him, like Nature, tells in action. Whom he takes he takes with firm sure grasp into live regions previously unattain'd—thenceforward is no rest—they see the space and ineffable sheen that turn the old spots and lights into dead vacuums. Now there shall be a man cohered out of tumult and chaos —the elder encourages the younger and shows him how— they two shall launch off fearlessly together till the new world fits an orbit for itself, and looks unabash'd on the lesser orbits of the stars, and sweeps through the ceaseless rings, and shall never be quiet again.

There will soon be no more priests. Their work is done. A new order shall arise, and they shall be the priests of man, and every man shall be his own priest. They shall find their inspiration in real objects to-day, symptoms of the past and future. They shall not deign to defend immortality or God, or the perfection of things, or liberty, or the exquisite beauty and reality of the soul. They shall arise in America, and be responded to from the remainder of the earth.

The English language befriends the grand American expression—it is brawny enough, and limber and full enough. On the tough stock of a race who through all change of circumstance was never without the idea of political liberty, which is the animus of all liberty, it has attracted the terms of daintier and gayer and subtler and more elegant tongues. It is the powerful language of resistance—it is the dialect of common sense. It is the speech of the proud and melancholy races, and of all who aspire. It is the chosen tongue to express growth, faith, self-esteem, freedom, justice, equality, friendliness, amplitude, prudence, decision, and courage. It is the medium that shall wellnigh express the inexpressible.

No great literature nor any like style of behavior or oratory, or social intercourse or household arrangements, or public institutions, or the treatment by bosses of employ'd people, nor executive detail, or detail of the army and navy, nor spirit of legislation or courts, or police or tuition or architecture, or songs or amusements, can long elude the jealous and passionate instinct of American standards. Whether or no the sign appears from the mouths of the people, it throbs a live interrogation in every freeman's and freewoman's heart, after that which passes by, or this built to remain. Is it uniform with my country? Are its disposals without ignominious distinctions? Is it for the ever-growing communes of brothers and lovers, large, well united, proud, beyond the old models, generous beyond all models? Is it something grown fresh out of the fields, or drawn from the sea for use to me to-day here? I know that what answers for me, an American, in Texas, Ohio, Canada, must answer for any individual or nation that serves for a part of my materials. Does this answer? Is it for the nursing of the young of the republic? Does it solve readily with the sweet milk of the nipples of the breasts of the Mother of Many Children?

America prepares with composure and good-will for the visitors that have sent word. It is not intellect that is to be their warrant and welcome. The talented, the artist, the ingenious, the editor, the statesman, the erudite, are not unappreciated—they fall in their place and do their work. The soul of the nation also does its work. It rejects none, it permits all. Only toward the like of itself will it advance half-way. An individual is as superb as a nation when he has the qualities which make a superb nation. The soul of the largest and wealthiest and proudest nation may well go half-way to meet that of its poets.

AMERICANISM IN LITERATURE

Thomas Wentworth Higginson

The voyager from Europe who lands upon our shores perceives a difference in the sky above his head; the height seems loftier, the zenith more remote, the horizon-wall more steep; the moon appears to hang in the middle air, beneath a dome that arches far beyond it. The sense of natural symbolism is so strong in us, that the mind seeks a spiritual significance in this glory of the atmosphere. It is not enough to find the sky enlarged, and not the mind,—*cœlum, non animum*. One wishes to be convinced that here the intellectual man inhales a deeper breath, and walks with bolder tread; that philosopher and artist are here more buoyant, more fresh, more fertile; that the human race has here escaped at one bound from the despondency of ages, as from their wrongs.

And the true and healthy Americanism is to be found, let us believe, in this attitude of hope; an attitude not necessarily connected with culture nor with the absence of culture, but with the consciousness of a new impulse given to all human progress. The most ignorant man may feel the full strength and heartiness of the American idea, and so may the most accomplished scholar. It is a matter of regret if thus far we have mainly had to look for our Americanism and our scholarship in very different quarters, and if it has been a rare delight to find the two in one.

It seems unspeakably important that all persons among us, and especially the student and the writer, should be pervaded with Americanism. Americanism includes the faith that national self-government is not a chimera, but that, with whatever inconsistencies and drawbacks, we are steadily establishing it here. It includes the faith that to this good thing all other good things must in time be added. When a man is heartily imbued with such a national sentiment as this, it is as marrow in his bones and blood in his veins. He may still need culture, but he has the basis of all culture. He is entitled to an imperturbable patience and hopefulness, born of a living faith. All that is scanty in our intellectual attainments, or poor in our artistic life, may then be cheerfully endured: if a man sees his house steadily rising on sure foundations, he can wait or let his children wait for the cornice and the frieze. But if one happens to be born or bred in America without this wholesome confidence, there is no happiness for him; he has his alternative between being unhappy at home and unhappy abroad; it is a choice of martyrdoms for himself, and a certainty of martyrdom for his friends.

Happily, there are few among our cultivated men in whom this oxygen of American life is wholly wanting. Where such exist, for them the path across the ocean is easy, and the return how hard! Yet our national character develops slowly; we are aiming at something better than our English fathers, and we pay for it by greater vacillations and vibrations of movement. The Englishman's strong point is a vigorous insularity which he carries with him, portable and sometimes insupportable. The American's more perilous gift is a certain power of assimilation, so that he acquires something from every man he meets, but runs the risk of parting with something in return. For the result, greater possibilities of culture, balanced by greater extremes of sycophancy and meanness. Emerson says that the Englishman of all men stands most firmly on his feet. But it is not the whole of man's mission to be found standing, even at the most important post. Let him take one step forward,—and in that advancing figure you have the American.

We are accustomed to say that the war and its results have made us a nation, subordinated local distinctions, cleared us of our chief shame, and given us the pride of a common career. This being the case, we may afford to treat ourselves to a little modest self-confidence. Those whose faith in the American people carried them hopefully through the long contest with slavery will not be daunted before any minor perplexities of Chinese immigrants or railway brigands or enfranchised women. We are equal to these things; and we shall also be equal to the creation of a literature. We need intellectual culture inexpressibly, but we need a hearty faith still more. "Never yet was there a great migration that did not result in a new form of national genius." But we must guard against both croakers and boasters; and above all, we must look beyond our little Boston or New York or Chicago or San Francisco, and be willing citizens of the great Republic.

The highest aim of most of our literary journals has thus far been to appear English, except where some diverging experimentalist has said, "Let us be German," or "Let us be French." This was inevitable; as inevitable as a boy's first imitations of Byron or Tennyson. But it necessarily implied that our literature must, during this epoch, be second-rate. We need to become national, not by any conscious effort, such as implies attitudinizing and constraint, but by simply accepting our own life. It is not desirable to go out of one's way to be original, but it is to be hoped that it may lie in one's way. Originality is simply a fresh pair of eyes. If you want to astonish the whole world, said Rahel, tell the simple truth. It is easier to excuse a thousand defects in the literary man who proceeds on this faith, than to forgive the one great defect of imitation in the purist who seeks only to be English. As Wasson has said, "The Englishman is undoubtedly a wholesome figure to the mental eye; but will not twenty million copies of him do, for the present?" We must pardon something to the spirit of liberty. We must run some risks, as all immature creatures do, in the effort to use our own limbs. Professor Edward Channing used to say that it was a bad sign for a college boy to write too well; there should be exuberances and inequalities. A nation which has but just begun to create a literature must sow some wild oats. The most tiresome vaingloriousness may be more hopeful than hypercriticism and spleen. The follies of the absurdest spread-eagle orator may be far more promising, because they smack more of the soil, than the neat Londonism of the city editor who dissects him.

It is but a few years since we have dared to be American in even the details and accessories of our literary work; to make our allusions to natural objects real not conventional; to ignore the nightingale and skylark, and look for the classic and romantic on our own soil. This change began mainly with Emerson. Some of us can recall the bewilderment with which his verses on the humblebee, for instance, were received, when the choice of subject caused as much wonder as the treatment. It was called "a foolish affectation of the familiar." Happily the atmosphere of distance forms itself rapidly in a new land, and the poem has now as serene a place in literature as if Andrew Marvell had written it. The truly cosmopolitan writer is not he who carefully denudes his work of everything occasional and temporary, but he who makes his local coloring forever classic through the fascination of the dream it tells. Reason, imagination, passion, are universal; but sky, climate, costume, and even type of human character, belong to some one spot alone till they find an artist potent enough to stamp their associations on the memory of all the world. Whether his work be picture or symphony, legend or lyric, is of little moment. The spirit of the execution is all in all.

As yet, we Americans have hardly begun to think of the details of execution in any art. We do not aim at perfection of detail even in engineering, much less in literature. In the haste of our national life, most of our intellectual work is done at a rush, is something inserted in the odd moments of the engrossing pursuit. The popular preacher becomes a novelist; the editor turns his paste-pot and scissors to the compilation of a history; the same man must be poet, wit, philanthropist, and genealogist. We find a sort of pleasure in seeing this variety of effort, just as the bystanders like to see a street-musician adjust every joint in his body to a separate instrument, and play a concerted piece with the whole of himself. To be sure, he plays each part badly, but it is such a wonder he should play them all! Thus, in our rather hurried and helter-skelter training, the man is brilliant, perhaps; his main work is well done; but his secondary work is slurred. The book sells, no doubt, by reason of the author's popularity in other fields; it is only the tone of our national literature that suffers. There is nothing in American life that can make concentration cease to be a virtue. Let a man choose his pursuit, and make all else count for recreation only. Goethe's advice to Eckermann is infinitely more important here than it ever was in Germany: "Beware of dissipating your powers; strive constantly to concentrate them. Genius thinks it can do whatever it sees others doing, but it is sure to repent of every ill-judged outlay."

In one respect, however, this desultory activity is an advantage: it makes men look in a variety of directions for a standard. As each sect in religion helps to protect us from some other sect, so every mental tendency is the limitation of some other. We need the English culture, but we do not need it more evidently than we need the German, the French, the Greek, the Oriental. In prose literature, for instance, the English contemporary models are not enough. There is an admirable vigor and heartiness, a direct and manly tone; King Richard still lives; but Saladin also had his fine sword-play; let us see him. There are the delightful French qualities,—the atmosphere where literary art means fineness of touch. "Où il n'y a point de délicatesse, il n'y a point de littérature. Un écrit où ne se recontrent que de la force et un certain feu sans éclat n'annonce que le caractère." But there is something in the English climate which seems to turn the fine edge of any very choice scymitar till it cuts Saladin's own fingers at last.

God forbid that I should disparage this broad Anglo-Saxon manhood which is the basis of our national life. I knew an American mother who sent her boy to Rugby School in England, in the certainty, as she said, that he would there learn two things,—to play cricket and to speak the truth. He acquired both thoroughly, and she brought him home for what she deemed, in comparison, the ornamental branches. We cannot spare the Englishman from our blood, but it is our business to make him more than an Englishman. That iron must become steel; finer, harder, more elastic, more polished. For this end the English stock was transferred from an island to a continent, and mixed with new ingredients, that it might lose its quality of coarseness, and take a more delicate grain.

As yet, it must be owned, this daring expectation is but feebly reflected in our books. In looking over any collection of American poetry, for instance, one is struck with the fact that it is not so much faulty as inadequate. Emerson set free the poetic intuition of America, Hawthorne its imagination. Both looked into the realm of passion, Emerson with distrust, Hawthorne with eager interest; but neither thrilled with its spell, and the American poet of passion is yet to come. How tame and manageable are wont to be the emotions of our bards, how placid and literary their allusions! There is no baptism of fire; no heat that breeds excess. Yet it is not life that is grown dull, surely; there are as many secrets in every heart, as many skeletons in every closet, as in any elder period of the world's career. It is the interpreters of life who are found wanting, and that not on this soil alone, but throughout the Anglo-Saxon race. It is not just to say, as someone has said, that our language has not in this generation produced a love-song, for it has produced Browning; but was it in England or in Italy that he learned to sound the depths of all human emotion?

And it is not to verse that this temporary check of ardor applies. It is often said that prose fiction now occupies the place held by the drama during the Elizabethan age. Certainly this modern product shows something of the brilliant profusion of that wondrous flowering of genius; but here the resemblance ends. Where in our imaginative literature does one find the concentrated utterance, the intense and breathing life, the triumphs and despairs, the depth of emotion, the tragedy, the thrill, that meet one everywhere in those Elizabethan pages? What impetuous and commanding men are these, what passionate women; how they love and hate, struggle and endure; how they play with the world; what a trail of fire they leave behind them as they pass by! Turn now to recent fiction. Dickens's people are amusing and lovable, no doubt; Thackeray's are wicked and witty; but how under-sized they look, and how they loiter on the mere surfaces of life, compared, I will not say with Shakespeare's, but even with Chapman's and Webster's men. Set aside Hawthorne in America, with perhaps Charlotte Brontë and George Eliot in England, and there would scarcely be a fact in prose literature to show that we modern Anglo-Saxons regard a profound human emotion as a thing worth the painting. Who now dares delineate a lover, except with good-natured pitying sarcasm, as in *David Copperfield* or *Pendennis?* In the Elizabethan period, with all its unspeakable coarseness, hot blood still ran in the veins of literature; lovers burned and suffered and were men. And what was true of love was true of all the passions of the human soul.

In this respect, as in many others, France has preserved more of the artistic tradition. The common criticism, however, is, that in modern French literature, as in the Elizabethan, the play of feeling is too naked and obvious, and that the Puritan self-restraint is worth more than all that dissolute wealth. I believe it; and here comes in the intellectual worth of America. Puritanism was a phase, a discipline, a hygiene; but we cannot remain always Puritans. The world needed that moral bracing, even for its art; but after all, life is not impoverished by being ennobled; and in a happier age, with a larger faith, we may again enrich ourselves with poetry and passion, while wearing that heroic girdle still around us. Then the next blossoming of the world's imagination need not bear within itself, like all the others, the seeds of an epoch of decay.

I utterly reject the position taken by Matthew Arnold, that the Puritan spirit in America was essentially hostile to literature and art. Of course the forest pioneer cannot compose orchestral symphonies, nor the founder of a state carve statues. But the thoughtful and scholarly men who created the Massachusetts Colony brought with them the traditions of their universities, and left these embodied in a college. The Puritan life was only historically inconsistent with culture; there was no logical antagonism. Indeed, that life had in it much that was congenial to art, in its enthusiasm and its truthfulness. Take these Puritan traits, employ them in a more genial sphere, add intellectual training and a sunny faith, and you have a soil suited to art above all others. To deny it is to see in art only something frivolous and insincere. The American writer in whom the artistic instinct was strongest came of unmixed Puritan stock. Major John Hathorne, in 1692, put his offenders on trial, and generally convicted and hanged them all. Nathaniel Hawthorne held his more spiritual tribunal two centuries later, and his keener scrutiny found some ground of vindication for each one. The fidelity, the thoroughness, the conscientious purpose, were the same in each. Both sought to rest their work, as all art and all law must rest, upon the absolute truth. The writer kept, no doubt, something of the somberness of the magistrate; each, doubtless, suffered in the woes he studied; and as the one "had a knot of pain in his forehead all winter" while meditating the doom of Arthur Dimmesdale, so may the other have borne upon his own brow the trace of Martha Corey's grief.

No, it does not seem to me that the obstacle to a new birth of literature and art in America lies in the Puritan tradition, but rather in the timid and faithless spirit that lurks in the circles of culture, and still holds something of literary and academic leadership in the homes of the Puritans. What are the ghosts of a myriad Blue Laws compared with the transplanted cynicism of one "Saturday Review"? How can any noble literature germinate where young men are habitually taught that there is no such thing as originality, and that nothing remains for us in this effete epoch of history but the mere recombining of thoughts which sprang first from braver brains? It is melancholy to see young men come forth from the college walls with less enthusiasm than they carried in; trained in a spirit which is in this respect worse than English toryism—that is, does not even retain a hearty faith in the past. It is better that a man should have eyes in the back of his head than that he should be taught to sneer at even a retrospective vision. One may believe that the golden age is behind us or before us, but alas for the forlorn wisdom of him who rejects it altogether! It is not the climax of culture that a college graduate should emulate the obituary praise bestowed by Cotton Mather on the Rev. John Mitchell of Cambridge, "a truly aged young man." Better a thousand times train a boy on Scott's novels or the Border Ballads than educate him to believe, on the one side, that chivalry was a cheat and the troubadours imbeciles, and on the other hand, that universal suffrage is an absurdity and the one real need is to get rid of our voters. A great crisis like a civil war brings men temporarily to their senses, and the young resume the attitude natural to their years, in spite of their teachers; but it is a sad thing when, in seeking for the generous impulses of youth, we have to turn from the public sentiment of the colleges to that of the workshops and the farms.

It is a thing not to be forgotten, that for a long series of years the people of our Northern States were habitually in advance of their institutions of learning, in courage and comprehensiveness of thought. There were long years during which the most cultivated scholar, so soon as he embraced an unpopular opinion, was apt to find the college doors closed against him, and only the country lyceum—the people's college—left open. Slavery had to be abolished before the most accomplished orator of the nation could be invited to address the graduates of his own university.

The first among American scholars was nominated year after year, only to be rejected, before the academic societies of his own neighborhood. Yet during all that time the rural lecture associations showered their invitations on Parker and Phillips; culture shunned them, but the common people heard them gladly. The home of real thought was outside, not inside, the college walls. It hardly embarrassed a professor's position if he defended slavery as a divine institution; but he risked his place if he denounced the wrong. In those days, if by any chance a man of bold opinions drifted into a reputable professorship, we listened sadly to hear his voice grow faint. He usually began to lose his faith, his courage, his toleration,—in short, his Americanism,—when he left the ranks of the uninstructed.

That time is past; and the literary class has now come more into sympathy with the popular heart. It is perhaps fortunate that there is as yet but little *esprit de corps* among our writers, so that they receive their best sympathy, not from each other, but from the people. Even the memory of our most original authors, as Thoreau, or Margaret Fuller Ossoli, is apt to receive its sharpest stabs from those of the same guild. When we American writers find grace to do our best, it is not so much because we are sustained by each other, as that we are conscious of a deep popular heart, slowly but surely answering back to ours, and offering a worthier stimulus than the applause of a coterie. If we once lose faith in our audience, the muse grows silent. Even the apparent indifference of this audience to culture and high finish may be in the end a wholesome influence, recalling us to those more important things, compared to which these are secondary qualities. The indifference is only comparative; our public prefers good writing, as it prefers good elocution; but it values energy, heartiness, and action more. The public is right; it is the business of the writer, as of the speaker, to perfect the finer graces without sacrificing things more vital. "She was not a good singer," says some novelist of his heroine, "but she sang with an inspiration such as good singers rarely indulge in." Given those positive qualities, and I think that a fine execution does not hinder acceptance in America, but rather aids it. Where there is beauty of execution alone, a popular audience, even in America, very easily goes to sleep. And in such matters, as the French actor, Samson, said to the young dramatist, "sleep is an opinion."

It takes more than grammars and dictionaries to make a literature. "It is the spirit in which we act that is the great matter," Goethe says. *Der Geist aus dem wir handeln ist das Höchste.* Technical training may give the negative merits of style, as an elocutionist may help a public speaker by ridding him of tricks. But the positive force of writing or of speech must come from positive sources,—ardor, energy, depth of feeling or of thought. No instruction ever gave these, only the inspiration of a great soul, a great need, or a great people. We all know that a vast deal of oxygen may go into the style of a man; we see in it not merely what books he has read, what company he has kept, but also the food he eats, the exercise he takes, the air he breathes. And so there is oxygen in the collective literature of a nation, and this vital element proceeds, above all else, from liberty. For want of this wholesome oxygen, the voice of Victor Hugo comes to us uncertain and spasmodic, as of one in an alien atmosphere where breath is pain; for want of it, the eloquent English tones that at first sounded so clear and bell-like now reach us only faint and muffled, and lose their music day by day. It is by the presence of this oxygen that American literature is to be made great. We are lost if we permit this inspiration of our nation's life to sustain only the journalist and the stump-speaker, while we allow the colleges and the books to be choked with the dust of dead centuries and to pant for daily breath.

Perhaps it may yet be found that the men who are contributing most to raise the tone of American literature are the men who have never yet written a book and have scarcely time to read one, but by their heroic energy in other spheres are providing exemplars for what our books shall one day be. The man who constructs a great mechanical work helps literature, for he gives a model which shall one day inspire us to construct literary works as great. I do not wish to be forever outdone by the carpet-machinery of Clinton or the grain-elevators of Chicago. We have not yet arrived at our literature,—other things must come first; we are busy with our railroads, perfecting the vast alimentary canal by which the nation assimilates raw immigrants at the rate of half a milion a year. We are not yet producing, we are digesting: food now, literary composition by and by: Shakespeare did not write *Hamlet* at the dinner-table. It is of course impossible to explain this to foreigners, and they still talk of convincing, while we talk of dining.

For one, I cannot dispense with the society which we call uncultivated. Democratic sympathies seem to be mainly a matter of vigor and health. It seems to be the first symptom of biliousness to think that only one's self and one's cousins are entitled to consideration and constitute the world. Every refined person is an aristocrat in his dyspeptic moments; when hearty and well, he demands a wider range of sympathy. It is so tedious to live only in one circle and have only a genteel acquaintance! Mrs. Trench, in her delightful letters, complains of the society in Dresden, about the year 1800, because of " the impossibility, without overstepping all bounds of social custom, or associating with any but *noblesse.*" We order that matter otherwise in America. I wish not only to know my neighbor, the man of fashion, who strolls to his club at noon, but also my neighbor, the wheelwright, who goes to his dinner at the same hour. One would not wish to be unacquainted with the fair maiden who drives by in her basket-wagon in the afternoon; nor with the other fair maiden, who may be seen at her washtub in the morning. Both are quite worth knowing; both are good, sensible, dutiful girls: the young laundress is the better mathematician, because she has gone through the grammar school; but the other has the better French accent, because she has spent half her life in Paris. They offer a variety, at least, and save from that monotony which besets any set of people when seen alone. There was much reason in Horace Walpole's coachman, who, having driven the maids of honor all his life, bequeathed his earnings to his son, on condition that he should never marry a maid of honor.

I affirm that democratic society, the society of the future, enriches and does not impoverish human life, and gives more, not less, material for literary art. Distributing culture through all classes, it diminishes class-distinction and develops individuality. Perhaps it is the best phenomenon of American life, thus far, that the word "gentleman," which in England still designates a social order, is here more apt to refer to personal character. When we describe a person as a gentleman, we usually refer to his manners, morals, and education, not to his property or birth; and this change alone is worth the transplantation across the Atlantic. The use of the word "lady" is yet more comprehensive, and therefore more honorable still; we sometimes see, in a shopkeeper's advertisement, "Saleslady wanted." No doubt the mere fashionable novelist loses terribly by the change: when all classes may wear the same dress-coat, what is left for him? But he who aims to depict passion and character gains in proportion; his material is increased tenfold. The living realities of American life ought to come in among the tiresome lay-figures of average English fiction like Steven Lawrence into the London drawing-room: tragedy must resume its grander shape, and no longer turn on the vexed question whether the daughter of this or that matchmaker shall marry the baronet. It is the characteristic of a real book that, though the scene be laid in courts, their whole machinery might be struck out and the essential interest of the plot remain the same. In Auerbach's *On the Heights,* for instance, the social heights might be abolished and the moral elevation would be enough. The play of human emotion is a thing so absorbing, that the petty distinctions of cottage and castle become as nothing in its presence. Why not waive these small matters in advance, then, and go straight to the real thing?

The greatest transatlantic successes which American novelists have yet attained—those won by Cooper and Mrs. Stowe—have come through a daring Americanism of subject, which introduced in each case a new figure to the European world,—first the Indian, then the negro. Whatever the merit of the work, it was plainly the theme which conquered. Such successes are not easily to be repeated, for they were based on temporary situations never to recur. But they prepare the way for higher triumphs to be won by a profounder treatment,—the introduction into literature, not of new tribes alone, but of the American spirit. To analyze combinations of character that only our national life produces, to portray dramatic situations that belong to a clearer social atmosphere,—this is the higher Americanism. Of course, to cope with such themes in such a spirit is less easy than to describe a foray or a tournament, or to multiply indefinitely such still-life pictures as the stereotyped English or French society affords; but the thing when once done is incomparably nobler. It may be centuries before it is done: no matter. It will be done, and with it will come a similar advance along the whole line of literary labor, like the elevation which we have seen in the whole quality of scientific work in this country within the last twenty years.

We talk idly about the tyranny of the ancient classics, as if there were some special peril about it, quite distinct from all other tyrannies. But if a man is to be stunted by the influence of a master, it makes no difference whether that master lived before or since the Christian epoch. One folio volume is as ponderous as another, if it crushes down the tender germs of thought. There is no great choice between the volumes of the Encyclopædia. It is not important to know whether a man reads Homer or Dante: the essential point is whether he believes the world to be young or old; whether he sees as much scope for his own inspiration as if never a book had appeared in the world. So long as he does this, he has the American spirit: no books, no travel, can overwhelm him, for these will only enlarge his thoughts and raise his standard of execution. When he loses this faith, he takes rank among the copyists and the secondary, and no accident can raise him to a place among the benefactors of mankind. He is like a man who is frightened in battle: you cannot exactly blame him, for it may be an affair of the temperament or of the digestion; but you are glad to let him drop to the rear, and to close up the ranks. Fields are won by those who believe in the winning.

[From *Americanism in Literature*. Copyright, 1871, by James R. Osgood & Co.]

THACKERAY IN AMERICA

George William Curtis

Mr. Thackeray's visit at least demonstrates that if we are unwilling to pay English authors for their books, we are ready to reward them handsomely for the opportunity of seeing and hearing them. If Mr. Dickens, instead of dining at other people's expense, and making speeches at his own, when he came to see us, had devoted an evening or two in the week to lecturing, his purse would have been fuller, his feelings sweeter, and his fame fairer. It was a Quixotic crusade, that of the Copyright, and the excellent Don has never forgiven the windmill that broke his spear.

Undoubtedly, when it was ascertained that Mr. Thackeray was coming, the public feeling on this side of the sea was very much divided as to his probable reception. "He'll come and humbug us, eat our dinners, pocket our money, and go home and abuse us, like that unmitigated snob Dickens," said Jonathan, chafing with the remembrance of that grand ball at the Park Theater and the Boz tableaux, and the universal wining and dining, to which the distinguished Dickens was subject while he was our guest.

"Let him have his say," said others, "and we will have our look. We will pay a dollar to hear him, if we can see him at the same time; and as for the abuse, why, it takes even more than two such cubs of the roaring British Lion to frighten the American Eagle. Let him come, and give him fair play."

He did come, and had fair play, and returned to England with a comfortable pot of gold holding $12,000, and with the hope and promise of seeing us again in September, to discourse of something not less entertaining than the witty men and sparkling times of Anne. We think there was no disappointment with his lectures. Those who knew his books found the author in the lecturer. Those who did not know his books were charmed in the lecturer by what is charming in the author—the unaffected humanity, the tenderness, the sweetness, the genial play of fancy, and the sad touch of truth, with that glancing stroke of satire which, lightning-like, illumines while it withers. The lectures were even more delightful than the books, because the tone of the voice and the appearance of the man, the general personal magnetism, explained and alleviated so much that would otherwise have seemed doubtful or unfair. For those who had long felt in the writings of Thackeray a reality quite inexpressible, there was a secret delight in finding it justified in his speaking; for he speaks as he writes—simply, directly, without flourish, without any cant of oratory, commending what he says by its intrinsic sense, and the sympathetic and humane way in which it was spoken. Thackeray is the kind of "stump orator" that would have pleased Carlyle. He never thrusts himself between you and his thought. If his conception of the time and his estimate of the men differ from your own, you have at least no doubt what his view is, nor how sincere and necessary it is to him. Mr. Thackeray considers Swift a misanthrope; he loves Goldsmith and Steele and Harry Fielding; he has no love for Sterne, great admiration for Pope, and alleviated admiration for Addison. How could it be otherwise? How could Thackeray not think Swift a misanthrope and Sterne a factitious sentimentalist? He is a man of instincts, not of thoughts: he sees and feels. He would be

Shakespeare's call-boy, rather than dine with the Dean of St. Patrick's. He would take a pot of ale with Goldsmith, rather than a glass of burgundy with the "Reverend Mr. Sterne," and that simply because he is Thackeray. He would have done it as Fielding would have done it, because he values one genuine emotion above the most dazzling thought; because he is, in fine, a Bohemian, "a minion of the moon," a great, sweet, generous heart.

We say this with more unction now that we have personal proof of it in his public and private intercourse while he was here.

The popular Thackeray-theory, before his arrival, was of a severe satirist, who concealed scalpels in his sleeves and carried probes in his waistcoat pockets; a wearer of masks; a scoffer and sneerer, and general infidel of all high aims and noble character. Certainly we are justified in saying that his presence among us quite corrected this idea. We welcomed a friendly, genial man; not at all convinced that speech is heaven's first law, but willing to be silent when there is nothing to say; who decidedly refused to be lionized—not by sulking, but by stepping off the pedestal and challenging the common sympathies of all he met; a man who, in view of the thirty-odd editions of Martin Farquhar Tupper, was willing to confess that every author should "think small-beer of himself." Indeed, he has this rare quality, that his personal impression deepens, in kind, that of his writings. The quiet and comprehensive grasp of the fact, and the intellectual impossibility of holding fast anything but the fact, is as manifest in the essayist upon the wits as in the author of *Henry Esmond* and *Vanity Fair*. Shall we say that this is the sum of his power, and the secret of his satire? It is not what might be, nor what we or other persons of well-regulated minds might wish, but it is the actual state of things that he sees and describes. How, then, can he help what we call satire, if he accept Mrs. Rawdon Crawley's invitation and describe her party? There was no more satire in it, so far as he is concerned, than in painting lilies white. A full-length portrait of the fair Lady Beatrix, too, must needs show a gay and vivid figure, superbly glittering across the vista of those stately days. Then, should Dab and Tab, the eminent critics, step up and demand that her eyes be a pale blue, and her stomacher higher around the neck? Do Dab and Tab expect to gather pears from peach-trees? Or, because their theory of dendrology convinces them that an ideal fruit-tree would supply any fruit desired upon application, do they denounce the non-pear-bearing peach-tree in the columns of their valuable journal? This is the drift of the fault found with Thackeray. He is not Fénelon, he is not Dickens, he is not Scott; he is not poetical, he is not ideal, he is not humane; he is not Tit, he is not Tat, complain the eminent Dabs and Tabs. Of course he is not, because he is Thackeray—a man who describes what he sees, motives as well as appearances—a man who believes that character is better than talent—that there is a worldly weakness superior to worldly wisdom—that Dick Steele may haunt the ale-house and be carried home muzzy, and yet be a more commendable character than the reverend Dean of St. Patrick's, who has genius enough to illuminate a century, but not sympathy enough to sweeten a drop of beer. And he represents this in a way that makes us see it as he does, and without exaggeration; for surely nothing could be more simple than his story of the life of "honest Dick Steele." If he allotted to that gentleman a consideration disproportioned to the space he occupies in literary history, it only showed the more strikingly how deeply the writer-lecturer's sympathy was touched by Steele's honest humanity.

An article in our April number complained that the tendency of his view of Anne's times was to a social laxity, which might be very exhilarating but was very dangerous; that the lecturer's warm commendation of fermented drinks, taken at a very early hour of the morning in tavern-rooms and club houses, was as deleterious to the moral health of enthusiastic young readers disposed to the literary life as the beverage itself to their physical health.

But this is not a charge to be brought against Thackeray. It is a quarrel with history and with the nature of literary life. Artists and authors have always been the good fellows of the world. That mental organization which predisposes a man to the pursuit of literature and art is made up of talent combined with ardent social sympathy, geniality, and passion, and leads him to taste every cup and try every experience. There is certainly no essential necessity that this class should be a dissipated and disreputable class, but by their very susceptibility to enjoyment .they will always be the pleasure lovers and seekers. And here is the social compensation to the literary man for the surrender of those chances of fortune which men of other pursuits enjoy. If he makes less money, he makes more juice out of what he does make. If he cannot drink burgundy he can quaff the nut-brown ale; while the most brilliant wit, the most salient fancy, the sweetest sympathy, the most genial culture, shall sparkle at his board more radiantly than a silver service, and give him the spirit of the tropics and the Rhine, whose fruits are on other tables. The golden light that transfigures talent and illuminates the world, and which we call genius, is erratic and erotic; and while in Milton it is austere, and in Wordsworth cool, and in Southey methodical, in Shakespeare it is fervent, with all the results of fervor; in Raphael lovely, with all the excesses of love; in Dante moody, with all the whims of caprice. The old quarrel of Lombard Street with Grub Street is as profound as that of Osiris and Typho—it is the difference of sympathy. The Marquis of Westminster will take good care that no superfluous shilling escapes. Oliver Goldsmith will still spend his last shilling upon a brave and unnecessary banquet to his friends.

Whether this be a final fact of human organization or not, it is certainly a fact of history. Every man instinctively believes that Shakespeare stole deer, just as he disbelieves that Lord-mayor Whittington ever told a lie; and the secret of that instinct is the consciousness of the difference in organization. "Knave, I have the power to hang ye," says somebody in one of Beaumont and Fletcher's plays. "And I do be hanged and scorn ye," is the airy answer. "I had a pleasant hour the other evening," said a friend to us, "over my cigar and a book." "What book was that?" "A treatise conclusively proving the awful consequences of smoking." De Quincey came up to London and declared war upon opium; but during a little amnesty, in which he lapsed into his old elysium, he wrote his best book depicting its horrors.

Our readers will not imagine that we are advocating the claims of drunkenness nor defending social excess. We are only recognizing a fact and stating an obvious tendency. The most brilliant illustrations of every virtue are to be found in the literary guild, as well as the saddest beacons of warning; yet it will often occur that the last in talent and the first in excess of a picked company will be a man around whom sympathy most kindly lingers. We love Goldsmith more at the head of an ill-advised feast than Johnson and his friends leaving it, thoughtful and generous as their conduct was. The heart despises prudence.

In the single-hearted regard we know that pity has a large share. Yet it is not so much that pity which is commisertion for misfortune and deficiency, as that which is recognition of a necessary worldly ignorance. The literary class is the most innocent of all. The contempt of practical men for the poets is based upon a consciousness that they are not bad enough for a bad world. To a practical man nothing is so absurd as the lack of worldly shrewdness. The very complaint of the literary life that it does not amass wealth and live in palaces is the scorn of the practical man, for he cannot understand that intellectual opacity which prevents the literary man from seeing the necessity of the different pecuniary condition. It is clear enough to the publisher who lays up fifty thousand a year why the author ends the year in debt. But the author is amazed that he who deals in ideas can only dine upon occasional chops, while the man who merely binds and sells ideas sits down to perpetual sirloin. If they should change places, fortune would change with them. The publisher turned author would still lay up his thousands; the publishing author would still directly lose thousands. It is simply because it is a matter of prudence, economy, and knowledge of the world. Thomas Hood made his ten thousand dollars a year, but if he lived at the rate of fifteen thousand he would hardly die rich. Mr. Jerdan, a gentleman who, in his *Autobiography,* advises energetic youth to betake themselves to the highway rather than to literature, was, we understand, in the receipt of an easy income, and was a welcome guest in pleasant houses; but living in a careless, shiftless, extravagant way, he was presently poor, and, instead of giving his memoirs the motto, *peccavi,* and inditing a warning, he dashes off a truculent defiance. Practical publishers and practical men of all sorts invest their earnings in Michigan Central or Cincinnati and Dayton instead, in steady works and devoted days, and reap a pleasant harvest of dividends. Our friends the authors invest in prime Havanas, Rhenish, in oyster suppers, love and leisure, and divide a heavy percentage of headache, dyspepsia, and debt.

This is as true a view, from another point, as the one we have already taken. If the literary life has the pleasures of freedom, it has also its pains. It may be willing to resign the queen's drawing-room, with the illustrious galaxy of stars and garters, for the chamber with a party nobler than the nobility. The author's success is of a wholly different kind from that of the publisher, and he is thoughtless who demands both. Mr. Roe, who sells sugar, naturally complains that Mr. Doe, who sells molasses, makes money more rapidly. But Mr. Tennyson, who writes poems, can hardly make the same complaint of Mr. Moxon, who publishes them, as was very fairly shown in a number of the *Westminster Review,* when noticing Mr. Jerdan's book.

What we have said is strictly related to Mr. Thackeray's lectures, which discuss literature. All the men he commemorated were illustrations and exponents of the career of letters. They all, in various ways, showed the various phenomena of the temperament. And when in treating of them the critic came to Steele, he found one who was one of the most striking illustrations of one of the most universal aspects of literary life—the simple-hearted, unsuspicious, gay gallant and genial gentleman; ready with his sword or his pen, with a smile or a tear, the fair representative of the social tendency of his life. It seems to us that the Thackeray theory—the conclusion that he is a man who loves to depict madness, and has no sensibilities to the finer qualities of character—crumbled quite away before that lecture upon Steele. We know that it was not considered the best; we know that many of the delighted audience were not sufficiently familiar with literary history fully to understand the position of the man in the lecturer's review; but, as a key to Thackeray, it was, perhaps, the most valuable of all. We know in literature of no more gentle treatment; we have not often encountered in men of the most rigorous and acknowledged virtue such humane tenderness; we have not often heard from the most clerical lips words of such genuine Christianity. Steele's was a character which makes weakness amiable: it was a weakness, if you will, but it was certainly amiability, and it was a combination more attractive than many full-panoplied excellences. It was not presented as a model. Captain Steele in the tap-room was not painted as the ideal of virtuous manhood; but it certainly was intimated that many admirable things were consonant with a free use of beer. It was frankly stated that if, in that character, virtue abounded, cakes and ale did much more abound. Captain Richard Steele might have behaved much better than he did, but we should then have never heard of him. A few fine essays do not float a man into immortality, but the generous character, the heart sweet in all excesses and under all chances, is a spectacle too beautiful and too rare to be easily forgotten. A man is better than many books. Even a man who is not immaculate may have more virtuous influence than the discreetest saint. Let us remember how fondly the old painters lingered round the story of Magdalen, and thank Thackeray for his full-length Steele.

We conceive this to be the chief result of Thackeray's visit, that he convinced us of his intellectual integrity; he showed us how impossible it is for him to see the world and describe it other than he does. He does not profess cynicism, nor satirize society with malice; there is no man more humble, none more simple; his interests are human and concrete, not abstract. We have already said that he looks through and through at the fact. It is easy enough, and at some future time it will be done, to deduce the peculiarity of his writings from the character of his mind.

There is no man who masks so little as he in assuming the author. His books are his observations reduced to writing. It seems to us as singular to demand that Dante should be like Shakespeare as to quarrel with Thackeray's want of what is called ideal portraiture. Even if you thought, from reading his *Vanity Fair,* that he had no conception of noble women, certainly after the lecture upon Swift, after all the lectures, in which every allusion to women was so manly and delicate and sympathetic, you thought so no longer. It is clear that his sympathy is attracted to women—to that which is essentially womanly, feminine. Qualities common to both sexes do not necessarily charm him because he finds them in women. A certain degree of goodness must always be assumed. It is only the rare flowering that inspires special praise. You call Amelia's fondness for George Osborne foolish, fond idolatry. Thackeray smiles, as if all love were not idolatry of the fondest foolishness. What was Hero's—what was Francesca da Rimini's—what was Juliet's? They might have been more brilliant women than Amelia, and their idols of a larger mold than George, but the love was the same old foolish, fond idolatry. The passion of love and a profound and sensible knowledge, regard based upon prodigious knowledge of character and appreciation of talent, are different things. What is the historic and poetic splendor of love but the very fact, which constantly appears in Thackeray's stories, namely, that it i a glory which dazzles and blinds. Men rarely love th women they ought to love, according to the ideal standards It is this that makes the plot and mystery of life. Is it no the perpetual surprise of all Jane's friends that she shoul love Timothy instead of Thomas? and is not the courtly an accomplished Thomas sure to surrender to some accident Lucy without position, wealth, style, worth, culture—wit out anything but heart? This is the fact, and it reappea in Thackeray, and it gives his books that air of reality which they possess beyond all modern story.

And it is this single perception of the fact which, simple as it is, is the rarest intellectual quality that made his lectures so interesting. The sun rose again upon the vanished century, and lighted those historic streets. The wits of Queen Anne ruled the hour, and we were bidden to their feast. Much reading of history and memoirs had not so sent the blood into those old English cheeks, and so moved those limbs in proper measure, as these swift glances through the eyes of genius. It was because, true to himself, Thackeray gave us his impression of those wits as men rather than authors. For he loves character more than thought. He is a man of the world, and not a scholar. He interprets the author by the man. When you are made intimate with young Swift, Sir William Temple's saturnine secretary, you more intelligently appreciate the Dean of St. Patrick's. When the surplice of Mr. Sterne is raised a little, more is seen than the reverend gentleman intends. Hogarth, the bluff Londoner, necessarily depicts a bluff, coarse, obvious morality. The hearty Fielding, the cool Addison, the genial Goldsmith, these are the figures that remain in memory, and their works are valuable as they indicate the man.

Mr. Thackeray's success was very great. He did not visit the West, nor Canada. He went home without seeing Niagara Falls. But wherever he did go he found a generous and social welcome, and a respectful and sympathetic hearing. He came to fulfill no mission, but he certainly knit more closely our sympathy with Englishmen. Heralded by various romantic memoirs, he smiled at them, stoutly asserted that he had been always able to command a good dinner, and to pay for it; nor did he seek to disguise that he hoped his American tour would help him to command and pay for more. He promised not to write a book about us, but we hope he will, for we can ill spare the criticism of such an observer. At least, we may be sure that the material gathered here will be worked up in some way. He found that we were not savages nor bores. He found that there were a hundred here for every score in England who knew well and loved the men of whom he spoke. He found that the same red blood colors all the lips that speak the language he so nobly praised. He found friends instead of critics. He found those who, loving the author, loved the man more. He found a quiet welcome from those who are waiting to welcome him again and as sincerely.

[From *Literary and Social Essays,* by George William Curtis. Copyright, 1894, by Harper & Brothers.]

OUR MARCH TO WASHINGTON

Theodore Winthrop

THROUGH THE CITY

At three o'clock in the afternoon of Friday, April 19, we took our peacemaker, a neat twelve-pound brass howitzer, down from the Seventh Regiment Armory, and stationed it in the rear of the building. The twin peacemaker is somewhere near us, but entirely hidden by this enormous crowd.

An enormous crowd! of both sexes, of every age and condition. The men offer all kinds of truculent and patriotic hopes; the women shed tears, and say, "God bless you, boys!"

This is a part of the town where baddish cigars prevail. But good or bad, I am ordered to keep all away from the gun. So the throng stands back, peers curiously over the heads of its junior members, and seems to be taking the measure of my coffin.

After a patient hour of this, the word is given, we fall in, our two guns find their places at the right of the line of march, we move on through the thickening crowd.

At a great house on the left, as we pass the Astor Library, I see a handkerchief waving for me. Yes! it is she who made the sandwiches in my knapsack. They were a trifle too thick, as I afterwards discovered, but otherwise perfection. Be these my thanks and the thanks of hungry comrades who had bites of them!

At the corner of Great Jones Street we halted for half

an hour,—then, everything ready, we marched down Broadway.

It was worth a life, that march. Only one who passed, as we did, through that tempest of cheers, two miles long, can know the terrible enthusiasm of the occasion. I could hardly hear the rattle of our own gun-carriages, and only once or twice the music of our band came to me muffled and quelled by the uproar. We knew now, if we had not before divined it, that our great city was with us as one man, utterly united in the great cause we were marching to sustain.

This grand fact I learned by two senses. If hundreds of thousands roared it into my ears, thousands slapped it into my back. My fellow-citizens smote me on the knapsack, as I went by at the gun-rope, and encouraged me each in his own dialect. "Bully for you!" alternated with benedictions, in the proportion of two "bullies" to one blessing.

I was not so fortunate as to receive more substantial tokens of sympathy. But there were parting gifts showered on the regiment, enough to establish a variety-shop. Handkerchiefs, of course, came floating down upon us from the windows, like a snow. Pretty little gloves pelted us with love-taps. The sterner sex forced upon us pocket-knives new and jagged, combs, soap, slippers, boxes of matches, cigars by the dozen and the hundred, pipes to smoke shag and pipes to smoke Latakia, fruit, eggs, and sandwiches. One fellow got a new purse with ten bright quarter-eagles.

At the corner of Grand Street, or thereabouts, a "bhoy" in red flannel shirt and black dress pantaloons, leaning back against the crowd with Herculean shoulders, called me,—
"Saäy, bully! take my dorg! he's one of the kind that holds till he draps." This gentleman, with his animal, was in-

stantly shoved back by the police, and the Seventh lost the "dorg."

These were the comic incidents of the march, but underlying all was the tragic sentiment that we might have tragic work presently to do. The news of the rascal attack in Baltimore on the Massachusetts Sixth had just come in. Ours might be the same chance. If there were any of us not in earnest before, the story of the day would steady us. So we said good-by to Broadway, moved down Cortlandt Street under a bower of flags, and at half-past six shoved off in the ferry-boat.

Everybody has heard how Jersey City turned out and filled up the Railroad Station, like an opera-house, to give God-speed to us as a representative body, a guaranty of the unquestioning loyalty of the "conservative" class in New York. Everybody has heard how the State of New Jersey, along the railroad line, stood through the evening and the night to shout their quota of good wishes. At every station the Jerseymen were there, uproarious as Jerseymen, to shake our hands and wish us a happy despatch. I think I did not see a rod of ground without its man, from dusk till dawn, from the Hudson to the Delaware.

Upon the train we made a jolly night of it. All knew that the more a man sings, the better he is likely to fight. So we sang more than we slept, and, in fact, that has been our history ever since.

PHILADELPHIA

At sunrise we were at the station in Philadelphia, and dismissed for an hour. Some hundreds of us made up Broad Street for the Lapierre House to breakfast. When I arrived, I found every place at table filled and every waiter ten deep with orders. So, being an old campaigner, I followed up the stream of provender to the fountain-head, the kitchen. Half a dozen other old campaigners were already there, most hospitably entertained by the cooks. They served us, hot and hot, with the best of their best, straight from the gridiron and the pan. I hope, if I live to breakfast again in the Lapierre House, that I may be allowed to help myself and choose for myself below-stairs.

When we rendezvoused at the train, we found that the orders were for every man to provide himself three days' rations in the neighborhood, and be ready for a start at a moment's notice.

A mountain of bread was already piled up in the station. I stuck my bayonet through a stout loaf, and, with a dozen comrades armed in the same way, went foraging about for other *vivers*.

It is a poor part of Philadelphia; but whatever they had in the shops or the houses seemed to be at our disposition.

I stopped at a corner shop to ask for pork, and was amicably assailed by an earnest dame,—Irish, I am pleased to say. She thrust her last loaf upon me, and sighed that it was not baked that morning for my " honor's service."

A little farther on, two kindly Quaker ladies compelled me to step in. " What could they do?" they asked eagerly. " They had no meat in the house; but could we eat eggs? They had in the house a dozen and a half, new-laid." So the pot to the fire, and the eggs boiled, and bagged by myself and that tall Saxon, my friend E., of the Sixth Company. While the eggs simmered, the two ladies thee-ed us prayerfully and tearfully, hoping that God would save our country from blood, unless blood must be shed to preserve Law and Liberty.

Nothing definite from Baltimore when we returned to the station. We stood by, waiting orders. About noon the Eighth Massachusetts Regiment took the train southward.

Our regiment was ready to a man to try its strength with the Plug Uglies. If there had been any voting on the subject, the plan to follow the straight road to Washington would have been accepted by acclamation. But the higher powers deemed that " the longest way round was the shortest way home," and no doubt their decision was wise. The event proved it.

At two o'clock came the word to " fall in." We handled our howitzers again, and marched down Jefferson Avenue to the steamer " Boston " to embark.

To embark for what port? For Washington, of course, finally; but by what route? That was to remain in doubt to us privates for a day or two.

The " Boston " is a steamer of the outside line from Philadelphia to New York. She just held our legion. We tramped on board, and were allotted about the craft from the top to the bottom story. We took tents, traps, and grub on board, and steamed away down the Delaware in the sweet afternoon of April. If ever the heavens smiled fair weather on any campaign, they have done so on ours.

THE " BOSTON "

Soldiers on shipboard are proverbially fish out of water. We could not be called by the good old nickname of " lobsters " by the crew. Our gray jackets saved the *sobriquet*. But we floundered about the crowded vessel like boiling victims in a pot. At last we found our places, and laid ourselves about the decks to tan or bronze or burn scarlet, according to complexion. There were plenty of cheeks of lobster-hue before next evening on the " Boston."

A thousand young fellows turned loose on shipboard were sure to make themselves merry. Let the reader imagine that! We were like any other excursionists, except that the stacks of bright guns were always present to remind us of our errand, and regular guard-mounting and drill went on all the time. The young citizens growled or laughed at the minor hardships of the hasty outfit, and toughened rapidly to business.

Sunday, the 21st, was a long and somewhat anxious day. While we were bowling along in the sweet sunshine and sweeter moonlight of the halcyon time, Uncle Sam might be dethroned by somebody in buckram, or Baltimore burnt by the boys from Lynn or Marblehead, revenging the massacre of their fellows. Everyone begins to comprehend the fiery eagerness of men who live in historic times. "I wish I had control of chain-lightning for a few minutes," says O., the droll fellow of our company. "I'd make it come thick and heavy and knock spots out of Secession."

At early dawn of Monday, the 22d, after feeling along slowly all night, we see the harbor of Annapolis. A frigate with sails unbent lies at anchor. She flies the stars and stripes. Hurrah!

A large steamboat is aground farther in. As soon as we can see anything, we catch the glitter of bayonets on board.

By and by boats come off, and we get news that the steamer is the "Maryland," a ferry-boat of the Philadelphia and Baltimore Railroad. The Massachusetts Eighth Regiment had been just in time to seize her on the north side of the Chesapeake. They learned that she was to be carried off by the crew and leave them blockaded. So they shot their Zouaves ahead as skirmishers. The fine fellows rattled on board, and before the steamboat had time to take a turn or open a valve, she was held by Massachusetts in trust for Uncle Sam. Hurrah for the most important prize thus far in the war! It probably saved the "Constitution," "Old Ironsides," from capture by the traitors. It probably

OUR MARCH TO WASHINGTON 247

saved Annapolis, and kept Maryland open without bloodshed.

As soon as the Massachusetts Regiment had made prize of the ferry-boat, a call was made for engineers to run her. Some twenty men at once stepped to the front. We of the New York Seventh afterwards concluded that whatever was needed in the way of skill or handicraft could be found among those brother Yankees. They were the men to make armies of. They could tailor for themselves, shoe themselves, do their own blacksmithing, gun-smithing, and all other work that calls for sturdy arms and nimble fingers. In fact, I have such profound confidence in the universal accomplishment of the Massachusetts Eighth, that I have no doubt, if the order were, " Poets to the front!" " Painters present arms!" " Sculptors charge bayonets!" a baker's dozen out of every company would respond.

Well, to go on with their story,—when they had taken their prize, they drove her straight downstream to Annapolis, the nearest point to Washington. There they found the Naval Academy in danger of attack, and " Old Ironsides "—serving as a practice-ship for the future midshipmen—also exposed. The call was now for seamen to man the old craft and save her from a worse enemy than her prototype met in the " Guerrière." Seamen? Of course! They were Marbleheaded men, Gloucester men, Beverly men, seamen all, *par excellence!* They clapped on the frigate to aid the middies, and by and by started her out into the stream. In doing this their own pilot took the chance to run them purposely on a shoal in the intricate channel. A great error of judgment on his part! as he perceived, when he found himself in irons and in confinement. " The days of trifling with traitors are over! " think the Eighth Regiment of Massachusetts.

But there they were, hard and fast on the shoal, when

we came up. Nothing to nibble on but knobs of anthracite. Nothing to sleep on softer or cleaner than coal-dust. Nothing to drink but the brackish water under their keel. "Rather rough!" so they afterward patiently told us.

Meantime the "Constitution" had got hold of a tug, and was making her way to an anchorage where her guns commanded everything and everybody. Good and true men chuckled greatly over this. The stars and stripes also were still up at the fort at the Naval Academy.

Our dread, that, while we were off at sea, some great and perhaps fatal harm had been suffered, was greatly lightened by these good omens. If Annapolis was safe, why not Washington safe also? If treachery had got head at the capital, would not treachery have reached out its hand and snatched this doorway? These were our speculations as we began to discern objects, before we heard news.

But news came presently. Boats pulled off to us. Our officers were put into communication with the shore. The scanty facts of our position became known from man to man. We privates have greatly the advantage in battling with the doubt of such a time. We know that we have nothing to do with rumors. Orders are what we go by. And orders are Facts.

We lay a long, lingering day, off Annapolis. The air was full of doubt, and we were eager to be let loose. All this while the "Maryland" stuck fast on the bar. We could see them, half a mile off, making every effort to lighten her. The soldiers tramped forward and aft, danced on her decks, shot overboard a heavy baggage-truck. We saw them start the truck for the stern with a cheer. It crashed down. One end stuck in the mud. The other fell back and rested on the boat. They went at it with axes, and presently it was clear.

As the tide rose, we gave our grounded friends a lift

with the hawser. No go! The "Boston" tugged in vain. We got near enough to see the whites of the Massachusetts eyes, and their unlucky faces and uniforms all grimy with their lodgings in the coal-dust. They could not have been blacker, if they had been breathing battle-smoke and dust all day. That experience was clear gain to them.

By and by, greatly to the delight of the impatient Seventh, the "Boston" was headed for shore. Never speak ill of the beast you bestraddle! Therefore *requiescat* "Boston"! may her ribs lie light on soft sand when she goes to pieces! may her engines be cut up into bracelets for the arms of the patriotic fair! good by to her, dear old, close, dirty, slow coach! She served her country well in a moment of trial. Who knows but she saved it? It was a race to see who should first get to Washington,—and we and the Virginia mob, in alliance with the District mob, were perhaps nip and tuck for the goal.

ANNAPOLIS

So the Seventh Regiment landed and took Annapolis. We were the first troops ashore.

The middies of the Naval Academy no doubt believe that they had their quarters secure. The Massachusetts boys are satisfied that they first took the town in charge. And so they did.

But the Seventh took it a little more. Not, of course, from its loyal men, but *for* its loyal men,—for loyal Maryland, and for the Union.

Has anybody seen Annapolis? It is a picturesque old place, sleepy enough, and astonished to find itself wide-awaked by a war, and obliged to take responsibility and share for good and ill in the movement of its time. The buildings of the Naval Academy stand parallel with the river Severn, with a green plateau toward the water and a lovely green lawn toward the town. All the scene was fresh and fair with April, and I fancied, as the " Boston " touched the wharf, that I discerned the sweet fragrance of apple-blossoms coming with the spring-time airs.

I hope that the companies of the Seventh, should the day arrive, will charge upon horrid batteries or serried ranks with as much alacrity as they marched ashore on the greensward of the Naval Academy. We disembarked, and were halted in line between the buildings and the river.

Presently, while we stood at ease, people began to arrive, —some with smallish fruit to sell, some with smaller news to give. Nobody knew whether Washington was taken. Nobody knew whether Jeff Davis was now spitting in the Presidential spittoon, and scribbling his distiches with the nib of the Presidential goose-quill. We were absolutely in doubt whether a seemingly inoffensive knot of rustics, on a mound without the inclosures, might not, at tap of drum, unmask a battery of giant columbiads, and belch blazes at us, raking our line.

Nothing so entertaining happened. It was a parade, not a battle. At sunset our band played strains sweet enough to pacify all Secession, if Secession had music in its soul. Coffee, hot from the coppers of the Naval School, and biscuit were served out to us; and while we supped, we talked with our visitors, such as were allowed to approach.

First the boys of the School—fine little blue-jackets—had their story to tell.

"Do you see that white farm-house, across the river?" says a brave pigmy of a chap in navy uniform. "That is head-quarters for Secession. They were going to take the School from us, Sir, and the frigate; but we've got ahead of 'em, now you and the Massachusetts boys have come down,"—and he twinkled all over with delight. "We can't study any more. We are on guard all the time. We've got

OUR MARCH TO WASHINGTON

howitzers, too, and we'd like you to see, to-morrow, on drill, how we can handle 'em. One of their boats came by our sentry last night," (a sentry probably five feet high), " and he blazed away, Sir. So they thought they wouldn't try us that time."

It was plain that these young souls had been well tried by the treachery about them. They, too, had felt the pang of the disloyalty of comrades. Nearly a hundred of the boys had been spoilt by the base example of their elders in the repudiating States, and had resigned.

After the middies, came anxious citizens from the town. Scared, all of them. Now that we were come and assured them that persons and property were to be protected, they ventured to speak of the disgusting tyranny to which they, American citizens, had been subjected. We came into contact here with utter social anarchy. No man, unless he was ready to risk assault, loss of property, exile, dared to act or talk like a freeman. " This great wrong must be righted," think the Seventh Regiment, as one man. So we tried to reassure the Annapolitans that we meant to do our duty as the nation's armed police, and mob-law was to be put down, so far as we could do it.

Here, too, voices of war met us. The country was stirred up. If the rural population did not give us a bastard imitation of Lexington and Concord, as we tried to gain Washington, all Pluguglydom would treat us *à la* Plugugly somewhere near the junction of the Annapolis and Baltimore and Washington Railroad. The Seventh must be ready to shoot.

At dusk we were marched up to the Academy and quartered about in the buildings,—some in the fort, some in the recitation-halls. We lay down on our blankets and knapsacks. Up to this time our sleep and diet had been severely scanty.

We stayed all next day at Annapolis. The "Boston" brought the Massachusetts Eighth ashore that night. Poor fellows! what a figure they cut, when we found them bivouacked on the Academy grounds next morning! To begin: They had come off in hot patriotic haste, half-uniformed and half-outfitted. Finding that Baltimore had been taken by its own loafers and traitors, and that the Chesapeake ferry was impracticable, had obliged them to change line of march. They were out of grub. They were parched dry for want of water on the ferry-boat. Nobody could decipher Caucasian, much less Bunker-Hill Yankee, in their grimy visages.

But, hungry, thirsty, grimy, these fellows were GRIT.

Massachusetts ought to be proud of such hardy, cheerful, faithful sons.

We of the Seventh are proud, for our part, that it was our privilege to share our rations with them, and to begin a fraternization which grows closer every day and will be *historical*.

But I must make a shorter story. We drilled and were reviewed that morning on the Academy parade. In the afternoon the Naval School paraded their last before they gave up their barracks to the coming soldiery. So ended the 23d of April.

Midnight, 24th. We were rattled up by an alarm,— perhaps a sham one, to keep us awake and lively. In a moment, the whole regiment was in order of battle in the moonlight on the parade. It was a most brilliant spectacle, as company after company rushed forward, with rifles glittering, to take their places in the array.

After this pretty spirt, we were rationed with pork, beef, and bread for three days, and ordered to be ready to march on the instant.

WHAT THE MASSACHUSETTS EIGHTH HAD BEEN DOING

MEANTIME General Butler's command, the Massachusetts Eighth, had been busy knocking disorder in the head.

Presently after their landing, and before they were refreshed, they pushed companies out to occupy the railroad-track beyond the town.

They found it torn up. No doubt the scamps who did the shabby job fancied that there would be no more travel that way until strawberry-time. They fancied the Yankees would sit down on the fences and begin to whittle white-oak toothpicks, darning the rebels, through their noses, meanwhile.

I know these men of the Eighth can whittle, and I presume they can say "Darn it," if occasion requires; but just now track-laying was the business on hand.

"Wanted, experienced track-layers!" was the word along the files.

All at once the line of the road became densely populated with experienced track-layers, fresh from Massachusetts.

Presto change! the rails were relaid, spiked, and the roadway leveled and better ballasted than any road I ever saw south of Mason and Dixon's line.

"We must leave a good job for these folks to model after," say the Massachusetts Eighth.

A track without a train is as useless as a gun without a man. Train and engine must be had. "Uncle Sam's mails and troops cannot be stopped another minute," our energetic friends conclude. So,—the railroad company's people being either frightened or false,—in marches Massachusetts to the station. "We, the People of the United States, want rolling-stock for the use of the Union," they said, or words to that effect.

The engine—a frowsy machine at the best—had been purposely disabled.

Here appeared the *deus ex machina,* Charles Homans, Beverly Light Guard, Company E, Eighth Massachusetts Regiment.

That is the man, name and titles in full, and he deserves well of his country.

He took a quiet squint at the engine,—it was as helpless as a boned turkey,—and he found "Charles Homans, his mark," written all over it.

The old rattletrap was an old friend. Charles Homans had had a share in building it. The machine and the man said, "How d'y' do?" at once. Homans called for a gang of engine-builders. Of course they swarmed out of the ranks. They passed their hands over the locomotive a few times, and presently it was ready to whistle and wheeze and rumble and gallop, as if no traitor had ever tried to steal the go and the music out of it.

This had all been done during the afternoon of the 23d. During the night, the renovated engine was kept cruising up and down the track to see all clear. Guards of the Eighth were also posted to protect passage.

Our commander had, I presume, been co-operating with General Butler in this business. The Naval Academy authorities had given us every despatch and assistance, and the middies, frank, personal hospitality. The day was halcyon, the grass was green and soft, the apple-trees were just in blossom: it was a day to be remembered.

Many of us will remember it, and show the marks of it for months, as the day we had our heads cropped. By evening there was hardly one poll in the Seventh tenable by anybody's grip. Most sat in the shade and were shorn by a barber. A few were honored with a clip by the artist hand of the *petit caporal* of our Engineer Company.

Our March to Washington

While I rattle off these trifling details, let me not fail to call attention to the grave service done by our regiment, by its arrival, at the nick of time, at Annapolis. No clearer special Providence could have happened. The country-people of the traitor sort were aroused. Baltimore and its mob were but two hours away. The "Constitution" had been hauled out of reach of a rush by the Massachusetts men,—first on the ground,—but was half manned and not fully secure. And there lay the "Maryland," helpless on the shoal, with six or seven hundred souls on board, so near the shore that the late Captain Rynders's gun could have sunk her from some ambush.

Yes! the Seventh Regiment at Annapolis was the Right Man in the Right Place!

OUR MORNING MARCH

REVEILLE. As nobody pronounces this word *à la française,* as everybody calls it "Revelee," why not drop it, as an affectation, and translate it the "Stir your Stumps," the "Peel your Eyes," the "Tumble Up," or literally the "Wake"?

Our snorers had kept up this call so lustily since midnight, that, when the drums sounded it, we were all ready.

The Sixth and Second Companies, under Captain Nevers, are detached to lead the van. I see my brother Billy march off with the Sixth, into the dusk, half moonlight, half dawn, and hope that no beggar of a Secessionist will get a pat shot at him, by the roadside, without his getting a chance to let fly in return. Such little possibilities intensify the earnest detestation we feel for the treasons we come to resist and to punish. There will be some bitter work done, if we ever get to blows in this war,—this needless, reckless, brutal assault upon the mildest of all governments.

Before the main body of the regiment marches, we learn that the "Baltic" and other transports came in last night with troops from New York and New England, enough to hold Annapolis against a square league of Plug Uglies. We do not go on without having our rear protected and our communications open. It is strange to be compelled to think of these things in peaceful America. But we really knew little more of the country before us than Cortés knew of Mexico. I have since learned from a high official, that thirteen different messengers were dispatched from Washington in the interval of anxiety while the Seventh was not forthcoming, and only one got through.

At half-past seven we take up our line of march, pass out of the charming grounds of the Academy, and move through the quiet, rusty, picturesque old town. It has a romantic dullness,—Annapolis,—which deserves a parting compliment.

Although we deem ourselves a fine-looking set, although our belts are blanched with pipe-clay and our rifles shine sharp in the sun, yet the townspeople stare at us in a dismal silence. They have already the air of men quelled by a despotism. None can trust his neighbor. If he dares to be loyal, he must take his life into his hands. Most would be loyal, if they dared. But the system of society which has ended in this present chaos had gradually eliminated the bravest and best men. They have gone in search of Freedom and Prosperity; and now the bullies cow the weaker brothers. "There must be an end of this mean tyranny," think the Seventh, as they march through old Annapolis and see how sick the town is with doubt and alarm.

Outside the town, we strike the railroad and move along, the howitzers in front, bouncing over the sleepers. When our line is fully disengaged from the town, we halt.

OUR MARCH TO WASHINGTON 257

Here the scene is beautiful. The van rests upon a high embankment, with a pool surrounded by pine-trees on the right, green fields on the left. Cattle are feeding quietly about. The air sings with birds. The chestnut-leaves sparkle. Frogs whistle in the warm spring morning. The regiment groups itself along the bank and the cutting. Several Marylanders of the half-price age—under twelve—come gaping up to see us harmless invaders. Each of these young gentry is armed with a dead spring frog, perhaps by way of tribute. And here—hollo! here comes Horace Greeley *in propria persona!* He marches through our groups with the Greeley walk, the Greeley hat on the back of his head, the Greeley white coat on his shoulders, his trousers much too short, and an absorbed, abstracted demeanor. Can it be Horace, reporting for himself? No; this is a Maryland production, and a little disposed to be sulky.

After a few minutes' halt, we hear the whistle of the engine. This machine is also an historic character in the war.

Remember it! "J. H. Nicholson" is its name. Charles Holmes drives, and on either side stands a sentry with fixed bayonet. New spectacles for America! But it is grand to know that the bayonets are to protect, not to assail, Liberty and Law.

The train leads off. We follow, by the track. Presently the train returns. We pass it and trudge on in light marching order, carrying arms, blankets, haversacks, and canteens. Our knapsacks are upon the train.

Fortunate for our backs that they do not have to bear any more burden! For the day grows sultry. It is one of those breezeless baking days which brew thunder-gusts. We march for some four miles, when, coming upon the guards of the Massachusetts Eighth, our howitzer is ordered to fall out and wait for the train. With a comrade of the Artillery, I am placed on guard over it.

ON GUARD WITH HOWITZER NO. TWO

Henry Bonnell is my fellow-sentry. He, like myself, is an old campaigner in such campaigns as our generation has known. So we talk California, Oregon, Indian life, the Plains, keeping our eyes peeled meanwhile, and ranging the country. Men that will tear up track are quite capable of picking off a sentry. A giant chestnut gives us little dots of shade from its pigmy leaves. The country about us is open and newly plowed. Some of the worm-fences are new, and ten rails high; but the farming is careless, and the soil thin.

Two of the Massachusetts men come back to the gun while we are standing there. One is my friend Stephen Morris, of Marblehead, Sutton Light Infantry. I had shared my breakfast yesterday with Stephe. So we re-fraternize.

His business is,—" I make shoes in winter and fishin' in summer." He gives me a few facts,—suspicious persons seen about the track, men on horseback in the distance. One of the Massachusetts guard last night challenged his captain. Captain replied, " Officer of the night." Whereupon, says Stephe, " the recruit let squizzle and jest missed his ear." He then related to me the incident of the railroad station. " The first thing they know'd," says he, " we bit right into the depot and took charge." " I don't mind," Stephe remarked,—" I don't mind life, nor yit death; but whenever I see a Massachusetts boy, I stick by him, and if them Secessionists attackt us to-night, or any other time, they'll get in debt."

Whistle, again! and the train appears. We are ordered

to ship our howitzer on a platform car. The engine pushes us on. This train brings our light baggage and the rear guard.

A hundred yards farther on is a delicious fresh spring below the bank. While the train halts, Stephe Morris rushes down to fill my canteen. "This a'n't like Marblehead," says Stephe, panting up; "but a man that can shin up *them* rocks can git right over *this* sand."

The train goes slowly on, as a rickety train should. At intervals we see the fresh spots of track just laid by our Yankee friends. Near the sixth mile, we began to overtake hot and uncomfortable squads of our fellows. The unseasonable heat of this most breathless day was too much for many of the younger men, unaccustomed to rough work, and weakened by want of sleep and irregular food in our hurried movements thus far.

Charles Homans's private carriage was, however, ready to pick up tired men, hot men, thirsty men, men with corns, or men with blisters. They tumbled into the train in considerable numbers.

An enemy that dared could have made a moderate bag of stragglers at this time. But they would not have been allowed to straggle, if any enemy had been about. By this time we were convinced that no attack was to be expected in this part of the way.

The main body of the regiment, under Major Shaler, a tall, soldierly fellow, with a mustache of the fighting color, tramped on their own pins to the watering-place, eight miles or so from Annapolis. There troops and train came to a halt, with the news that a bridge over a country road was broken a mile farther on.

It had been distinctly insisted upon, in the usual Southern style, that we were not to be allowed to pass through Maryland, and that we were to be " welcomed to hospitable graves." The broken bridge was a capital spot for a skirmish. Why not look for it here?

We looked; but got nothing. The rascals could skulk about by night, tear up rails, and hide them where they might be found by a man with half an eye, or half destroy a bridge; but there was no shoot in them. They have not faith enough in their cause to risk their lives for it, even behind a tree or from one of these thickets, choice spots for ambush.

So we had no battle there, but a battle of the elements. The volcanic heat of the morning was followed by a furious storm of wind and a smart shower. The regiment wrapped themselves in their blankets and took their wetting with more or less satisfaction. They were receiving samples of all the different little miseries of a campaign.

And here let me say a word to my fellow-volunteers, actual and prospective, in all the armies of all the States:—

A soldier needs, besides his soldierly drill,

I. Good Feet.

II. A good Stomach.

III. And after these, come the good Head and the good Heart.

But Good Feet are distinctly the first thing. Without them you cannot get to your duty. If a comrade, or a horse, or a locomotive, takes you on its back to the field, you are useless there. And when the field is lost, you cannot retire, run away, and save your bacon.

Good shoes and plenty of walking make good feet. A man who pretends to belong to an infantry company ought always to keep himself in training, so that any moment he can march twenty or thirty miles without feeling a pang or raising a blister. Was this the case with even a decimation of the army who rushed to defend Washington? Were you so trained, my comrades of the Seventh?

A captain of a company, who will let his men march with such shoes as I have seen on the feet of some poor fellows in this war, ought to be garroted with shoe-strings, or at least compelled to play Pope and wash the feet of the whole army of the Apostles of Liberty.

If you find a foot-soldier lying beat out by the roadside, desperate as a sea-sick man, five to one his heels are too high, or his soles too narrow or too thin, or his shoe is not made straight on the inside, so the great toe can spread into its place as he treads.

I am an old walker over Alps across the water, and over Cordilleras, Sierras, Deserts and Prairies at home; I have done my near sixty miles a day without discomfort,—and speaking from large experience, and with painful recollections of the suffering and death I have known for want of good feet on the march, I say to every volunteer:—

Trust in God; BUT KEEP YOUR SHOES EASY!

THE BRIDGE

When the frenzy of the brief tempest was over, it began to be a question, "What to do about the broken bridge?" The gap was narrow; but even Charles Homans could not promise to leap the "J. H. Nicholson" over it. Who was to be our Julius Cæsar in bridge-building? Who but Sergeant Scott, Armorer of the Regiment, with my fellow-sentry of the morning, Bonnell, as First Assistant?

Scott called for a working party. There were plenty of handy fellows among our Engineers and in the Line. Tools were plenty in the Engineers' chest. We pushed the platform car upon which howitzer No. 1 was mounted down to the gap, and began operations.

"I wish," says the *petit caporal* of the Engineer Company, patting his howitzer gently on the back, "that I could get this Putty Blower pointed at the enemy, while you fellows are bridge-building."

The inefficient destructives of Maryland had only half spoilt the bridge. Some of the old timbers could be used,—and for new ones, there was the forest.

Scott and his party made a good and a quick job of it. Our friends of the Massachusetts Eighth had now come up. They lent a ready hand, as usual. The sun set brilliantly. By twilight there was a practicable bridge. The engine was dispatched back to keep the road open. The two platform cars, freighted with our howitzers, were rigged with the gun-ropes for dragging along the rail. We passed through the files of the Massachusetts men, resting by the way, and eating by the fires of the evening the suppers we had in great part provided them; and so begins our night-march.

THE NIGHT-MARCH

O GOTTSCHALK! what a poetic *Marche de Nuit* we then began to play, with our heels and toes, on the railroad track!

It was full-moonlight and the night inexpressibly sweet and serene. The air was cool and vivified by the gust and shower of the afternoon. Fresh spring was in every breath. Our fellows had forgotten that this morning they were hot and disgusted. Everyone hugged his rifle as if it were the arm of the Girl of his Heart, and stepped out gayly for the promenade. Tired or foot-sore men, or even lazy ones, could mount upon the two freight-cars we were using for artillery-wagons. There were stout arms enough to tow the whole.

The scouts went ahead under First Lieutenant Farnham of the Second Company. We were at school together,—I am afraid to say how many years ago. He is just the same

Our March to Washington

cool, dry, shrewd fellow he was as a boy, and a most efficient officer.

It was an original kind of march. I suppose a battery of howitzers never before found itself mounted upon cars, ready to open fire at once and bang away into the offing with shrapnel or into the bushes with canister. Our line extended a half-mile along the track. It was beautiful to stand on the bank above a cutting, and watch the files strike from the shadow of a wood into a broad flame of moonlight, every rifle sparkling up alert as it came forward. A beautiful sight to see the barrels writing themselves upon the dimness, each a silver flash.

By and by, "Halt!" came, repeated along from the front, company after company. "Halt! a rail gone."

It was found without difficulty. The imbeciles who took it up probably supposed we would not wish to wet our feet by searching for it in the dewy grass of the next field. With incredible doltishness they had also left the chairs and spikes beside the track. Bonnell took hold, and in a few minutes had the rail in place and firm enough to pass the engine. Remember, we were not only hurrying on to succor Washington, but opening the only convenient and practicable route between it and the loyal States.

A little farther on, we came to a village,—a rare sight in this scantily peopled region. Here Sergeant Keeler, of our company, the tallest man in the regiment, and one of the handiest, suggested that we should tear up the rails at a turn-out by the station, and so be prepared for chances. So "Out crowbars!" was the word. We tore up and bagged half a dozen rails, with chairs and spikes complete. Here too, some of the engineers found a keg of spikes. This was also bagged and loaded on our cars. We fought the chaps with their own weapons, since they would not meet us with ours.

These things made delay, and by and by there was a long halt, while the Colonel communicated, by orders sounded along the line, with the engine. Homans's drag was hard after us, bringing our knapsacks and traps.

After I had admired for some time the beauty of our moonlit line, and listened to the orders as they grew or died along the distance, I began to want excitement. Bonnell suggested that he and I should scout up the road and see if any rails were wanting. We traveled along into the quiet night.

A mile ahead of the line we suddenly caught the gleam of a rifle-barrel. "Who goes there?" one of our own scouts challenged smartly.

We had arrived at the nick of time. Three rails were up. Two of them were easily found. The third was discovered by beating the bush thoroughly. Bonnell and I ran back for tools, and returned at full trot with crowbar and sledge on our shoulders. There were plenty of willing hands to help,—too many, indeed,—and with the aid of a huge Massachusetts man we soon had the rail in place.

From this time on we were constantly interrupted. Not a half-mile passed without a rail up. Bonnell was always at the front laying track, and I am proud to say that he accepted me as aide-de-camp. Other fellows, unknown to me in the dark, gave hearty help. The Seventh showed that it could do something else than drill.

At one spot, on a high embankment over standing water, the rail was gone, sunk probably. Here we tried our rails brought from the turn-out. They were too short. We supplemented with a length of plank from our stores. We rolled our cars carefully over. They passed safe. But Homans shook his head. He could not venture a locomotive on that frail stuff. So we lost the society of the "J. H. Nicholson." Next day the Massachusetts commander called for someone to dive in the pool for the lost rail. Plump into the water went a little wiry chap and grappled the rail. "When I come up," says the brave fellow afterwards to me, "our officer out with a twenty-dollar gold-piece and wanted me to take it. 'That a'n't what I come for,' says I. 'Take it,' says he, 'and share with the others.' 'That a'n't what they come for,' says I. But I took a big cold," the diver continued, "and I'm condemned hoarse yit,"—which was the fact.

Farther on we found a whole length of track torn up, on both sides, sleepers and all, and the same thing repeated with alternations of breaks of single rails. Our howitzer-ropes came into play to hoist and haul. We were not going to be stopped.

But it was becoming a *Noche Triste* to some of our comrades. We had now marched some sixteen miles. The distance was trifling. But the men had been on their legs pretty much all day and night. Hardly anyone had had any full or substantial sleep or meal since we started from New York. They napped off, standing, leaning on their guns, dropping down in their tracks on the wet ground, at every halt. They were sleepy, but plucky. As we passed through deep cuttings, places, as it were, built for defense, there was a general desire that the tedium of the night should be relieved by a shindy.

During the whole night I saw our officers moving about the line, doing their duty vigorously, despite exhaustion, hunger and sleeplessness.

About midnight our friends of the Eighth had joined us, and our whole little army struggled on together. I find that I have been rather understating the troubles of the march. It seems impossible that such difficulty could be encountered within twenty miles of the capital of our nation. But we were making a rush to put ourselves in that capital, and we could not proceed in the slow, systematic way of an advancing army. We must take the risk and stand the suffering, whatever it was. So the Seventh Regiment went through its bloodless *Noche Triste*.

MORNING

At last we issued from the damp woods, two miles below the railroad junction. Here was an extensive farm. Our vanguard had halted and borrowed a few rails to make fires. These were, of course, carefully paid for at their proprietor's own price. The fires were bright in the gray dawn. About them the whole regiment was now halted. The men tumbled down to catch forty winks. Some, who were hungrier for food than sleep, went off foraging among the farm-houses. They returned with appetizing legends of hot breakfast in hospitable abodes, or scanty fare given grudgingly in hostile ones. All meals, however, were paid for.

Here, as at other halts below, the country-people came up to talk to us. The traitors could easily be distinguished by their insolence disguised as obsequiousness. The loyal men were still timid, but more hopeful at last. All were very lavish with the monosyllable, Sir. It was an odd coincidence, that the vanguard, halting off at a farm in the morning, found it deserted for the moment by its tenants, and protected only by an engraved portrait of our (former) Colonel Duryea, serenely smiling over the mantel-piece.

From this point, the railroad was pretty much all gone. But we were warmed and refreshed by a nap and a bite, and besides had daylight and open country.

We put our guns on their own wheels, all dropped into ranks as if on parade, and marched the last two miles to the station. We still had no certain information. Until we actually saw the train awaiting us, and the Washington companies, who had come down to escort us, drawn up, we did not know whether our Uncle Sam was still a resident of the capital.

We packed into the train, and rolled away to Washington.

WASHINGTON

We marched up to the White House, showed ourselves to the President, made our bow to him as our host, and then marched up to the Capitol, our grand lodgings.

There we are now, quartered in the Representatives' Chamber.

And here I must hastily end this first sketch of the Great Defense. May it continue to be as firm and faithful as it is this day!

I have scribbled my story with a thousand men stirring about me. If any of my sentences miss their aim, accuse my comrades and the bewilderment of this martial crowd. For here are four or five thousand others on the same business as ourselves, and drums are beating, guns are clanking, companies are tramping, all the while. Our friends of the Eighth Massachusetts are quartered under the dome, and cheer us whenever we pass.

Desks marked John Covode, John Cochran, and Anson Burlingame have allowed me to use them as I wrote.

CALVIN

A STUDY OF CHARACTER

Charles Dudley Warner

Calvin is dead. His life, long to him, but short for the rest of us, was not marked by startling adventures, but his character was so uncommon and his qualities were so worthy of imitation, that I have been asked by those who personally knew him to set down my recollections of his career.

His origin and ancestry were shrouded in mystery; even his age was a matter of pure conjecture. Although he was of the Maltese race, I have reason to suppose that he was American by birth as he certainly was in sympathy. Calvin was given to me eight years ago by Mrs. Stowe, but she knew nothing of his age or origin. He walked into her house one day out of the great unknown and became at once at home, as if he had been always a friend of the family. He appeared to have artistic and literary tastes, and it was as if he had inquired at the door if that was the residence of the author of *Uncle Tom's Cabin*, and, upon being assured that it was, had decided to dwell there. This is, of course, fanciful, for his antecedents were wholly unknown, but in his time he could hardly have been in any household where he would not have heard *Uncle Tom's Cabin* talked about. When he came to Mrs. Stowe, he was as large as he ever was, and apparently as old as he ever became. Yet there was in him no appearance of age; he was in the happy maturity of all his powers, and you would rather have said that in that maturity he had found the secret of perpetual youth. And it was as difficult to believe that he would ever be aged as it was to imagine that he had ever been in immature youth. There was in him a mysterious perpetuity.

After some years, when Mrs. Stowe made her winter home in Florida, Calvin came to live with us. From the first moment, he fell into the ways of the house and assumed a recognized position in the family,—I say recognized, because after he became known he was always inquired for by visitors, and in the letters to the other members of the family he always received a message. Although the least obtrusive of beings, his individuality always made itself felt.

His personal appearance had much to do with this, for he was of royal mould, and had an air of high breeding. He was large, but he had nothing of the fat grossness of the celebrated Angora family; though powerful, he was exquisitely proportioned, and as graceful in every movement as a young leopard. When he stood up to open a door—he opened all the doors with old-fashioned latches—he was portentously tall, and when stretched on the rug before the fire he seemed too long for this world—as indeed he was. His coat was the finest and softest I have ever seen, a shade of quiet Maltese; and from his throat downward, underneath, to the white tips of his feet, he wore the whitest and most delicate ermine; and no person was ever more fastidiously neat. In his finely formed head you saw something of his aristocratic character; the ears were small and cleanly cut, there was a tinge of pink in the nostrils, his face was handsome, and the expression of his countenance exceedingly intelligent—I should call it even a sweet expression if the term were not inconsistent with his look of alertness and sagacity.

It is difficult to convey a just idea of his gayety in connection with his dignity and gravity, which his name expressed. As we know nothing of his family, of course it will be understood that Calvin was his Christian name. He had times of relaxation into utter playfulness, delighting in a ball of yarn, catching sportively at stray ribbons when his mistress was at her toilet, and pursuing his own tail, with hilarity, for lack of anything better. He could amuse himself by the hour, and he did not care for children; perhaps something in his past was present to his memory. He had absolutely no bad habits, and his disposition was perfect. I never saw him exactly angry, though I have seen his tail grow to an enormous size when a strange cat appeared upon his lawn. He disliked cats, evidently regarding them as feline and treacherous, and he had no association with them. Occasionally there would be heard a night concert in the shrubbery. Calvin would ask to have the door opened, and then you would hear a rush and a "pestzt," and the concert would explode, and Calvin would quietly come in and resume his seat on the hearth. There was no trace of anger in his manner, but he wouldn't have any of that about the house. He had the rare virtue of magnanimity. Although he had fixed notions about his own rights, and extraordinary persistency in getting them, he never showed temper at a repulse; he simply and firmly persisted till he had what he wanted. His diet was one point; his idea was that of the scholars about dictionaries,—to " get the best." He knew as well as anyone what was in the house, and would refuse beef if turkey was to be had; and if there were oysters, he would wait over the turkey to see if the oysters would not be forthcoming. And yet he was not a gross gourmand; he would eat bread if he saw me eating it, and thought he was not being imposed on. His habits of feeding, also, were refined; he never used a knife, and he would put up his hand and draw the fork down to his mouth as gracefully as a grown person. Unless necessity compelled, he would not eat in the kitchen, but insisted upon his meals in the dining-room, and would wait patiently, unless a stranger were present; and then he was sure to importune the visitor, hoping that the latter was ignorant of the rule of the house, and would give him something. They used to say that he preferred as his table-cloth on the floor a certain well-known church journal; but this was said by an Episcopalian. So far as I know, he had no religious prejudices, except that he did not like the association with Romanists. He tolerated the servants, because they belonged to the house, and would sometimes linger by the kitchen stove; but the moment visitors came in he arose, opened the door, and marched into the drawing-room. Yet he enjoyed the company of his equals, and never withdrew, no matter how many callers—whom he recognized as of his society—might come into the drawing-room. Calvin was fond of company, but he wanted to choose it; and I have no doubt that his was an aristocratic fastidiousness rather than one of faith. It is so with most people.

The intelligence of Calvin was something phenomenal, in his rank of life. He established a method of communicating his wants, and even some of his sentiments; and he could help himself in many things. There was a furnace register in a retired room, where he used to go when he wished to be alone, that he always opened when he desired more heat; but never shut it, any more than he shut the door after himself. He could do almost everything but speak; and you would declare sometimes that you could see a pathetic longing to do that in his intelligent face. I have no desire to overdraw his qualities, but if there was one thing in him more noticeable than another, it was his fondness for nature. He could content himself for hours at a low window, looking into the ravine and at the great trees, noting the smallest stir there; he delighted, above all things, to accompany me walking about the garden, hearing the birds, getting the smell of the fresh earth, and rejoicing in the sunshine. He followed me and gamboled like a dog, rolling over on the turf and exhibiting his delight in a hundred ways. If I worked, he sat and watched me, or looked off over the bank, and kept his ear open to the twitter in the cherry-trees. When it stormed, he was sure to sit at the window, keenly watching the rain or the snow, glancing up and down at its falling; and a winter tempest always delighted him. I think he was genuinely fond of birds, but, so far as I know, he usually confined himself to one a day; he never killed, as some sportsmen do, for the sake of killing, but only as civilized people do,—from necessity. He was intimate with the flying-squirrels who dwell in the chestnut-trees,—too intimate, for almost every day in the summer he would bring in one, until he nearly discouraged them. He was, indeed, a superb hunter, and would have been a devastating one, if his bump of destructiveness had not been offset by a bump of moderation. There was very little of the brutality of the lower animals about him; I don't think he enjoyed rats for themselves, but he knew his business, and for the first few months of his residence with us he waged an awful campaign against the horde, and after that his simple presence was sufficient to deter them from coming on the premises. Mice amused him, but he usually considered them too small game to be taken seriously; I have seen him play for an hour with a mouse, and then let him go with a royal condescension. In this whole matter of "getting a living," Calvin was a great contrast to the rapacity of the age in which he lived.

I hesitate a little to speak of his capacity for friendship

and the affectionateness of his nature, for I know from his own reserve that he would not care to have it much talked about. We understood each other perfectly, but we never made any fuss about it; when I spoke his name and snapped my fingers, he came to me; when I returned home at night, he was pretty sure to be waiting for me near the gate, and would rise and saunter along the walk, as if his being there were purely accidental,—so shy was he commonly of showing feeling; and when I opened the door he never rushed in, like a cat, but loitered, and lounged, as if he had had no intention of going in, but would condescend to. And yet, the fact was, he knew dinner was ready, and he was bound to be there. He kept the run of dinner-time. It happened sometimes, during our absence in the summer, that dinner would be early, and Calvin, walking about the grounds, missed it and came in late. But he never made a mistake the second day. There was one thing he never did,—he never rushed through an open doorway. He never forgot his dignity. If he had asked to have the door opened, and was eager to go out, he always went deliberately; I can see him now, standing on the sill, looking about at the sky as if he was thinking whether it were worth while to take an umbrella, until he was near having his tail shut in.

His friendship was rather constant than demonstrative. When we returned from an absence of nearly two years, Calvin welcomed us with evident pleasure, but showed his satisfaction rather by tranquil happiness than by fuming about. He had the faculty of making us glad to get home. It was his constancy that was so attractive. He liked companionship, but he wouldn't be petted, or fussed over, or sit in anyone's lap a moment; he always extricated himself from such familiarity with dignity and with no show of temper. If there was any petting to be done, however, he chose to do it. Often he would sit looking at me, and then, moved by a delicate affection, come and pull at my coat and sleeve until he could touch my face with his nose, and then go away contented. He had a habit of coming to my study in the morning, sitting quietly by my side or on the table for hours, watching the pen run over the paper, occasionally swinging his tail round for a blotter, and then going to sleep among the papers by the inkstand. Or, more rarely, he would watch the writing from a perch on my shoulder. Writing always interested him, and, until he understood it, he wanted to hold the pen.

He always held himself in a kind of reserve with his friend, as if he had said, "Let us respect our personality, and not make a 'mess' of friendship." He saw, with Emerson, the risk of degrading it to trivial conveniency. "Why insist on rash personal relations with your friend?" "Leave this touching and clawing." Yet I would not give an unfair notion of his aloofness, his fine sense of the sacredness of the me and the not-me. And, at the risk of not being believed, I will relate an incident, which was often repeated. Calvin had the practice of passing a portion of the night in the contemplation of its beauties, and would come into our chamber over the roof of the conservatory through the open window, summer and winter, and go to sleep on the foot of my bed. He would do this always exactly in this way; he never was content to stay in the chamber if we compelled him to go upstairs and through the door. He had the obstinacy of General Grant. But this is by the way. In the morning, he performed his toilet and went down to breakfast with the rest of the family. Now, when the mistress was absent from home, and at no other time, Calvin would come in the morning, when the bell rang, to the head of the bed, put up his feet and look into my face, follow me about when I rose, "assist" at the dressing, and in many purring ways show his fondness, as if he had plainly said, "I know that she has gone away, but I am here." Such was Calvin in rare moments.

He had his limitations. Whatever passion he had for nature, he had no conception of art. There was sent to him once a fine and very expressive cat's head in bronze, by Frémiet. I placed it on the floor. He regarded it intently, approached it cautiously and crouchingly, touched it with his nose, perceived the fraud, turned away abruptly, and never would notice it afterward. On the whole, his life was not only a successful one, but a happy one. He never had but one fear, so far as I know: he had a mortal and a reasonable terror of plumbers. He would never stay in the house when they were here. No coaxing could quiet him. Of course he didn't share our fear about their charges, but he must have had some dreadful experience with them in that portion of his life which is unknown to us. A plumber was to him the devil, and I have no doubt that, in his scheme, plumbers were foreordained to do him mischief.

In speaking of his worth, it has never occurred to me to estimate Calvin by the worldly standard. I know that it is customary now, when anyone dies, to ask how much he was worth, and that no obituary in the newspapers is considered complete without such an estimate. The plumbers in our house were one day overheard to say that, "They say that *she* says that *he* says that he wouldn't take a hundred dollars for him." It is unnecessary to say that I never made such a remark, and that, so far as Calvin was concerned, there was no purchase in money.

As I look back upon it, Calvin's life seems to me a fortunate one, for it was natural and unforced. He ate when he was hungry, slept when he was sleepy, and enjoyed existence to the very tips of his toes and the end of his expressive and slow-moving tail. He delighted to roam about the garden, and stroll among the trees, and to lie on the green grass and luxuriate in all the sweet influences of summer. You could never accuse him of idleness, and yet he knew the secret of repose. The poet who wrote so prettily of him that his little life was rounded with a sleep, understated his felicity; it was rounded with a good many. His conscience never seemed to interfere with his slumbers. In fact, he had good habits and a contented mind. I can see him now walk in at the study door, sit down by my chair, bring his tail artistically about his feet, and look up at me with unspeakable happiness in his handsome face. I often thought that he felt the dumb limitation which denied him the power of language. But since he was denied speech, he scorned the inarticulate mouthings of the lower animals. The vulgar mewing and yowling of the cat species was beneath him; he sometimes uttered a sort of articulate and well-bred ejaculation, when he wished to call attention to something that he considered remarkable, or to some want of his, but he never went whining about. He would sit for hours at a closed window, when he desired to enter, without a murmur, and when it was opened he never admitted that he had been impatient by "bolting" in. Though speech he had not, and the unpleasant kind of utterance given to his race he would not use, he had a mighty power of purr to express his measureless content with congenial society. There was in him a musical organ with stops of varied power and expression, upon which I have no doubt he could have performed Scarlatti's celebrated cat's-fugue.

Whether Calvin died of old age, or was carried off by one of the diseases incident to youth, it is impossible to say; for his departure was as quiet as his advent was mysterious. I only know that he appeared to us in this world in his perfect stature and beauty, and that after a time, like

Lohengrin, he withdrew. In his illness there was nothing more to be regretted than in all his blameless life. I suppose there never was an illness that had more of dignity and sweetness and resignation in it. It came on gradually, in a kind of listlessness and want of appetite. An alarming symptom was his preference for the warmth of a furnace-register to the lively sparkle of the open wood-fire. Whatever pain he suffered, he bore it in silence, and seemed only anxious not to obtrude his malady. We tempted him with the delicacies of the season, but it soon became impossible for him to eat, and for two weeks he ate or drank scarcely anything. Sometimes he made an effort to take something, but it was evident that he made the effort to please us. The neighbors—and I am convinced that the advice of neighbors is never good for anything—suggested catnip. He wouldn't even smell it. We had the attendance of an amateur practitioner of medicine, whose real office was the cure of souls, but nothing touched his case. He took what was offered, but it was with the air of one to whom the time for pellets was passed. He sat or lay day after day almost motionless, never once making a display of those vulgar convulsions or contortions of pain which are so disagreeable to society. His favorite place was on the brightest spot of a Smyrna rug by the conservatory, where the sunlight fell and he could hear the fountain play. If we went to him and exhibited our interest in his condition, he always purred in recognition of our sympathy. And when I spoke his name, he looked up with an expression that said, " I understand it, old fellow, but it's no use." He was to all who came to visit him a model of calmness and patience in affliction.

I was absent from home at the last, but heard by daily postal-card of his failing condition; and never again saw him alive. One sunny morning, he rose from his rug, went into the conservatory (he was very thin then), walked around it deliberately, looking at all the plants he knew, and then went to the bay-window in the dining-room, and stood a long time looking out upon the little field, now brown and sere, and toward the garden, where perhaps the happiest hours of his life had been spent. It was a last look. He turned and walked away, laid himself down upon the bright spot in the rug, and quietly died.

It is not too much to say that a little shock went through the neighborhood when it was known that Calvin was dead, so marked was his individuality; and his friends, one after another, came in to see him. There was no sentimental nonsense about his obsequies; it was felt that any parade would have been distasteful to him. John, who acted as undertaker, prepared a candle-box for him, and I believe assumed a professional decorum; but there may have been the usual levity underneath, for I heard that he remarked in the kitchen that it was the "dryest wake he ever attended." Everybody, however, felt a fondness for Calvin, and regarded him with a certain respect. Between him and Bertha there existed a great friendship, and she apprehended his nature; she used to say that sometimes she was afraid of him, he looked at her so intelligently; she was never certain that he was what he appeared to be.

When I returned, they had laid Calvin on a table in an upper chamber by an open window. It was February. He reposed in a candle-box, lined about the edge with evergreen, and at his head stood a little wine-glass with flowers. He lay with his head tucked down in his arms,—a favorite position of his before the fire,—as if asleep in the comfort of his soft and exquisite fur. It was the involuntary exclamation of those who saw him, "How natural he looks!" As for myself, I said nothing. John buried him under the twin hawthorn-trees,—one white and the other pink,—in a spot where Calvin was fond of lying and listening to the hum of summer insects and the twitter of birds.

Perhaps I have failed to make appear the individuality of character that was so evident to those who knew him. At any rate, I have set down nothing concerning him but the literal truth. He was always a mystery. I did not know whence he came; I do not know whither he has gone. I would not weave one spray of falsehood in the wreath I lay upon his grave.

[From *My Summer in a Garden*, by Charles Dudley Warner. Copyright, 1870, by Fields, Osgood & Co. Copyright, 1898, by Charles Dudley Warner. Copyright, 1912, by Susan Lee Warner.]

FIVE AMERICAN CONTRIBUTIONS TO CIVILIZATION

Charles William Eliot

Looking back over forty centuries of history, we observe that many nations have made characteristic contributions to the progress of civilization, the beneficent effects of which have been permanent, although the races that made them may have lost their national form and organization, or their relative standing among the nations of the earth. Thus, the Hebrew race, during many centuries, made supreme contributions to religious thought; and the Greek, during the brief climax of the race, to speculative philosoophy, architecture, sculpture, and the drama. The Roman people developed military colonization, aqueducts, roads and bridges, and a great body of public law, large parts of which still survive; and the Italians of the middle ages and the Renaissance developed ecclesiastical organization and the fine arts, as tributary to the splendor of the church and to municipal luxury. England, for several centuries, has contributed to the institutional development of representative government and public justice; the Dutch, in the sixteenth century, made a superb struggle for free thought and free government; France, in the eighteenth century, taught the doctrine of individual freedom and the theory of human rights; and Germany, at two periods within the nineteenth century, fifty years apart, proved the vital force of the sentiment of nationality. I ask you to consider with me what characteristic and durable contributions the American people have been making to the progress of civilization.

The first and principal contribution to which I shall ask your attention is the advance made in the United States, not in theory only, but in practice, toward the abandonment of war as the means of settling disputes between nations, the substitution of discussion and arbitration, and the avoidance of armaments. If the intermittent Indian fighting and the brief contest with the Barbary corsairs be disregarded, the United States have had only four years and a quarter of international war in the one hundred and seven years since the adoption of the Constitution. Within the same period the United States have been a party to forty-seven arbitrations—being more than half of all that have taken place in the modern world. The questions settled by these arbitrations have been just such as have commonly caused wars, namely, questions of boundary, fisheries, damage caused by war or civil disturbances, and injuries to commerce. Some of them were of great magnitude, the four made under the treaty of Washington (May 8, 1871) being the most important that have ever taken place. Confident in their strength, and relying on their ability to adjust international differences, the United States have habitually maintained, by voluntary enlistment for short terms, a standing army and a fleet which, in proportion to the population, are insignificant.

The beneficent effects of this American contribution to civilization are of two sorts: in the first place, the direct evils of war and of preparations for war have been diminished; and secondly, the influence of the war spirit on the perennial conflict between the rights of the single personal unit and the powers of the multitude that constitute organized society—or, in other words, between individual freedom and collective authority—has been reduced to the lowest terms. War has been, and still is, the school of collectivism, the warrant of tyranny. Century after century, tribes, clans, and nations have sacrificed the liberty of the individual to the fundamental necessity of being strong for combined defense or attack in war. Individual freedom is crushed in war, for the nature of war is inevitably despotic. It says to the private person: " Obey without a question, even unto death; die in this ditch, without knowing why; walk into that deadly thicket; mount this embankment, behind which are men who will try to kill you, lest you should kill them; make part of an immense machine for blind destruction, cruelty, rapine, and killing." At this moment every young man in Continental Europe learns the lesson of absolute military obedience, and feels himself subject to this crushing power of militant society, against which no rights of the individual to life, liberty, and the pursuit of happiness avail anything. This pernicious influence, inherent in the social organization of all Continental Europe during many centuries, the American people have for generations escaped, and they show other nations how to escape it. I ask your attention to the favorable conditions under which this contribution of the United States to civilization has been made.

There has been a deal of fighting on the American continent during the past three centuries; but it has not been of the sort which most imperils liberty. The first European colonists who occupied portions of the coast of North America encountered in the Indians men of the Stone Age, who ultimately had to be resisted and quelled by force. The Indian races were at a stage of development thousands of years behind that of the Europeans. They could not be assimilated; for the most part they could not be taught or even reasoned with; with a few exceptions they had to be driven away by prolonged fighting, or subdued by force so that they would live peaceably with the whites. This warfare, however, always had in it for the whites a large element of self-defense—the homes and families of the settlers were to be defended against a stealthy and pitiless foe. Constant exposure to the attacks of savages was only one of the formidable dangers and difficulties which for a hundred years the early settlers had to meet, and which developed in them courage, hardiness, and persistence. The French and English wars on the North American continent, always more or less mixed with Indian warfare, were characterized by race hatred and religious animosity—two of the commonest causes of war in all ages; but they did not tend to fasten upon the English colonists any objectionable public authority, or to contract the limits of individual liberty. They furnished a school of martial qualities at small cost to liberty. In the War of Independence there was a distinct hope and purpose to enlarge individual liberty. It made possible a confederation of the colonies, and, ultimately, the adoption of the Constitution of the United States. It gave to the thirteen colonies a lesson in collectivism, but it was a needed lesson on the necessity of combining their forces to resist an oppressive external authority. The war of 1812 is properly called the Second War of Independence, for it was truly a fight for liberty and for the rights of neutrals, in resistance to the impressment of seamen and other oppressions growing out of European conflicts. The civil war of 1861-65 was waged, on the side of the North, primarily, to prevent the dismemberment of the country, and, secondarily and incidentally, to destroy the institution of slavery. On the Northern side it therefore called forth a generous element of popular ardor in defense of free institutions; and though it temporarily caused centralization of great powers in the government, it did as much to promote individual freedom as it did to strengthen public authority.

In all this series of fightings the main motives were self-defense, resistance to oppression, the enlargement of liberty, and the conservation of national acquisitions. The war with Mexico, it is true, was of a wholly different type. That was a war of conquest, and of conquest chiefly in the interest of African slavery. It was also an unjust attack made by a powerful people on a feeble one; but it lasted less than two years, and the number of men engaged in it was at no time large. Moreover, by the treaty which ended the war, the conquering nation agreed to pay the conquered eighteen million dollars in partial compensation for some of the territory wrested from it, instead of demanding a huge war-indemnity, as the European way is. Its results contradicted the anticipations both of those who advocated and of those who opposed it. It was one of the wrongs which prepared the way for the great rebellion; but its direct evils were of moderate extent, and it had no effect on the perennial conflict between individual liberty and public power.

In the meantime, partly as the results of Indian fighting and the Mexican war, but chiefly through purchases and arbitrations, the American people had acquired a territory so extensive, so defended by oceans, gulfs, and great lakes, and so intersected by those great natural highways, navigable rivers, that it would obviously be impossible for any enemy to overrun or subdue it. The civilized nations of Europe, western Asia, and northern Africa have always been liable to hostile incursions from without. Over and over again barbarous hordes have overthrown established civilizations; and at this moment there is not a nation of Europe which does not feel obliged to maintain monstrous armaments for defense against its neighbors. The American people have long been exempt from such terrors, and are now absolutely free from this necessity of keeping in readiness to meet heavy assaults. The absence of a great standing army and of a large fleet has been a main characteristic of the United States, in contrast with the other civilized nations; this has been a great inducement to immigration, and a prime cause of the country's rapid increase in wealth. The United States have no formidable neighbor, except Great Britain in Canada. In April, 1817, by a convention made between Great Britain and the United States, without much public discussion or observation, these two powerful nations agreed that each should keep on the Great Lakes only a few police vessels of insignificant size and armament. This agreement was made but four years after Perry's naval victory on Lake Erie, and only three years after the burning of Washington by a British force. It was one of the first acts of Monroe's first administration, and it would be difficult to find in all history a more judicious or effectual agreement between two powerful neighbors. For eighty years this beneficent convention has helped to keep the peace. The European way would have been to build competitive fleets, dock-yards, and fortresses, all of which would have helped to bring on war during the periods of mutual exasperation which have occurred since 1817. Monroe's second administration was signalized, six years later, by the declaration that the United States would consider any attempt on the part of the Holy Alliance to extend their system to any portion of this hemisphere as dangerous to the peace and safety of the United States. This announcement was designed to prevent the introduction on the American continent of the horrible European system— with its balance of power, its alliances offensive and defensive in opposing groups, and its perpetual armaments on an enormous scale. That a declaration expressly intended to promote peace and prevent armaments should now be perverted into an argument for arming and for a belligerent public policy is an extraordinary perversion of the true American doctrine.

The ordinary causes of war between nation and nation have been lacking in America for the last century and a quarter. How many wars in the world's history have been due to contending dynasties; how many of the most cruel and protracted wars have been due to religious strife; how many to race hatred! No one of these causes of war has been efficacious in America since the French were overcome in Canada by the English in 1759. Looking forward into the future, we find it impossible to imagine circumstances under which any of these common causes of war can take effect on the North American continent. Therefore, the ordinary motives for maintaining armaments in time of peace, and concentrating the powers of government in such a way as to interfere with individual liberty, have not been in play in the United States as among the nations of Europe, and are not likely to be.

Such have been the favorable conditions under which America has made its best contribution to the progress of our race.

There are some people of a perverted sentimentality who occasionally lament the absence in our country of the ordinary inducements to war, on the ground that war develops certain noble qualities in some of the combatants, and gives opportunity for the practice of heroic virtues, such as courage, loyalty, and self-sacrifice. It is further said that prolonged peace makes nations effeminate, luxurious, and materialistic, and substitutes for the high ideals of the patriot soldier the low ideals of the farmer, manufacturer, tradesman, and pleasure-seeker. This view seems to me to err in two opposite ways. In the first place, it forgets that war, in spite of the fact that it develops some splendid virtues, is the most horrible occupation that human beings can possibly engage in. It is cruel, treacherous, and murderous. Defensive warfare, particularly on the part of a weak nation against powerful invaders or oppressors, excites a generous sympathy; but for every heroic defense there must be an attack by a preponderating force, and war, being the conflict of the two, must be judged by its moral effects not on one party, but on both parties. Moreover, the weaker party may have the worse cause. The immediate ill effects of war are bad enough, but its after effects are generally worse, because indefinitely prolonged and indefinitely wasting and damaging. At this moment, thirty-one years after the end of our civil war, there are two great evils afflicting our country which took their rise in that war, namely, (1) the belief of a large proportion of our people in money without intrinsic value, or worth less than its face, and made current solely by act of Congress, and (2) the payment of immense annual sums in pensions. It is the paper-money delusion born of the civil war which generated and supports the silver-money delusion of to-day. As a consequence of the war, the nation has paid $2,000,000,000 in pensions within thirty-three years. So far as pensions are paid to disabled persons, they are a just and inevitable, but unproductive expenditure; so far as they are paid to persons who are not disabled,—men or women, —they are in the main not only unproductive but demoralizing; so far as they promote the marriage of young women to old men, as a pecuniary speculation, they create a grave social evil. It is impossible to compute or even imagine the losses and injuries already inflicted by the fiat-money delusion; and we know that some of the worst evils of the pension system will go on for a hundred years to come, unless the laws about widows' pensions are changed for the better. It is a significant fact that of the existing pensioners of the war of 1812 only twenty-one are surviving soldiers or sailors, while 3826 are widows.[1]

War gratifies, or used to gratify, the combative instinct of mankind, but it gratifies also the love of plunder, destruction, cruel discipline, and arbitrary power. It is doubtful whether fighting with modern appliances will continue to gratify the savage instinct of combat; for it is not likely that in the future two opposing lines of men can ever meet, or any line or column reach an enemy's intrenchments. The machine-gun can only be compared to the scythe, which cuts off every blade of grass within its sweep. It has made cavalry charges impossible, just as the modern ironclad has made impossible the manœuvers of one of Nelson's fleets. On land, the only mode of approach of one line to another must hereafter be by concealment, crawling, or surprise. Naval actions will henceforth be conflicts between opposing machines, guided, to be sure, by men; but it will be the best machine that wins, and not necessarily the most enduring men. War will become a contest between treasuries or war-chests; for now that 10,000 men can fire away a million dollars' worth of ammunition in an hour, no poor nation can long resist a rich one, unless there be some extraordinary difference between the two in mental and moral strength.

The view that war is desirable omits also the consideration that modern social and industrial life affords ample opportunities for the courageous and loyal discharge of duty, apart from the barbarities of warfare. There are many serviceable occupations in civil life which call for all the courage and fidelity of the best soldier, and for more than his independent responsibility, because not pursued in masses or under the immediate command of superiors. Such

[1] June 30, 1895.

occupations are those of the locomotive engineer, the electric lineman, the railroad brakeman, the city fireman, and the policeman. The occupation of the locomotive engineer requires constantly a high degree of skill, alertness, fidelity, and resolution, and at any moment may call for heroic self-forgetfulness. The occupation of a lineman requires all the courage and endurance of a soldier, whose lurking foe is mysterious and invisible. In the two years, 1893 and 1894, there were 34,000 trainmen killed and wounded on the railroads of the United States, and 25,000 other railroad employés besides. I need not enlarge on the dangers of the fireman's occupation, or on the disciplined gallantry with which its risks are habitually incurred. The policeman in large cities needs every virtue of the best soldier, for in the discharge of many of his most important duties he is alone. Even the feminine occupation of the trained nurse illustrates every heroic quality which can possibly be exhibited in war; for she, simply in the way of duty, without the stimulus of excitement or companionship, runs risks from which many a soldier in hot blood would shrink. No one need be anxious about the lack of opportunities in civilized life for the display of heroic qualities. New industries demand new forms of fidelity and self-sacrificing devotion. Every generation develops some new kind of hero. Did it ever occur to you that the " scab " is a creditable type of nineteenth century hero? In defense of his rights as an individual, he deliberately incurs the reprobation of many of his fellows, and runs the immediate risk of bodily injury, or even of death. He also risks his livelihood for the future, and thereby the well-being of his family. He steadily asserts in action his right to work on such conditions as he sees fit to make, and, in so doing, he exhibits remarkable courage, and renders a great service to his fellow-men. He is generally a quiet, unpretending, silent person, who values his personal freedom more than the society and approbation of his mates. Often he is impelled to work by family affection, but this fact does not diminish his heroism. There are file-closers behind the line of battle of the bravest regiment. Another modern personage who needs heroic endurance, and often exhibits it, is the public servant who steadily does his duty against the outcry of a party press bent on perverting his every word and act. Through the telegram, cheap postage, and the daily newspaper, the forces of hasty public opinion can now be concentrated and expressed with a rapidity and intensity unknown to preceding generations. In consequence, the independent thinker or actor, or the public servant, when his thoughts or acts run counter to prevailing popular or party opinions, encounters sudden and intense obloquy, which, to many temperaments, is very formidable. That habit of submitting to the opinion of the majority which democracy fosters renders the storm of detraction and calumny all the more difficult to endure—makes it, indeed, so intolerable to many citizens, that they will conceal or modify their opinions rather than endure it. Yet the very breath of life for a democracy is free discussion, and the taking account, of all opinions honestly held and reasonably expressed. The unreality of the vilification of public men in the modern press is often revealed by the sudden change when an eminent public servant retires or dies. A man for whom no words of derision or condemnation were strong enough yesterday is recognized to-morrow as an honorable and serviceable person, and a credit to his country. Nevertheless, this habit of partizan ridicule and denunciation in the daily reading-matter of millions of people calls for a new kind of courage and toughness in public men, and calls for it, not in brief moments of excitement only, but steadily, year in and year out. Clearly, there is no need of bringing on wars in order to breed heroes. Civilized life affords plenty of opportunities for heroes, and for a better kind than war or any other savagery has ever produced. Moreover, none but lunatics would set a city on fire in order to give opportunities for heroism to firemen, or introduce the cholera or yellow fever to give physicians and nurses opportunity for practicing disinterested devotion, or condemn thousands of people to extreme poverty in order that some well-to-do persons might practice a beautiful charity. It is equally crazy to advocate war on the ground that it is a school for heroes.

Another misleading argument for war needs brief notice. It is said that war is a school of national development—that a nation, when conducting a great war, puts forth prodigious exertions to raise money, supply munitions, enlist troops, and keep them in the field, and often gets a clearer conception and a better control of its own material and moral forces while making these unusual exertions. The nation which means to live in peace necessarily foregoes, it is said, these valuable opportunities of abnormal activity. Naturally, such a nation's abnormal activities devoted to destruction would be diminished; but its normal and abnormal activities devoted to construction and improvement ought to increase.

One great reason for the rapid development of the United States since the adoption of the Constitution is the comparative exemption of the whole people from war, dread of war, and preparations for war. The energies of the people have been directed into other channels. The progress of applied science during the present century, and the new ideals concerning the well-being of human multitudes, have opened great fields for the useful application of national energy. This immense territory of ours, stretching from ocean to ocean, and for the most part but imperfectly developed and sparsely settled, affords a broad field for the beneficent application of the richest national forces during an indefinite period. There is no department of national activity in which we could not advantageously put forth much more force than we now expend; and there are great fields which we have never cultivated at all. As examples, I may mention the post-office, national sanitation, public works, and education. Although great improvements have been made during the past fifty years in the collection and delivery of mail matter, much still remains to be done both in city and country, and particularly in the country. In the mail facilities secured to our people, we are far behind several European governments, whereas we ought to be far in advance of every European government except Switzerland, since the rapid interchange of ideas, and the promotion of family, friendly, and commercial intercourse, are of more importance to a democracy than to any other form of political society. Our national government takes very little pains about the sanitation of the country, or its deliverance from injurious insects and parasites; yet these are matters of gravest interest, with which only the general government can deal, because action by separate States or cities is necessarily ineffectual. To fight pestilences needs quite as much energy, skill, and courage as to carry on war; indeed, the foes are more insidious and awful, and the means of resistance less obvious. On the average and the large scale, the professions which heal and prevent disease, and mitigate suffering, call for much more ability, constancy, and devotion than the professions which inflict wounds and death and all sorts of human misery. Our government has never touched the important subject of national roads, by which I mean not railroads, but common highways; yet here is a great subject for beneficent action through government, in which we need only go for our

FIVE AMERICAN CONTRIBUTIONS TO CIVILIZATION 293

lessons to little republican Switzerland. Inundations and droughts are great enemies of the human race, against which government ought to create defenses, because private enterprise cannot cope with such wide-spreading evils. Popular education is another great field in which public activity should be indefinitely enlarged, not so much through the action of the Federal government,—though even there a much more effective supervision should be provided than now exists,—but through the action of States, cities, and towns. We have hardly begun to apprehend the fundamental necessity and infinite value of public education, or to appreciate the immense advantages to be derived from additional expenditure for it. What prodigious possibilities of improvement are suggested by the single statement that the average annual expenditure for the schooling of a child in the United States is only about eighteen dollars! Here is a cause which requires from hundreds of thousands of men and women keen intelligence, hearty devotion to duty, and a steady uplifting and advancement of all its standards and ideals. The system of public instruction should embody for coming generations all the virtues of the mediæval church. It should stand for the brotherhood and unity of all classes and conditions; it should exalt the joys of the intellectual life above all material delights; and it should produce the best constituted and most wisely directed intellectual and moral host that the world has seen. In view of such unutilized opportunities as these for the beneficent application of great public forces, does it not seem monstrous that war should be advocated on the ground that it gives occasion for rallying and using the national energies?

The second eminent contribution which the United States have made to civilization is their thorough acceptance, in theory and practice, of the widest religious toleration. As a means of suppressing individual liberty, the collective authority of the Church, when elaborately organized in a hierarchy directed by one head and absolutely devoted in every rank to its service, comes next in proved efficiency to that concentration of powers in government which enables it to carry on war effectively. The Western Christian Church, organized under the Bishop of Rome, acquired, during the middle ages, a centralized authority which quite overrode both the temporal ruler and the rising spirit of nationality. For a time Christian Church and Christian States acted together, just as in Egypt, during many earlier centuries, the great powers of civil and religious rule had been united. The Crusades marked the climax of the power of the Church. Thereafter, Church and State were often in conflict; and during this prolonged conflict the seeds of liberty were planted, took root, and made some sturdy growth. We can see now, as we look back on the history of Europe, how fortunate it was that the colonization of North America by Europeans was deferred until after the period of the Reformation, and especially until after the Elizabethan period in England, the Luther period in Germany, and the splendid struggle of the Dutch for liberty in Holland. The founders of New England and New York were men who had imbibed the principles of resistance both to arbitrary civil power and to universal ecclesiastical authority. Hence it came about that within the territory now covered by the United States no single ecclesiastical organization ever obtained a wide and oppressive control, and that in different parts of this great region churches very unlike in doctrine and organization were almost simultaneously established. It has been an inevitable consequence of this condition of things that the Church, as a whole, in the United States has not been an effective opponent of any form of human rights. For generations it has been divided into numerous sects and denominations, no one of which has been able to claim more than a tenth of the population as its adherents; and the practices of these numerous denominations have been profoundly modified by political theories and practices, and by social customs natural to new communities formed under the prevailing conditions of free intercourse and rapid growth. The constitutional prohibition of religious tests as qualifications for office gave the United States the leadership among the nations in dissociating theological opinions and political rights. No one denomination or ecclesiastical organization in the United States has held great properties, or has had the means of conducting its ritual with costly pomp or its charitable works with imposing liberality. No splendid architectural exhibitions of Church power have interested or overawed the population. On the contrary, there has prevailed in general a great simplicity in public worship, until very recent years. Some splendors have been lately developed by religious bodies in the great cities; but these splendors and luxuries have been almost simultaneously exhibited by religious bodies of very different, not to say opposite, kinds. Thus, in New York city, the Jews, the Greek Church, the Catholics, and the Episcopalians have all erected, or undertaken to erect, magnificent edifices. But these recent demonstrations of wealth and zeal are so distributed among differing religious organizations that they cannot be imagined to indicate a coming centralization of ecclesiastical influence adverse to individual liberty.

In the United States, the great principle of religious toleration is better understood and more firmly established than in any other nation of the earth. It is not only embodied in legislation, but also completely recognized in the habits and customs of good society. Elsewhere it may be a long road from legal to social recognition of religious liberty, as the example of England shows. This recognition alone would mean, to any competent student of history, that the United States had made an unexampled contribution to the reconciliation of just governmental power with just freedom for the individual, inasmuch as the partial establishment of religious toleration has been the main work of civilization during the past four centuries. In view of this characteristic and infinitely beneficent contribution to human happiness and progress, how pitiable seem the temporary outbursts of bigotry and fanaticism which have occasionally marred the fair record of our country in regard to religious toleration! If anyone imagines that this American contribution to civilization is no longer important,—that the victory for toleration has been already won,—let him recall the fact that the last years of the nineteenth century have witnessed two horrible religious persecutions, one by a Christian nation, the other by a Moslem—one, of the Jews by Russia, and the other, of the Armenians by Turkey.

The third characteristic contribution which the United States have made to civilization has been the safe development of a manhood suffrage nearly universal. The experience of the United States has brought out several principles with regard to the suffrage which have not been clearly apprehended by some eminent political philosophers. In the first place, American experience has demonstrated the advantages of a gradual approach to universal suffrage, over a sudden leap. Universal suffrage is not the first and only means of attaining democratic government; rather, it is the ultimate goal of successful democracy. It is not a specific for the cure of all political ills; on the contrary, it may itself easily be the source of great political evils. The people of the United States feel its dangers to-day. When constituencies are large, it aggravates the well-known difficulties of party government; so that many of the ills which threaten democratic communities at this moment, whether in Europe or America, proceed from the breakdown of party government rather than from failures of universal suffrage. The methods of party government were elaborated where suffrage was limited and constituencies were small. Manhood suffrage has not worked perfectly well in the United States, or in any other nation where it has been adopted, and it is not likely very soon to work perfectly anywhere. It is like freedom of the will for the individual—the only atmosphere in which virtue can grow, but an atmosphere in which sin can also grow. Like freedom of the will, it needs to be surrounded with checks and safeguards, particularly in the childhood of the nation; but, like freedom of the will, it is the supreme good, the goal of perfected democracy. Secondly, like freedom of the will, universal suffrage has an educational effect, which has been mentioned by many writers, but has seldom been clearly apprehended or adequately described. This educational effect is produced in two ways: In the first place, the combination of individual freedom with social mobility, which a wide suffrage tends to produce, permits the capable to rise through all grades of society, even within a single generation; and this freedom to rise is intensely stimulating to personal ambition. Thus every capable American, from youth to age, is bent on bettering himself and his condition. Nothing can be more striking than the contrast between the mental condition of an average American belonging to the laborious classes, but conscious that he can rise to the top of the social scale, and that of a European mechanic, peasant, or tradesman, who knows that he cannot rise out of his class, and is content with his hereditary classification. The state of mind of the American prompts to constant struggle for self-improvement and the acquisition of all sorts of property and power. In the second place, it is a direct effect of a broad suffrage that the voters become periodically interested in the discussion of grave public problems, which carry their minds away from the routine of their daily labor and household experience out into larger fields. The instrumentalities of this prolonged education have been multiplied and improved enormously within the last fifty years. In no field of human endeavor have the fruits of the introduction of steam and electrical power been more striking than in the methods of reaching multitudes of people with instructive narratives, expositions, and arguments. The multiplication of newspapers, magazines, and books is only one of the immense developments in the means of reaching the people. The advocates of any public cause now have it in their power to provide hundreds of newspapers with the same copy, or the same plates, for simultaneous issue. The mails provide the means of circulating millions of leaflets and pamphlets. The interest in the minds of the people which prompts to the reading of these multiplied communications comes from the frequently recurring elections. The more difficult the intellectual problem presented in any given election, the more educative the effect of the discussion. Many modern industrial and financial problems are extremely difficult, even for highly-educated men. As subjects of earnest thought and discussion on the farm, and in the work-shop, factory, rolling-mill, and mine, they supply a mental training for millions of adults, the like of which has never before been seen in the world.

In these discussions, it is not only the receptive masses that are benefited; the classes that supply the appeals to the masses are also benefited in a high degree. There is no better mental exercise for the most highly trained man than the effort to expound a difficult subject in so clear a way that the untrained man can understand it. In a republic in which the final appeal is to manhood suffrage, the educated minority of the people is constantly stimulated to exertion, by the instinct of self-preservation as well as by love of country. They see dangers in proposals made to universal suffrage, and they must exert themselves to ward off those dangers. The position of the educated and well-to-do classes is a thoroughly wholesome one in this respect: they cannot depend for the preservation of their advantages on land-owning, hereditary privilege, or any legislation not equally applicable to the poorest and humblest citizen. They must maintain their superiority by being superior. They cannot live in a too safe corner.

I touch here on a misconception which underlies much of the criticism of universal suffrage. It is commonly said that the rule of the majority must be the rule of the most ignorant and incapable, the multitude being necessarily uninstructed as to taxation, public finance, and foreign relations, and untrained to active thought on such difficult subjects. Now, universal suffrage is merely a convention as to where the last appeal shall lie for the decision of public questions; and it is the rule of the majority only in this sense. The educated classes are undoubtedly a minority; but it is not safe to assume that they monopolize the good sense of the community. On the contrary, it is very clear that native good judgment and good feeling are not proportional to education, and that among a multitude of men who have only an elementary education, a large proportion will possess both good judgment and good feeling. Indeed, persons who can neither read nor write may possess a large share of both, as is constantly seen in regions where the opportunities for education in childhood have been scanty or inaccessible. It is not to be supposed that the cultivated classes, under a régime of universal suffrage, are not going to try to make their cultivation felt in the discussion and disposal of public questions. Any result under universal suffrage is a complex effect of the discussion of the public question in hand by the educated classes in the presence of the comparatively uneducated, when a majority of both classes taken together is ultimately to settle the question. In practice, both classes divide on almost every issue. But, in any case, if the educated classes cannot hold their own with the uneducated, by means of their superior physical, mental, and moral qualities, they are obviously unfit to lead society. With education should come better powers of argument and persuasion, a stricter sense of honor, and a greater general effectiveness. With these advantages, the educated classes must undoubtedly appeal to the less educated, and try to convert them to their way of thinking; but this is a process which is good for both sets of people. Indeed, it is the best possible process for the training of freemen, educated or uneducated, rich or poor.

It is often assumed that the educated classes become impotent in a democracy, because the representatives of those classes are not exclusively chosen to public office. This argument is a very fallacious one. It assumes that the public offices are the places of greatest influence; whereas, in the United States, at least, that is conspicuously not the case. In a democracy, it is important to discriminate influence from authority. Rulers and magistrates may or may not be persons of influence; but many persons of influence never become rulers, magistrates, or representatives in parliaments or legislatures. The complex industries of a modern state, and its innumerable corporation services, offer great fields for administrative talent which were entirely unknown to preceding generations; and these new activities attract many ambitious and capable men more strongly than the public service. These men are not on that account lost to their country or to society. The present generation has wholly escaped from the conditions of earlier centuries, when able men who were not great land-owners had but three outlets for their ambition—the army, the church, or the national civil service. The national service, whether in an empire, a limited monarchy, or a republic, is now only one of many fields which offer to able and patriotic men an honorable and successful career. Indeed, legislation and public administration necessarily have a very second-hand quality; and more and more legislators and administrators become dependent on the researches of scholars, men of science, and historians, and follow in the footsteps of inventors, economists, and political philosophers. Political leaders are very seldom leaders of thought; they are generally trying to induce masses of men to act on principles thought out long before. Their skill is in the selection of practicable approximations to the ideal; their arts are arts of exposition and persuasion; their honor comes from fidelity under trying circumstances to familiar principles of public duty. The real leaders of American thought in this century have been preachers, teachers, jurists, seers, and poets. While it is of the highest importance, under any form of government, that the public servants should be men of intelligence, education, and honor, it is no objection to any given form, that under it large numbers of educated and honorable citizens have no connection with the public service.

Well-to-do Europeans, when reasoning about the working of democracy, often assume that under any government the property-holders are synonymous with the intelligent and educated class. That is not the case in the American democracy. Anyone who has been connected with a large American university can testify that democratic institutions produce plenty of rich people who are not educated and plenty of educated people who are not rich, just as mediæval society produced illiterate nobles and cultivated monks.

Persons who object to manhood suffrage as the last resort for the settlement of public questions are bound to show where, in all the world, a juster or more practicable regulation or convention has been arrived at. The objectors ought at least to indicate where the ultimate decision should, in their judgment, rest—as, for example, with the landowners, or the property-holders, or the graduates of secondary schools, or the professional classes. He would be a bold political philosopher who, in these days, should propose that the ultimate tribunal should be constituted in any of these ways. All the experience of the civilized world fails to indicate a safe personage, a safe class, or a safe minority, with which to deposit this power of ultimate decision. On the contrary, the experience of civilization indicates that no select person or class can be trusted with that power, no matter what the principle of selection. The convention that the majority of males shall decide public questions has obviously great recommendations. It is apparently fairer than the rule of any minority, and it is sure to be supported by an adequate physical force. Moreover, its decisions are likely to enforce themselves. Even in matters of doubtful prognostication, the fact that a majority of the males do the prophesying tends to the fulfillment of the prophecy. At any rate, the adoption or partial adoption of universal male suffrage by several civilized nations is coincident with unexampled ameliorations in the condition of the least fortunate and most numerous classes of the population. To this general amelioration many causes have doubtless contributed; but it is reasonable to suppose that the acquisition of the power which comes with votes has had something to do with it.

Timid or conservative people often stand aghast at the

possible directions of democratic desire, or at some of the predicted results of democratic rule; but meantime the actual experience of the American democracy proves: 1, that property has never been safer under any form of government; 2, that no people have ever welcomed so ardently new machinery, and new inventions generally; 3, that religious toleration was never carried so far, and never so universally accepted; 4, that nowhere have the power and disposition to read been so general; 5, that nowhere has governmental power been more adequate, or more freely exercised, to levy and collect taxes, to raise armies and to disband them, to maintain public order, and to pay off great public debts—national, State, and town; 6, that nowhere have property and well-being been so widely diffused; and 7, that no form of government ever inspired greater affection and loyalty, or prompted to greater personal sacrifices in supreme moments. In view of these solid facts, speculations as to what universal suffrage would have done in the seventeenth and eighteenth centuries, or may do in the twentieth, seem futile indeed. The most civilized nations of the world have all either adopted this final appeal to manhood suffrage, or they are approaching that adoption by rapid stages. The United States, having no customs or traditions of an opposite sort to overcome, have led the nations in this direction, and have had the honor of devising, as a result of practical experience, the best safeguards for universal suffrage, safeguards which, in the main, are intended to prevent hasty public action, or action based on sudden discontents or temporary spasms of public feeling. These checks are intended to give time for discussion and deliberation, or, in other words, to secure the enlightenment of the voters before the vote. If, under new conditions, existing safeguards prove insufficient, the only wise course is to devise new safeguards.

The United States have made to civilization a fourth contribution of a very hopeful sort, to which public attention needs to be directed, lest temporary evils connected therewith should prevent the continuation of this beneficent action. The United States have furnished a demonstration that people belonging to a great variety of races or nations are, under favorable circumstances, fit for political freedom. It is the fashion to attribute to the enormous immigration of the last fifty years some of the failures of the American political system, and particularly the American failure in municipal government, and the introduction in a few States of the rule of the irresponsible party foremen known as "bosses." Impatient of these evils, and hastily accepting this improbable explanation of them, some people wish to depart from the American policy of welcoming immigrants. In two respects the absorption of large numbers of immigrants from many nations into the American commonwealth has been of great service to mankind. In the first place, it has demonstrated that people who at home have been subject to every sort of aristocratic or despotic or military oppression become within less than a generation serviceable citizens of a republic; and, in the second place, the United States have thus educated to freedom many millions of men. Furthermore, the comparatively high degree of happiness and prosperity enjoyed by the people of the United States has been brought home to multitudes in Europe by friends and relatives who have emigrated to this country, and has commended free institutions to them in the best possible way. This is a legitimate propaganda vastly more effective than any annexation or conquest of unwilling people, or of people unprepared for liberty.

It is a great mistake to suppose that the process of assimilating foreigners began in this century. The eighteenth century provided the colonies with a great mixture of peoples, although the English race predominated then, as now. When the Revolution broke out, there were already English, Irish, Scotch, Dutch, Germans, French, Portuguese, and Swedes in the colonies. The French were, to be sure, in small proportion, and were almost exclusively Huguenot refugees, but they were a valuable element in the population. The Germans were well diffused, having established themselves in New York, Pennsylvania, Virginia, and Georgia. The Scotch were scattered through all the colonies. Pennsylvania, especially, was inhabited by an extraordinary mixture of nationalities and religions. Since steam-navigation on the Atlantic and railroad transportation on the North American continent became cheap and easy, the tide of immigration has greatly increased; but it is very doubtful if the amount of assimilation going on in the nineteenth century has been any larger, in proportion to the population and wealth of the country, than it was in the eighteenth. The main difference in the assimilation going on in the two centuries is this, that in the eighteenth century the newcomers were almost all Protestants, while in the nineteenth century a considerable proportion have been Catholics. One result, however, of the importation of large numbers of Catholics into the United States has been a profound modification of the Roman Catholic Church in regard to the manners and customs of both the clergy and the laity, the scope of the authority of the priest, and the attitude of the Catholic Church toward public education. This American modification of the Roman Church has reacted strongly on the Church in Europe.

Another great contribution to civilization made by the United States is the diffusion of material well-being among the population. No country in the world approaches the United States in this respect. It is seen in that diffused elementary education which implants for life a habit of reading, and in the habitual optimism which characterizes the common people. It is seen in the housing of the people and of their domestic animals, in the comparative costliness of their food, clothing, and household furniture, in their implements, vehicles, and means of transportation, and in the substitution, on a prodigious scale, of the work of machinery for the work of men's hands. This last item in American well-being is quite as striking in agriculture, mining, and fishing, as it is in manufactures. The social effects of the manufacture of power, and of the discovery of means of putting that power just where it is wanted, have been more striking in the United States than anywhere else. Manufactured and distributed power needs intelligence to direct it: the bicycle is a blind horse, and must be steered at every instant; somebody must show a steam-drill where to strike and how deep to go. So far as men and women can substitute for the direct expenditure of muscular strength the more intelligent effort of designing, tending, and guiding machines, they win promotion in the scale of being, and make their lives more interesting as well as more productive. It is in the invention of machinery for producing and distributing power, and at once economizing and elevating human labor, that American ingenuity has been most conspicuously manifested. The high price of labor in a sparsely-settled country has had something to do with this striking result; but the genius of the people and of their government has had much more to do with it. As proof of the general proposition, it suffices merely to mention the telegraph and telephone, the sewing-machine, the cotton-gin, the mower, reaper, and threshing-machine, the dish-washing machine, the river steamboat, the sleeping-car, the boot and shoe machinery, and the watch machinery. The ultimate effects of these and kindred inventions are quite as much intellectual as physical, and they are developing and increasing with a portentous rapidity which sometimes suggests a doubt whether the bodily forces of men and women are adequate to resist the new mental strains brought upon them. However this may prove to be in the future, the clear result in the present is an unexampled diffusion of well-being in the United States.

These five contributions to civilization—peace-keeping, religious toleration, the development of manhood suffrage, the welcoming of newcomers, and the diffusion of well-being—I hold to have been eminently characteristic of our country, and so important that, in spite of the qualifications and deductions which every candid citizen would admit with regard to every one of them, they will ever be held in the grateful remembrance of mankind. They are reasonable grounds for a steady, glowing patriotism. They have had much to do, both as causes and as effects, with the material prosperity of the United States; but they are all five essentially moral contributions, being triumphs of reason, enterprise, courage, faith, and justice, over passion, selfishness, inertness, timidity, and distrust. Beneath each one of these developments there lies a strong ethical sentiment, a strenuous moral and social purpose. It is for such work that multitudinous democracies are fit.

In regard to all five of these contributions, the characteristic policy of our country has been from time to time threatened with reversal—is even now so threatened. It is for true patriots to insist on the maintenance of these historic purposes and policies of the people of the United States. Our country's future perils, whether already visible or still unimagined, are to be met with courage and constancy founded firmly on these popular achievements in the past.

I TALK OF DREAMS

W. D. Howells

But it is mostly my own dreams I talk of, and that will somewhat excuse me for talking of dreams at all. Everyone knows how delightful the dreams are that one dreams one's self, and how insipid the dreams of others are. I had an illustration of the fact, not many evenings ago, when a company of us got telling dreams. I had by far the best dreams of any; to be quite frank, mine were the only dreams worth listening to; they were richly imaginative, delicately fantastic, exquisitely whimsical, and humorous in the last degree; and I wondered that when the rest could have listened to them they were always eager to cut in with some silly, senseless, tasteless thing that made me sorry and ashamed for them. I shall not be going too far if I say that it was on their part the grossest betrayal of vanity that I ever witnessed.

But the egotism of some people concerning their dreams is almost incredible. They will come down to breakfast and bore everybody with a recital of the nonsense that has passed through their brains in sleep, as if they were not bad enough when they were awake; they will not spare the slightest detail; and if, by the mercy of Heaven, they have forgotten something, they will be sure to recollect it, and go back and give it all over again with added circumstance. Such people do not reflect that there is something so purely and intensely personal in dreams that they can rarely interest anyone but the dreamer, and that to the dearest friend, the closest relation or connection, they can seldom be otherwise than tedious and impertinent. The habit husbands and wives have of making each other listen to their dreams is especially cruel. They have each other quite helpless, and for this reason they should all the more carefully guard themselves from abusing their advantage. Parents should not afflict their offspring with the rehearsal of their mental maunderings in sleep, and children should learn that one of the first duties a child owes its parents is to spare them the anguish of hearing what it has dreamed about overnight. A like forbearance in regard to the community at large should be taught as the first trait of good manners in the public schools, if we ever come to teach good manners there.

I

Certain exceptional dreams, however, are so imperatively significant, so vitally important, that it would be wrong to withhold them from the knowledge of those who happened not to dream them, and I feel some such quality in my own dreams so strongly that I could scarcely forgive myself if I did not, however briefly, impart them. It was only the last week, for instance, that I found myself one night in the company of the Duke of Wellington, the great Duke, the Iron one, in fact; and after a few moments of agreeable conversation on topics of interest among gentlemen, his Grace said that now, if I pleased, he would like a couple of those towels. We had not been speaking of towels, that I remember, but it seemed the most natural thing in the world that he should mention them in the connection, whatever it was, and I went at once to get them for him. At the place where they gave out towels, and where I found some very civil people, they told me that what I wanted was not towels, and they gave me instead two bath-gowns, of rather scanty measure, butternut in color and Turkish in texture. The garments made somehow a very strong impression upon me, so that I could draw them now, if I could draw anything, as they looked when they were held up to me. At the same moment, for no reason that I can allege, I passed from a social to a menial relation to the Duke, and foresaw that when I went back to him with those bath-gowns he would not thank me as one gentleman would another, but would offer me a tip as if I were a servant. This gave me no trouble, for I at once dramatized a little scene between myself and the Duke, in which I should bring him the bath-gowns, and he should offer me the tip, and I should refuse it with a low bow, and say that I was an American. What I did not dramatize, or what seemed to enter into the dialogue quite without my agency, was the Duke's reply to my proud speech. It was foreshown me that he would say, He did not see why that should make any difference. I suppose it was in the hurt I felt at this wound to our national dignity that I now instantly invented the society of some ladies, whom I told of my business with those bath-gowns (I still had them in my hands), and urged them to go with me and call upon the Duke. They expressed, somehow, that they would rather not, and then I urged that the Duke was very handsome. This seemed to end the whole affair, and I passed on to other visions, which I cannot recall.

I have not often had a dream of such international import, in the offense offered through me to the American character and its well-known superiority to tips, but I have had others quite as humiliating to me personally. In fact, I am rather in the habit of having such dreams, and I think I may not unjustly attribute to them the disciplined modesty which the reader will hardly fail to detect in the present essay. It has more than once been my fate to find myself during sleep

I Talk of Dreams

in battle, where I behave with so little courage as to bring discredit upon our flag and shame upon myself. In these circumstances I am not anxious to make even a showing of courage; my one thought is to get away as rapidly and safely as possible. It is said that this is really the wish of all novices under fire, and that the difference between a hero and a coward is that the hero hides it, with a duplicity which finally does him honor, and that the coward frankly runs away. I have never really been in battle, and if it is anything like a battle in dreams I would not willingly qualify myself to speak by the card on this point. Neither have I ever really been upon the stage, but in dreams I have often been there, and always in a great trouble of mind at not knowing my part. It seems a little odd that I should not sometimes be prepared, but I never am, and I feel that when the curtain rises I shall be disgraced beyond all reprieve. I dare say it is the suffering from this that awakens me in time, or changes the current of my dreams so that I have never yet been actually hooted from the stage.

II

But I do not so much object to these ordeals as to some social experiences which I have in dreams. I cannot understand why one should dream of being slighted or snubbed in society, but this is what I have done more than once, though never perhaps so signally as in the instance I am about to give. I found myself in a large room, where people were sitting at lunch or supper around small tables, as is the custom, I am told, at parties in the houses of our nobility and gentry. I was feeling very well; not too proud, I hope, but in harmony with the time and place. I was very well dressed, for me; and as I stood talking to some ladies at one of the tables I was saying some rather brilliant things, for me; I lounged easily on one foot, as I have observed men of fashion do, and as I talked, I flipped my gloves, which I held in one hand, across the other; I remember thinking that this was a peculiarly distinguished action. Upon the whole I comported myself like one in the habit of such affairs, and I turned to walk away to another table, very well satisfied with myself and with the effect of my splendor upon the ladies. But I had got only a few paces off when I perceived (I could not see with my back turned) one of the ladies lean forward, and heard her say to the rest in a tone of killing condescension and patronage: "*I* don't see why that person isn't as well as another."

I say that I do not like this sort of dreams, and I never would have them if I could help. They make me ask myself if I am really such a snob when I am waking, and this in itself is very unpleasant. If I am, I cannot help hoping that it will not be found out; and in my dreams I am always less sorry for the misdeeds I commit than for their possible discovery. I have done some very bad things in dreams which I have no concern for whatever, except as they seem to threaten me with publicity or bring me within the penalty of the law; and I believe this is the attitude of most other criminals, remorse being a fiction of the poets, according to the students of the criminal class. It is not agreeable to bring this home to one's self, but the fact is not without its significance in another direction. It implies that both in the case of the dream-criminal and the deed-criminal there is perhaps the same taint of insanity; only in the deed-criminal it is active, and in the dream-criminal it is passive. In both, the inhibitory clause that forbids evil is off, but the dreamer is not bidden to do evil as the maniac is, or as the malefactor often seems to be. The dreamer is purely unmoral; good and bad are the same to his conscience; he has no more to do with right and wrong than the animals; he is reduced to the state of the merely natural man; and perhaps the primitive men were really like what we all are now in our dreams. Perhaps all life to them was merely dreaming, and they never had anything like our waking consciousness, which seems to be the offspring of conscience, or else the parent of it. Until men passed the first stage of being, perhaps that which we call the soul, for want of a better name, or a worse, could hardly have existed, and perhaps in dreams the soul is mostly absent now. The soul, or the principle that we call the soul, is the supernal criticism of the deeds done in the body, which goes perpetually on in the waking mind. While this watches, and warns or commands, we go right; but when it is off duty we go neither right nor wrong, but are as the beasts that perish.

A common theory is that the dreams which we remember are those we have in the drowse which precedes sleeping and waking; but I do not altogether accept this theory. In fact, there is very little proof of it. We often wake from a dream, literally, but there is no proof that we did not dream in the middle of the night the dream which is quite as vividly with us in the morning as the one we wake from. I should think that the dream which has some color of conscience in it was the drowse-dream, and that the dream which has none is the sleep-dream; and I believe that the most of our dreams will be found by this test to be sleep-dreams. It is in these we may know what we would be without our souls, without their supernal criticism of the mind; for the mind keeps on working in them, with the lights of waking knowledge, both experience and observation, but ruthlessly, remorselessly. By them we may know what the state of the habitual criminal is, what the state of the lunatic, the animal, the devil is. In them the personal character ceases; the dreamer is remanded to his type.

III

It is very strange, in the matter of dreadful dreams, how the body of the terror is, in the course of often dreaming, reduced to a mere convention. For a long time I was tormented with a nightmare of burglars, and at first I used to dramatize the whole affair in detail, from the time the burglars approached the house till they mounted the stairs and the light of their dark-lanterns shone under the door into my room. Now I have blue-penciled all that introductory detail; I have a light shining in under my door at once; I know that it is my old burglars; and I have the effect of nightmare without further ceremony. There are other nightmares that still cost me a great deal of trouble in their construction, as, for instance, the nightmare of clinging to the face of a precipice or the eaves of a lofty building; I have to take as much pains with the arrangement of these as if I were now dreaming them for the first time and were hardly more than an apprentice in the business.

Perhaps the most universal dream of all is that disgraceful dream of appearing in public places and in society with very little or nothing on. This dream spares neither age nor sex, I believe, and I daresay the innocency of wordless infancy is abused by it and dotage pursued to the tomb. I have not the least doubt Adam and Eve had it in Eden; though, up to the moment the fig-leaf came in, it is difficult to imagine just what plight they found themselves in that seemed improper; probably there was some plight. The most amusing thing about this dream is the sort of defensive process that goes on in the mind in search of self-justification or explanation. Is there not some peculiar circumstance or special condition in whose virtue it is wholly right and proper for one to come to a fashionable assembly clad simply in a towel, or to go about the street in nothing but a pair of kid gloves, or of pajamas at the most? This, or something like it, the mind of the dreamer struggles to establish, with a good deal of anxious appeal to the bystanders and a final sense of the hopelessness of the cause.

One may easily laugh off this sort of dream in the morning, but there are other shameful dreams whose inculpation projects itself far into the day, and whose infamy often lingers about one till lunch-time. Everyone, nearly, has had them, but it is not the kind of dream that anyone is fond of telling: the gross vanity of the most besotted dreamteller keeps that sort back. During the forenoon, at least, the victim goes about with the dim question whether he is not really that kind of man harassing him, and a sort of remote fear that he may be. I fancy that as to his nature and as to his mind he is so, and that but for the supernal criticism, but for his soul, he might be that kind of man in very act and deed.

The dreams we sometimes have about other people are not without a curious suggestion; and the superstitious (of those superstitious who like to invent their own superstitions) might very well imagine that the persons dreamed of had a witting complicity in their facts, as well as the dreamer. This is a conjecture that must, of course, not be forced to any conclusion. One must not go to one of these persons and ask, however much one would like to ask: " Sir, have you no recollection of such and such a thing, at such and such a time and place, which happened to us in my dream?" Any such person would be fully justified in not answering the question. It would be, of all interviewing, the most intolerable species. Yet a singular interest, a curiosity not altogether indefensible, will attach to these persons in the dreamer's mind, and he will not be without the sense, ever after, that he and they have a secret in common. This is dreadful, but the only thing that I can think to do about it is to urge people to keep out of other people's dreams by every means in their power.

IV

There are things in dreams very awful, which would not be at all so in waking—quite witless and aimless things, which at the time were of such baleful effect that it remains forever. I remember dreaming when I was quite a small boy, not more than ten years old, a dream which is vivider in my mind now than anything that happened at the time. I suppose it came remotely from my reading of certain "Tales of the Grotesque and the Arabesque," which had just then fallen into my hands; and it involved simply an action of the fire-company in the little town where I lived. They were working the brakes of the old fire-engine, which would seldom respond to their efforts, and as their hands rose and fell they set up the heart-shaking and soul-desolating cry of "Arms Poe! arms Poe! arms Poe!" This and nothing more was the body of my horror; and if the reader is not moved by it the fault is his and not mine; for I can assure him that nothing in my experience had been more dreadful to me.

I can hardly except the dismaying apparition of a clown whom I once saw, somewhat later in life, rise through the air in a sitting posture and float lightly over the house-roof, snapping his fingers and vaguely smiling, while the antennæ on his forehead, which clowns have in common with some other insects, nodded elasticity. I do not know why this portent should have been so terrifying, or indeed that it was a portent at all, for nothing ever came of it; what I know is that it was to the last degree threatening and awful. I never got anything but joy out of the circuses where this dream must have originated, but the pantomime of "Don

Giovanni," which I saw at the theater, was as grewsome to me waking as it was to me dreaming. The statue of the Commendatore, in getting down from his horse to pursue the wicked hero (I think that is what he gets down for), set an example by which a long line of statues afterward profited in my dreams. For many years, and I do not know but quite up to the time when I adopted burglars as the theme of my nightmares, I was almost always chased by a marble statue with an uplifted arm, and almost always I ran along the verge of a pond to escape it. I believe that I got this pond out of my remote childhood, and that it may have been a fish-pond embowered by weeping-willows which I used to admire in the door-yard of a neighbor. I have somehow a greater respect for the material of this earlier nightmare than I have for that of the later ones, and no doubt the reader will agree with me that it is much more romantic to be pursued by a statue than to be threatened by burglars. It is but a few hours ago, however, that I saved myself from these inveterate enemies by waking up just in time for breakfast. They did not come with that light of the dark-lanterns shining under the door, or I should have known them at once, and not had so much bother; but they intimated their presence in the catch of the lock, which would not close securely, and there was some question at first whether they were not ghosts. I thought of tying the doorknob on the inside of my room to my bedpost (a bedpost that has not been in existence for fifty years), but after suffering awhile I decided to speak to them from an upper window. By this time they had turned into a trio of harmless, necessary tramps, and at my appeal to them, absolutely nonsensical as I now believe it to have been, to regard the peculiar circumstances, whatever they were or were not, they did really get up from the back porch where they were seated and go quietly away.

Burglars are not always so easily to be entreated. On one occasion, when I found a party of them digging at the corner of my house on Concord Avenue in Cambridge, and opened the window over them to expostulate, the leader looked up at me in well-affected surprise. He lifted his hand, with a twenty-dollar note in it, toward me, and said: "Oh! Can you change me a twenty-dollar bill?" I expressed a polite regret that I had not so much money about me, and then he said to the rest, "Go ahead, boys," and they went on undermining my house. I do not know what came of it all.

Of ghosts I have seldom dreamed, so far as I can remember; in fact, I have never dreamed of the kind of ghosts that we are all more or less afraid of, though I have dreamed rather often of the spirits of departed friends. But I once dreamed of dying, and the reader, who has never died yet, may be interested to know what it is like. According to this experience of mine, which I do not claim is typical, it is like a fire kindling in an air-tight stove with paper and shavings; the gathering smoke and gases suddenly burst into flame and puff the door out, and all is over.

I have not yet been led to execution for the many crimes I have committed in my dreams, but I was once in the hands of a barber who added to the shaving and shampooing business the art of removing his customers' heads in treatment for headache. As I took my seat in his chair I had some lingering doubts as to the effect of a treatment so drastic, and I ventured to mention the case of a friend of mine, a gentleman somewhat eminent in the law, who after several weeks was still going about without his head. The barber did not attempt to refute my position. He merely said: "Oh, well, he had such a very thick sort of a head, anyway."

This was a sarcasm, but I think it was urged as a reason,

though it may not have been. We rarely bring away from sleep the things that seem so brilliant to us in our dreams. Verse is especially apt to fade away, or turn into doggerel in the memory, and the witty sayings which we contrive to remember will hardly bear the test of daylight. The most perfect thing of the kind out of my own dreams was something that I seemed to wake with the very sound of in my ears. It was after a certain dinner, which had been rather uncommonly gay, with a good deal of very good talk, which seemed to go on all night, and when I woke in the morning someone was saying: "Oh, I shouldn't at all mind his robbing Peter to pay Paul, if I felt sure that Paul would get the money." This I think really humorous, and an extremely neat bit of characterization; I feel free to praise it, because it was not I who said it.

V

Apparently the greater part of dreams have no more mirth than sense in them. This is perhaps because the man is in dreams reduced to the brute condition, and is the lawless inferior of the waking man intellectually, as the lawless in waking are always the inferiors of the lawful. Some loose thinkers suppose that if we give the rein to imagination it will do great things, but it will really do little things, foolish and worthless things, as we witness in dreams, where it is quite unbridled. It must keep close to truth, and it must be under the law if it would work strongly and sanely. The man in his dreams is really lower than the lunatic in his deliriums. These have a logic of their own; but the dreamer has not even a crazy logic.

"Like a dog, he hunts in dreams,"

and probably his dreams and the dog's are not only alike, but are of the same quality. In his wicked dreams the man is not only animal, he is devil, so wholly is he let into his evils, as the Swedenborgians say. The wrong is indifferent to him until the fear of detection and punishment steals in upon him. Even then he is not sorry for his misdeed, as I have said before; he is only anxious to escape its consequences.

It seems probable that when this fear makes itself felt he is near to waking; and probably when we dream, as we often do, that the thing is only a dream, and hope for rescue from it by waking, we are always just about to wake. This double effect is very strange, but still more strange is the effect which we are privy to in the minds of others when they not merely say things to us which are wholly unexpected, but think things that we know they are thinking, and that they do not express in words. A great many years ago, when I was young, I dreamed that my father, who was in another town, came into the room where I was really lying asleep and stood by my bed. He wished to greet me, after our separation, but he reasoned that if he did so I should wake, and he turned and left the room without touching me. This process in his mind, which I knew as clearly and accurately as if it had apparently gone on in my own, was apparently confined to his mind as absolutely as anything could be that was not spoken or in any wise uttered.

Of course, it was of my agency, like any other part of the dream, and it was something like the operation of the novelist's intention through the mind of his characters. But in this there is the author's consciousness that he is doing it all himself, while in my dream this reasoning in the mind of another was something that I felt myself mere witness of. In fact, there is no analogy, so far as I can make out, between the process of literary invention and the process of dreaming. In the invention, the critical faculty is vividly

I Talk of Dreams

and constantly alert; in dreaming, it seems altogether absent. It seems absent, too, in what we call day-dreaming, or that sort of dramatizing action which perhaps goes on perpetually in the mind, or some minds. But this day-dreaming is not otherwise any more like night-dreaming than invention is; for the man is never more actively and consciously a man, and never has a greater will to be fine and high and grand than in his day-dreams, while in his night-dreams he is quite willing to be a miscreant of any worst sort.

It is very remarkable, in view of this fact, that we have now and then, though ever so much more rarely, dreams that are as angelic as those others are demoniac. Is it possible that then the dreamer is let into his goods (the word is Swedenborg's again) instead of his evils? It may be supposed that in sleep the dreamer lies passive, while his proper soul is away, and other spirits, celestial and infernal, have free access to his mind, and abuse it to their own ends in the one case, and use it in his behalf in the other.

That would be an explanation, but nothing seems quite to hold in regard to dreams. If it is true, why should the dreamer's state so much oftener be imbued with evil than with good? It might be answered that the evil forces are much more positive and aggressive than the good; or that the love of the dreamer, which is his life, being mainly evil, invites the wicked spirits oftener. But that is a point which I would rather leave each dreamer to settle for himself. The greater number of everyone's dreams, like the romantic novel, I fancy, concern incident rather than character, and I am not sure, after all, that the dream which convicts the dreamer of an essential baseness is commoner than the dream that tells in his favor morally.

I daresay every reader of this book has had dreams so amusing that he has wakened himself from them by laughing, and then not found them so very funny, or perhaps not been able to recall them at all. I have had at least one of this sort, remarkable for other reasons, which remains perfect in my mind, though it is now some ten years old. One of the children had been exposed to a very remote chance of scarlet-fever at the house of a friend, and had been duly scolded for the risk, which was then quite forgotten. I dreamed that this friend, however, was giving a ladies' lunch, at which I was unaccountably and invisibly present, and the talk began to run upon the scarlet-fever cases in her family. She said that after the last she had fumigated the whole house for seventy-two hours (the period seemed very significant and important in my dream), and had burned everything she could lay her hands on.

"And what did the nurse burn?" asked one of the other ladies.

The hostess began to laugh. "The nurse didn't burn a thing!"

Then all the rest burst out laughing at the joke, and the laughter woke me, to see the boy sitting up in his bed and hear him saying: "Oh, I am so sick!"

It was the nausea which announces scarlet-fever, and for six weeks after that we were in quarantine. Very likely the fear of the contagion had been in my nether mind all the time, but, so far as consciousness could testify of it, I had wholly forgotten it.

VI

One rarely loses one's personality in dreams; it is rather intensified, with all the proper circumstances and relations of it, but I have had at least one dream in which I seemed to transcend my own circumstance and condition with remarkable completeness. Even my epoch, my precious present, I left behind (or ahead, rather), and in my unity with the persons of my dream I became strictly mediæval.

In fact, I have always called it my mediæval dream, to such as I could get to listen to it; and it had for its scene a feudal tower in some waste place, a tower open at the top and with a deep, clear pool of water at the bottom, so that it instantly became known to me, as if I had always known it, for the Pool Tower. While I stood looking into it, in a mediæval dress and a mediæval mood, there came flying in at the open door of the ruin beside me the duke's hunchback, and after him, furious and shrieking maledictions, the swarthy beauty whom I was aware the duke was tired of. The keeping was now not only ducal, but thoroughly Italian, and it was suggested somehow to my own subtle Italian perception that the hunchback had been set on to tease the girl and provoke her so that she would turn upon him and try to wreak her fury on him and chase him into the Pool Tower and up the stone stairs that wound round its hollow to the top, where the solemn sky showed. The fearful spire of the steps was unguarded, and when I had lost the pair from sight, with the dwarf's mocking laughter and the girl's angry cries in my ears, there came fluttering from the height, like a bird wounded and whirling from a lofty tree, the figure of the girl, while far aloof the hunchback peered over at her fall. Midway in her descent her head struck against the edge of the steps, with a *kish,* such as an egg-shell makes when broken against the edge of a platter, and then plunged into the dark pool at my feet, where I could presently see her lying in the clear depths and the blood curling upward from the wound in her skull like a dark smoke. I was not sensible of any great pity; I accepted the affair, quite mediævally, as something that might very well have happened, given the girl, the duke and the dwarf, and the time and place.

I am rather fond of a mediæval setting for those

"Dreams that wave before the half-shut eye,"

just closing for an afternoon nap. Then I invite to my vision a wide landscape, with a cold, wintry afternoon light upon it, and over this plain I have bands and groups of people scurrying, in mediæval hose of divers colors and mediæval leathern jerkins, hugging themselves against the frost, and very miserable. They affect me with a profound compassion; they represent to me, somehow, the vast mass of humanity, the mass that does the work, and earns the bread, and goes cold and hungry through all the ages. I should be at a loss to say why this was the effect, and I am utterly unable to say why these fore-dreams, which I partially solicit, should have such a tremendous significance as they seem to have. They are mostly of the most evanescent and intangible character, but they have one trait in common. They always involve the attribution of ethical motive and quality to material things, and in their passage through my brain they promise me a solution of the riddle of the painful earth in the very instant when they are gone forever. They are of innumerable multitude, chasing each other with the swiftness of light, and never staying to be seized by the memory, which seems already drugged with sleep before their course begins. One of these dreams, indeed, I did capture, and I found it to be the figure 8, but lying on its side, and in that posture involving the mystery and the revelation of the mystery of the universe. I leave the reader to imagine why.

As we grow older, I think we are less and less able to remember our dreams. This is perhaps because the experience of youth is less dense, and the empty spaces of the young consciousness are more hospitable to these airy visitants. A few dreams of my later life stand out in strong relief, but for the most part they blend in an indistinguishable mass, and pass away with the actualities into a common oblivion. I should say that they were more frequent with me than they used to be; it seems to me that now I dream whole nights through, and much more about the business of my waking life than formerly. As I earn my living by weaving a certain sort of dreams into literary form, it might be supposed that I would some time dream of the personages in these dreams, but I cannot remember that I have ever done so. The two kinds of inventing, the voluntary and the involuntary, seem absolutely and finally distinct.

Of the prophetic dreams which people sometimes have I have mentioned the only one of mine which had any dramatic interest, but I have verified in my own experience the theory of Ribot that approaching disease sometimes intimates itself in dreams of the disorder impending, before it is otherwise declared in the organism. In actual sickness I think that I dream rather less than in health. I had a malarial fever when I was a boy, and I had a sort of continuous dream in it that distressed me greatly. It was of gliding down the school-house stairs without touching my feet to the steps, and this was indescribably appalling.

The anguish of mind that one suffers from the imaginary dangers of dreams is probably of the same quality as that inspired by real peril in waking. A curious proof of this happened within my knowledge not many years ago. One of the neighbor's children was coasting down a long hill with a railroad at the foot of it, and as he neared the bottom an express-train rushed round the curve. The flagman ran forward and shouted to the boy to throw himself off his sled, but he kept on and ran into the locomotive, and was so hurt that he died. His injuries, however, were to the spine, and they were of a kind that rendered him insensible to pain while he lived. He talked very clearly and calmly of his accident, and when he was asked why he did not throw himself off his sled, as the flag-man bade him, he said: "*I thought it was a dream*" The reality had, through the mental stress, no doubt transmuted itself to the very substance of dreams, and he had felt the same kind and quality of suffering as he would have done if he had been dreaming. The Norwegian poet and novelist Björnstjerne Björnson was at my house shortly after this happened, and he was greatly struck by the psychological implications of the incident; it seemed to mean for him all sorts of possibilities in the obscure realm where it cast a fitful light.

But such a glimmer soon fades, and the darkness thickens round us again. It is not with the blindfold sense of sleep that we shall ever find out the secret of life, I fancy, either in the dreams which seem personal to us each one, or those universal dreams which we apparently share with the whole race. Of the race-dream, as I may call it, there is one hardly less common than that dream of going about insufficiently clad, which I have already mentioned, and that is the dream of suddenly falling from some height and waking with a start. The experience before the start is extremely dim, and latterly I have condensed this dread almost as much as the preliminary passages of my burglar-dream. I am aware of nothing but an instant of danger, and then comes the jar or jolt that wakens me. Upon the whole, I find this a great saving of emotion, and I do not know but there is a tendency, as I grow older, to shorten up the detail of what may be styled the conventional dream, the dream which we have so often that it is like a story read before. Indeed, the plots of dreams are not much more varied than the plots of romantic novels, which are notoriously stale and hackneyed. It would be interesting, and possibly important, if some observer would note the recurrence of this sort of dreams and classify their varieties. I think we should all be astonished to find how few and slight the variations were.

VII

If I come to speak of dreams concerning the dead, it must be with a tenderness and awe that all who have had them will share with me. Nothing is more remarkable in them than the fact that the dead, though they are dead, yet live, and are, to our commerce with them, quite like all other living persons. We may recognize, and they may recognize, that they are no longer in the body, but they are as verily living as we are. This may be merely an effect from the doctrine of immortality which we all hold or have held, and yet I would fain believe that it may be something like proof of it. No one really knows, or can know, but one may at least hope, without offending science, which indeed no longer frowns so darkly upon faith. This persistence of life in those whom we mourn as dead, may not it be a witness of the fact that the consciousness cannot accept the notion of death at all, and,

"Whatever crazy sorrow saith,"

that we have never truly felt them lost? Sometimes those who have died come back in dreams as parts of a common life which seems never to have been broken; the old circle is restored without a flaw; but whether they do this, or whether it is acknowledged between them and us that they have died, and are now disembodied spirits, the effect of life is the same. Perhaps in those dreams they and we are alike disembodied spirits, and the soul of the dreamer, which so often seems to abandon the body to the animal, is then the conscious entity, the thing which the dreamer feels to be himself, and is mingling with the souls of the departed on something like the terms which shall hereafter be constant.

I think very few of those who have lost their beloved have failed to receive some sign or message from them in dreams, and often it is of deep and abiding consolation. It may be that this is our anguish compelling the echo of love out of the darkness where nothing is, but it may be that there is something there which answers to our throe with pity and with longing like our own. Again, no one knows, but in a matter impossible of definite solution I will not refuse the comfort which belief can give. Unbelief can be no gain, and belief no loss. But those dreams are so dear, so sacred, so interwoven with the finest and tenderest tissues of our being that one cannot speak of them freely, or indeed more than most vaguely. It is enough to say that one has had them, and to know that almost everyone else has had them, too. They seem to be among the universal dreams, and a strange quality of them is that, though they deal with a fact of universal doubt, they are, to my experience at least, not nearly so fantastic or capricious as the dreams that deal with the facts of every-day life and with the affairs of people still in this world.

I do not know whether it is common to dream of faces or figures strange to our waking knowledge, but occasionally I have done this. I suppose it is much the same kind of invention that causes the person we dream of to say or do a thing unexpected to us. But this is rather common, and the creation of a novel aspect, the physiognomy of a stranger, in the person we dream of, is rather rare. In all my dreams I can recall but one presence of the kind. I have never dreamed of any sort of monster foreign to my knowledge, or even of any grotesque thing made up of elements familiar to it; the grotesqueness has always been in the motive or circumstance of the dream. I have very seldom dreamed of animals, though once, when I was a boy, for a time after I had passed a corn-field where there were some bundles of snakes, writhen and knotted together in the cold of an early spring day, I had dreams infested by like images of those loathsome reptiles. I suppose that everyone has had dreams of finding his way through unnamable filth and of feeding upon hideous carnage; these are clearly the punishment of gluttony, and are the fumes of a rebellious stomach.

I have heard people say they have sometimes dreamed of a thing, and awakened from their dream and then fallen asleep and dreamed of the same thing; but I believe that this is all one continuous dream; that they did not really awaken, but only dreamed that they awakened. I have never had any such dream, but at one time I had a recurrent dream, which was so singular that I thought no one else had ever had a recurrent dream till I proved that it was rather common by starting the inquiry in the Contributors' Club in the *Atlantic Monthly,* when I found that great numbers of people have recurrent dreams. My own recurrent dreams began to come during the first year of my consulate at Venice, where I had hoped to find the same kind of poetic dimness on the phases of American life, which I wished to treat in literature, as the distance in time would have given. I should not wish any such dimness now; but those were my romantic days, and I was sorely baffled by its absence. The disappointment began to haunt my nights as well as my days, and a dream repeated itself from week to week for a matter of eight or ten months to one effect. I dreamed that I had gone home to America, and that people met me and said, " Why, you have given up your place!" and I always answered: " Certainly not; I haven't done at all what I mean to do there, yet. I am only here on my ten days' leave." I meant the ten days which a consul might take each quarter without applying to the Department of State; and then I would reflect how impossible it was that I should make the visit in that time. I saw that I should be found out and dismissed from my office and publicly disgraced. Then, suddenly, I was not consul at Venice, and had not been, but consul at Delhi, in India; and the distress I felt would all end in a splendid Oriental phantasmagory of elephants and native princes, with their retinues in procession, which I suppose was mostly out of my reading of De Quincey. This dream, with no variation that I can recall, persisted till I broke it up by saying, in the morning after it had recurred, that I had dreamed that dream again; and so it began to fade away, coming less and less frequently, and at last ceasing altogether.

I am rather proud of that dream; it is really my battle-horse among dreams, and I think I will ride away on it.

[From *Impressions and Experiences*, by W. D. Howells. Copyright, 1896, by W. D. Howells.]

AN IDYL OF THE HONEY-BEE

John Burroughs

THERE is no creature with which man has surrounded himself that seems so much like a product of civilization, so much like the result of development on special lines and in special fields, as the honey-bee. Indeed, a colony of bees, with their neatness and love of order, their division of labor, their public-spiritedness, their thrift, their complex economies, and their inordinate love of gain, seems as far removed from a condition of rude nature as does a walled city or a cathedral town. Our native bee, on the other hand, the " burly, dozing humblebee," affects one more like the rude, untutored savage. He has learned nothing from experience. He lives from hand to mouth. He luxuriates in time of plenty, and he starves in times of scarcity. He lives in a rude nest, or in a hole in the ground, and in small communities; he builds a few deep cells or sacks in which he stores a little honey and bee-bread for his young, but as a worker in wax he is of the most primitive and awkward. The Indian regarded the honey-bee as an ill-omen. She was the white man's fly. In fact she was the epitome of the white man himself. She has the white man's craftiness, his industry, his architectural skill, his neatness and love of system, his foresight; and, above all, his eager, miserly habits. The honey-bee's great ambition is to be rich, to lay up great stores, to possess the sweet of every flower that blooms. She is more than provident. Enough will not satisfy her; she must have all she can get by hook or by crook. She comes from the oldest country, Asia, and thrives best in the most fertile and long-settled lands.

Yet the fact remains that the honey-bee is essentially a wild creature, and never has been and cannot be thoroughly domesticated. Its proper home is the woods, and thither every new swarm counts on going; and thither many do go in spite of the care and watchfulness of the bee-keeper. If the woods in any given locality are deficient in trees with suitable cavities, the bees resort to all sorts of makeshifts; they go into chimneys, into barns and outhouses, under stones, into rocks, and so forth. Several chimneys in my locality with disused flues are taken possession of by colonies of bees nearly every season. One day, while bee-hunting, I developed a line that went toward a farmhouse where I had reason to believe no bees were kept. I followed it up and questioned the farmer about his bees. He said he kept no bees, but that a swarm had taken possession of his chimney, and another had gone under the clapboards in the gable end of his house. He had taken a large lot of honey out of both places the year before. Another farmer told me that one day his family had seen a number of bees examining a knothole in the side of his house; the next day, as they were sitting down to dinner, their attention was attracted by a loud humming noise, when they discovered a swarm of bees settling upon the side of the house and pouring into the knothole. In subsequent years other swarms came to the same place.

Apparently every swarm of bees, before it leaves the parent hive, sends out exploring parties to look up the future home. The woods and groves are searched through and through, and no doubt the privacy of many a squirrel and many a wood-mouse is intruded upon. What cozy nooks and retreats they do spy out, so much more attractive than the painted hive in the garden, so much cooler in summer and so much warmer in winter!

The bee is in the main an honest citizen: she prefers legitimate to illegitimate business; she is never an outlaw until her proper sources of supply fail; she will not touch honey as long as honey yielding flowers can be found; she always prefers to go to the fountain-head, and dislikes to take her sweets at second hand. But in the fall, after the flowers have failed, she can be tempted. The bee-hunter takes advantage of this fact; he betrays her with a little honey. He wants to steal her stores, and he first encourages her to steal his, then follows the thief home with her booty. This is the whole trick of the bee-hunter. The bees never suspect his game, else by taking a circuitous route they could easily baffle him. But the honey-bee has absolutely no wit or cunning outside of her special gifts as a gatherer and storer of honey. She is a simple-minded creature, and can be imposed upon by any novice. Yet it is not every novice that can find a bee-tree. The sportsman may track his game to its retreat by the aid of his dog, but in hunting the honey-bee one must be his own dog, and track his game through an element in which it leaves no trail. It is a task for a sharp, quick eye, and may test the resources of the best woodcraft. One autumn, when I devoted much time to this pursuit, as the best means of getting at nature and the open-air exhilaration, my eye became so trained that bees were nearly as easy to it as birds. I saw and heard bees wherever I went. One day, standing on a street corner in a great city, I saw above the trucks and the traffic a line of bees carrying off sweets from some grocery or confectionery shop.

One looks upon the woods with a new interest when he suspects they hold a colony of bees. What a pleasing secret it is,—a tree with a heart of comb honey, a decayed oak or maple with a bit of Sicily or Mount Hymettus stowed away in its trunk or branches; secret chambers where lies hidden the wealth of ten thousand little freebooters, great nuggets and wedges of precious ore gathered with risk and labor from every field and wood about!

But if you would know the delights of bee-hunting, and how many sweets such a trip yields beside honey, come with me some bright, warm, late September or early October day. It is the golden season of the year, and any errand or pursuit that takes us abroad upon the hills or by the painted woods and along the amber-colored streams at such a time is enough. So, with haversacks filled with grapes and peaches and apples and a bottle of milk,—for we shall not be home to dinner,—and armed with a compass, a hatchet, a pail, and a box with a piece of comb honey neatly fitted into it,—any box the size of your hand with a lid will do nearly as well as the elaborate and ingenious contrivance of the regular bee-hunter,—we sally forth. Our course at first lies along the highway under great chestnut-trees whose nuts are just dropping, then through an orchard and across a little creek, thence gently rising through a long series of cultivated fields toward some high uplying land behind which rises a rugged wooded ridge or mountain, the most sightly point in all this section. Behind this ridge for several miles the country is wild, wooded, and rocky, and is no doubt the home of many wild swarms of bees. What a gleeful uproar the robins, cedar-birds, high-holes, and cow blackbirds make amid the black cherry trees as we pass along! The raccoons, too, have been here after black cherries, and we see their marks at various points. Several crows are walking about a newly sowed wheatfield we pass through, and we pause to note their graceful movements and glossy coats. I have seen no bird walk the ground with just the same air the crow does. It

An Idyl of the Honey-Bee

is not exactly pride; there is no strut or swagger in it, though perhaps just a little condescension; it is the contented, complaisant, and self-possessed gait of a lord over his domains. All these acres are mine, he says, and all these crops; men plow and sow for me, and I stay here or go there, and find life sweet and good wherever I am. The hawk looks awkward and out of place on the ground; the game-birds hurry and skulk; but the crow is at home, and treads the earth as if there were none to molest or make him afraid.

The crows we have always with us, but it is not every day or every season that one sees an eagle. Hence I must preserve the memory of one I saw the last day I went bee-hunting. As I was laboring up the side of a mountain at the head of a valley, the noble bird sprang from the top of a dry tree above me and came sailing directly over my head. I saw him bend his eye down upon me, and I could hear the low hum of his plumage as if the web of every quill in his great wings vibrated in his strong, level flight. I watched him as long as my eye could hold him. When he was fairly clear of the mountain he began that sweeping spiral movement in which he climbs the sky. Up and up he went, without once breaking his majestic poise, till he appeared to sight some far-off alien geography, when he bent his course thitherward and gradually vanished in the blue depths. The eagle is a bird of large ideas; he embraces long distances; the continent is his home. I never look upon one without emotion; I follow him with my eye as long as I can. I think of Canada, of the Great Lakes, of the Rocky Mountains, of the wild and sounding seacoast. The waters are his, and the woods and the inaccessible cliffs. He pierces behind the veil of the storm, and his joy is height and depth and vast spaces.

We go out of our way to touch at a spring run in the

edge of the woods, and are lucky to find a single scarlet lobelia lingering there. It seems almost to light up the gloom with its intense bit of color. Beside a ditch in a field beyond, we find the great blue lobelia, and near it, amid the weeds and wild grasses and purple asters, the most beautiful of our fall flowers, the fringed gentian. What a rare and delicate, almost aristocratic look the gentian has amid its coarse, unkempt surroundings! It does not lure the bee, but it lures and holds every passing human eye. If we strike through the corner of yonder woods, where the ground is moistened by hidden springs, and where there is a little opening amid the trees, we shall find the closed gentian, a rare flower in this locality. I had walked this way many times before I chanced upon its retreat, and then I was following a line of bees. I lost the bees, but I got the gentians. How curious this flower looks with its deep blue petals folded together so tightly,— a bud and yet a blossom! It is the nun among our wild flowers,—a form closely veiled and cloaked. The buccaneer bumblebee sometimes tries to rifle it of its sweets. I have seen the blossom with the bee entombed in it. He had forced his way into the virgin corolla as if determined to know its secret, but he had never returned with the knowledge he had gained.

After a refreshing walk of a couple of miles we reach a point where we will make our first trial,—a high stone wall that runs parallel with the wooded ridge referred to, and separated from it by a broad field. There are bees at work there on that goldenrod, and it requires but little manœuvering to sweep one into our box. Almost any other creature rudely and suddenly arrested in its career, and clapped into a cage in this way, would show great confusion and alarm. The bee is alarmed for a moment, but the bee has a passion stronger than its love of life or fear of death, namely, desire for honey, not simply to eat, but to carry home as booty. "Such rage of honey in their bosom beats," says Virgil. It is quick to catch the scent of honey in the box, and as quick to fall to filling itself. We now set the box down upon the wall and gently remove the cover. The bee is head and shoulders in one of the half-filled cells, and is oblivious to everything else about it. Come rack, come ruin, it will die at work. We step back a few paces, and sit down upon the ground so as to bring the box against the blue sky as a background. In two or three minutes the bee is seen rising slowly and heavily from the box. It seems loath to leave so much honey behind, and it marks the place well. It mounts aloft in a rapidly increasing spiral, surveying the near and minute objects first, then the larger and more distant, till, having circled above the spot five or six times and taken all its bearings, it darts away for home. It is a good eye that holds fast to the bee till it is fairly off. Sometimes one's head will swim following it, and often one's eyes are put out by the sun. This bee gradually drifts down the hill, then strikes away toward a farmhouse half a mile away where I know bees are kept. Then we try another and another, and the third bee, much to our satisfaction, goes straight toward the woods. We could see the brown speck against the darker background for many yards. The regular bee-hunter professes to be able to tell a wild bee from a tame one by the color, the former, he says, being lighter. But there is no difference; they are both alike in color and in manner. Young bees are lighter than old, and that is all there is of it. If a bee lived many years in the woods it would doubtless come to have some distinguishing marks, but the life of a bee is only a few months at the farthest, and no change is wrought in this brief time.

Our bees are all soon back, and more with them, for we

have touched the box here and there with the cork of a bottle of anise oil, and this fragrant and pungent oil will attract bees half a mile or more. When no flowers can be found, this is the quickest way to obtain a bee.

It is a singular fact that when the bee first finds the hunter's box, its first feeling is one of anger; it is as mad as a hornet; its tone changes, it sounds its shrill war trumpet and darts to and fro, and gives vent to its rage and indignation in no uncertain manner. It seems to scent foul play at once. It says, " Here is robbery; here is the spoil of some hive, may be my own," and its blood is up. But its ruling passion soon comes to the surface, its avarice gets the better of its indignation, and it seems to say, " Well, I had better take possession of this and carry it home." So after many feints and approaches and dartings off with a loud angry hum as if it would none of it, the bee settles down and fills itself.

It does not entirely cool off and get soberly to work till it has made two or three trips home with its booty. When other bees come, even if all from the same swarm, they quarrel and dispute over the box, and clip and dart at each other like bantam cocks. Apparently the ill feeling which the sight of the honey awakens is not one of jealousy or rivalry, but wrath.

A bee will usually make three or four trips from the hunter's box before it brings back a companion. I suspect the bee does not tell its fellows what it has found, but that they smell out the secret; it doubtless bears some evidence with it upon its feet or proboscis that it has been upon honeycomb and not upon flowers, and its companions take the hint and follow, arriving always many seconds behind. Then the quantity and quality of the booty would also betray it. No doubt, also, there are plenty of gossips about a hive that note and tell everything. " Oh, did you see that? Peggy Mel came in a few moments ago in great haste, and one of the upstairs packers says she was loaded till she groaned with apple-blossom honey, which she deposited, and then rushed off again like mad. Apple-blossom honey in October! Fee, fi, fo, fum! I smell something! Let's after."

In about half an hour we have three well-defined lines of bees established,—two to farmhouses and one to the woods, and our box is being rapidly depleted of its honey. About every fourth bee goes to the woods, and now that they have learned the way thoroughly they do not make the long preliminary whirl above the box, but start directly from it. The woods are rough and dense and the hill steep, and we do not like to follow the line of bees until we have tried at least to settle the problem as to the distance they go into the woods,—whether the tree is on this side of the ridge or into the depth of the forest on the other side. So we shut up the box when it is full of bees and carry it about three hundred yards along the wall from which we are operating. When liberated, the bees, as they always will in such cases, go off in the same directions they have been going; they do not seem to know that they have been moved. But other bees have followed our scent, and it is not many minutes before a second line to the woods is established. This is called cross-lining the bees. The new line makes a sharp angle with the other line, and we know at once that the tree is only a few rods into the woods. The two lines we have established form two sides of a triangle of which the wall is the base; at the apex of the triangle, or where the two lines meet in the woods, we are sure to find the tree. We quickly follow up these lines, and where they cross each other on the side of the hill we scan every tree closely. I pause at the foot of an oak and examine a hole near the root; now the bees are in this tree and their entrance is on the upper side near the ground not two feet from the hole I peer into, and yet so quiet and secret is their going and coming that I fail to discover them and pass on up the hill. Failing in this direction I return to the oak again, and then perceive the bees going out in a small crack in the tree. The bees do not know they are found out and that the game is in our hands, and are as oblivious of our presence as if we were ants or crickets. The indications are that the swarm is a small one, and the store of honey trifling. In "taking up" a bee-tree it is usual first to kill or stupefy the bees with the fumes of burning sulphur or with tobacco smoke. But this course is impracticable on the present occasion, so we boldly and ruthlessly assault the tree with an ax we have procured. At the first blow the bees set up a loud buzzing, but we have no mercy, and the side of the cavity is soon cut away and the interior with its white-yellow mass of comb honey is exposed, and not a bee strikes a blow in defense of its all. This may seem singular, but it has nearly always been my experience. When a swarm of bees are thus rudely assaulted with an ax they evidently think the end of the world has come, and, like true misers as they are, each one seizes as much of the treasure as it can hold; in other words, they all fall to and gorge themselves with honey, and calmly await the issue. While in this condition they make no defense, and will not sting unless taken hold of. In fact they are as harmless as flies. Bees are always to be managed with boldness and decision. Any half-way measures, any timid poking about, any feeble attempts to reach their honey, are sure to be quickly resented. The popular notion that bees have a special antipathy toward certain persons and a liking for certain others has only this fact at the bottom of it: they will sting a person who is afraid of them and goes skulking and dodging about, and they will not sting a person who faces them boldly and has no dread of them. They are like dogs. The way to disarm a vicious dog is to show him you do not fear him; it is his turn to be afraid then. I never had any dread of bees and am seldom stung by them. I have climbed up into a large chestnut that contained a swarm in one of its cavities and chopped them out with an ax, being obliged at times to pause and brush the bewildered bees from my hands and face, and not been stung once. I have chopped a swarm out of an apple-tree in June, and taken out the cards of honey and arranged them in a hive, and then dipped out the bees with a dipper, and taken the whole home with me in pretty good condition, with scarcely any opposition on the part of the bees. In reaching your hand into the cavity to detach and remove the comb you are pretty sure to get stung, for when you touch the "business end" of a bee, it will sting even though its head be off. But the bee carries the antidote to its own poison. The best remedy for bee sting is honey, and when your hands are besmeared with honey, as they are sure to be on such occasions, the wound is scarcely more painful than the prick of a pin. Assault your bee-tree, then, boldly with your ax, and you will find that when the honey is exposed every bee has surrendered and the whole swarm is cowering in helpless bewilderment and terror. Our tree yields only a few pounds of honey, not enough to have lasted the swarm till January, but no matter: we have the less burden to carry.

In the afternoon we go nearly half a mile farther along the ridge to a cornfield that lies immediately in front of the highest point of the mountain. The view is superb; the ripe autumn landscape rolls away to the east, cut through by the great placid river; in the extreme north the wall of the Catskills stands out clear and strong, while in the south the mountains of the Highlands bound the view. The day is warm, and the bees are very busy there in that neglected corner of the field, rich in asters, fleabane, and goldenrod. The corn has been cut, and upon a stout but a few rods from the woods, which here drop quickly down from the precipitous heights, we set up our bee-box, touched again with the pungent oil. In a few moments a bee has found it; she comes up to leeward, following the scent. On leaving the box, she goes straight toward the woods. More bees quickly come, and it is not long before the line is well established. Now we have recourse to the same tactics we employed before, and move along the ridge to another field to get our cross line. But the bees still go in almost the same direction they did from the corn stout. The tree is then either on the top of the mountain or on the other or west side of it. We hesitate to make the plunge into the woods and seek to scale those precipices, for the eye can plainly see what is before us. As the afternoon sun gets lower, the bees are seen with wonderful distinctness. They fly toward and under the sun, and are in a strong light, while the near woods which form the background are in deep shadow. They look like large luminous motes. Their swiftly vibrating, transparent wings surround their bodies with a shining nimbus that makes them visible for a long distance. They seem magnified many times. We see them bridge the little gulf between us and the woods, then rise up over the treetops with their burdens, swerving neither to the right hand nor to the left. It is almost pathetic to see them labor so, climbing the mountain and unwittingly guiding us to their treasures. When the sun gets down so that his direction corresponds exactly with the course of the bees, we make the plunge. It proves even harder climbing than we had anticipated; the mountain is faced by a broken and irregular wall of rock, up which we pull ourselves slowly and cautiously by main strength,

An Idyl of the Honey-Bee

In half an hour, the perspiration streaming from every pore, we reach the summit. The trees here are all small, a second growth, and we are soon convinced the bees are not here. Then down we go on the other side, clambering down the rocky stairways till we reach quite a broad plateau that forms something like the shoulder of the mountain. On the brink of this there are many large hemlocks, and we scan them closely and rap upon them with our ax. But not a bee is seen or heard; we do not seem as near the tree as we were in the fields below; yet, if some divinity would only whisper the fact to us, we are within a few rods of the coveted prize, which is not in one of the large hemlocks or oaks that absorb our attention, but in an old stub or stump not six feet high, and which we have seen and passed several times without giving it a thought. We go farther down the mountain and beat about to the right and left, and get entangled in brush and arrested by precipices, and finally, as the day is nearly spent, give up the search and leave the woods quite baffled, but resolved to return on the morrow. The next day we come back and commence operations in an opening in the woods well down on the side of the mountain where we gave up the search. Our box is soon swarming with the eager bees, and they go back toward the summit we have passed. We follow back and establish a new line, where the ground will permit; then another and still another, and yet the riddle is not solved. One time we are south of them, then north, then the bees get up through the trees and we cannot tell where they go. But after much searching, and after the mystery seems rather to deepen than to clear up, we chance to pause beside the old stump. A bee comes out of a small opening like that made by ants in decayed wood, rubs its eyes and examines its antennæ, as bees always do before leaving their hive, then takes flight. At the same instant several bees come by us loaded with our honey and settle home with that peculiar low, complacent buzz of the well-filled insect. Here, then, is our idyl, our bit of Virgil and Theocritus, in a decayed stump of a hemlock-tree. We could tear it open with our hands, and a bear would find it an easy prize, and a rich one, too, for we take from it fifty pounds of excellent honey. The bees have been here many years, and have of course sent out swarm after swarm into the wilds. They have protected themselves against the weather and strengthened their shaky habitation by a copious use of wax.

When a bee-tree is thus "taken up" in the middle of the day, of course a good many bees are away from home and have not heard the news. When they return and find the ground flowing with honey, and piles of bleeding combs lying about, they apparently do not recognize the place, and their first instinct is to fall to and fill themselves; this done, their next thought is to carry it home, so they rise up slowly through the branches of the trees till they have attained an altitude that enables them to survey the scene, when they seem to say, "Why, *this* is home," and down they come again; beholding the wreck and ruins once more, they still think there is some mistake, and get up a second or a third time and then drop back pitifully as before. It is the most pathetic sight of all, the surviving and bewildered bees struggling to save a few drops of their wasted treasures.

Presently, if there is another swarm in the woods, robber bees appear. You may know them by their saucy, chiding, devil-may-care hum. It is an ill wind that blows nobody good, and they make the most of the misfortune of their neighbors, and thereby pave the way for their own ruin. The hunter marks their course and the next day looks them up. On this occasion the day was hot and the honey very fragrant, and a line of bees was soon established

An Idyl of the Honey-Bee

S. S. W. Though there was much refuse honey in the old stub, and though little golden rills trickled down the hill from it, and the near branches and saplings were besmeared with it where we wiped our murderous hands, yet not a drop was wasted. It was a feast to which not only honey-bees came, but bumblebees, wasps, hornets, flies, ants. The bumblebees, which at this season are hungry vagrants with no fixed place of abode, would gorge themselves, then creep beneath the bits of empty comb or fragments of bark and pass the night, and renew the feast next day. The bumble-bee is an insect of which the bee-hunter sees much. There are all sorts and sizes of them. They are dull and clumsy compared with the honey-bee. Attracted in the fields by the bee-hunter's box, they will come up the wind on the scent and blunder into it in the most stupid, lubberly fashion.

The honey-bees that licked up our leavings on the old stub belonged to a swarm, as it proved, about half a mile farther down the ridge, and a few days afterward fate overtook them, and their stores in turn became the prey of another swarm in the vicinity, which also tempted Providence and were overwhelmed. The first-mentioned swarm I had lined from several points, and was following up the clew over rocks and through gulleys, when I came to where a large hemlock had been felled a few years before, and a swarm taken from a cavity near the top of it; fragments of the old comb were yet to be seen. A few yards away stood another short, squatty hemlock, and I said my bees ought to be there. As I paused near it, I noticed where the tree had been wounded with an ax a couple of feet from the ground many years before. The wound had partially grown over, but there was an opening there that I did not see at the first glance. I was about to pass on when a bee passed me making that peculiar shrill, discordant hum that a bee makes when besmeared with honey. I saw it alight in the partially closed wound and crawl home; then came others and others, little bands and squads of them heavily freighted with honey from the box. The tree was about twenty inches through and hollow at the butt, or from the ax-mark down. This space the bees had completely filled with honey. With an ax we cut away the outer ring of live wood and exposed the treasure. Despite the utmost care, we wounded the comb so that little rills of the golden liquid issued from the root of the tree and trickled down the hill.

The other bee-tree in the vicinity to which I have referred we found one warm November day in less than half an hour after entering the woods. It also was a hemlock that stood in a niche in a wall of hoary, moss-covered rocks thirty feet high. The tree hardly reached to the top of the precipice. The bees entered a small hole at the root, which was seven or eight feet from the ground. The position was a striking one. Never did apiary have a finer outlook or more rugged surroundings. A black, wood-embraced lake lay at our feet; the long panorama of the Catskills filled the far distance, and the more broken outlines of the Shawangunk range filled the rear. On every hand were precipices and a wild confusion of rocks and trees.

The cavity occupied by the bees was about three feet and a half long and eight or ten inches in diameter. With an ax we cut away one side of the tree, and laid bare its curiously wrought heart of honey. It was a most pleasing sight. What winding and devious ways the bees had through their palace! What great masses and blocks of snow-white comb there were! Where it was sealed up, presenting that slightly dented, uneven surface, it looked like some precious ore. When we carried a large pailful of it out of the woods it seemed still more like ore.

An Idyl of the Honey-Bee

Your native bee-hunter predicates the distance of the tree by the time the bee occupies in making its first trip. But this is no certain guide. You are always safe in calculating that the tree is inside of a mile, and you need not as a rule look for your bee's return under ten minutes. One day I picked up a bee in an opening in the woods and gave it honey, and it made three trips to my box with an interval of about twelve minutes between them; it returned alone each time; the tree, which I afterward found, was about half a mile distant.

In lining bees through the woods the tactics of the hunter are to pause every twenty or thirty rods, lop away the branches or cut down the trees, and set the bees to work again. If they still go forward, he goes forward also and repeats his observations till the tree is found, or till the bees turn and come back upon the trail. Then he knows he has passed the tree, and he retraces his steps to a convenient distance and tries again, and thus quickly reduces the space to be looked over till the swarm is traced home. On one occasion, in a wild rocky wood, where the surface alternated between deep gulfs and chasms filled with thick, heavy growths of timber and sharp, precipitous, rocky ridges like a tempest-tossed sea, I carried my bees directly under their tree, and set them to work from a high, exposed ledge of rocks not thirty feet distant. One would have expected them under such circumstances to have gone straight home, as there were but few branches intervening, but they did not; they labored up through the trees and attained an altitude above the woods as if they had miles to travel, and thus baffled me for hours. Bees will always do this. They are acquainted with the woods only from the top side, and from the air above; they recognize home only by landmarks here, and in every instance they rise aloft to take their bearings. Think how familiar to them the topography of the forest summits must be,—an umbrageous sea or plain where every mark and point is known.

Another curious fact is that generally you will get track of a bee-tree sooner when you are half a mile from it than when you are only a few yards. Bees, like us human insects, have little faith in the near at hand; they expect to make their fortune in a distant field, they are lured by the remote and the difficult, and hence overlook the flower and the sweet at their very door. On several occasions I have unwittingly set my box within a few paces of a bee-tree and waited long for bees without getting them, when, on removing to a distant field or opening in the woods, I have got a clew at once.

I have a theory that when bees leave the hive, unless there is some special attraction in some other direction, they generally go against the wind. They would thus have the wind with them when they returned home heavily laden, and with these little navigators the difference is an important one. With a full cargo, a stiff head-wind is a great hindrance, but fresh and empty-handed they can face it with more ease. Virgil says bees bear gravel stones as ballast, but their only ballast is their honey-bag. Hence, when I go bee-hunting, I prefer to get to windward of the woods in which the swarm is supposed to have refuge.

Bees, like the milkman, like to be near a spring. They do water their honey, especially in a dry time. The liquid is then of course thicker and sweeter, and will bear diluting. Hence old bee-hunters look for bee-trees along creeks and near spring runs in the woods. I once found a tree a long distance from any water, and the honey had a peculiar bitter flavor, imparted to it, I was convinced, by rainwater sucked from the decayed and spongy hemlock-tree in which the swarm was found. In cutting into the tree, the north side of it was found to be saturated with water like a spring, which ran out in big drops, and had a bitter flavor. The bees had thus found a spring or a cistern in their own house.

Bees are exposed to many hardships and many dangers. Winds and storms prove as disastrous to them as to other navigators. Black spiders lie in wait for them as do brigands for travelers. One day, as I was looking for a bee amid some goldenrod, I spied one partly concealed under a leaf. Its baskets were full of pollen, and it did not move. On lifting up the leaf I discovered that a hairy spider was ambushed there and had the bee by the throat. The vampire was evidently afraid of the bee's sting, and was holding it by the throat till quite sure of its death. Virgil speaks of the painted lizard, perhaps a species of salamander, as an enemy of the honey-bee. We have no lizard that destroys the bee; but our tree-toad, ambushed among the apple and cherry blossoms, snaps them up wholesale. Quick as lightning that subtle but clammy tongue darts forth, and the unsuspecting bee is gone. Virgil also accuses the titmouse and the woodpecker of preying upon the bees, and our kingbird has been charged with the like crime, but the latter devours only the drones. The workers are either too small and quick for it or else it dreads their sting.

Virgil, by the way, had little more than a child's knowledge of the honey-bee. There is little fact and much fable in his fourth Georgic. If he had ever kept bees himself, or even visited an apiary, it is hard to see how he could have believed that the bee in its flight abroad carried a gravel stone for ballast.

> "And as when empty barks on billows float,
> With sandy ballast sailors trim the boat;
> So bees bear gravel stones, whose poising weight
> Steers through the whistling winds their steady flight;"

or that, when two colonies made war upon each other, they issued forth from their hives led by their kings and fought in the air, strewing the ground with the dead and dying:—

> "Hard hailstones lie not thicker on the plain,
> Nor shaken oaks such show'rs of acorns rain."

It is quite certain he had never been bee-hunting. If he had we should have had a fifth Georgic. Yet he seems to have known that bees sometimes escaped to the woods:—

> "Nor bees are lodged in hives alone, but found
> In chambers of their own beneath the ground:
> Their vaulted roofs are hung in pumices,
> And in the rotten trunks of hollow trees."

Wild honey is as near like tame as wild bees are like their brothers in the hive. The only difference is, that wild honey is flavored with your adventure, which makes it a little more delectable than the domestic article.

[From *Pepacton,* by John Burroughs. Copyright, 1881, 1895, and 1909, by John Burroughs.]

CUT-OFF COPPLES'S

Clarence King

One October day, as Kaweah and I traveled by ourselves over a lonely foothill trail, I came to consider myself the friend of woodpeckers. With rather more reserve as regards the bluejay, let me admit great interest in his worldly wisdom. As an instance of co-operative living the partnership of these two birds is rather more hopeful than most mundane experiments. For many autumn and winter months such food as their dainty taste chooses is so rare throughout the Sierras that in default of any climatic temptation to migrate the birds get in harvests with annual regularity and surprising labor. Oak and pine mingle in open growth. Acorns from the one are their grain; the soft pine bark is granary; and this the process:

Armies of woodpeckers drill small, round holes in the bark of standing pine-trees, sometimes perforating it thickly up to twenty or thirty and even forty feet above the ground; then about equal numbers of woodpeckers and jays gather acorns, rejecting always the little cup, and insert the gland tightly in the pine bark with its tender base outward and exposed to the air.

A woodpecker, having drilled a hole, has its exact measure in mind, and after examining a number of acorns makes his selection, and never fails of a perfect fit. Not so the jolly, careless jay, who picks up any sound acorn he finds, and, if it is too large for a hole, drops it in the most offhand way as if it were an affair of no consequence; utters one of his dry, chuckling squawks, and either tries another or loafs about, lazily watching the hard-working woodpeckers.

Thus they live, amicably harvesting, and with this sequel: those acorns in which grubs form become the sole property of woodpeckers, while all sound ones fall to the jays. Ordinarily chances are in favor of woodpeckers, and when there are absolutely no sound nuts the jays sell short, to to speak, and go over to Nevada and speculate in juniper-berries.

The monotony of hill and glade failing to interest me, and in default of other diversion, I all day long watched the birds, recalling how many gay and successful jays I knew who lived, as these, on the wit and industry of less ostentatious woodpeckers; thinking, too, what naïvely dogmatic and richly worded political economy Mr. Ruskin would phrase from my feathered friends. Thus I came to Ruskin, wishing I might see the work of his idol, and after that longing for some equal artist who should arise and choose to paint our Sierras as they are with all their color-glory, power of innumerable pine and countless pinnacle, gloom of tempest, or splendor, where rushing light shatters itself upon granite crag, or burns in dying rose upon far fields of snow.

Had I rubbed Aladdin's lamp? A turn in the trail brought suddenly into view a man who sat under shadow of oaks, painting upon a large canvas.

As I approached, the artist turned half round upon his stool, rested palette and brushes upon one knee, and in familiar tone said, "Dern'd if you ain't just naturally ketched me at it! Get off and set down. You ain't going for no doctor, I know."

My artist was of short, good-natured, butcher-boy make-up, dressed in what had formerly been black broadcloth, with an enlivening show of red flannel shirt about the throat, wrists, and a considerable display of the same where his waistcoat might once have overlapped a strained but as yet coherent waistband. The cut of these garments, by length of coat-tail and voluminous leg, proudly asserted a " Bay " origin. His small feet were squeezed into tight, short boots, with high, raking heels.

A round face, with small, full mouth, non-committal nose, and black, protruding eyes, showed no more sign of the ideal temperament than did the broad daub upon his square yard of canvas.

" Going to Copples's? " inquired my friend.

That was my destination, and I answered, " Yes."

" That's me," he ejaculated. " Right over there, down below those two oaks! Ever there? "

" No."

" My *studio* 's there now;" giving impressive accent to the word.

All the while these few words were passing he scrutinized me with unconcealed curiosity, puzzled, as well he might be, by my dress and equipment. Finally, after I had tied Kaweah to a tree and seated myself by the easel, and after he had absently rubbed some raw sienna into his little store of white, he softly ventured: " Was you looking out a ditch? "

" No," I replied.

He neatly rubbed up the white and sienna with his " blender," unconsciously adding a dash of Veronese green, gazed at my leggings, then at the barometer, and again meeting my eye with a look as if he feared I might be a disguised duke, said in slow tone, with hyphens of silence between each two syllables, giving to his language all the dignity of an unabridged Webster, " I would take pleasure in stating that my name is Hank G. Smith, artist; " and, seeing me smile, he relaxed a little, and, giving the blender another vigorous twist, added, "I would request yours."

Mr. Smith having learned my name, occupation, and that my home was on the Hudson, near New York, quickly assumed a familiar me-and-you-old-fel' tone, and rattled on merrily about his winter in New York spent in "going through the Academy,"—a period of deep moment to one who before that painted only wagons for his livelihood.

Storing away canvas, stool, and easel in a deserted cabin close by, he rejoined me, and, leading Kaweah by his lariat, I walked beside Smith down the trail toward Copples's.

He talked freely, and as if composing his own biography, beginning:

"California-born and mountain-raised, his nature soon drove him into a painter's career." Then he reverted fondly to New York and his experience there.

"Oh, no!" he mused in pleasant irony, "he never spread his napkin over his legs and partook French victuals up to old Delmonico's. 'Twasn't H. G. which took *her* to the theater."

In a sort of stage-aside to me, he added, "*She* was a *model!* Stood for them sculptors, you know; perfectly virtuous, and built from the ground up." Then, as if words failed him, made an expressive gesture with both hands over his shirt-bosom to indicate the topography of her figure, and, sliding them down sharply against his waistband, he added, "Anatomical torso!"

Mr. Smith found relief in meeting one so near himself, as he conceived me to be, in habit and experience. The long-pent-up emotions and ambitions of his life found ready utterance, and a willing listener.

I learned that his aim was to become a characteristically California painter, with special designs for making himself famous as the delineator of mule-trains and ox-wagons; to be, as he expressed it, "the Pacific Slope Bonheur."

"There," he said, "is old Eastman Johnson; he's made the riffle on barns, and that everlasting girl with the ears of corn; but it ain't *life,* it ain't got the real git-up.

"If you want to see *the* thing, just look at a Gérôme; his Arab folks and Egyptian dancing-girls, they ain't assuming a pleasant expression and looking at spots while their likenesses is took.

"H. G. will discount Eastman yet."

He avowed his great admiration of Church, which, with a little leaning toward Mr. Gifford, seemed his only hearty approval.

"It's all Bierstadt, and Bierstadt, and Bierstadt nowadays! What has he done but twist and skew and distort and discolor and belittle and be-pretty this whole dog-gonned country? Why, his mountains are too high and too slim; they'd blow over in one of our fall winds.

"I've herded colts two summers in Yosemite, and honest now, when I stood right up in front of his picture, I didn't know it.

"He hasn't what old Ruskin calls for."

By this time the station buildings were in sight, and far down the cañon, winding in even grade round spur after spur, outlined by a low, clinging cloud of red dust, we could see the great Sierra mule-train,—that industrial gulf-stream flowing from California plains over into arid Nevada, carrying thither materials for life and luxury. In a vast, perpetual caravan of heavy wagons, drawn by teams of from eight to fourteen mules, all the supplies of many cities and villages were hauled across the Sierra at an immense cost, and with such skill of driving and generalship of mules as the world has never seen before.

Our trail descended toward the grade, quickly bringing us to a high bank immediately overlooking the trains a few rods below the group of station buildings.

I had by this time learned that Copples, the former station-proprietor, had suffered amputation of the leg three times, receiving from the road men, in consequence, the name of "Cut-off," and that, while his doctors disagreed as to whether they had better try a fourth, the kindly hand of death had spared him that pain, and Mrs. Copples an added extortion in the bill.

The dying "Cut-off" had made his wife promise she would stay by and carry on the station until all his debts, which were many and heavy, should be paid, and then do as she chose.

The poor woman, a New Englander of some refinement, lingered, sadly fulfilling her task, though longing for liberty.

When Smith came to speak of Sarah Jane, her niece, a new light kindled in my friend's eye.

"You never saw Sarah Jane?" he inquired.

I shook my head.

He went on to tell me that he was living in hope of making her Mrs. H. G., but that the bar-keeper also indulged a hope, and as this important functionary was a man of ready cash, and of derringers and few words, it became a delicate matter to avow open rivalry; but it was evident my friend's star was ascendant, and, learning that he considered himself to possess the "dead-wood," and to have "gaited" the bar-keeper, I was more than amused, even comforted.

It was pleasure to sit there leaning against a vigorous old oak while Smith opened his heart to me, in easy confidence, and, with quick eye watching the passing mules, penciled in a little sketch-book a leg, a head, or such portions of body and harness as seemed to him useful for future works.

"These are notes," he said, "and I've pretty much made up my mind to paint my great picture on a *gee-pull*. I'll scumble in a sunset effect, lighting up the dust, and striking across the backs of team and driver, and I'll paint a come-up-there-d'n-you look on the old teamster's face, and the mules will be just a-humping their little selves and laying down to work like they'd expire. And the wagon! Don't you see what fine color-material there is in the heavy load and canvas-top with sunlight and shadow in the folds? And that's what's the matter with H. G. Smith.

"Orders, sir, orders; that's what I'll get then, and I'll take my little old Sarah Jane and light out for New York, and you'll see *Smith* on a studio doorplate, and folks 'll say, 'Fine feeling for nature, has Smith!'"

I let this singular man speak for himself in his own vernacular, pruning nothing of its idiom or slang, as you shall choose to call it. In this faithful transcript there are words I could have wished to expunge, but they are his, not mine, and illustrate his mental construction.

The breath of most Californians is as unconsciously charged with slang as an Italian's of garlic, and the two, after all, have much the same function; you touch the bowl or your language, but should never let either be fairly recognized in salad or conversation. But Smith's English was the well undefiled when compared with what I every moment heard from the current of teamsters which set constantly by us in the direction of Copples's.

Close in front came a huge wagon piled high with cases of freight, and drawn along by a team of twelve mules, whose heavy breathing and drenched skins showed them hard-worked and well tired out. The driver looked anxiously ahead at a soft spot in the road, and on at the station, as if calculating whether his team had courage left to haul through.

He called kindly to them, cracked his black-snake whip, and all together they strained bravely on.

The great van rocked, settled a little on the near side, and stuck fast.

With a look of despair the driver got off and laid the lash freely among his team; they jumped and jerked, frantically tangled themselves up, and at last all sulked and became stubbornly immovable. Meanwhile, a mile of teams behind, unable to pass on the narrow grade, came to an unwilling halt.

About five wagons back I noticed a tall Pike, dressed in checked shirt, and pantaloons tucked into jack-boots. A soft felt hat, worn on the back of his head, displayed long locks of flaxen hair, which hung freely about a florid pink countenance, noticeable for its pair of violent little blue eyes, and facial angle rendered acute by a sharp, long nose.

This fellow watched the stoppage with impatience, and at last, when it was more than he could bear, walked up by the other teams with a look of wrath absolutely devilish. One would have expected him to blow up with rage; yet withal his gait and manner were cool and soft in the extreme. In a bland, almost tender voice, he said to the unfortunate driver, " My friend, perhaps I can help you;" and his gentle way of disentangling and patting the leaders as he headed them round in the right direction would have given him a high office under Mr. Bergh. He leisurely examined the embedded wheel, and cast an eye along the road ahead. He then began in rather excited manner to swear, pouring it out louder and more profane, till he utterly eclipsed the most horrid blasphemies I ever heard, piling them up thicker and more fiendish till it seemed as if the very earth must open and engulf him.

I noticed one mule after another give a little squat, bringing their breasts hard against the collars, and straining traces, till only one old mule, with ears back and dangling chain, still held out. The Pike walked up and yelled one gigantic oath; her ears sprang forward, she squatted in terror, and the iron links grated under her strain. He then stepped back and took the rein, every trembling mule looking out of the corner of its eye and listening at *qui vive*.

With a peculiar air of deliberation and of childlike simplicity, he said in every-day tones, "Come up there, mules!"

One quick strain, a slight rumble, and the wagon rolled on to Copples's.

Smith and I followed, and as we neared the house he punched me familiarly and said, as a brown petticoat disappeared in the station door, "There's Sarah Jane! When I see that girl I feel like I'd reach out and gather her in;" then clasping her imaginary form as if she was about to dance with him, he executed a couple of waltz turns, softly intimating, "That's what's the matter with H. G."

Kaweah being stabled, we betook ourselves to the office, which was of course bar-room as well. As I entered, the unfortunate teamster was about paying his liquid compliment to the florid Pike. Their glasses were filled. "My respects," said the little driver. The whiskey became lost to view, and went eroding its way through the dust these poor fellows had swallowed. He added, "Well, Billy, you *can* swear."

"Swear?" repeated the Pike in a tone of incredulous questioning. "Me swear?" as if the compliment were greater than his modest desert. "No, I can't blaspheme worth a cuss. You'd jest orter hear Pete Green. *He can exhort the impenitent mule.* I've known a ten-mule-team to renounce the flesh and haul thirty-one thousand through a foot of clay mud under one of his outpourings."

As a hotel, Copples's is on the Mongolian plan, which means that dining-room and kitchen are given over to the mercies—never very tender—of Chinamen; not such Chinamen as learned the art of pig-roasting that they might be served up by Elia, but the average John, and a sadly low average that John is. I grant him a certain general air of thrift, admitting, too, that his lack of sobriety never makes itself apparent in loud Celtic brawl. But he is, when all is said, and in spite of timid and fawning obedience, a very poor servant.

Now and then at one friend's house it has happened to me that I dined upon artistic Chinese cookery, and all they who come home from living in China smack their lips over the relishing *cuisine*. I wish they had sat down that day at Copples's. No; on second thought I would spare them.

John may go peacefully to North Adams and make shoes for us, but I shall not solve the awful domestic problem by bringing him into my kitchen; certainly so long as Howells's "Mrs. Johnson" lives, nor even while I can get an Irish lady to torment me, and offer the hospitality of my home to her cousins.

After the warning bell, fifty or sixty teamsters inserted their dusty heads in buckets of water, turned their once white neck-handkerchiefs inside out, producing a sudden effect of clean linen, and made use of the two mournful wrecks of combs which hung on strings at either side the Copples's mirror. Many went to the bar and partook of a "dust-cutter." There was then such clearing of throats, and such loud and prolonged blowing of noses as may not often be heard upon this globe.

In the calm which ensued, conversation sprang up on

"lead harness," the "Stockton wagon that had went off the grade," with here and there a sentiment called out by two framed lithographic belles, who in great richness of color and scantiness of raiment flanked the bar-mirror;—a dazzling reflector, chiefly destined to portray the barkeeper's back hair, which work of art involved much affectionate labor.

A second bell and rolling away of doors revealed a long dining-room, with three parallel tables, cleanly set and watched over by Chinamen, whose fresh, white clothes and bright, olive-buff skin made a contrast of color which was always chief among my yearnings for the Nile.

While I loitered in the background every seat was taken, and I found myself with a few dilatory teamsters destined to await a second table.

The dinner-room communicated with a kitchen beyond by means of two square apertures cut in the partition wall. Through these portholes a glare of red light poured, except when the square framed a Chinese cook's head, or discharged hundreds of little dishes.

The teamsters sat down in patience; a few of the more elegant sort cleaned their nails with the three-tine forks, others picked their teeth with them, and nearly all speared with this implement small specimens from the dishes before them, securing a pickle or a square inch of pie or even that luxury, a dried apple; a few, on tilted-back chairs, drummed upon the bottom of their plates the latest tune of the road.

When fairly under way the scene became active and animated beyond belief. Waiters, balancing upon their arms twenty or thirty plates, hurried along and shot them dexterously over the teamsters' heads with crash and spatter.

Beans swimming in fat, meats slimed with pale, ropy

gravy, and over everything a faint Mongol odor,—the flavor of moral degeneracy and of a disintegrating race.

Sharks and wolves may no longer be figured as types of prandial haste. My friends, the teamsters, stuffed and swallowed with a rapidity which was alarming but for the dexterity they showed, and which could only have come of long practice.

In fifteen minutes the room was empty, and those fellows who were not feeding grain to their mules lighted cigars and lingered round the bar.

Just then my artist rushed in, seized me by the arm, and said in my ear, " We'll have *our* supper over to Mrs. Copples's. O no, I guess not—Sarah Jane—arms peeled —cooking up stuff—old woman gone into the milk-room with a skimmer." He then added that if I wanted to see what I had been spared, I might follow him.

We went round an angle of the building and came upon a high bank, where, through wide-open windows, I could look into the Chinese kitchen.

By this time the second table of teamsters were under way, and the waiters yelled their orders through to the three cooks.

This large, unpainted kitchen was lighted up by kerosene lamps. Through clouds of smoke and steam dodged and sprang the cooks, dripping with perspiration and grease, grabbing a steak in the hand and slapping it down on the gridiron, slipping and sliding around on the damp floor, dropping a card of biscuits and picking them up again in their fists, which were garnished by the whole bill of fare. The red papers with Chinese inscriptions, and little joss-sticks here and there pasted upon each wall, the spry devils themselves, and that faint, sickening odor of China which pervaded the room, combined to produce a sense of deep, sober gratitude that I had not risked their fare.

"Now," demanded Smith, "you see that there little white building yonder?"

I did.

He struck a contemplative position, leaned against the house, extending one hand after the manner of the minstrel sentimentalist, and softly chanted:

> "''Tis, O, 'tis the cottage of me love;'

"and there's where they're getting up as nice a little supper as can be found on this road or any other. Let's go over!"

So we strolled across an open space where were two giant pines towering somber against the twilight, a little mountain brooklet, and a few quiet cows.

"Stop," said Smith, leaning his back against a pine, and encircling my neck affectionately with an arm; "I told you, as regards Sarah Jane, how my feelings stand. Well, now, you just bet she's on the reciprocate! When I told old woman Copples I'd like to invite you over,—Sarah Jane she passed me in the doorway,—and said she, 'Glad to see *your* friends.'"

Then *sotto voce*, for we were very near, he sang again:

> "''Tis, O, 'tis the cottage of me love;'

"and C. K.," he continued familiarly, "you're a judge of wimmen," chucking his knuckles into my ribs, whereat I jumped; when he added, "There, I knew you was. Well, Sarah Jane is a derned magnificent female; number three boot, just the height for me. *Venus de* Copples, I call her, and would make the most touching artist's wife in this planet. If I design to paint a head, or a foot, or an arm, get my little old Sarah Jane to peel the particular charm, and just whack her in on the canvas."

We passed in through low doors, turned from a small, dark entry into the family sitting-room, and were alone there in presence of a cheery log fire, which good-naturedly bade us welcome, crackling freely and tossing its sparks out upon floor of pine and coyote-skin rug. A few old framed prints hung upon dark walls, their faces looking serenely down upon the scanty, old-fashioned furniture and windows full of flowering plants. A low-cushioned chair, not long since vacated, was drawn close by the centre-table, whereon were a lamp and a large, open Bible, with a pair of silver-bowed spectacles lying upon its lighted page.

Smith made a gesture of silence toward the door, touched the Bible, and whispered, "*Here's* where old woman Copples lives, and it is a good thing; I read it aloud to her evenings, and I can just feel the high, local lights of it. It'll fetch H. G. yet!"

At this juncture the door opened; a pale, thin, elderly woman entered, and with tired smile greeted me. While her hard, labor-stiffened, needle-roughened hand was in mine, I looked into her face and felt something (it may be, it must be, but little, yet something) of the sorrow of her life; that of a woman large in sympathy, deep in faith, eternal in constancy, thrown away on a rough, worthless fellow. All things she hoped for had failed her; the tenderness which never came, the hopes years ago in ashes, the whole world of her yearnings long buried, leaving only the duty of living and the hope of Heaven. As she sat down, took up her spectacles and knitting, and closed the Bible, she began pleasantly to talk to us of the warm, bright autumn nights, of Smith's work, and then of my own profession, and of her niece, Sarah Jane. Her genuinely sweet spirit and natively gentle manner were very beautiful, and far overbalanced all traces of rustic birth and mountain life.

O, that unquenchable Christian fire, how pure the gold of its result! It needs no practiced elegance, no social greatness, for its success; only the warm human heart, and out of it shall come a sacred calm and gentleness, such as no power, no wealth, no culture may ever hope to win.

No words of mine would outline the beauty of that plain, weary old woman, the sad, sweet patience of those gray eyes, nor the spirit of overflowing goodness which cheered and enlivened the half hour we spent there.

H. G. might perhaps be pardoned for showing an alacrity when the door again opened and Sarah Jane rolled—I might almost say trundled—in, and was introduced to me.

Sarah Jane was an essentially Californian product, as much so as one of those vast potatoes or massive pears; she had a suggestion of State-Fair in the fullness of her physique, yet withal was pretty and modest.

If I could have rid myself of a fear that her buttons might sooner or later burst off and go singing by my ear, I think I might have felt as H. G. did, that she was a "magnificent female," with her smooth, brilliant skin and ropes of soft brown hair.

H. G., in presence of the ladies, lost something of his original flavor, and rose into studied elegance, greatly to the comfort of Sarah, whose glow of pride as his talk ran on came without show of restraint.

The supper was delicious.

But Sarah was quiet, quiet to H. G. and to me, until after tea, when the old lady said, "You young folks will have to excuse me this evening," and withdrew to her chamber.

More logs were then piled on the sitting-room hearth, and we three gathered in a semi-circle.

Presently H. G. took the poker and twisted it about among coals and ashes, prying up the oak sticks, as he announced, in a measured, studied way, "An artist's wife, that is," he explained, "an Academician's wife orter, well she'd orter *sabe* the beautiful, and take her regular æsthetics; and then again," he continued in explanatory tone, "she'd orter to know how to keep a hotel, derned if she hadn't, for it's rough like furst off, 'fore a feller gets his name up. But then when he does, tho', she's got a salubrious old time of it. It's touch a little bell" (he pressed the andiron-top to show us how the thing was done), "and 'Brooks, the morning paper!' Open your regular Herald:

"'ART NOTES.—Another of H. G. Smith's tender works, entitled, "Off the Grade," so full of out-of-doors and subtle feeling of nature, is now on exhibition at Goupil's.'

"Look down a little further:

"'ITALIAN OPERA.—Between the acts all eyes turned to the *distingué* Mrs. H. G. Smith, who looked,'"—then turning to me, and waving his hand at Sarah Jane, "I leave it to you if she don't."

Sarah Jane assumed the pleasing color of the sugar-beet, without seeming inwardly unhappy.

"It's only a question of time with H. G.," continued my friend. "Art is long, you know—derned long—and it may be a year before I paint my great picture, but after that Smith works in lead harness."

He used the poker freely, and more and more his flow of hopes turned a shade of sentiment to Sarah Jane, who smiled broader and broader, showing teeth of healthy whiteness.

At last I withdrew and sought my room, which was H. G.'s also, and his studio. I had gone with a candle round the walls whereon were tacked studies and sketches, finding here and there a bit of real merit among the profusion of trash, when the door burst open and my friend entered, kicked off his boots and trousers, and walked up and down at a sort of quadrille step, singing:

> "'Yes, it's the cottage of me love;
> You bet, it's the cottage of me love,'

"and, what's more, H. G. has just had his genteel goodnight kiss; and when and where is the good old bar-keep?"

I checked his exuberance as best I might, knowing full well that the quiet and elegant dispenser of neat and mixed beverages hearing this inquiry would put in an appearance in person and offer a few remarks designed to provoke ill-feeling. So I at last got Smith in bed and the lamp out. All was quiet for a few moments, and when I had almost gotten asleep I heard my room-mate in low tones say to himself,—

"Married, by the Rev. Gospel, our talented California artist, Mr. H. G. Smith, to Miss Sarah Jane Copples. No cards."

A, pause, and then with more gentle utterance, "and that's what's the matter with H. G."

Slowly from this atmosphere of art I passed away into the tranquil land of dreams.

[From *Mountaineering in the Sierra Nevada,* by Clarence King. Copyright, 1871, by James R. Osgood & Co. Copyright, 1902, by Charles Scribner's Sons.]

THE THÉÂTRE FRANÇAIS

Henry James

M. Francisque Sarcey, the dramatic critic of the Paris "Temps," and the gentleman who, of the whole journalistic fraternity, holds the fortune of a play in the hollow of his hand, has been publishing during the last year a series of biographical notices of the chief actors and actresses of the first theater in the world. *Comédiens et Comédiennes: la Comédie Française*—such is the title of this publication, which appears in monthly numbers of the "Librairie des Bibliophiles," and is ornamented on each occasion with a very prettily etched portrait, by M. Gaucherel, of the artist to whom the number is devoted. By lovers of the stage in general and of the Théâtre Français in particular the series will be found most interesting; and I welcome the pretext for saying a few words about an institution which—if such language be not hyperbolical—I passionately admire. I must add that the portrait is incomplete, though for the present occasion it is more than sufficient. The list of M. Sarcey's biographies is not yet filled up; three or four, those of Madame Favart and of MM. Fèbvre and Delaunay, are still wanting. Nine numbers, however, have appeared—the first being entitled *La Maison de Molière,* and devoted to a general account of the great theater; and the others treating of its principal *sociétaires* and *pensionnaires* in the following order:

Regnier,
Got,
Sophie Croizette,
Sarah Bernhardt,
Coquelin,
Madeleine Brohan,
Bressant,
Madame Plessy.

(This order, by the way, is purely accidental; it is not that of age or of merit.) It is always entertaining to encounter M. Francisque Sarcey, and the reader who, during a Paris winter, has been in the habit, of a Sunday evening, of unfolding his " Temps " immediately after unfolding his napkin, and glancing down first of all to see what this sturdy *feuilletoniste* has found to his hand—such a reader will find him in great force in the pages before us. It is true that, though I myself confess to being such a reader, there are moments when I grow rather weary of M. Sarcey, who has in an eminent degree both the virtues and the defects which attach to the great French characteristic—the habit of taking terribly *au sérieux* anything that you may set about doing. Of this habit of abounding in one's own sense, of expatiating, elaborating, reiterating, refining, as if for the hour the fate of mankind were bound up with one's particular topic, M. Sarcey is a capital and at times an almost comical representative. He talks about the theater once a week as if—honestly, between himself and his reader—the theater were the only thing in this frivolous world that is worth seriously talking about. He has a religious respect for his theme and he holds that if a thing is to be done at all it must be done in detail as well as in the gross.

It is to this serious way of taking the matter, to his thoroughly businesslike and professional attitude, to his unwearying attention to detail, that the critic of the " Temps " owes his enviable influence and the weight of his words. Add to this that he is sternly incorruptible. He has his admirations, but they are honest and discriminating; and whom he loveth he very often chasteneth. He is not ashamed to commend Mlle. X., who has only had a curtsy to make, if her curtsy has been the ideal curtsy of the situation; and he is not afraid to overhaul M. A., who has delivered the *tirade* of the play, if M. A., has failed to hit the mark. Of course his judgment is good; when I have had occasion to measure it I have usually found it excellent. He has the scenic sense—the theatrical eye. He knows at a glance what will do, and what will not do. He is shrewd and sagacious and almost tiresomely in earnest, and this is his principal brilliancy. He is homely, familiar and colloquial; he leans his elbows on his desk and does up his weekly budget into a parcel the reverse of coquettish. You can fancy him a grocer retailing tapioca and hominy—full weight for the price; his style seems a sort of integument of brown paper. But the fact remains that if M. Sarcey praises a play the play has a run; and that if M. Sarcey says it will not do it does not do at all. If M. Sarcey devotes an encouraging line and a half to a young actress, mademoiselle is immediately *lancée;* she has a career. If he bestows a quiet "bravo" on an obscure comedian, the gentleman may forthwith renew his engagement. When you make and unmake fortunes at this rate, what matters it whether you have a little elegance the more or the less? Elegance is for M. Paul de St. Victor, who does the theaters in the " Moniteur," and who, though he writes a style only a trifle less pictorial than that of Théophile Gautier himself, has never, to the best of my belief, brought clouds or sunshine to any playhouse. I may add, to finish with M. Sarcey, that he contributes a daily political article—generally devoted to watching and showing up the "game" of the clerical party—to Edmond About's journal, the "XIXième Siècle"; that he gives a weekly *conférence* on current literature; that he " confers " also on those excellent Sunday morning performances now so common in the French theaters, during which examples of the classic reportory are presented, accompanied by a light lecture upon the history and character of the play. As the commentator on these occasions M. Sarcey is in great demand, and he officiates sometimes in small provincial towns. Lastly, frequent playgoers in Paris observe that the very slenderest novelty is sufficient to insure at a theater the (very considerable) physical presence of the conscientious critic of the " Temps." If he were remarkable for nothing else he would be remarkable for the fortitude with which he exposes himself to the pestiferous climate of the Parisian temples of the drama.

For these agreeable " notices " M. Sarcey appears to have mended his pen and to have given a fillip to his fancy. They are gracefully and often lightly turned; occasionally, even, the author grazes the epigrammatic. They deal, as is proper, with the artistic and not with the private physiognomy of the ladies and gentlemen whom they commemorate; and though they occasionally allude to what the French call " intimate " matters, they contain no satisfaction for the lovers of scandal. The Théâtre Français, in the face it presents to the world, is an austere and venerable establishment, and a frivolous tone about its affairs would be almost as much out of keeping as if applied to the Académie herself. M. Sarcey touches upon the organization of the theater, and gives some account of the different phases through which it has passed during these latter years. Its chief functionary is a general administrator, or director, appointed by the State, which enjoys this right in virtue of the considerable subsidy which it pays to the house; a subsidy amounting, if I am not mistaken (M. Sarcey does not mention the sum), to 250,000 francs. The director, however, is not an absolute but a constitutional ruler; for he shares his powers with the society itself, which has always had a large deliberative voice.

Whence, it may be asked, does the society derive its light and its inspiration? From the past, from precedent, from tradition—from the great unwritten body of laws which no one has in his keeping but many have in their memory, and all in their respect. The principles on which the Théâtre Français rests are a good deal like the Common Law of England—a vaguely and inconveniently registered mass of regulations which time and occasion have welded together and from which the recurring occasion can usually manage to extract the rightful precedent. Napoleon I., who had a finger in every pie in his dominion, found time during his brief and disastrous occupation of Moscow to send down a decree remodeling and regulating the constitution of the theater. This document has long been a dead letter, and the society abides by its older traditions. The *traditions* of the Comédie Française—that is the sovereign word, and that is the charm of the place—the charm that one never ceases to feel, however often one may sit beneath the classic, dusky dome. One feels this charm with peculiar intensity as a newly arrived foreigner. The Théâtre Français has had the good fortune to be able to allow its traditions to accumulate. They have been preserved, transmitted, respected, cherished, until at last they form the very atmosphere, the vital air, of the establishment. A stranger feels their superior influence the first time he sees the great curtain go up; he feels that he is in a theater that is not as other theaters are. It is not only better, it is different. It has a peculiar perfection—something consecrated, historical, academic. This impression is delicious, and he watches the performance in a sort of tranquil ecstasy.

Never has he seen anything so smooth and harmonious, so artistic and complete. He has heard all his life of attention to detail, and now, for the first time, he sees something that deserves the name. He sees dramatic effort refined to a point with which the English stage is unacquainted. He sees that there are no limits to possible "finish," and that so trivial an act as taking a letter from a servant or placing one's hat on a chair may be made a suggestive and interesting incident. He sees these things and a great many more besides, but at first he does not analyze them; he gives himself up to sympathetic contemplation. He is in an ideal and exemplary world—a world that has managed to attain all the felicities that the world we live in misses. The people do the things that we should like to do; they are gifted as we should like to be; they have mastered the accomplishments that we have had to give up. The women are not all beautiful—decidedly not, indeed—but they are graceful, agreeable, sympathetic, ladylike; they have the best manners possible and they are delightfully well dressed. They have charming musical voices and they speak with irreproachable purity and sweetness; they walk with the most elegant grace and when they sit it is a pleasure to see their attitudes. They go out and come in, they pass across the stage, they talk, and laugh, and cry, they deliver long *tirades* or remain statuesquely mute; they are tender or tragic, they are comic or conventional; and through it all you never observe an awkwardness, a roughness, an accident, a crude spot, a false note.

As for the men, they are not handsome either; it must be confessed, indeed, that at the present hour manly beauty is but scantily represented at the Théâtre Français. Bressant, I believe, used to be thought handsome; but Bressant has retired, and among the gentlemen of the troupe I can think of no one but M. Mounet-Sully who may be positively commended for his fine person. But M. Mounet-Sully is, from the scenic point of view, an Adonis of the first magnitude. To be handsome, however, is for an actor one of the last necessities; and these gentlemen are mostly handsome enough. They look perfectly what they are intended to look, and in cases where it is proposed that they shall seem handsome, they usually succeed. They are as well mannered and as well dressed as their fairer comrades and their voices are no less agreeable and effective. They represent gentlemen and they produce the illusion. In this endeavour they deserve even greater credit than the actresses, for in modern comedy, of which the repertory of the Théâtre Français is largely composed, they have nothing in the way of costume to help to carry it off. Half-a-dozen ugly men, in the periodic coat and trousers and stove-pipe hat, with blue chins and false mustaches, strutting before the footlights, and pretending to be interesting, romantic, pathetic, heroic, certainly play a perilous game. At every turn they suggest prosaic things and the usual liability to awkwardness is meantime increased a thousandfold. But the comedians of the Théâtre Français are never awkward, and when it is necessary they solve triumphantly the problem of being at once realistic to the eye and romantic to the imagination.

I am speaking always of one's first impression of them. There are spots on the sun, and you discover after a while that there are little irregularities at the Théâtre Français. But the acting is so incomparably better than any that you have seen that criticism for a long time is content to lie dormant. I shall never forget how at first I was under the charm. I liked the very incommodities of the place; I am not sure that I did not find a certain mystic salubrity in the bad ventilation. The Théâtre Français, it is known, gives you a good deal for your money. The performance, which rarely ends before midnight, and sometimes transgresses it, frequently begins by seven o'clock. The first hour or two is occupied by secondary performers; but not for the world at this time would I have missed the first rising of the curtain. No dinner could be too hastily swallowed to enable me to see, for instance, Madame Nathalie in Octave Feuillet's charming little comedy of "Le Village." Madame Nathalie was a plain, stout old woman, who did the mothers and aunts and elderly wives; I use the past tense because she retired from the stage a year ago, leaving a most conspicuous vacancy. She was an admirable actress and a perfect mistress of laughter and tears. In "Le Village" she played an old provincial bourgeoise whose husband takes it into his head, one winter night, to start on the tour of Europe with a roving bachelor friend, who has dropped down on him at supper-time, after the lapse of years, and has gossiped him into momentary discontent with his fireside existence. My pleasure was in Madame Nathalie's figure when she came in dressed to go out to vespers across the *place*. The two foolish old cronies are over their wine, talking of the beauty of the women on the Ionian coast; you hear the church-bell in the distance. It was the quiet felicity of the old lady's dress that used to charm me; the Comédie Française was in every fold of it. She wore a large black silk mantilla, of a peculiar cut, which looked as if she had just taken it tenderly out of some old wardrobe where it lay folded in lavender, and a large dark bonnet, adorned with handsome black silk loops and bows. Her big pale face had a softly frightened look, and in her hand she carried her neatly kept breviary. The extreme suggestiveness, and yet the taste and temperance of this costume, seemed to me inimitable; the bonnet alone, with its handsome, decent, virtuous bows, was worth coming to see. It expressed all the rest, and you saw the excellent, pious woman go pick her steps churchward among the puddles, while Jeannette, the cook, in a high white cap, marched before her in sabots with a lantern.

Such matters are trifles, but they are representative trifles, and they are not the only ones that I remember. It used to please me, when I had squeezed into my stall—the stalls at the Français are extremely uncomfortable—to remember of how great a history the large, dim *salle* around me could boast; how many great things had happened there; how the air was thick with associations. Even if I had never seen Rachel, it was something of a consolation to think that those very footlights had illumined her finest moments and that the echoes of her mighty voice were sleeping in that dingy dome. From this to musing upon the "traditions" of the place, of which I spoke just now, was of course but a step. How were they kept? by whom, and where? Who trims the undying lamp and guards the accumulated treasure? I never found out—by sitting in the stalls; and very soon I ceased to care to know. One may be very fond of the stage and yet care little for the green-room; just as one may be very fond of pictures and books and yet be no frequenter of studios and authors' dens. They might pass on the torch as they would behind the scenes; so long as during my time they did not let it drop I made up my mind to be satisfied. And that one could depend upon their not letting it drop became a part of the customary comfort of Parisian life. It became certain that the "traditions" were not mere catchwords, but a most beneficent reality.

Going to the other Parisian theaters helps you to believe in them. Unless you are a voracious theater-goer you give the others up; you find they do not "pay"; the Français does for you all that they do and so much more besides. There are two possible exceptions—the Gymnase and the Palais Royal. The Gymnase, since the death of Mademoiselle Desclée, has been under a heavy cloud; but occasionally, when a month's sunshine rests upon it, there is a savor of excellence in the performance. But you feel that you are still within the realm of accident; the delightful security of the Rue de Richelieu is wanting. The young lover is liable to be common and the beautifully dressed heroine to have an unpleasant voice. The Palais Royal has always been in its way very perfect; but its way admits of great imperfection. The actresses are classically bad, though usually pretty, and the actors are much addicted to taking liberties. In broad comedy, nevertheless, two or three of the latter are not to be surpassed, and (counting out the women) there is usually something masterly in a Palais Royal performance. In its own line it has what is called style, and it therefore walks, at a distance, in the footsteps of the Français. The Odéon has never seemed to me in any degree a rival of the Théâtre Français, though it is a smaller copy of that establishment. It receives a subsidy from the State, and is obliged by its contract to play the classic repertory one night in the week. It is on these nights, listening to Molière or Marivaux, that you may best measure the superiority of the greater theater. I have seen actors at the Odéon, in the classic repertory, imperfect in their texts; a monstrously insupposable case at the Comédie Française. The function of the Odéon is to operate as a *pépinière* or nursery for its elder—to try young talents, shape them, make them flexible and then hand them over to the upper house. The more especial nursery of the Français, however, is the Conservatoire Dramatique, an institution dependent upon the State, through the Ministry of the Fine Arts, whose budget is charged with the remuneration of its professors. Pupils graduating from the Conservatoire with a prize have *ipso facto* the right to *débuter* at the Théâtre Français, which retains them or lets them go, according to its discretion. Most of the first subjects of the Français have done their two years' work at the Conservatoire, and M. Sarcey holds that an actor who has not had that fundamental training which is only to be acquired there never obtains a complete mastery of his resources. Nevertheless some of the best actors of the day have owed nothing to the Conservatoire—Bressant, for instance, and Aimée Desclée, the latter of whom, indeed, never arrived at the Français. (Molière and Balzac were not of the Academy, and so Mlle. Desclée, the first actress after Rachel, died without acquiring the privilege which M. Sarcey says is the day-dream of all young theatrical women—that of printing on their visiting-cards, after their name, *de la Comédie Française.*)

The Théâtre Français has, moreover, the right to do as Molière did—to claim its property wherever it finds it. It may stretch out its long arm and break the engagement of a promising actor at any of the other theaters; of course after a certain amount of notice given. So, last winter, it notified to the Gymnase its design of appropriating Worms, the admirable *jeune premier,* who, returning from a long sojourn in Russia and taking the town by surprise, had begun to retrieve the shrunken fortunes of that establishment.

On the whole, it may be said that the great talents find their way, sooner or later, to the Théâtre Français. This is of course not a rule that works unvaryingly, for there are a great many influences to interfere with it. Interest as well as merit—especially in the case of the actresses—weighs in the scale; and the ire that may exist in celestial minds has been known to manifest itself in the councils of the Comédie. Moreover, a brilliant actress may prefer to reign supreme at one of the smaller theaters; at the Français, inevitably, she shares her dominion. The honor is less, but the comfort is greater.

Nevertheless, at the Français, in a general way, there is in each case a tolerably obvious artistic reason for membership; and if you see a clever actor remain outside for years, you may be pretty sure that, though private reasons count, there are artistic reasons as well. The first half dozen times I saw Mademoiselle Fargueil, who for years ruled the roost, as the vulgar saying is, at the Vaudeville, I wondered that so consummate and accomplished an actress should not have a place on the first French stage. But I presently grew wiser, and perceived that, clever as Mademoiselle Fargueil is, she is not for the Rue de Richelieu, but for the Boulevards; her peculiar, intensely Parisian intonation would sound out of place in the Maison de Molière. (Of course if Mademoiselle Fargueil has ever received overtures from the Français, my sagacity is at fault—I am looking through a millstone. But I suspect she has not.) Frédéric Lemaître, who died last winter, and who was a very great actor, had been tried at the Français and found wanting—for those particular conditions. But it may probably be said that if Frédéric was wanting, the theater was too, in this case. Frédéric's great force was his extravagance, his fantasticality; and the stage of the Rue de Richelieu was a trifle too academic. I have even wondered whether Desclée, if she had lived, would have trod that stage by right, and whether it would have seemed her proper element. The negative is not impossible. It is very possible that in that classic atmosphere her great charm—her intensely modern quality, her super-subtle realism—would have appeared an anomaly. I can imagine even that her strange, touching, nervous voice would not have seemed the voice of the house. At the Français you must know how to acquit yourself of a *tirade;* that has always been the touchstone of capacity. It would probably have proved Desclée's stumbling-block, though she could utter speeches of six words as no one else surely has ever done. It is true that Mademoiselle Croizette, and in a certain sense Mademoiselle Sarah Bernhardt, are rather weak at their *tirades;* but then old theater-goers will tell you that these young ladies, in spite of a hundred attractions, have no business at the Français.

In the course of time the susceptible foreigner passes from that superstitious state of attention which I just now sketched to that greater enlightenment which enables him to understand such a judgment as this of the old theater-goers. It is borne in upon him that, as the good Homer sometimes nods, the Théâtre Français sometimes lapses from its high standard. He makes various reflections. He thinks that Mademoiselle Favart rants. He thinks M. Mounet-Sully, in spite of his delicious voice, insupportable. He thinks that M. Parodi's five-act tragedy, "Rome Vaincue," presented in the early part of the present winter, was better done certainly than it would have been done upon any English stage, but by no means so much better done as might have been expected. (Here, if I had space, I would open a long parenthesis, in which I should aspire to demonstrate that the incontestable superiority of average French acting to English is by no means so strongly marked in tragedy as in comedy—is indeed sometimes not strongly marked at all. The reason of this is in a great measure, I think, that we have had Shakespeare to exercise ourselves upon, and that an inferior dramatic instinct exercised upon Shakespeare may become more flexible than a superior one exercised upon Corneille and Racine. When it comes to ranting—ranting even in a modified and comparatively reasonable sense—we do, I suspect, quite as well as the French, if not rather better.) Mr. G. H. Lewes, in his entertaining little book upon *Actors and the Art of Acting*, mentions M. Talbot, of the Français, as a surprisingly incompetent performer. My memory assents to his judgment at the same time that it proposes an amendment. This actor's special line is the buffeted, bemuddled, besotted old fathers, uncles and guardians of classic comedy, and he plays them with his face much more than with his tongue. Nature has endowed him with a visage so admirably adapted, once for all, to his rôle, that he has only to sit in a chair, with his hands folded on his stomach, to look like a monument of bewildered senility. After that it does not matter what he says or how he says it.

The Comédie Française sometimes does weaker things than in keeping M. Talbot. Last autumn,* for instance, it was really depressing to see Mademoiselle Dudley brought all the way from Brussels (and with not a little flourish either) to "create" the guilty vestal in " Rome Vaincue." As far as the interests of art are concerned, Mademoiselle Dudley had much better have remained in the Flemish capital, of whose language she is apparently a perfect mistress. It is hard, too, to forgive M. Perrin (M. Perrin is the present director of the Théâtre Français) for bringing out "L'Ami Fritz" of M. Erckmann-Chatrian. The two gentlemen who write under this name have a double claim to kindness. In the first place, they have produced some delightful little novels; everyone knows and admires *Le Conscrit de 1813;* everyone admires, indeed, the charming tale on which the play in question is founded. In the second place, they were, before the production of their piece, the objects of a scurrilous attack by the "Figaro" newspaper, which held the authors up to reprobation for

* 1876.

having "insulted the army," and did its best to lay the train for a hostile manifestation on the first night. (It may be added that the good sense of the public outbalanced the impudence of the newspaper, and the play was simply advertised into success.) But neither the novels nor the persecutions of M. Erckmann-Chatrian avail to render "L'Ami Fritz," in its would-be dramatic form, worthy of the first French stage. It is played as well as possible, and upholstered even better; but it is, according to the vulgar phrase, too "thin" for the locality. Upholstery has never played such a part at the Théâtre Français as during the reign of M. Perrin, who came into power, if I mistake not, after the late war. He proved very early that he was a radical, and he has introduced a hundred novelties. His administration, however, has been brilliant, and in his hands the Théâtre Français has made money. This it had rarely done before, and this, in the conservative view, is quite beneath its dignity. To the conservative view I should humbly incline. An institution so closely protected by a rich and powerful State ought to be able to cultivate art for art.

The first of M. Sarcey's biographies, to which I have been too long in coming, is devoted to Regnier, a veteran actor, who left the stage four or five years since, and who now fills the office of oracle to his younger comrades. It is the indispensable thing, says M. Sarcey, for a young aspirant to be able to say that he has had lessons of M. Regnier, or that M. Regnier had advised him, or that he has talked such and such a point over with M. Regnier. (His comrades always speak of him as M. Regnier—never as simple Regnier.) I have had the fortune to see him but once; it was the first time I ever went to the Théâtre Français. He played Don Annibal in Emile Augier's romantic comedy of "L'Aventurière," and I have not forgotten the exquisite humor of the performance. The part is that of a sort of seventeenth century Captain Costigan, only the Miss Fotheringay in the case is the gentleman's sister and not his daughter. This lady is moreover an ambitious and designing person, who leads her thread-bare braggart of a brother quite by the nose. She has entrapped a worthy gentleman of Padua, of mature years, and he is on the eve of making her his wife, when his son, a clever young soldier, beguiles Don Annibal into supping with him, and makes him drink so deep that the prating adventurer at last lets the cat out of the bag and confides to his companion that the fair Clorinde is not the virtuous gentlewoman she appears, but a poor strolling actress who has had a lover at every stage of her journey. The scene was played by Bressant and Regnier, and it has always remained in my mind as one of the most perfect things I have seen on the stage. The gradual action of the wine upon Don Annibal, the delicacy with which his deepening tipsiness was indicated, its intellectual rather than physical manifestation, and, in the midst of it, the fantastic conceit which made him think that he was winding his fellow drinker round his fingers—all this was exquisitely rendered. Drunkenness on the stage is usually both dreary and disgusting; and I can remember besides this but two really interesting pictures of intoxication (excepting always, indeed, the immortal tipsiness of Cassio in "Othello," which a clever actor can always make touching). One is the beautiful befuddlement of Rip Van Winkle, as Mr. Joseph Jefferson renders it, and the other (a memory of the Théâtre Français) the scene in the "Duc Job," in which Got succumbs to mild inebriation, and dozes in his chair just boosily enough for the young girl who loves him to make it out.

It is to this admirable Émile Got that M. Sarcey's second notice is devoted. Got is at the present hour unquestionably the first actor at the Théâtre Français, and I have personally no hesitation in accepting him as the first of living actors. His younger comrade, Coquelin, has, I think, as much talent and as much art; as the older man Got has the longer and fuller record and may therefore be spoken of as the master. If I were obliged to rank the half-dozen *premiers sujets* of the last few years at the Théâtre Français in their absolute order of talent (thank Heaven, I am not so obliged!) I think I should make up some such little list as this: Got, Coquelin, Madame Plessy, Sarah Bernhardt, Mademoiselle Favart, Delaunay. I confess that I have no sooner written it than I feel as if I ought to amend it, and wonder whether it is not a great folly to put Delaunay after Mademoiselle Favart. But this is idle.

As for Got, he is a singularly interesting actor. I have often wondered whether the best definition of him would not be to say that he is really a *philosophic* actor. He is an immense humorist and his comicality is sometimes colossal; but his most striking quality is the one on which M. Sarcey dwells—his sobriety and profundity, his underlying element of manliness and melancholy, the impression he gives you of having a general conception of human life and of seeing the relativity, as one may say, of the character he represents. Of all the comic actors I have seen he is the least trivial—at the same time that for richness of detail his comic manner is unsurpassed. His repertory is very large and various, but it may be divided into two equal halves—the parts that belong to reality and the parts that belong to fantasy. There is of course a great deal of fantasy in his realistic parts and a great deal of reality in his fantastic ones, but the general division is just; and at times, indeed, the two faces of his talent seem to have little in common. The Duc Job, to which I just now alluded, is one of the things he does most perfectly. The part, which is that of a young man, is a serious and tender one. It is amazing that the actor who plays it should also be able to carry off triumphantly the frantic buffoonery of Maître Pathelin, or should represent the Sganarelle of the "Médecin Malgré Lui" with such an unctuous breadth of humor. The two characters, perhaps, which have given me the liveliest idea of Got's power and fertility are the Maître Pathelin and the M. Poirier who figures in the title to the comedy which Emile Augier and Jules Sandeau wrote together. M. Poirier, the retired shopkeeper who marries his daughter to a marquis and makes acquaintance with the incommodities incidental to such a piece of luck, is perhaps the actor's most elaborate creation; it is difficult to see how the portrayal of a type and an individual can have a larger sweep and a more minute completeness. The *bonhomme* Poirier, in Got's hands, is really great; and half-a-dozen of the actor's modern parts that I could mention are hardly less brilliant. But when I think of him I instinctively think first of some rôle in which he wears the cap and gown of a period as regards which humorous invention may fairly take the bit in its teeth. This is what Got lets it do in Maître Pathelin, and he leads the spectator's exhilarated fancy a dance to which the latter's aching sides on the morrow sufficiently testify.

The piece is a *réchauffé* of a mediæval farce which has the credit of being the first play not a "mystery" or a miracle-piece in the records of the French drama. The plot is extremely bald and primitive. It sets forth how a cunning lawyer undertook to purchase a dozen ells of cloth for nothing. In the first scene we see him in the market-place, bargaining and haggling with the draper, and then marching off with the roll of cloth, with the understanding that the shopman shall call at his house in the course of an hour for the money. In the next act we have Maître Pathelin at his fireside with his wife, to whom he relates his trick and its projected sequel, and who greets them with Homeric laughter. He gets into bed, and the innocent draper arrives. Then follows a scene of which the liveliest description must be ineffective. Pathelin pretends to be out of his head, to be overtaken by a mysterious malady which has made him delirious, not to know the draper from Adam, never to have heard of the dozen ells of cloth, and to be altogether an impossible person to collect a debt from. To carry out this character he indulges in a series of indescribable antics, out-Bedlams Bedlam, frolics over the room dressed out in the bed-clothes and chanting the wildest gibberish, bewilders the poor draper to within an inch of his own sanity and finally puts him utterly to rout. The spectacle could only be portentously flat or heroically successful, and in Got's hands this latter was its fortune. His Sganarelle, in the " Médicin Malgré Lui," and half-a-dozen of his characters from Molière besides—such a part, too, as his Tibia, in Alfred de Musset's charming bit of romanticism, the " Caprices de Marianne "—have a certain generic resemblance with his treatment of the figure I have sketched. In all these things the comicality is of the exuberant and tremendous order, and yet in spite of its richness and flexibility it suggests little connection with high animal spirits. It seems a matter of invention, of reflection and irony. You cannot imagine Got representing a fool pure and simple—or at least a passive and unsuspecting fool. There must always be an element of shrewdness and even of contempt; he must be the man who knows and judges—or at least who pretends. It is a compliment, I take it, to an actor, to say that he prompts you to wonder about his private personality; and an observant spectator of M. Got is at liberty to guess that he is both obstinate and proud.

In Coquelin there is perhaps greater spontaneity, and there is a not inferior mastery of his art. He is a wonderfully brilliant, elastic actor. He is but thirty-five years old, and yet his record is most glorious. He too has his "actual" and his classical repertory, and here also it is hard to choose. As the young *valet de comédie* in Molière and Regnard and Marivaux he is incomparable. I shall never forget the really infernal brilliancy of his Mascarille in "L'Étourdi." His volubility, his rapidity, his impudence and gayety, his ringing, penetrating voice and the shrill trumpet-note of his laughter, make him the ideal of the classic serving-man of the classic young lover—half rascal and half good fellow. Coquelin has lately had two or three immense successes in the comedies of the day. His Duc de Sept-Monts, in the famous "Étrangère" of Alexandre Dumas, last winter, was the capital creation of the piece; and in the revival, this winter, of Augier's "Paul Forestier," his Adolphe de Beaubourg, the young man about town, consciously tainted with *commonness,* and trying to shake off the incubus, seemed while one watched it and listened to it the last word of delicately humorous art. Of Coquelin's eminence in the old comedies M. Sarcey speaks with a certain pictorial force: "No one is better cut out to represent those bold and magnificent rascals of the old repertory, with their boisterous gayety, their brilliant fancy and their superb extravagance, who give to their buffoonery *je ne sais quoi d'épique*. In these parts one may say of Coquelin that he is incomparable. I prefer him to Got in such cases, and even to Regnier, his master. I never saw Monrose, and cannot speak of him. But good judges have assured me that there was much that was factitious in the manner of this eminent comedian, and that his vivacity was a trifle mechanical. There is nothing whatever of this in Coquelin's manner. The eye, the nose, and the voice—the voice above all—are his most powerful means of action. He launches his *tirades* all in one breath, with full lungs, without troubling himself too much over the shading of details, in large masses, and he possesses himself only the more strongly of the public, which has a great sense of *ensemble.* The words that must be detached, the words that must decisively 'tell,' glitter in this delivery with the sonorous ring of a brand-new louis d'or. Crispin, Scapin, Figaro, Mascarille have never found a more valiant and joyous interpreter."

I should say that this was enough about the men at the Théâtre Français, if I did not remember that I have not spoken of Delaunay. But Delaunay has plenty of people to speak for him; he has, in especial, the more eloquent half of humanity—the ladies. I suppose that of all the actors of the Comédie Française he is the most universally appreciated and admired; he is the popular favorite. And he has certainly earned this distinction, for there was never a more amiable and sympathetic genius. He plays the young lovers of the past and the present, and he acquits himself of his difficult and delicate task with extraordinary grace and propriety. The danger I spoke of a while since —the danger, for the actor of a romantic and sentimental part, of being compromised by the coat and trousers, the hat and umbrella of the current year—are reduced by Delaunay to their minimum. He reconciles in a marvelous fashion the love-sick gallant of the ideal world with the "gentlemanly man" of to-day; and his passion is as far removed from rant as his propriety is from stiffness. He has been accused of late years of falling into a mannerism, and I think there is some truth in the charge. But the fault in Delaunay's situation is certainly venial. How can a man of fifty, to whom, as regards face and figure, Nature has been stingy, play an amorous swain of twenty without taking refuge in a mannerism? His mannerism is a legitimate device for diverting the spectator's attention from certain incongruities. Delaunay's juvenility, his ardor, his passion, his good taste and sense of fitness, have always an irresistible charm. As he has grown older he has increased his repertory by parts of greater weight and sobriety—he has played the husbands as well as the lovers. One of his most recent and brilliant "creations" of this kind is his Marquis de Presles in "Le Gendre de M. Poirier"—a piece of acting superb for its lightness and *désinvolture*. It cannot be better praised than by saying it was worthy of Got's inimitable rendering of the part opposed to it. But I think I shall remember Delaunay best in the picturesque and romantic comedies—as the Duc de Richelieu in "Mlle. De Belle-Isle"; as the joyous, gallant, exuberant young hero, his plumes and love knots fluttering in the breath of his gushing improvisation, of Corneille's "Menteur"; or, most of all, as the melodious swains of those charmingly poetic, faintly, naturally Shakespearean little comedies of Alfred de Musset.

To speak of Delaunay ought to bring us properly to Mademoiselle Favart, who for so many years invariably represented the object of his tender invocations. Mademoiselle Favart at the present time rather lacks what the French call "actuality." She has recently made an attempt to recover something of that large measure of it which she once possessed; but I doubt whether it has been completely successful. M. Sarcey has not yet put forth his notice of her; and when he does so it will be interesting to see how he treats her. She is not one of his high admirations. She is a great talent that has passed into eclipse. I call her a great talent, although I remember the words in which M. Sarcey somewhere speaks of her: "Mlle. Favart, who, to happy natural gifts, *soutenus par un travail acharné,* owed a distinguished place," etc. Her talent is great, but the impression that she gives of a *travail acharné* and of an insatiable ambition is perhaps even greater. For many years she reigned supreme, and I believe she is accused of not having always reigned generously. However that may be, there came a day when Mesdemoiselles Croizette and Sarah Bernhardt passed to the front and the elder actress receded, if not into the background, at least into what painters call the middle distance. The private history of these events has, I believe, been rich in heart-burnings; but it is only with the public history that we are concerned. Mademoiselle Favart has always seemed to me a powerful rather than an interesting actress; there is usually something mechanical and overdone in her manner. In some of her parts there is a kind of audible creaking of the machinery. If Delaunay is open to the reproach of having let a mannerism get the better of him, this accusation is much more fatally true of Mademoiselle Favart. On the other hand, she knows her trade as no one does—no one, at least, save Madame Plessy. When she is bad she is extremely bad, and sometimes she is interruptedly bad for a whole evening. In the revival of Scribe's clever comedy of "Une Chaine," this winter (which, by the way, though the cast included both Got and Coquelin, was the nearest approach to mediocrity I have ever seen at the Théâtre Français), Mademoiselle Favart was, to my sense, startlingly bad. The part had originally been played by Madame Plessy; and I remember how M. Sarcey in his *feuilleton* treated its actual representative. "Mademoiselle Favart does Louise. Who does not recall the exquisite delicacy and temperance with which Mme. Plessy rendered that difficult scene in the second act?" etc. And nothing more. When, however, Mademoiselle Favart is at her best, she is remarkably strong. She rises to great occasions. I doubt whether such parts as the desperate heroine of the " Supplice d'une Femme," or as Julie in Octave Feuillet's lugubrious drama of that name, could be more effectively played than she plays them. She can carry a great weight without flinching; she has what the French call " authority "; and in declamation she sometimes unrolls her fine voice, as it were, in long harmonious waves and cadences the sustained power of which her younger rivals must often envy her.

I am drawing to the close of these rather desultory observations without having spoken of the four ladies commemorated by M. Sarcey in the publication which lies before me; and I do not know that I can justify my tardiness otherwise than by saying that writing and reading about artists of so extreme a personal brilliancy is poor work, and that the best the critic can do is to wish his reader may see them, from a quiet *fauteuil,* as speedily and as often as possible. Of Madeleine Brohan, indeed, there is little to say. She is a delightful person to listen to, and she is still delightful to look at, in spite of that redundancy of contour which time has contributed to her charms. But she has never been ambitious and her talent has had no particularly original quality. It is a long time since she created an important part; but in the old repertory her rich, dense voice, her charming smile, her mellow, tranquil gayety, always give extreme pleasure. To hear her sit and *talk,* simply, and laugh and play with her fan, along with Madame Plessy, in Molière's " Critique de l'École des Femmes," is an entertainment to be remembered. For Madame Plessy I should have to mend my pen and begin a new chapter; and for Mademoiselle Sarah Bernhardt no less a ceremony would suffice. I saw Madame Plessy for the first time in Émile Augier's " Aventurière," when, as I mentioned, I first saw Regnier. This is considered by many persons her best part, and she certainly carries it off with a high hand;

but I like her better in characters which afford more scope to her talents for comedy. These characters are very numerous, for her activity and versatility have been extraordinary. Her comedy of course is "high"; it is of the highest conceivable kind, and she has often been accused of being too mincing and too artificial. I should never make this charge, for, to me, Madame Plessy's *minauderies,* her grand airs and her arch-refinements, have never been anything but the odorous swayings and queenly tossings of some splendid garden flower. Never had an actress grander manners. When Madame Plessy represents a duchess you have no allowances to make. Her limitations are on the side of the pathetic. If she is brilliant, she is cold; and I cannot imagine her touching the source of tears. But she is in the highest degree accomplished; she gives an impression of intelligence and intellect which is produced by none of her companions—excepting always the extremely exceptional Sarah Bernhardt. Madame Plessy's intellect has sometimes misled her—as, for instance, when it whispered to her, a few years since, that she could play Agrippine in Racine's "Britannicus," on that tragedy being presented for the *débuts* of Mounet-Sully. I was verdant enough to think her Agrippine very fine. But M. Sarcey reminds his readers of what he said of it the Monday after the first performance. "I will not say"—he quotes himself—"that Madame Plessy is indifferent. With her intelligence, her natural gifts, her great situation, her immense authority over the public, one cannot be indifferent in anything. She is therefore not indifferently bad. She is bad to a point that cannot be expressed and that would be distressing for dramatic art if it were not that in this great shipwreck there rise to the surface a few floating fragments of the finest qualities that nature has ever bestowed upon an artist."

Madame Plessy retired from the stage six months ago

and it may be said that the void produced by this event is irreparable. There is not only no prospect, but there is no hope of filling it up. The present conditions of artistic production are directly hostile to the formation of actresses as consummate and as complete as Madame Plessy. One may not expect to see her like, any more than one may expect to see a new manufacture of old lace and old brocade. She carried off with her something that the younger generation of actresses will consistently lack—a certain largeness of style and robustness of art. (These qualities are in a modified degree those of Mademoiselle Favart.) But if the younger actresses have the success of Mesdemoiselles Croizette and Sarah Bernhardt, will they greatly care whether they are not "robust"? These young ladies are children of a later and eminently contemporary type, according to which an actress undertakes not to interest but to fascinate. They are charming—"awfully" charming; strange, eccentric, imaginative. It would be needless to speak specifically of Mademoiselle Croizette; for although she has very great attractions I think she may (by the cold impartiality of science) be classified as a secondary, a less inspired and (to use the great word of the day) a more "brutal" Sarah Bernhardt. (Mademoiselle Croizette's "brutality" is her great card.) As for Mademoiselle Sarah Bernhardt, she is simply, at present, in Paris, one of the great figures of the day. It would be hard to imagine a more brilliant embodiment of feminine success; she deserves a chapter for herself.

December, 1876.

THEOCRITUS ON CAPE COD

Hamilton Wright Mabie

Cape Cod lies at the other end of the world from Sicily not only in distance, but in the look of it, the lay of it, the way of it. It is so far off that it offers a base from which one may get a fresh view of Theocritus.

There are very pleasant villages on the Cape, in the wide shade of ancient elms, set deep in the old-time New England quiet. For there was a time before the arrival of the Syrians, the Armenians, and the automobile, when New England was in a meditative mood. But Cape Cod is really a ridge of sand with a backbone of soil, rashly thrust into the Atlantic, and as fluent and volatile, so to speak, as one of those far Western rivers that are shifting currents sublimely indifferent to private ownership. The Cape does not lack stability, but it shifts its lines with easy disregard of charts and boundaries, and remains stable only at its center; it is always fraying at the edges. It lies, too, on the western edge of the ocean stream, where the forces of land and sea are often at war and the palette of colors is limited. The sirocco does not sift fine sand through every crevice and fill the heart of man with murderous impulses; but the east wind diffuses a kind of elemental depression.

Sicily, on the other hand, is high-built on rocky foundations, and is the wide-spreading reach of a great volcano sloping broadly and leisurely to the sea. It is often shaken at its center, but the sea does not take from nor add to its substance at will. It lies in the very heart of a sea of such ravishing color that by sheer fecundity of beauty it has given birth to a vast fellowship of gods and divinely fashioned creatures; its slopes are white with billowy masses of almond blossoms in that earlier spring which is late winter on Cape Cod; while gray-green, gnarled, and twisted olive-trees bear witness to the passionate moods of the Mediterranean, mother of poetry, comedy, and tragedy, often asleep in a dream of beauty in which the shadowy figures of the oldest time move, often as violent as the North Atlantic when March torments it with furious moods. For the Mediterranean is as seductive, beguiling, and uncertain of temper as Cleopatra, as radiant as Hera, as voluptuous as Aphrodite. Put in terms of color, it is as different from the sea round Cape Cod as a picture by Sorolla is different from a picture by Mauve.

Theocritus is interested in the magic of the island rather than in the mystery of the many-sounding sea, and to him the familiar look of things is never edged like a photograph; it is as solid and real as a report of the Department of Agriculture, but a mist of poetry is spread over it, in which, as in a Whistler nocturne, many details harmonize in a landscape at once actual and visionary. There is no example in literature of the unison of sight and vision more subtly and elusively harmonious than the report of Sicily in the *Idylls*. In its occupations the island was as prosaic as Cape Cod, and lacked the far-reaching consciousness of the great world which is the possession of every populated sand-bar in the Western world; but it was enveloped in an atmosphere in which the edges of things were lost in a sense of their rootage in poetic relations, and of interrelations so elusive and immaterial that a delicate but persistent charm exhaled from them.

Sicily was a solid and stubborn reality thousands of years before Theocritus struck his pastoral lyre; but its most obvious quality was atmospheric. It was compacted of facts, but they were seen not as a camera sees, but as an artist sees; not in sharp outline and hard actuality, but softened by a flood of light which melts all hard lines in a landscape vibrant and shimmering. Our landscape-painters are now reporting Nature as Theocritus saw her in Sicily; the value of the overtone matching the value of the undertone, to quote an artist's phrase, " apply these tones in right proportions," writes Mr. Harrison, " and you will find that the sky painted with the perfectly matched tone will fly away indefinitely, will be bathed in a perfect atmosphere." We who have for a time lost the poetic mood and strayed from the poet's standpoint paint the undertones with entire fidelity; but we do not paint in the overtones, and the landscape loses the luminous and vibrant quality which comes into it when the sky rains light upon it. We see with the accuracy of the camera; we do not see with the vision of the poet, in which reality is not sacrificed, but subdued to larger uses. We insist on the scientific fact; the poet is intent on the visual fact. The one gives the bare structure of the landscape; the other gives us its color, atmosphere, charm. Here, perhaps, is the real difference between Cape Cod and Sicily. It is not so much a contrast between encircling seas and the sand-ridge and rock-ridge as between the two ways of seeing, the scientific and the poetic.

The difference of soils must also be taken into account. The soil of history on Cape Cod is almost as thin as the physical soil, which is so light and detached that it is blown about by all the winds of heaven. In Sicily, on the other hand, the soil is so much a part of the substance of the island that the sirocco must bring from the shores of Africa the fine particles with which it tortures men. On Cape Cod there are a few colonial traditions, many heroic memories of brave deeds in awful seas, some records of prosperous daring in fishing-ships, and then the advent of the summer colonists; a creditable history, but of so recent date that it has not developed the fructifying power of a rich soil, out of which atmosphere rises like an exhalation. In Sicily, on the other hand, the soil of history is so deep that the spade of the archæologist has not touched bottom, and even the much-toiling Freeman found four octavo volumes too cramped to tell the whole story, and mercifully stopped at the death of Agathocles.

Since the beginning of history, which means only the brief time since we began to remember events, everybody has gone to Sicily, and most people have stayed there until they were driven on, or driven out, by later comers; and almost everybody has been determined to keep the island for himself, and set about it with an ingenuity and energy of slaughter which make the movement toward universal peace seem pallid and nerveless. It is safe to say that on no bit of ground of equal area has more history been enacted than in Sicily; and when Theocritus was young, Sicily was already venerable with years and experience.

Now, history, using the word as signifying things which have happened, although enacted on the ground, gets into the air, and one often feels it before he knows it. In this volatile and pervasive form it is diffused over the landscape and becomes atmospheric; and atmosphere, it must be remembered, bears the same relation to air that the countenance bears to the face: it reveals and expresses what is behind the physical features. There is hardly a half-mile of Sicily below the upper ridges of Ætna that has not been fought over; and the localities are few which cannot show the prints of the feet of the gods or of the heroes who were their children.

It was a very charming picture on which the curtain was rolled up when history began, but the island was not a theater in which men sat at ease and looked at Persephone in the arms of Pluto; it was an arena in which race followed close upon race, like the waves of the sea, each rising a little higher and gaining a little wider sweep, and each leaving behind not only wreckage, but layers of soil potent in vitality. The island was as full of strange music, of haunting presences, of far-off memories of tragedy, as the island of the *Tempest:* it bred its *Calibans,* but it bred also its *Prosperos.* For the imagination is nourished by rich associations as an artist is fed by a beautiful landscape; and in Sicily men grew up in an invisible world of memories that spread a heroic glamor over desolate places and kept Olympus within view of the mountain pastures where rude shepherds cut their pipes:

"A pipe discoursing through nine mouths I made, full fair to view;
The wax is white thereon, the line of this and that edge true."

The soil of history may be so rich that it nourishes all manner of noxious things side by side with flowers of glorious beauty; this is the price we pay for fertility. A thin soil, on the other hand, sends a few flowers of delicate structure and haunting fragrance into the air, like the arbutus and the witchiana, which express the clean, dry sod of Cape Cod, and are symbolic of the poverty and purity of its history. Thoreau reports that in one place he saw advertised, "Fine sand for sale here," and he ventures the suggestion that "some of the street" had been sifted. And, possibly, with a little tinge of malice after his long fight with winds and shore-drifts, he reports that "in some pictures of Provincetown the persons of the inhabitants are not drawn below the ankles, so much being supposed to be buried in the sand." "Nevertheless," he continues, "natives of Provincetown assured me that they could walk in the middle of the road without trouble, even in slippers, for they had learned how to put their feet down and lift them up without taking in any sand." On a soil so light and porous there is a plentiful harvesting of health and substantial comfort, but not much chance of poetry.

In the country of Theocritus there was great chance for poetry; not because anybody was taught anything, but because everybody was born in an atmosphere that was a diffused poetry. If this had not been true, the poet could not have spread a soft mist of poesy over the whole island: no man works that kind of magic unaided; he compounds his potion out of simples culled from the fields round him. Theocritus does not disguise the rudeness of the life he describes; goat-herds and he-goats are not the conventional properties of the poetic stage. The poet was without a touch of the drawing-room consciousness of crude things, though he knew well softness and charm of life in Syracuse under a tyrant who did not "patronize the arts," but was instructed by them. To him the distinction between poetic and unpoetic things was not in the appearance, but in the root. He was not ashamed of Nature as he found her, and he never apologized for her coarseness by avoiding things not fit for refined eyes. His shepherds and goat-herds are often gross and unmannerly, and as stuffed with noisy abuse as Shakespeare's people in "Richard III." Lacon and Cometas, rival poets of the field, are having a controversy, and this is the manner of their argument:

"LACON

"When learned I from thy practice or thy preaching aught that's right,
Thou puppet, thou mis-shapen lump of ugliness and spite?

"COMETAS

"When? When I beat thee, wailing sore; your goats looked on with glee,
And bleated; and were dealt with e'en as I had dealt with thee."

And then, without a pause, the landscape shines through the noisy talk:

> "Nay, here are oaks and galingale: the hum of housing bees
> Makes the place pleasant, and the birds are piping in the trees,
> And here are two cold streamlets; here deeper shadows fall
> Than yon place owns, and look what cones drop from the pine tree tall."

Thoreau, to press the analogy from painting a little further, lays the undertones on with a firm hand: " It is a wild, rank place and there is no flattery in it. Strewn with crabs, horse-shoes, and razor-clams, and whatever the sea casts up,—a vast *morgue*, where famished dogs may range in packs, and cows come daily to glean the pittance which the tide leaves them. The carcasses of men and beasts together lie stately up upon its shelf, rotting and bleaching in the sun and waves, and each tide turns them in their beds, and tucks fresh sand under them. There is naked Nature,—inhumanely sincere, wasting no thought on man, nibbling at the cliffy shore where gulls wheel amid the spray."

It certainly is naked Nature with a vengeance, and it was hardly fair to take her portrait in that condition. Theocritus would have shown us Acteon surprising Artemis, not naked, but nude; and there is all the difference between nakedness and nudity that yawns between a Greek statue and a Pompeiian fresco indiscreetly preserved in the museum at Naples. Theocritus shows Nature nude, but not naked; and it is worth noting that the difference between the two lies in the presence or absence of consciousness. In Greek mythology, nudity passes without note or comment; the moment it begins to be noted and commented upon it becomes nakedness.

Theocritus sees Nature nude, as did all the Greek poets,

but he does not surprise her when she is naked. He paints the undertones faithfully, but he always lays on the overtones, and so spreads the effulgence of the sky-stream over the undertones, and the picture becomes vibrant and luminous. The fact is never slurred or ignored; it gets full value, but not as a solitary and detached thing untouched by light, unmodified by the landscape. Is there a more charming impression of a landscape bathed in atmosphere, exhaling poetry, breathing in the very presence of divinity, than this, in Calverley's translation:

> "I ceased. He, smiling sweetly as before,
> Gave me the staff, 'the Muses'' parting gift,
> And leftward sloped toward Pyxa. We the while
> Bent us to Phrasydene's, Eucritus and I,
> And baby-faced Amyntas: there we lay
> Half-buried in a couch of fragrant reed
> And fresh-cut vine leaves, who so glad as we?
> A wealth of elm and poplar shook o'erhead;
> Hard by, a sacred spring flowed gurgling on
> From the Nymphs' grot, and in the somber boughs
> The sweet cicada chirped laboriously.
> Hid in the thick thorn-bushes far away
> The tree frog's note was heard; the crested lark
> Sang with the goldfinch; turtles made their moan;
> And o'er the fountain hung the gilded bee.
> All of rich summer smacked, of autumn all:
> Pears at our feet, and apples at our side
> Rolled in luxuriance; branches on the ground
> Sprawled, overweighted with damsons; while we brushed
> From the cask's head the crust of four long years.
> Say, ye who dwell upon Parnassian peaks,
> Nymphs of Castalia, did old Chiron e'er
> Set before Hercules a cup so brave
> In Pholus' cavern—did as nectarous draughts
> Cause that Anapian shepherd, in whose hand
> Rocks were as pebbles, Polypheme the strong,
> Featly to foot it o'er the cottage lawns:—
> As, ladies, ye bid flow that day for us
> All by Demeter's shrine at harvest-home?
> Beside whose corn-stacks may I oft again
> Plant my broad fan: while she stands by and smiles,
> Poppies and corn-sheaves on each laden arm."

Here is the landscape seen with a poet's eye; and the color and shining quality of a landscape, it must be remembered, are in the exquisitely sensitive eye that sees, not in the structure and substance upon which it rests. The painter and poet create nature as really as they create art, for in every clear sight of the world we are not passive receivers of impressions, but partners in that creative work which makes nature as contemporaneous as the morning newspaper.

It is true, Sicily was poetic in its very structure while Cape Cod is poetic only in oases, bits of old New England shade and tracery of elms, the peace of ancient sincerity and content honestly housed, the changing color of marshes in whose channels the tides are singing or mute; but the Sicily of Theocritus was seen by the poetic eye. In every complete vision of a landscape what is behind the eye is as important as what lies before it, and behind the eyes that looked at Sicily in the third century, B.C., there were not only the memories of many generations, but there was also a faith in visible and invisible creatures which peopled the world with divinities. The text of Theocritus is starred with the names of gods and goddesses, of heroes and poets: it is like a rich tapestry, on the surface of which history has been woven in beautiful colors; the flat surface dissolves in a vast distance, and the dull warp and woof glows with moving life.

The *Idylls* are saturated with religion, and as devoid of piety as a Bernard Shaw play. Gods and men differ only in their power, not at all in their character. What we call morals were as conspicuously absent from Olympus as from Sicily. In both places life and the world are taken in their obvious intention; there was no attempt, apart from the philosophers, who are always an inquisitive folk, to discover either the mind or the heart of things. In the

Greek Bible, which Homer composed and recited to crowds of people on festive occasions, the fear of the gods and their vengeance are set forth in a text of unsurpassed force and vitality of imagination; but no god in his most dissolute mood betrays any moral consciousness, and no man repents of sins. That things often go wrong was as obvious then as now, but there was no sense of sin. There were Greeks who prayed, but none who put dust on his head and beat his breast and cried, "Woe unto me, a sinner!" There were disasters by land and sea, but no newspaper spread them out in shrieking type, and by skillful omission and selection of topics wore the semblance of an official report of a madhouse; there were diseases and deaths, but patent-medicine advertisements had not saturated the common mind with ominous symptoms; old age was present with its monitions of change and decay:

> "Age o'ertakes us all;
> Our tempers first; then on o'er cheek and chin,
> Slowly and surely, creep the frosts of Time.
> Up and go somewhere, ere thy limbs are sere."

Theocritus came late in the classical age, and the shadows had deepened since Homer's time. The torches on the tombs were inverted, the imagery of immortality was faint and dim; but the natural world was still naturally seen, and, if age was coming down the road, the brave man went bravely forward to meet the shadow.

It was different on Cape Cod. Even Thoreau, who had escaped from the morasses of theology into the woods and accomplished the reversion to paganism in the shortest possible manner, never lost the habit of moralizing, which is a survival of the deep-going consciousness of sin. Describing the operations of a sloop dragging for anchors and chains, he gives his text those neat, hard touches of fancy which he had at command even in his most uncompromising, semi-scientific moments: "To hunt to-day in pleasant weather for anchors which had been lost,—the sunken faith and hope of mariners, to which they trusted in vain; now, perchance it is the rusty one of some old pirate ship or Norman fisherman, whose cable parted here two hundred years ago, and now the best bower anchor of a Canton or California ship which has gone about her business."

And then he drops into the depths of the moral subconsciousness from which the clear, clean waters of Walden Pond could not wash him: "If the roadsteads of the spiritual ocean could be thus dragged, what rusty flukes of hope deceived and parted chain-cables of faith might again be windlassed aboard! enough to sink the finder's craft, or stock new navies to the end of time. The bottom of the sea is strewn with anchors, some deeper and some shallower, and alternately covered and uncovered by the sand, perchance with a small length of iron cable still attached, to which where is the other end? . . . So, if we had diving bells adapted to the spiritual deeps, we should see anchors with their cables attached, as thick as eels in vinegar, all wriggling vainly toward their holding ground. But that is not treasure for us which another man has lost; rather it is for us to seek what no other man has found or can find." The tone is light, almost trifling, when one takes into account the imagery and the idea, and the subconsciousness is wearing thin; but it is still there.

Thoreau's individual consciousness was a very faint reflection of an ancestral consciousness of the presence of sin, and of moral obligations of an intensity almost inconceivable in these degenerate days. There was a time in a Cape Cod community when corporal punishment was inflicted on all residents who denied the Scriptures, and all persons who stood outside the meeting-house during the time of divine service were set in the stocks. The way of righteousness was not a straight and narrow path, but a macadamized thoroughfare, and woe to the man who ventured on a by-path! One is not surprised to learn that "hysteric fits" were very common, and that congregations were often thrown into the utmost confusion; for the preaching was far from quieting. "Some think sinning ends with this life," said a well-known preacher, "but it is a mistake. The creature is held under an everlasting law; the damned increase in sin in hell. Possibly, the mention of this may please thee. But, remember, there shall be no pleasant sins there; no eating, drinking, singing, dancing; wanton dalliance, and drinking stolen waters; but damned sins, bitter, hellish sins; sins exasperated by torments; cursing God, spite, rage, and blasphemy. The guilt of all thy sins shall be laid upon thy soul, and be made so many heaps of fuel. . . . He damns sinners heaps upon heaps."

It is not surprising to learn that as a result of such preaching the hearers were several times greatly alarmed, and "on one occasion a comparatively innocent young man was frightened nearly out of his wits." One wonders in what precise sense the word "comparatively" was used; it is certain that those who had this sense of the sinfulness of things driven into them were too thoroughly frightened to see the world with the poet's eye.

In Sicily nobody was concerned for the safety of his soul; nobody was aware that he had a soul to be saved. Thoughtful people knew that certain things gave offense to the gods; that you must not flaunt your prosperity after the fashion of some American millionaires, who have discovered in recent years that there is a basis of fact for the Greek feeling that it is wise to hold great possessions modestly;

that certain family and state relations are sacred, and that the fate of Œdipus was a warning: but nobody was making observations of his own frame of mind; there were no thermometers to take the spiritual temperature.

In his representative capacity as poet, Theocritus, speaking for his people, might have said with Gautier, " I am a man for whom the visible world exists." It is as impossible to cut the visible world loose from the invisible as to see the solid stretch of earth without seeing the light that streams upon it and makes the landscape; but Gautier came as near doing the impossible as any man could, and the goat-herds and pipe-players of Theocritus measurably approached this instable position. On Cape Cod, it is true, they looked " up and not down," but it is also true that they " looked in and not out "; in Sicily they looked neither up nor down, but straight ahead. The inevitable shadows fell across the fields whence the distracted Demeter sought Persephone, and Enceladus, uneasily bearing the weight of Ætna, poured out the vials of his wrath on thriving vineyards and on almond orchards white as with sea-foam; but the haunting sense of disaster in some other world beyond the dip of the sea was absent. If the hope of living with the gods was faint and far, and the forms of vanished heroes were vague and dim, the fear of retribution beyond the gate of death was a mere blurring of the landscape by a mist that came and went.

The two workmen whose talk Theocritus overhears and reports in the *Tenth Idyll* are not discussing the welfare of their souls; they are not even awake to the hard conditions of labor, and take no thought about shorter hours and higher wages: they are interested chiefly in Bombyca, " lean, dusk, a gypsy,"

". . . twinkling dice thy feet,
Poppies thy lips, thy ways none knows how sweet!"

And they lighten the hard task of the reaper of the stubborn corn in this fashion:

> "O rich in fruit and corn-blade: be this field
> Tilled well, Demeter, and fair fruitage yield!
>
> "Bind the sheaves, reapers: lest one, passing, say—
> 'A fig for these, they're never worth their pay!'
>
> "Let the mown swathes look northward, ye who mow,
> Or westward—for the ears grow fattest so.
>
> "Avoid a noon-tide nap, ye threshing men:
> The chaff flies thickest from the corn-ears then.
>
> "Wake when the lark wakes; when he slumbers close
> Your work, ye reapers: and at noontide doze.
>
> "Boys, the frogs' life for me! They need not him
> Who fills the flagon, for in drink they swim.
>
> "Better boil herbs, thou toiler after gain,
> Than, splitting cummin, split thy hand in twain."

In Sicily no reckoning of the waste of life had been kept, and armies and fleets had been spent as freely in the tumultuous centuries of conquest as if, in the over-abundance of life, these losses need not be entered in the book of account. Theocritus distils this sense of fertility from the air, and the leaves of the *Idylls* are fairly astir with it. The central myth of the island has a meaning quite beyond the reach of accident; poetic as it is, its symbolism seems almost scientific. Under skies so full of the light which, in a real sense, creates the landscape, encircled by a sea which was fecund of gods and goddesses, Sicily was the teeming mother of flower-strewn fields and trees heavy with fruit, trunks and boughs made firm by winds as the fruit grew mellow in the sun. Demeter moved through harvest-fields and across the grassy slopes where herds are fed, a smiling goddess,

> "Poppies and corn-sheaves on each laden arm."

Forgetfulness of the ills of life, dreams of Olympian beauty and tempered energy in the fields—are not these the secrets of the fair world which survives in the *Idylls?*

The corn and wine were food for the gods who gave them as truly as for the men who plucked the ripened grain and pressed the fragrant grape. If there was a sense of awe in the presence of the gods, there was no sense of moral separation, no yawning chasm of unworthiness. The gods obeyed their impulses not less readily than the men and women they had created; both had eaten of the fruit of the tree of life, but neither had eaten of the tree of knowledge of good and evil. Anybody might happen upon Pan in some deeply shadowed place, and the danger of surprising Diana at her bath was not wholly imaginary. Religion was largely the sense of being neighbor to the gods; they were more prosperous than men and had more power, but they were different only in degree, and one might be on easy terms with them. They were created by the poetic mind, and they repaid it a thousand-fold with the consciousness of a world haunted by near, familiar, and radiant divinity. The heresy which shattered the unity of life by dividing it between the religious and the secular had not come to confuse the souls of the good and put a full half of life in the hands of sinners; religion was as natural as sunlight and as easy as breathing.

There was little philosophy and less science in Sicily as Theocritus reports it. The devastating passion for knowledge had not brought self-consciousness in like a tide, nor had the desire to know about things taken the place of knowledge of the things themselves. The beauty of the world was a matter of experience, not of formal observation, and was seen directly as artists see a landscape before they bring technical skill to reproduce it. So far as the men and women who work and sing and make love in the

Idylls were concerned, the age was delightfully unintellectual and, therefore, normally poetic. The vocabulary of names for things was made up of descriptive rather than analytical words, and things were seen in wholes rather than in parts.

From this point of view religion was as universal and all-enfolding as air, and the gods were as concrete and tangible as trees and rocks and stars. They were companionable with all sorts and conditions of men, and if one wished to represent them, he used symbols and images of divinely fashioned men and women, not philosophical ideas or scientific formulæ. In this respect the Roman Catholic Church has been both a wise teacher and a tender guardian of lonely and sorrowful humanity. Homer was not a formal theologian, but the harvest of the seed of thought he sowed is not even now fully gathered. He peopled the whole world of imagination. Christianity is not only concrete but historic, and some day, when the way of abstraction has been abandoned for that way of vital knowledge, which is the path of the prophets, the saints, and the artists, it will again set the imagination aflame. Meantime Theocritus is a charming companion for those who hunger and thirst for beauty, and who long from time to time to hang up the trumpet of the reformer, and give themselves up to the song of the sea and the simple music of the shepherd's pipe.

COLONIALISM IN THE UNITED STATES *

Henry Cabot Lodge

NOTHING is more interesting than to trace, through many years and almost endless wanderings and changes, the fortunes of an idea or habit of thought. The subject is a much-neglected one, even in these days of sweeping and minute investigation, because the inherent difficulties are so great, and the necessary data so multifarious, confused, and sometimes contradictory, that absolute proof and smooth presentation seem well-nigh impossible. Yet the ideas, the opinions, even the prejudices of men, impalpable and indefinite as they are, have at times a wonderful vitality and force and are not without meaning and importance when looked at with considerate eyes. The conditions under which they have been developed may change, or pass utterly

* This essay appeared originally in the *Atlantic Monthly* for May, 1883. During the thirty years which have elapsed since it was written the manifestations of the colonial spirit then apparent in the United States have not only altered in character but, I am glad to say, have weakened, diminished, and become less noticeable. Since 1883, also, there has been much achieved by Americans in Art and Literature, in painting, in sculpture, in music, and particularly in architecture. Success in all these fields has, with few exceptions, been won by men working in the spirit which is not colonial, but which it was the purpose of this essay to inculcate as the true one to which alone we could look for fine and enduring achievement. I have called attention to the date at which the essay was written in order that those who read it may remember that it applies in certain points to the conditions of thirty years ago and not to those of the present day.

away, while they, mere shadowy creations of the mind, will endure for generations. Long after the world to which it belonged has vanished, a habit of thought will live on, indelibly imprinted upon a race or nation, like the footprint of some extinct beast or bird upon a piece of stone. The solemn bigotry of the Spaniard is the fossil trace of the fierce struggle of eight hundred years with the Moors. The theory of the Lord's day peculiar to the English race all over the world is the deeply branded sign of the brief reign of Puritanism. A certain fashion of thought prevailed half a century ago; another is popular to-day. There is a resemblance between the two, the existence of both is recognized, and both, without much consideration, are set down as sporadic and independent, which is by no means a safe conclusion. We have all heard of those rivers which are suddenly lost to sight in the bowels of the earth, and, coming as suddenly again to the surface, flow onward to the sea as before. Or the wandering stream may turn aside into fresh fields, and, with new shapes and colors, seem to have no connection with the waters of its source or with those which finally mingle with the ocean. Yet, despite the disappearances and the changes, it is always the same river. It is exactly so with some kinds of ideas and modes of thought,—those that are wholly distinct from the countless host of opinions which perish utterly, and are forgotten in a few years, or which are still oftener the creatures of a day, or an hour, and die by myriads, like the short-lived insects whose course is run between sunrise and sunset.

The purpose of this essay is to discuss briefly certain opinions which belong to the more enduring class. They are sufficiently well known. When they are mentioned everyone will recognize them, and will admit their existence at the particular period to which they belong. The point which is overlooked is their connection and relationship.

They all have the same pedigree, a marked resemblance to each other, and they derive their descent from a common ancestor. My intention is merely to trace the pedigree and narrate the history of this numerous and interesting family of ideas and habits of thought. I have entitled them collectively "Colonialism in the United States," a description which is perhaps more comprehensive than satisfactory or exact.

In the year of grace 1776, we published to the world our Declaration of Independence. Six years later, England assented to the separation. These are tolerably familiar facts. That we have been striving ever since to make that independence real and complete, and that the work is not yet entirely finished, are not, perhaps, equally obvious truisms. The hard fighting by which we severed our connection with the mother-country was in many ways the least difficult part of the work of building up a great and independent nation. The decision of the sword may be rude, but it is pretty sure to be speedy. Armed revolution is quick. A South American, in the exercise of his constitutional privileges, will rush into the street and declare a revolution in five minutes. A Frenchman will pull down one government to-day, and set up another to-morrow, besides giving new names to all the principal streets of Paris during the intervening night. We English-speaking people do not move quite so fast. We come more slowly to the boiling point; we are not fond of violent changes, and when we make them we consume a considerable time in the operation. Still, at the best, a revolution by force of arms is an affair of a few years. We broke with England in 1776, we had won our victory in 1782, and by the year 1789 we had a new national government fairly started.

But if we are slower than other people in the conduct of revolutions, owing largely to our love of dogged fighting and inability to recognize defeat, we are infinitely more deliberate than our neighbors in altering, or even modifying, our ideas and modes of thought. The slow mind and ingrained conservatism of the English race are the chief causes of their marvelous political and material success. After much obstinate fighting in the field, they have carried through the few revolutions which they have seen fit to engage in; but when they have undertaken to extend these revolutions to the domain of thought, there has arisen a spirit of stubborn and elusive resistance, which has seemed to set every effort, and even time itself, at defiance.

By the treaty of Paris our independence was acknowledged, and in name and theory was complete. We then entered upon the second stage in the conflict, that of ideas and opinions. True to our race and to our instincts, and with a wisdom which is one of the glories of our history, we carefully preserved the principles and forms of government and law, which traced an unbroken descent and growth from the days of the Saxon invasion. But while we kept so much that was of inestimable worth, we also retained, inevitably, of course, something which it would have been well for us to have shaken off together with the rule of George III. and the British Parliament. This was the colonial spirit in our modes of thought.

The word "colonial" is preferable to the more obvious word "provincial," because the former is absolute, while the latter, by usage, has become in a great measure relative. We are very apt to call an opinion, a custom, or a neighbor "provincial," because we do not like the person or thing in question; and in this way the true value of the word has of late been frittered away. "Colonialism," moreover, has in this connection historical point and value, while "provincialism" is general and meaningless. Colonialism is also susceptible of accurate definition. A colony is an off-shoot from a parent stock, and its chief characteristic is dependence. In exact proportion as dependence lessens, the colony changes its nature and advances toward national existence. For a hundred and fifty years we were English colonies. Just before the revolution, in everything but the affairs of practical government, the precise point at which the break came, we were still colonies in the fullest sense of the term. Except in matters of food and drink, and of the wealth which we won from the soil and the ocean, we were in a state of complete material and intellectual dependence. Every luxury, and almost every manufactured article, came to us across the water. Our politics, except those which were purely local, were the politics of England, and so also were our foreign relations. Our books, our art, our authors, our commerce, were all English; and this was true of our colleges, our professions, our learning, our fashions, and our manners. There is no need here to go into the details which show the absolute supremacy of the colonial spirit and our entire intellectual dependence. When we sought to originate, we simply imitated. The conditions of our life could not be overcome.

The universal prevalence of the colonial spirit at that period is shown most strongly by one great exception, just as the flash of lightning makes us realize the intense darkness of a thunder-storm at night. In the midst of the provincial and barren waste of our intellectual existence in the eighteenth century there stands out in sharp relief the luminous genius of Franklin. It is true that Franklin was cosmopolitan in thought, that his name and fame and achievements in science and literature belonged to mankind; but he was all this because he was genuinely and intensely American. His audacity, his fertility, his adaptability, are all characteristic of America, and not of an English colony. He moved with an easy and assured step, with a poise and balance which nothing could shake, among the great men of the world; he stood before kings and princes and courtiers, unmoved and unawed. He was strongly averse to breaking with England; but when the war came he was the one man who could go forth and represent to Europe the new nationality without a touch of the colonist about him. He met them all, great ministers and great sovereigns, on a common ground, as if the colonies of yesterday had been an independent nation for generations. His autobiography is the corner-stone, the first great work of American literature. The plain, direct style, almost worthy of Swift, the homely, forcible language, the humor, the observation, the knowledge of men, the worldly philosophy of that remarkable book, are familiar to all; but its best and, considering its date, its most extraordinary quality is its perfect originality. It is American in feeling, without any taint of English colonialism. Look at Franklin in the midst of that excellent Pennsylvania community; compare him and his genius with his surroundings, and you get a better idea of what the colonial spirit was in America in those days, and how thoroughly men were saturated with it, than in any other way.

In general terms it may be said that, outside of politics and the still latent democratic tendencies, the entire intellectual life of the colonists was drawn from England, and that to the mother country they looked for everything pertaining to the domain of thought. The colonists in the eighteenth century had, in a word, a thoroughly and deeply rooted habit of mental dependence. The manner in which we have gradually shaken off this dependence, retaining of the past only that which is good, constitutes the history of the decline of the colonial spirit in the United States. As this spirit existed everywhere at the outset, and brooded over the whole realm of intellect, we can in most cases trace its history best in the recurring and successful revolts against it, which, breaking out now here, now there, have at last brought it so near to final extinction.

In 1789, after the seven years of disorder and demoralization which followed the close of the war, the United States government was established. Every visible political tie which bound us to England had been severed, and we were apparently entirely independent. But the shackles of the colonial spirit, which had been forging and welding for a century and a half, were still heavy upon us, and fettered all our mental action. The work of making our independence real and genuine was but half done, and the first struggle of the new national spirit with that of the colonial past was in the field of politics, and consumed twenty-five years before victory was finally obtained. We still felt that our fortunes were inextricably interwoven with those of Europe. We could not realize that what affected us nearly when we were a part of the British Empire no longer touched us as an independent nation. We can best understand how strong this feeling was by the effect which was produced here by the French revolution. That tremendous convulsion, it may be said, was necessarily felt everywhere; but one much greater might take place in Europe to-day without producing here anything at all resembling the excitement of 1790. We had already achieved far more than the French revolution ever accomplished. We had gone much farther on the democratic road than any other nation. Yet worthy men in the United States put on cockades and liberty caps, erected trees of liberty, called each other "Citizen Brown" and "Citizen Smith," drank confusion to tyrants, and sang the wild songs of Paris. All this was done in a country where every privilege and artificial distinction had been swept away, and where the government was the creation of the people themselves. These ravings and symbols had a terrific reality in Paris and in Europe, and so, like colonists, we felt that they must have a meaning to us, and that the fate and fortunes of our ally were our fate and fortunes. A part of the people engaged in an imitation that became here the shallowest nonsense, while the other portion of the community, which was hostile to French ideas, took up and propagated the notion that the welfare of civilized society lay with England and with English opinions. Thus we had two great parties in the United States, working themselves up to white heat over the politics of England and France. The first heavy blow to the influence of foreign politics was Washington's proclamation of neutrality. It seems a very simple and obvious thing now, this policy of non-interference in the affairs of Europe which that proclamation inaugurated, and yet at the time men marveled at the step, and thought it very strange. Parties divided over it. People could not conceive how we could keep clear of the great stream of European events. One side disliked the proclamation as hostile to France, while the other approved it for the same reason. Even the Secretary of State, Thomas Jefferson, one of the most representative men of American democracy, resisted the neutrality policy in the genuine spirit of the colonist. Yet Washington's proclamation was simply the sequel to the Declaration of Independence. It merely amounted to saying: We have created a new nation, and England not only cannot govern us, but English and European politics are none of our business, and we propose to be independent of them and not meddle in them. The neutrality policy of Washington's administration was a great advance toward independence and a severe blow to colonialism in politics. Washington himself exerted a powerful influence against the colonial spirit. The principle of nationality, then just entering upon its long struggle with state's rights, was in its very nature hostile to everything colonial; and Washington, despite his Virginian traditions, was thoroughly imbued with the national spirit. He believed himself, and insensibly impressed his belief upon the people, that true nationality could only be obtained by keeping ourselves aloof from the conflicts and the politics of the Old World. Then, too, his splendid personal dignity, which still holds us silent and respectful after the lapse of a hundred years, communicated itself to his office, and thence to the nation of which he was the representative. The colonial spirit withered away in the presence of Washington.

The only thorough-going nationalist among the leaders of that time was Alexander Hamilton. He was not born in the States, and was therefore free from all local influences; and he was by nature imperious in temper and imperial in his views. The guiding principle of that great man's public career was the advancement of American nationality. He was called " British " Hamilton by the very men who wished to throw us into the arms of the French republic, because he was wedded to the principles and the forms of constitutional English government and sought to preserve them here adapted to new conditions. He desired to put our political inheritance to its proper use, but this was as far removed from the colonial spirit as possible. Instead of being " British," Hamilton's intense eagerness for a strong national government made him the deadliest foe of the colonial spirit, which he did more to strangle and crush out than any other man of his time. The objects at which he aimed were continental supremacy, and complete independence in business, politics, and industry. In all these departments he saw the belittling effects of dependence, and so he assailed it by his reports and by his whole policy, foreign and domestic. So much of his work as he carried through had a far-reaching effect, and did a great deal to weaken the colonial spirit. But the strength of that spirit was best shown in the hostility or indifference which was displayed toward his projects. The great cause of opposition to Hamilton's financial policy proceeded, undoubtedly, from state jealousy of the central government; but the resistance to his foreign policy arose from the colonial ignorance which could not understand the real purpose of neutrality, and which thought that Hamilton was simply and stupidly endeavoring to force us toward England as against France.

Washington, Hamilton, and John Adams, notwithstanding his New England prejudices, all did much while they were in power, as the heads of the Federalist party, to cherish and increase national self-respect, and thereby eradicate colonialism from our politics. The lull in Europe, after the fall of the Federalists, led to a truce in the contests over foreign affairs in the United States, but with the renewal of war the old conflict broke out. The years from 1806 to 1812 are among the least creditable in our history. The Federalists ceased to be a national party and the fierce reaction against the French revolution drove them into an unreasoning admiration of England. They looked to England for the salvation of civilized society. Their chief interest centered in English politics, and the resources of England formed the subject of their thoughts and studies, and furnished the theme of conversation at their dinner tables. It was just as bad on the other side. The Republicans still clung to their affection for France, notwithstanding the despotism of the empire. They regarded Napoleon with reverential awe, and shivered at the idea of plunging into hostilities with anyone. The foreign policy of Jefferson was that of a thorough colonist. He shrank with horror from war. He would have had us confine ourselves to agriculture, and to our flocks and herds, because our commerce, the commerce of a nation, was something with which other powers were likely to interfere. He wished us to exist in a state of complete commercial and industrial dependence, and allow England to carry for us and manufacture for us, as she did when we were colonies weighed down by the clauses of the navigation acts. His plans of resistance did not extend beyond the old colonial scheme of non-importation and non-intercourse agreements. Read the bitter debates in Congress of those years, and you find them filled with nothing but the politics of other nations. All the talk is saturated with colonial feeling. Even the names of opprobrium which the hostile parties applied to each other were borrowed. The Republicans called the Federalists "Tories" and a "British faction," while the Federalists retorted by stigmatizing their opponents as Jacobins. During these sorry years, however, the last in which our politics bore the colonial character, a new party was growing up, which may be called the national party, not as distinguished from the party of state's rights, but as the opposition to colonial ideas. This new movement was headed and rendered illustrious by such men as Henry Clay, John Quincy Adams, the brilliant group from South Carolina, comprising Calhoun, Langdon Cheves, and William Lowndes, and at a later period by Daniel Webster. Clay and the South Carolinians were the first to push forward the resistance to colonialism. Their policy was crude and ill-defined. They struck out blindly against the evil influence which, as they felt, was choking the current of national life, for they were convinced that, to be truly independent, the United States must fight somebody. Who that somebody should be was a secondary question. Of all the nations which had been kicking and cuffing us, England was, on the whole, the most arrogant, and offensive; and so the young nationalists dragged the country into the war of 1812. We were wonderfully successful at sea and at New Orleans, but in other respects this war was neither very prosperous nor very creditable, and the treaty of Ghent was absolutely silent as to the objects for which we had expressly declared war. Nevertheless, the real purpose of the war was gained, despite the silent and almost meaningless treaty which concluded it. We had proved to the world and to ourselves that we existed as a nation. We had demonstrated the fact that we had ceased to be colonies. We had torn up colonialism in our public affairs by the roots, and we had crushed out the colonial spirit in our politics. After the war of 1812 our politics might be good, bad, or indifferent, but they were our own politics, and not those of Europe. The wretched colonial spirit which had belittled and warped them for twenty-five years had perished utterly, and with the treaty of Ghent it was buried so deeply that not even its ghost has since then crossed our political pathway.

Besides being the field where the first battle with the colonial spirit was fought out, politics then offered almost the only intellectual interest of the country, outside of commerce, which was still largely dependent in character, and very different in its scope from the great mercantile combinations of to-day. Religious controversy was of the past, and except in New England, where the liberal revolt against Calvinism was in progress, there was no great interest in theological questions. When the Constitution went into operation the professions of law and medicine were in their infancy. There was no literature, no art, no science, none of the multifarious interests which now divide and absorb the intellectual energies of the community. In the quarter of a century which closed with the treaty of Ghent we can trace the development of the legal and medical professions, and their advance towards independence and originality. But in the literary efforts of the time we see the colonial spirit displayed more strongly than anywhere else, and in apparently undiminished vigor.

Our first literature was political, and sprang from the discussions incident to the adoption of the Constitution. It was, however, devoted to our own affairs, and aimed at the foundation of a nation, and was therefore fresh, vigorous, often learned, and thoroughly American in tone. Its masterpiece was the *Federalist,* which marks an era in the history of constitutional discussion, and which was the conception of the thoroughly national mind of Hamilton. After the new government was established, our political writings, like our politics, drifted back to provincialism of thought, and were absorbed in the affairs of Europe; but the first advance on the road to literary independence was made by the early literature of the Constitution.

It is to this period also, which covers the years from 1789 to 1815, that Washington Irving, the first of our great writers, belongs. This is not the place to enter into an analysis of Irving's genius, but it may be fairly said that while in feeling he was a thorough American, in literature he was a cosmopolitan. His easy style, the tinge of romance, and the mingling of the story-teller and the antiquarian remind us of his great contemporary, Walter Scott. In his quiet humor and gentle satire, we taste the flavor of Addison. In the charming legends with which he has consecrated the beauties of the Hudson River valley, and thrown over that beautiful region the warm light of his imagination, we find the genuine love of country and of home. In like manner we perceive his historical taste and his patriotism in the last work of his life, the biography of his great namesake. But he wrought as well with the romance of Spain and of England. He was too great to be colonial; he did not find enough food for his imagination in the America of that day to be thoroughly American. He stands apart, a notable gift from America to English literature, but not a type of American literature itself. He had imitators and friends, whom it has been the fashion to call a school, but he founded no school, and died as he had lived, alone. He broke through the narrow trammels of colonialism himself, but the colonial spirit hung just as heavily upon the feeble literature about him. In those years also came the first poem of William Cullen Bryant, the first American poem with the quality of life and which was native and not of imported origin.

In that same period too there flourished another literary man, who was far removed in every way from the brilliant editor of Diedrich Knickerbocker, but who illustrated by his struggle with colonialism the strength of that influence far better than Irving, who soared so easily above it. Noah Webster, poor, sturdy, independent, with a rude but surprising knowledge of philology, revolted in every nerve and fiber of his being against the enervating influence of the colonial past. The spirit of nationality had entered into his soul. He felt that the nation which he saw growing up about him was too great to take its orthography or its pronunciation blindly and obediently from the mother land. It was a new country and a new nation, and Webster determined that so far as in him lay it should have linguistic independence. It was an odd idea, but it came from his heart, and his national feeling found natural expression in the study of language, to which he devoted his life. He went into open rebellion against British tradition. He was snubbed, laughed at, and abused. He was regarded as little better than a madman to dare to set himself up against Johnson and his successors. But the hard-headed New Englander pressed on, and finally brought out his dictionary, —a great work, which has fitly preserved his name. His knowledge was crude, his general theory mistaken; his system of changes has not stood the test of time, and was in itself contradictory; but the stubborn battle which he fought for literary independence and the hard blows he struck should never be forgotten, while the odds against which he contended and the opposition he aroused are admirable illustrations of the overpowering influence of the colonial spirit in our early literature.

What the state of our literature was, what the feelings of our few literary men apart from these few exceptions, and what the spirit with which Webster did battle, all come out in a few lines written by an English poet. We can see everything as by a sudden flash of light, and we do not need to look farther to understand the condition of American literature in the early years of the century. In the waste of barbarism called the United States, the only oasis discovered by the delicate sensibilities of Mr. Thomas Moore was in the society of Mr. Joseph Dennie, a clever editor and essayist, and his little circle of friends in Philadelphia. The lines commonly quoted in this connection are those in the epistle to Spencer, beginning,—

> "Yet, yet, forgive me, O ye sacred few,
> Whom late by Delaware's green banks I knew;"

which describe the poet's feelings toward America, and his delight in the society of Mr. Dennie and his friends. But the feelings and opinions of Moore are of no moment. The really important passage describes not the author, but what Dennie and his companions said and thought, and has in this way historical if not poetic value. The lines occur among those addressed to the "Boston frigate" when the author was leaving Halifax:—

> "Farewell to the few I have left with regret;
> May they sometimes recall, what I cannot forget,
> The delight of those evenings,—too brief a delight,
> When in converse and song we have stol'n on the night;
> When they've asked me the manners, the mind, or the mien,
> Of some bard I had known or some chief I had seen,

Whose glory, though distant, they long had adored,
Whose name had oft hallowed the wine-cup they poured.
And still, as with sympathy humble but true
I have told of each bright son of fame all I knew,
They have listened, and sighed that the powerful stream
Of America's empire should pass like a dream,
Without leaving one relic of genius, to say
How sublime was the tide which had vanished away!"

The evils apprehended by these excellent gentlemen are much more strongly set forth in the previous epistle, but here we catch sight of the men themselves. There they sit adoring Englishmen, and eagerly inquiring about them of the gracious Mr. Moore, while they are dolefully sighing that the empire of America is to pass away and leave no relic of genius. In their small way they were doing what they could toward such a consummation. It may be said that this frame of mind was perfectly natural under the circumstances; but it is not to the purpose to inquire into causes and motives; it is enough to state the fact. Here was a set of men of more than average talents and education; not men of real talent and quality, like Irving, but clever men, forming one of the two or three small groups of literary persons in the United States. They come before us as true provincials, steeped to the eyes in colonialism, and they fairly represent the condition of American literature at that time. They were slaves to the colonial spirit, which bowed before England and Europe. They have not left a name or a line which is remembered or read, except to serve as a historical illustration, and they will ultimately find their fit resting-place in the foot-notes of the historian.

With the close of the English war the United States entered upon the second stage of their development. The new era, which began in 1815, lasted until 1861. It was a period of growth, not simply in the direction of a vast material prosperity and a rapidly increasing population, but in national sentiment, which made itself felt everywhere. Wherever we turn during those years, we discover a steady decline of the colonial influence. Politics had become wholly national and independent. The law was illustrated by great names, which take high rank in the annals of English jurisprudence. Medicine began to have its schools, and to show practitioners who no longer looked across the sea for inspiration. The Monroe doctrine bore witness to the strong foreign policy of an independent people. The tariff gave evidence of the eager desire for industrial independence, which found practical expression in the fast-growing native manufactures. Internal improvements were a sign of the general faith and interest in the development of the national resources. The rapid multiplication of inventions resulted from the natural genius of America in that important field, where it took almost at once a leading place. Science began to have a home at our seats of learning, and in the land of Franklin found a congenial soil.

But the colonial spirit, cast out from our politics and fast disappearing from business and the professions, still clung closely to literature, which must always be the best and last expression of a national mode of thought. In the admirable *Life of Cooper,* recently published, by Professor Lounsbury, the condition of our literature in 1820 is described so vividly and so exactly that it cannot be improved. It is as follows:—

"The intellectual dependence of America upon England at that period is something that it is now hard to understand. Political supremacy had been cast off, but the supremacy of opinion remained absolutely unshaken. Of creative literature there was then very little of any value produced; and to that little a foreign stamp was necessary, to give currency outside of the petty circle in which it originated. There was slight encouragement for the author to write; there was still less for the publisher to print. It was, indeed, a positive injury, ordinarily, to the commercial credit of a bookseller to bring out a volume of poetry or of prose fiction which had been written by an American; for it was almost certain to fail to pay expenses. A sort of critical literature was struggling, or rather gasping, for a life that was hardly worth living; for its most marked characteristic was its servile deference to English judgment and dread of English censure. It requires a painful and penitential examination of the reviews of the period to comprehend the utter abasement of mind with which the men of that day accepted the foreign estimate upon works written here, which had been read by themselves, but which it was clear had not been read by the critics whose opinions they echoed. Even the meekness with which they submitted to the most depreciatory estimate of themselves was outdone by the anxiety with which they hurried to assure the world that they, the most cultivated of the American race, did not presume to have so high an opinion of the writings of some one of their countrymen as had been expressed by enthusiasts, whose patriotism had proved too much for their discernment. Never was any class so eager to free itself from charges that imputed to it the presumption of holding independent views of its own. Out of the intellectual character of many of those who at that day pretended to be the representatives of the highest education in this country, it almost seemed that the element of manliness had been wholly eliminated; and that, along with its sturdy democracy, whom no obstacles thwarted and no dangers daunted, the New World was also to give birth to a race of literary cowards and parasites."

The case is vigorously stated, but is not at all overcharged. Far stronger, indeed, than Professor Lounsbury's statement is the commentary furnished by Cooper's first book. This novel, now utterly forgotten, was entitled *Precaution*. Its scene was laid wholly in England; its characters were drawn from English society, chiefly from the aristocracy of that favored land; its conventional phrases were all English; worst and most extraordinary of all, it professed to be by an English author, and was received on that theory without suspicion. In such a guise did the most popular of American novelists and one of the most eminent among modern writers of fiction first appear before his countrymen and the world. If this were not so pitiable, it would be utterly ludicrous and yet the most melancholy feature of the case is that Cooper was not in the least to blame, and no one found fault with him, for his action was regarded by everyone as a matter of course. In other words, the first step of an American entering upon a literary career was to pretend to be an Englishman, in order that he might win the approval, not of Englishmen, but of his own countrymen.

If this preposterous state of public opinion had been a mere passing fashion it would hardly be worth recording. But it represented a fixed and settled habit of mind, and is only one example of a long series of similar phenomena. We look back to the years preceding the revolution, and there we find this mental condition flourishing and strong. At that time it hardly calls for comment, because it was so perfectly natural. It is when we find such opinions existing in the year 1820 that we are conscious of their significance. They belong to colonists, and yet they are uttered by the citizens of a great and independent state. The sorriest part of it is that these views were chiefly held by the best educated portion of the community. The great body of the American people, who had cast out the colonial spirit from their politics and their business, and were fast destroying it in the professions, was sound and true. The parasitic literature of that day makes the boastful and rhetorical patriotism then in the exuberance of youth seem actually noble and fine, because, with all its faults, it was honest, genuine, and inspired by a real love of country.

Yet it was during this period, between the years 1815 and 1861, that we began to have a literature of our own, and one in which any people could take a just pride. Cooper himself was the pioneer. In his second novel, *The Spy,* he threw off the wretched spirit of the colonist, and the story, which at once gained a popularity that broke down all barriers, was read everywhere with delight and approbation. The chief cause of the difference between the fate of this novel and that of its predecessor lies in the fact that *The Spy* was of genuine native origin. Cooper knew and loved American scenery and life. He understood certain phases of American character on the prairie and the ocean, and his genius was no longer smothered by the dead colonialism of the past. *The Spy,* and those of Cooper's novels which belong to the same class, have lived and will live, and certain American characters which he drew will likewise endure. He might have struggled all his life in the limbo of intellectual servitude to which Moore's friends consigned themselves, and no one would have cared for him then or remembered him now. But, with all his foibles, Cooper was inspired by an intense patriotism, and he had a bold, vigorous, aggressive nature. He freed his talents at a stroke, and giving them full play attained at once a world-wide reputation, which no man of colonial mind could ever have dreamed of reaching. Yet his countrymen, long before his days of strife and unpopularity, seem to have taken singularly little patriotic pride in his achievements, and the well bred and well educated shuddered to hear him called the " American Scott"; not because they thought this truly colonial description inappropriate and misapplied, but because it was a piece of irreverent audacity toward a great light of English literature.

Cooper was the first, after the close of the war of 1812, to cast off the colonial spirit and take up his position as a representative of genuine American literature; but he soon had companions, who carried still higher the standard which he had raised. To this period, which closed with our civil war, belong many of the names which are to-day among those most cherished by English-speaking people everywhere. We see the national spirit in Longfellow turning from the themes of the Old World to those of the New. In the beautiful creations of the sensitive and delicate imagination of Hawthorne, there was a new tone and a rich originality, and the same influence may be detected in the remarkable poems and the wild fancies of Poe. We find a like native strength in the sparkling verses of Holmes, in the pure and gentle poetry of Whittier, and in the firm, vigorous work of Lowell. A new leader of independent thought arises in Emerson, destined to achieve a world-wide reputation. A new school of historians appears, adorned by the talents of Prescott, Bancroft, and Motley. Many of these distinguished men were far removed in point of time from the beginning of the new era, but they all belonged to and were the result of the national movement, which began its onward march as soon as we had shaken ourselves clear from the influence of the colonial spirit upon our public affairs by the struggle which culminated in " Madison's war," as the Federalists loved to call it.

These successes in the various departments of intellectual activity were all due to an instinctive revolt against colonialism. But, nevertheless, the old and time-worn spirit which made Cooper pretend to be an Englishman in 1820 was very strong, and continued to impede our progress toward intellectual independence. We find it clinging to the lesser and weaker forms of literature. We see it in fashion and society and in habits of thought, but we find the best proof of its vitality in our sensitiveness to foreign opinion. This was a universal failing. The body of the people showed it by bitter resentment; the cultivated and highly educated by abject submission and deprecation, or by cries of pain.

As was natural in a very young nation, just awakened to its future destiny, just conscious of its still undeveloped strength, there was at this time a vast amount of exuberant self-satisfaction, of cheap rhetoric, and of noisy self-glorification. There was a corresponding readiness to take offense at the unfavorable opinion of outsiders, and at the same time an eager and insatiable curiosity to hear foreign opinions of any kind. We were, of course, very open to satire and attack. We were young, undeveloped, with a crude, almost raw civilization, and a great inclination to be boastful and conceited. Our English cousins, who had failed to conquer us, bore us no good will, and were quite ready to take all the revenge which books of travel and criticism could afford. It is to these years that Marryat, Trollope, Hamilton, Dickens, and a host of others belong. Most of their productions are quite forgotten now. The only ones which are still read, probably, are the *American Notes* and *Martin Chuzzlewit:* the former preserved by the fame of the author, the latter by its own merit as a novel. There was abundant truth in what Dickens said, to take the great novelist as the type of this group of foreign critics. It was an age in which Elijah Pogram and Jefferson Brick flourished rankly. It is also true that all that Dickens wrote was poisoned by his utter ingratitude, and that to describe the United States as populated by nothing but Bricks and Pograms was one-sided and malicious, and not true to facts. But the truth or the falsehood, the value or the worthlessness, of these criticisms are not of importance now. The striking fact, and the one we are in search of, is the manner in which we bore these censures when they appeared. We can appreciate contemporary feeling at that time only by delving in much forgotten literature; and even then we can hardly comprehend fully what we find, so completely has our habit of mind altered since those days. We received these strictures with a howl of anguish and a scream of mortified vanity. We winced and writhed, and were almost ready to go to war, because English travelers and writers abused us. It is usual now to refer these ebullitions of feeling to our youth, probably from analogy with the youth of an individual. But the analogy is misleading. Sensitiveness to foreign opinion is not especially characteristic of a youthful nation, or, at least, we have no cases to prove it, and in the absence of proof the theory falls. On the other hand, this excessive and almost morbid sensibility is a characteristic of provincial, colonial, or dependent states, especially in regard to the mother country. We raged and cried out against adverse English criticism, whether it was true or false, just or unjust, and we paid it this unnatural attention because the spirit of the colonist still lurked in our hearts and affected our mode of thought. We were advancing fast on the road to intellectual and moral independence, but we were still far from the goal.

This second period in our history closed, as has been said, with the struggle generated by a great moral question, which finally absorbed all the thoughts and passions of the people, and culminated in a terrible civil war. We fought to preserve the integrity of the Union; we fought for our national life, and nationality prevailed. The magnitude of the conflict, the dreadful suffering which it caused for the sake of principle, the uprising of a great people, elevated and ennobled the whole country. The flood-gates were opened, and the tremendous tide of national feeling swept away every meaner emotion. We came out of the battle, after an experience which brought a sudden maturity with it, stronger than ever, but much graver and soberer than before. We came out self-poised and self-reliant, with a true sense of dignity and of our national greatness, which years of peaceful development could not have given us. The sensitiveness to foreign opinion which had been the marked feature of our mental condition before the war had disappeared. It had vanished in the smoke of battle, as the colonial spirit disappeared from our politics in the war of 1812. Englishmen and Frenchmen have come and gone, and written their impressions of us, and made little splashes in the current of every-day topics, and have been forgotten. Just now it is the fashion for every Englishman who visits this country, particularly if he is a man of any note, to go home and tell the world what he thinks of us. Some of these writers do this without taking the trouble to come here first. Sometimes we read what they have to say out of curiosity. We accept what is true, whether unpalatable or not, philosophically, and smile at what is false. The general feeling is one of wholesome indifference. We no longer see salvation and happiness in favorable foreign opinion, or misery in the reverse. The colonial spirit in this direction also is practically extinct.

But while this is true of the mass of the American people whose mental health is good, and is also true of the great body of sound public opinion in the United States, it has some marked exceptions; and these exceptions constitute the lingering remains of the colonial spirit, which survives, and shows itself here and there even at the present day, with a strange vitality.

In the years which followed the close of the war, it seemed

as if colonialism had been utterly extinguished: but, unfortunately, this was not the case. The multiplication of great fortunes, the growth of a class rich by inheritance, and the improvement in methods of travel and communication, all tended to carry large numbers of Americans to Europe. The luxurious fancies which were born of increased wealth, and the intellectual tastes which were developed by the advance of the higher education, and to which an old civilization offers peculiar advantages and attractions, combined to breed in many persons a love of foreign life and foreign manners. These tendencies and opportunities have revived the dying spirit of colonialism. We see it most strongly in the leisure class, which is gradually increasing in this country. During the miserable ascendancy of the Second Empire, a band of these persons formed what was known as the "American colony," in Paris. Perhaps they still exist; if so, their existence is now less flagrant and more decent. When they were notorious they presented the melancholy spectacle of Americans admiring and aping the manners, habits, and vices of another nation, when that nation was bent and corrupted by the cheap, meretricious, and rotten system of the third Napoleon. They furnished a very offensive example of peculiarly mean colonialism. This particular phase has departed, but the same sort of Americans are, unfortunately, still common in Europe. I do not mean, of course, those persons who go abroad to buy social consideration, nor the women who trade on their beauty or their wits to gain a brief and dishonoring notoriety. These last are merely adventurers and adventuresses, who are common to all nations. The people referred to here form that large class, comprising many excellent men and women, no doubt, who pass their lives in Europe, mourning over the inferiority of their own country, and who become thoroughly denationalized. They do not change into Frenchmen or Englishmen, but are simply disfigured and deformed Americans.

We find the same wretched habit of thought in certain groups among the rich and idle people of our great eastern cities, especially in New York, because it is the metropolis. These groups are for the most part made up of young men who despise everything American and admire everything English. They talk and dress and walk and ride in certain ways, because they imagine that the English do these things after that fashion. They hold their own country in contempt, and lament the hard fate of their birth. They try to think that they form an aristocracy, and become at once ludicrous and despicable. The virtues which have made the upper classes in England what they are, and which take them into public affairs, into literature and politics, are forgotten, for Anglo-Americans imitate the vices or the follies of their models, and stop there. If all this were merely a fleeting fashion, an attack of Anglo-mania or of Gallo-mania, of which there have been instances enough everywhere, it would be of no consequence. But it is a recurrence of the old and deep-seated malady of colonialism. It is a lineal descendant of the old colonial family. The features are somewhat dim now, and the vitality is low, but there is no mistaking the hereditary traits. The people who thus despise their own land, and ape English manners, flatter themselves with being cosmopolitans, when in truth they are genuine colonists, petty and provincial to the last degree.

We see a like tendency in the same limited but marked way in our literature. Some of our cleverest fiction is largely devoted to studying the character of our countrymen abroad; that is, either denationalized Americans or Americans with a foreign background. At times this species of literature resolves itself into an agonized effort to show

how foreigners regard us, and to point out the defects which jar upon foreign susceptibilities even while it satirizes the denationalized American. The endeavor to turn ourselves inside out in order to appreciate the trivialities of life which impress foreigners unpleasantly is very unprofitable exertion, and the Europeanized American is not worth either study or satire. Writings of this kind, again, are intended to be cosmopolitan in tone, and to evince a knowledge of the world, and yet they are in reality steeped in colonialism. We cannot but regret the influence of a spirit which wastes fine powers of mind and keen perceptions in a fruitless striving and a morbid craving to know how we appear to foreigners, and to show what they think of us.

We see, also, men and women of talent going abroad to study art and remaining there. The atmosphere of Europe is more congenial to such pursuits, and the struggle as nothing to what must be encountered here. But when it leads to an abandonment of America, the result is wholly vain. Sometimes these people become tolerably successful French artists, but their nationality and individuality have departed, and with them originality and force. The admirable school of etching which has arisen in New York; the beautiful work of American wood-engraving; the Chelsea tiles of Low, which have won the highest prizes at English exhibitions; the silver of Tiffany, specimens of which were bought by the Japanese commissioners at the Paris Exposition, are all strong, genuine work, and are doing more for American art, and for all art, than a wilderness of over-educated and denationalized Americans who are painting pictures and carving statues and writing music in Europe or in the United States, in the spirit of colonists, and bowed down by a wretched dependence.

There is abundance of splendid material all about us here for the poet, the artist, or the novelist. The conditions are not the same as in Europe, but they are not on that account inferior. They are certainly as good. They may be better. Our business is not to grumble because they are different, for that is colonial. We must adapt ourselves to them, for we alone can use properly our own resources; and no work in art or literature ever has been, or ever will be, of any real or lasting value which is not true, original, and independent.

If these remnants of the colonial spirit and influence were, as they look at first sight, merely trivial accidents, they would not be worth mentioning. But the range of their influence, although limited, affects an important class. It appears almost wholly among the rich or the highly educated in art and literature; that is, to a large extent among men and women of talent and refined sensibilities. The follies of those who imitate English habits belong really to but a small portion of even their own class. But as these follies are contemptible, the wholesome prejudice which they excite is naturally, but thoughtlessly, extended to all who have anything in common with those who are guilty of them. In this busy country of ours, the men of leisure and education, although increasing in number, are still few, and they have heavier duties and responsibilities than anywhere else. Public charities, public affairs, politics, literature, all demand the energies of such men. To the country which has given them wealth and leisure and education they owe the duty of faithful service, because they, and they alone, can afford to do that work which must be done without pay. The few who are imbued with the colonial spirit not only fail in their duty, and become contemptible and absurd, but they injure the influence and thwart the activity of the great majority of those who are similarly situated, and who are also patriotic and public spirited.

In art and literature the vain struggle to be somebody

or something other than an American, the senseless admiration of everything foreign, and the morbid anxiety about our appearance before foreigners have the same deadening effect. Such qualities were bad enough in 1820. They are a thousand times meaner and more foolish now. They retard the march of true progress, which here, as elsewhere, must be in the direction of nationality and independence. This does not mean that we are to expect or to seek for something utterly different, something new and strange, in art, literature, or society. Originality is thinking for one's self. Simply to think differently from other people is eccentricity. Some of our English cousins, for instance, have undertaken to hold Walt Whitman up as the herald of the coming literature of American democracy, not because he was a genius, not for his merits alone, but largely because he departed from all received forms, and indulged in barbarous eccentricities. They mistake difference for originality. Whitman was a true and a great poet, but it was his power and imagination which made him so, not his eccentricities. When Whitman did best, he was, as a rule, nearest to the old and well-proved forms. We, like our contemporaries everywhere, are the heirs of the ages, and we must study the past, and learn from it, and advance from what has been already tried and found good. That is the only way to success anywhere, or in anything. But we cannot enter upon that or any other road until we are truly national and independent intellectually, and are ready to think for ourselves, and not look to foreigners in order to find out what they think.

To those who grumble and sigh over the inferiority of America we may commend the opinion of a distinguished Englishman, as they prefer such authority. Mr. Herbert Spencer said, recently, "I think that whatever difficulties they may have to surmount, and whatever tribulations they may have to pass through, the Americans may reasonably look forward to a time when they will have produced a civilization grander than any the world has known." Even the Englishmen whom our provincials of to-day adore, even those who are most hostile, pay a serious attention to America. That keen respect for success and anxious deference to power so characteristic of Great Britain find expression every day, more and more, in the English interest in the United States, now that we do not care in the least about it; and be it said in passing, no people despises more heartily than the English a man who does not love his country. To be despised abroad, and regarded with contempt and pity at home, is not a very lofty result of so much effort on the part of our lovers of the British. But it is the natural and fit reward of colonialism. Members of a great nation instinctively patronize colonists.

It is interesting to examine the sources of the colonial spirit, and to trace its influence upon our history and its gradual decline. The study of a habit of mind, with its tenacity of life, is an instructive and entertaining branch of history. But if we lay history and philosophy aside, the colonial spirit as it survives to-day, although curious enough, is a mean and noxious thing, which cannot be too quickly or too thoroughly stamped out. It is the dying spirit of dependence, and wherever it still clings it injures, weakens, and degrades. It should be exorcised rapidly and completely, so that it will never return. I cannot close more fitly than with the noble words of Emerson:—

"Let the passion for America cast out the passion for Europe. They who find America insipid, they for whom London and Paris have spoiled their own homes, can be spared to return to those cities. I not only see a career at home for more genius than we have, but for more than there is in the world."

NEW YORK AFTER PARIS

W. C. Brownell

No American, not a commercial or otherwise hardened traveler, can have a soul so dead as to be incapable of emotion when, on his return from a long trip abroad, he catches sight of the low-lying and insignificant Long Island coast. One's excitement begins, indeed, with the pilot-boat. The pilot-boat is the first concrete symbol of those native and normal relations with one's fellow-men, which one has so long observed in infinitely varied manifestation abroad, but always as a spectator and a stranger, and which one is now on the eve of sharing himself. As she comes up swiftly, white and graceful, drops her pilot, crosses the steamer's bows, tacks, and picks up her boat in the foaming wake, she presents a spectacle beside which the most picturesque Mediterranean craft, with colored sails and lazy evolutions, appear mistily in the memory as elements of a feeble and conventional ideal. The ununiformed pilot clambers on board, makes his way to the bridge, and takes command with an equal lack of French manner and of English affectation distinctly palpable to the sense, sharpened by long absence into observing native characteristics as closely as foreign ones. If the season be right the afternoon is bright, the range of vision apparently limitless, the sky nearly cloudless and, by contrast with the European firmament, almost colorless, the July sun such as no Parisian or Londoner ever saw. The French reproach us for having no word for "patrie" as distinct from "pays"; we have the thing at all events, and cherish it, and it needs only the proximity of the foreigner, from whom in general we are so widely separated, to give our patriotism a tinge of the veriest chauvinism that exists in France itself.

We fancy the feeling old-fashioned, and imagine ours to be the most cosmopolitan, the least prejudiced temperament in the world. It is reasonable that it should be. The extreme sensitiveness noticed in us by all foreign observers during the antebellum epoch, and ascribed by Tocqueville to our self-distrust, is naturally inconsistent with our position and circumstances to-day. A population greater than that of any of the great nations, isolated by the most enviable geographical felicity in the world from the narrowing influences of international jealousy apparent to every American who travels in Europe, is increasingly less concerned at criticism than a struggling provincial republic of half its size. And along with our self-confidence and our carelessness of "abroad," it is only with the grosser element among us that national conceit has deepened; in general, we are apt to fancy we have become cosmopolitan in proportion as we have lost our provincialism. With us surely the individual has not withered, and if the world has become more and more to him, it is because it is the world at large and not the pent-up confines of his own country's history and extent. "La patrie" in danger would be quickly enough rescued—there is no need to prove that over again, even to our own satisfaction; but in general "la patrie" not being in any danger, being on the contrary apparently on the very crest of the wave of the world, it is felt not to need much of one's active consideration, and passively indeed is viewed by many people, probably, as a comfortable and gigantic contrivance for securing a free field in which the individual may expand and develop. "America," says Emerson, "America is Opportunity." After all, the average American of the present day says, a country stands or falls by the number of properly expanded and developed individuals it possesses. But the happening of any one of a dozen things unexpectedly betrays that all this cosmopolitanism is in great measure, and so far as sentiment is concerned, a veneer and a disguise. Such a happening is the very change from blue water to gray that announces to the returning American the nearness of that country which he sometimes thinks he prizes more for what it stands for than for itself. It is not, he then feels with a sudden flood of emotion, that America is home, but that home is America. America comes suddenly to mean what it never meant before.

Unhappily for this exaltation, ordinary life is not composed of emotional crises. It is ordinary life with a vengeance which one encounters in issuing from the steamer dock and facing again his native city. Paris never looked so lovely, so exquisite to the sense as it now appears in the memory. All that Parisian regularity, order, decorum, and beauty into which, although a stranger, your own activities fitted so perfectly that you were only half-conscious of its existence, was not, then, merely normal, wholly a matter of course. Emerging into West Street, amid the solicitations of hackmen, the tinkling jog-trot of the most ignoble horse-cars you have seen since leaving home, the dry dust blowing into your eyes, the gaping black holes of broken pavements, the unspeakable filth, the line of red brick buildings prematurely decrepit, the sagging multitude of telegraph wires, the clumsy electric lights depending before the beer saloon and the groggery, the curious confusion of spruceness and squalor in the aspect of these latter, which also seem legion—confronting all this for the first time in three years, say, you think with wonder of your disappointment at not finding the Tuileries Gardens a mass of flowers, and with a blush of the times you have told Frenchmen that

New York was very much like Paris. New York is at this moment the most foreign-looking city you have ever seen; in going abroad the American discounts the unexpected; returning after the insensible orientation of Europe, the contrast with things recently familiar is prodigious, because one is so entirely unprepared for it. One thinks to be at home, and finds himself at the spectacle. New York is less like any European city than any European city is like any other. It is distinguished from them all—even from London—by the ignoble character of the *res publicæ,* and the refuge of taste, care, wealth, pride, self-respect even, in private and personal regions. A splendid carriage, liveried servants without and Paris dresses within, rattling over the scandalous paving, splashed by the neglected mud, catching the rusty drippings of the hideous elevated railway, wrenching its axle in the tram-track in avoiding a mountainous wagon load of commerce on this hand and a garbage cart on that, caught in a jam of horse-cars and a blockade of trucks, finally depositing its dainty freight to pick its way across a sidewalk eloquent of official neglect and private contumely, to a shop door or a residence stoop—such a contrast as this sets us off from Europe very definitely and in a very marked degree.

There is no palpable New York in the sense in which there is a Paris, a Vienna, a Milan. You can touch it at no point. It is not even ocular. There is instead a Fifth Avenue, a Broadway, a Central Park, a Chatham Square. How they have dwindled, by the way. Fifth Avenue might be any one of a dozen London streets in the first impression it makes on the retina and leaves on the mind. The opposite side of Madison Square is but a step away. The spacious hall of the Fifth Avenue Hotel has shrunk to stifling proportions. Thirty-fourth Street is a lane; the City Hall a band-box; the Central Park a narrow strip of elegant landscape whose lateral limitations are constantly forced upon the sense by the Lenox Library on one side and a monster apartment house on the other. The American fondness for size—for pure bigness—needs explanation, it appears; we care for size, but inartistically; we care nothing for proportion, which is what makes size count, Everything is on the same scale; there is no play, no movement. An exception should be made in favor of the big business building and the apartment house which have arisen within a few years, and which have greatly accentuated the grotesqueness of the city's sky-line as seen from either the New Jersey or the Long Island shore. They are perhaps rather high than big; many of them were built before the authorities noticed them and followed unequally in the steps of other civilized municipal governments, from that of ancient Rome down, in prohibiting the passing of a fixed limit. But bigness has also evidently been one of their architectonic motives, and it is to be remarked that they are so far out of scale with the surrounding buildings as to avoid the usual commonplace, only by creating a positively disagreeable effect. The aspect of Fifty-seventh Street between Broadway and Seventh Avenue, for example, is certainly that of the world upside down: a Gothic church utterly concealed, not to say crushed, by contiguous flats, and confronted by the overwhelming " Osborne," which towers above anything in the neighborhood, and perhaps makes the most powerful impression that the returned traveler receives during his first week or two of strange sensations. Yet the " Osborne's " dimensions are not very different from those of the Arc de l'Étoile. It is true it does not face an avenue of majestic buildings a mile and a half long and two hundred and thirty feet wide, but the association of these two structures, one a private enterprise and the other a public monument, together with the obvious suggestions of each, furnish a not misleading illustration of both the spectacular and the moral contrast between New York and Paris, as it appears unduly magnified no doubt to the sense surprised to notice it at all.

Still another reason for the foreign aspect of the New Yorker's native city is the gradual withdrawing of the American element into certain quarters, its transformation or essential modification in others, and in the rest the presence of the lees of Europe. At every step you are forced to realize that New York is the second Irish and the third or fourth German city in the world. However great our success in drilling this foreign contingent of our social army into order and reason and self-respect—and it is not to be doubted that this success gives us a distinction wholly new in history—nevertheless our effect upon its members has been in the direction of development rather than of assimilation. We have given them our opportunity, permitted them the expansion denied them in their own several feudalities, made men of serfs, demonstrated the utility of self-government under the most trying conditions, proved the efficacy of our elastic institutions on a scale truly grandiose; but evidently, so far as New York is concerned, we have done this at the sacrifice of a distinct and obvious nationality. To an observant sense New York is nearly as little national as Port Said. It contrasts absolutely in this respect with Paris, whose assimilating power is prodigious; every foreigner in Paris eagerly seeks Parisianization.

Ocularly, therefore, the "note" of New York seems that of characterless individualism. The monotony of the chaotic composition and movement is, paradoxically, its most abiding impression. And as the whole is destitute of definiteness, of distinction, the parts are, correspondingly, individually insignificant. Where in the world are all the types? one asks one's self in renewing his old walks and desultory wanderings. Where is the New York counterpart of that astonishing variety of types which makes Paris what it is morally and pictorially, the Paris of Balzac as well as the Paris of M. Jean Béraud. Of a sudden the lack of nationality in our familiar literature and art becomes luminously explicable. One perceives why Mr. Howells is so successful in confining himself to the simplest, broadest, most representative representatives, why Mr. James goes abroad invariably for his *mise-en-scène,* and often for his characters, why Mr. Reinhart lives in Paris, and Mr. Abbey in London. New York is this and that, it is incontestably unlike any other great city, but compared with Paris, its most impressive trait is its lack of that organic quality which results from variety of types. Thus compared, it seems to have only the variety of individuals which results in monotony. It is the difference between noise and music. Pictorially, the general aspect of New York is such that the mind speedily takes refuge in insensitiveness. Its expansiveness seeks exercise in other directions—business, dissipation, study, æstheticism, politics. The life of the senses is no longer possible. This is why one's sense for art is so stimulated by going abroad, and one's sense for art in its freest, frankest, most universal and least special, intense and enervated development, is especially exhilarated by going to Paris. It is why, too, on one's return one can note the gradual decline of his sensitiveness, his severity—the progressive atrophy of a sense no longer called into exercise. "I had no conception before," said a Chicago broker to me one day in Paris, with intelligent eloquence, "of a finished city!" Chicago undoubtedly presents a greater contrast to Paris than does New York, and so, perhaps, better prepares one to appreciate the Parisian quality, but the *returned* New Yorker cannot fail to be deeply impressed with the finish, the organic perfection, the elegance, and reserve

New York After Paris

of the Paris mirrored in his memory. Is it possible that the uniformity, the monotony of Paris architecture, the prose note in Parisian taste, should once have weighed upon his spirit? Riding once on the top of a Paris tramway, betraying an understanding of English by reading an American newspaper, that sub-consciousness of moral isolation which the foreigner feels in Paris as elsewhere, was suddenly and completely destroyed by my next neighbor, who remarked with contemptuous conviction and a Manhattan accent: " When you've seen one block of this infernal town you've seen it all!" He felt sure of sympathy in advance. Probably few New Yorkers would have differed with him. The universal light stone and brown paint, the wide sidewalks, the asphalt pavement, the indefinitely multipled kiosks, the prevalence of a few marked kinds of vehicles, the uniformed workmen and workwomen, the infinite reduplication, in a word, of easily recognized types, is at first mistaken by the New Yorker for that dead level of uniformity which is, of all things in the world, the most tiresome to him in his own city. After a time, however, he begins to realize three important facts: In the first place these phenomena, which so vividly force themselves on his notice that their reduplication strikes him more than their qualities, are nevertheless of a quality altogether unexampled in his experience for fitness and agreeableness; in the second place, they are details of a whole, members of an organism, and not they, but the city which they compose, the " finished city " of the acute Chicagoan, is the spectacle; in the third place they serve as a background for the finest group of monuments in the world. On his return he perceives these things with a melancholy *a non lucendo* luminousness. The dead level of Murray Hill uniformity he finds the most agreeable aspect in the city.

And the reason is that Paris has habituated him to the

exquisite, the rational, pleasure to be derived from that organic spectacle a " finished city," far more than that Murray Hill is respectable and appropriate, and that almost any other prospect, except in spots of very limited area which emphasize the surrounding ugliness, is acutely displeasing. This latter is certainly very true. We have long frankly reproached ourselves with having no art commensurate with our distinction in other activities, resignedly attributing the lack to our hitherto necessary material preoccupation. But what we are really accounting for in this way is our lack of Titians and Bramantes. We are for the most part quite unconscious of the character of the American æsthetic substratum, so to speak. As a matter of fact, we do far better in the production of striking artistic personalities than we do in the general medium of taste and culture. We figure well invariably at the *Salon*. At home the artist is simply either driven in upon himself, or else awarded by a *naïve clientèle,* an eminence so far out of perspective as to result unfortunately both for him and for the community. He pleases himself, follows his own bent, and prefers salience to conformability for his work, because his chief aim is to make an effect. This is especially true of those of our architects who have ideas. But these are the exceptions, of course, and the general aspect of the city is characterized by something far less agreeable than mere lack of symmetry; it is characterized mainly by an all-pervading bad taste in every detail into which the element of art enters or should enter—that is to say, nearly everything that meets the eye.

However, on the other hand, Parisian uniformity may depress exuberance, it is the condition and often the cause of the omnipresent good taste. Not only is it true that, as Mr. Hamerton remarks, " in the better quarters of the city a building hardly ever rises from the ground unless it has been designed by some architect who knows what art is, and endeavors to apply it to little things as well as great"; but it is equally true that the national sense of form expresses itself in every appurtenance of life as well as in the masses and details of architecture. In New York our noisy diversity not only prevents any effect of *ensemble* and makes, as I say, the old commonplace brown stone regions the most reposeful and rational prospects of the city, but it precludes also, in a thousand activities and aspects, the operation of that salutary constraint and conformity without which the most acutely sensitive individuality inevitably declines to a lower level of form and taste. *La mode,* for example, seems scarcely to exist at all; or at any rate to have taken refuge in the chimney-pot hat and the *tournure.* The dude, it is true, has been developed within a few years, but his distinguishing trait of personal extinction has had much less success and is destined to a much shorter life than his appellation, which has wholly lost its original significance in gaining its present popularity. Every woman one meets in the street has a different bonnet. Every street car contains a millinery museum. And the mass of them may be judged after the circumstance that one of the most fashionable Fifth Avenue *modistes* flaunts a sign of enduring brass announcing " English Round Hats and Bonnets." The enormous establishments of ready-made men's clothing seem not yet to have made their destined impression in the direction of uniformity. The contrast in dress of the working classes with those of Paris is as conspicuously unfortunate æsthetically, as politically and socially it may be significant; ocularly, it is a substitution of a cheap, faded, and ragged imitation of *bourgeois* costume for the marvel of neatness and propriety which composes the uniform of the Parisian *ouvrier* and *ouvrière.* Broadway below Tenth Street is a forest of signs which obscure the thoroughfare, conceal the buildings, overhang the sidewalks, and exhibit severally and collectively a taste in harmony with the Teutonic and Semitic enterprise which, almost exclusively, they attest. The shop-windows' show, which is one of the great spectacles of Paris, is niggard and shabby; that of Philadelphia has considerably more interest, that of London nearly as much. Our clumsy coinage and countrified currency; our eccentric book-bindings; that class of our furniture and interior decoration which may be described as American rococo; that multifariously horrible machinery devised for excluding flies from houses and preventing them from alighting on dishes, for substituting a draught of air for stifling heat, for relieving an entire population from that surplusage of old-fashioned breeding involved in shutting doors, for rolling and rattling change in shops, for enabling you to " put only the exact fare in the box "; the racket of pneumatic tubes, of telephones, of aërial trains; the practice of reticulating pretentious façades with fire-escapes in lieu of fire-proof construction; the vast mass of our nickel-plated paraphernalia; our zinc cemetery monuments; our comic valentines and serious Christmas cards, and grocery labels, and " fancy " job-printing and theater posters; our conspicuous cuspadores and our conspicuous need of more of them; the " tone " of many articles in our most popular journals, their references to each other, their illustrations; the Sunday panorama of shirt-sleeved ease and the week-day fatigue costume of curl papers and " Mother Hubbards " general in some quarters; our sumptuous new bar-rooms, decorated perhaps on the principle that *le mauvais goût mène au crime*—all these phenomena, the list of which might be indefinitely extended, are so many witnesses of a general taste, public and private, which differs cardinally from that prevalent in Paris.

In fine, the material spectacle of New York is such that at last, with some anxiety, one turns from the external vile-ness of every prospect to seek solace in the pleasure that man affords. But even after the wholesome American reaction has set in, and your appetite for the life of the senses is starved into indifference for what begins to seem to you an unworthy ideal; after you are patriotically readjusted and feel once more the elation of living in the future owing to the dearth of sustenance in the present—you are still at the mercy of perceptions too keenly sharpened by your Paris sojourn to permit blindness to the fact that Paris and New York contrast as strongly in moral atmosphere as in material aspect. You become contemplative, and speculate pensively as to the character and quality of those native and normal conditions, those Relations, which finally you have definitely resumed. What is it—that vague and pervasive moral contrast which the American feels so potently on his return from abroad? How can we define that apparently undefinable difference which is only the more sensible for being so elusive? Book after book has been written about Europe from the American standpoint—about America from the European standpoint. None of them has specified what everyone has experienced. The spectacular and the material contrasts are easily enough characterized, and it is only the unreflecting or the superficial who exaggerate the importance of them. We are by no means at the mercy of our appreciation of Parisian spectacle, of the French machinery of life. We miss or we do not miss the Salon Carré, the view of the south transept of Notre Dame as one descends the rue St. Jacques, the Théâtre Français, the concerts, the Luxembourg Gardens, the excursions to the score of charming suburban places, the library at the corner, the convenient cheap cab, the manners of the people, the quiet, the climate, the constant entertainment of the senses. We have in general too much work to do to waste much time in regretting these things. In general, work is by natural selection so invariable a concomitant of our unrivaled opportunity to work profitably, that it absorbs our energies so far as this palpable sphere is concerned. But what is it that throughout the hours of busiest work and closest application, as well as in the preceding and following moments of leisure and the occasional intervals of relaxation, makes everyone vaguely perceive the vast moral difference between life here at home and life abroad—notably life in France? What is the subtle influence pervading the moral atmosphere in New York, which so markedly distinguishes what we call life here from life in Paris or even in Pennedepie?

It is, I think, distinctly traceable to the intense individualism which prevails among us. Magnificent results have followed our devotion to this force; incontestably, we have spared ourselves both the acute and the chronic misery for which the tyranny of society over its constituent parts is directly responsible. We have, moreover, in this way not only freed ourselves from the tyranny of despotism, such for example as is exerted socially in England and politically in Russia, but we have undoubtedly developed a larger number of self-reliant and potentially capable social units than even a democratic system like that of France, which sacrifices the unit to the organism, succeeds in producing. We may truly say that, material as we are accused of being, we turn out more *men* than any other nationality. And if some Frenchman points out that we attach an esoteric sense to the term " man," and that at any rate our men are not better adapted than some others to a civilized environment which demands other qualities than honesty, energy, and intelligence, we may be quite content to leave him his objection, and to prefer what seems to us manliness, to civilization itself. At the same time we cannot pretend that individualism has done everything for us that could be desired. In giving us the man it has robbed us of the *milieu*. Morally speaking, the *milieu* with us scarcely exists. Our difference from Europe does not consist in the difference between the European *milieu* and ours; it consists in the fact that, comparatively speaking of course, we have no *milieu*. If we are individually developed, we are also individually isolated to a degree elsewhere unknown. Politically we have parties who, in Cicero's phrase, "think the same things concerning the republic," but concerning very little else are we agreed in any mass of any moment. The number of our sauces is growing, but there is no corresponding diminution in the number of our religions. We have no communities. Our villages even are apt, rather, to be aggregations. Politics aside, there is hardly an American view of any phenomenon or class of phenomena. Every one of us likes, reads, sees, does what he chooses. Often dissimilarity is affected as adding piquancy of paradox. The judgment of the ages, the consensus of mankind, exercise no tyranny over the individual will. Do you believe in this or that, do you like this or that, are questions which, concerning the most fundamental matters, nevertheless form the staple of conversation in many circles. We live all of us apparently in a divine state of flux. The question asked at dinner by a lady in a neighboring city of a literary stranger, "What do you think of Shakespeare?" is not exaggeratedly peculiar. We all think differently of Shakespeare, of Cromwell, of Titian, of Browning, of George Washington. Concerning matters as to which we must be fundamentally disinterested, we permit ourselves not only prejudice but passion. At the most we have here and there groups of personal acquaintance only, whose members are in accord in regard to some one thing, and quickly crystallize and precipitate at the mention of something that is really a corollary of the force which unites them. The efforts that have been made in New York, within the past twenty years, to establish various special *milieus,* so to speak, have been pathetic in their number and resultlessness. Efforts of this sort are of course doomed to failure, because the essential trait of the *milieu* is spontaneous existence, but their failure discloses the mutual repulsion which keeps the molecules of our society from uniting. How can it be otherwise when life is so speculative, so experimental, so wholly dependent on the personal force and idiosyncrasies of the individual? How shall we accept any general verdict pronounced by persons of no more authority than ourselves, and arrived at by processes in which we are equally expert? We have so little consensus as to anything, because we dread the loss of personality involved in submitting to conventions, and because personality operates centrifugally alone. We make exceptions in favor of such matters as the Copernican system and the greatness of our own future. There *are* things which we take on the credit of the consensus of authorities, for which we may not have all the proofs at hand. But as to conventions of all sorts, our attitude is apt to be one of suspicion and uncertainty. Mark Twain, for example, first won his way to the popular American heart by exposing the humbugs of the Cinque-cento. Specifically the most teachable of people, nervously eager for information, Americans are nevertheless wholly distrustful of generalizations made by anyone else, and little disposed to receive blindly formularies and classifications of phenomena as to which they have had no experience. And of experience we have necessarily had, except politically, less than any civilized people in the world.

We are infinitely more at home amid universal mobility. We want to act, to exert ourselves, to be, as we imagine, nearer to nature. We have our tastes in painting as in confectionery. Some of us prefer Tintoretto to Rembrandt, as we do chocolate to cocoanut. In respect of taste it would be impossible for the gloomiest skeptic to deny that this is an exceedingly free country. " I don't know anything about the subject (whatever the subject may be), but I know what I like," is a remark which is heard on every hand, and which witnesses the sturdiness of our struggle against the tyranny of conventions and the indomitable nature of our independent spirit. In criticism the individual spirit fairly runs a-muck; it takes its lack of concurrence as credentials of impartiality often. In constructive art everyone is occupied less with nature than with the point of view. Mr. Howells himself displays more delight in his naturalistic attitude than zest in his execution, which, compared with that of the French naturalists, is in general faint-hearted enough. Everyone writes, paints, models, exclusively the point of view. Fidelity in following out nature's suggestions, in depicting the emotions nature arouses, a sympathetic submission to nature's sentiment, absorption into nature's moods and subtle enfoldings, are extremely rare. The artist's eye is fixed on the treatment. He is " creative " by main strength. He is penetrated with a desire to get away from " the same old thing," to " take it " in a new way, to draw attention to himself, to shine. One would say that every American nowadays who handles a brush or designs a building, was stimulated by the secret ambition of founding a school. We have in art thus, with a vengeance, that personal element which is indeed its savor, but which it is fatal to make its substance. We have it still more conspicuously in life. What do you think of him, or her? is the first question asked after every introduction. Of every new individual we meet we form instantly some personal impression. The criticism of character is nearly the one disinterested activity in which we have become expert. We have for this a peculiar gift, apparently, which we share with gypsies and money-lenders, and other people in whom the social instinct is chiefly latent. Our gossip takes on the character of personal judgments rather than of tittle-tattle. It concerns not what So-and-So has done, but what kind of a person So-and-So is. It would hardly be too much to say that So-and-So never leaves a group of which he is not an intimate without being immediately, impartially but fundamentally, discussed. To a degree not at all suspected by the author of the phrase, he "leaves his character" with them on quitting any assemblage of his acquaintance.

The great difficulty with our individuality and independence is that differentiation begins so soon and stops so far short of real importance. In no department of life has the law of the survival of the fittest, that principle in virtue of whose operation societies become distinguished and admirable, had time to work. Our social characteristics are inventions, discoveries, not survival. Nothing with us has passed into the stage of instinct. And for this reason some of our "best people," some of the most "thoughtful" among us, have less of that quality best characterized as social maturity than a Parisian washerwoman or *concierge*. Centuries of sifting, ages of gravitation toward harmony and homogeneity, have resulted for the French in a delightful immunity from the necessity of "proving all things" remorselessly laid on every individual of our society. Very many matters, at any rate, which to the French are matters of course, our self-respect pledges us to a personal examination of. The idea of sparing ourselves trouble in thinking occurs to us far more rarely than to other peoples. We have certainly an insufficient notion of the superior results reached by economy and system in this respect.

In one of Mr. Henry James's cleverest sketches, *Lady Barberina*, the English heroine marries an American and comes to live in New York. She finds it dull. She is homesick without quite knowing why. Mr. James is at his best in exhibiting at once the intensity of her disgust and the intangibility of its provocation. We are not all like "Lady Barb." We do not all like London, whose materialism is only more splendid, not less uncompromising than our own; but we cannot help perceiving that what that unfortunate lady missed in New York was the *milieu*—an environment sufficiently developed to permit spontaneity and free play of thought and feeling, and a certain domination of shifting merit by fixed relations which keeps one's mind off that disagreeable subject of contemplation, one's self. Everyone seems acutely self-conscious; and the self-consciousness of the unit is fatal, of course, to the composure of the *ensemble*. The number of people intently minding their P's and Q's, reforming their orthoepy, practicing new discoveries in etiquette, making over their names, and in general exhibiting that activity of the amateur known as "going through the motions" to the end of bringing themselves up, as it were, is very noticeable in contrast with French oblivion to this kind of personal exertion. Even our simplicity is apt to be *simplesse*. And the conscientiousness in educating others displayed by those who are so fortunate as to have reached perfection nearly enough to permit relaxation in self-improvement, is only equaled by the avidity in acquisitiveness displayed by the learners themselves. Meantime the composure born of equality, as well as that springing from unconsciousness, suffers. Our society is a kind of Jacob's ladder, to maintain equilibrium upon which requires an amount of effort on the part of the personally estimable gymnasts perpetually ascending and descending, in the highest degree hostile to spontaneity, to serenity, and stability.

Naturally, thus, everyone is personally preoccupied to a degree unknown in France. And it is not necessary that this preoccupation should concern any side of that multifarious monster we know as "business." It may relate strictly to the paradox of seeking employment for leisure. Even the latter is a terribly conscious proceeding. We go about it with a mental deliberateness singularly in contrast with our physical precipitancy. But it is mainly "business," perhaps, that accentuates our individualism. The condition of *désœuvrement* is positively disreputable. It arouses the suspicion of acquaintance and the anxiety of friends. Occupation to the end of money-getting is our normal condition, any variation from which demands explanation, as little likely to be entirely honorable. Such occupation is, as I said, the inevitable sequence of the opportunity for it, and is the wiser and more dignified because of its necessity to the end of securing independence. What the Frenchman can secure merely by the exercise of economy is with us only the reward of energy and enterprise in acquisition—so comparatively speculative and hazardous is the condition of our business. And whereas with us money is far harder to keep, and is moreover something which it is far harder to be without than is the case in France, the ends of self-respect, freedom from mortification, and getting the most out of life, demand that we should take constant advantage of the fact that it is easier to get. Consequently everyone who is, as we say, worth anything, is with us adjusted to the prodigious dynamic condition which characterizes our existence. And such occupation is tremendously absorbing. Our opportunity is fatally handicapped by this remorseless necessity of embracing it. It yields us fruit after its kind, but it rigorously excludes us from tasting any other. Everyone is engaged in preparing the working drawings of his own fortune. There is no co-operation possible, because competition is the life of enterprise.

In the resultant manners the city illustrates Carlyle's "anarchy plus the constable." Never was the struggle for existence more palpable, more naked, and more unpictorial. "It is the art of mankind to polish the world," says Thoreau somewhere, "and everyone who works is scrubbing in some part." Everyone certainly is here at work, yet was there ever such scrubbing with so little resultant polish? The disproportion would be tragic if it were not grotesque. Amid all "the hurry and rush of life along the sidewalks," as the newspapers say, one might surely expect to find the unexpected. The spectacle ought certainly to have the interest of picturesqueness which is inherent in the fortuitous. Unhappily, though there is hurry and rush enough, it is the bustle of business, not the dynamics of what is properly to be called life. The elements of the picture lack dignity—so completely as to leave the *ensemble* quite without accent. More incidents in the drama of real life will happen before midnight to the individuals who compose the orderly Boulevard procession in Paris than those of its chaotic Broadway counterpart will experience in a month. The latter are not really more impressive because they are apparently all running errands and include no *flâneurs*. The *flâneur* would fare ill should anything draw him into the stream. Everything being adjusted to the motive of looking out for one's self, any of the sidewalk civility and mutual interest which obtain in Paris would throw the entire machine out of gear. Whoever is not in a hurry is in the way. A man running after an omnibus at the Madeleine would come into collision with fewer people and cause less disturbance than one who should stop on Fourteenth Street to apologize for an inadvertent jostle, or to give a lady any surplusage of passing room. He would be less ridiculous. A friend recently returned from Paris told me that, on several street occasions, his involuntary "Excuse me!" had been mistaken for a salutation and answered by a "How do you do?" and a stare of speculation. Apologies of this class sound to us, perhaps, like a subtle and deprecatory impeachment of our large tolerance and universal good nature.

In this way our undoubted self-respect undoubtedly loses something of its bloom. We may prefer being jammed into street-cars and pressed against the platform rails of the elevated road to the tedious waiting at Paris 'bus stations—to mention one of the perennial and principal points of contrast which monopolize the thoughts of the average American sojourner in the French capital. But it is terribly vulgarizing. The contact and pressure are abominable. To a Parisian the daily experience in this respect of those of our women who have no carriages of their own, would seem as singular as the latter would find the Oriental habit of regarding the face as more important than other portions of the female person to keep concealed. But neither men nor women can persist in blushing at the intimacy of rudeness to which our crowding subjects them in common. The only resource is in blunted sensibility. And the manners thus negatively produced we do not quite appreciate in their enormity because the edge of our appreciation is thus necessarily dulled. The conductor scarcely ceases whistling to poke you for your fare. Other whistlers apparently go on forever. Loud talking follows naturally from the impossibility of personal seclusion in the presence of others. Our Sundays have lost secular decorum very much in proportion as they have lost Puritan observance. If we have nothing quite comparable with a London bank holiday, or with the conduct of the popular cohorts of the Epsom army; if only in " political picnics " and the excursions of " gangs " of " toughs " we illustrate absolute barbarism, it is nevertheless true that, from Central Park to Coney Island, our people exhibit a conception of the fitting employment of periodical leisure which would seem indecorous to a crowd of Belleville *ouvriers*. If we have not the cad, we certainly possess in abundance the species "hoodlum," which, though morally far more refreshing, is yet æsthetically intolerable; and the hoodlum is nearly as rare in Paris as the cad. Owing to his presence and to the atmosphere in which he thrives, we find ourselves, in spite of the most determined democratic convictions, shunning crowds whenever it is possible to shun them. The most robust of us easily get into the frame of mind of a Boston young woman, to whom the Champs-Élysées looked like a railway station, and who wished the people would get up from the benches and go home. Our life becomes a life of the interior; wherefore, in spite of a climate that permits walks abroad, we confine out-door existence to Newport lawns and camps in the Adirondacks; and whence proceeds that carelessness of the exterior which subordinates architecture to "household art," and makes of our streets such mere thoroughfares lined with "homes."

The manners one encounters in street and shop in Paris are, it is well known, very different from our own. But no praise of them ever quite prepares an American for their agreeableness and simplicity. We are always agreeably surprised at the absence of elaborate manner which eulogists of French manners in general omit to note; and indeed it is an extremely elusive quality. Nothing is further removed from that intrusion of the national *gemüthlichkeit* into so impersonal a matter as affairs, large or small, which to an occasional sense makes the occasional German manner enjoyable. Nothing is farther from the obsequiousness of the London shopman, which rather dazes the American than pleases him. Nothing, on the other hand, is farther from our own bald dispatch. With us every shopper expects, or at any rate is prepared for, obstruction rather than facilitation on the seller's side. The drygoods counter, especially when the attendant is of the gentler sex, is a kind of *chevaux-de-frise*. The retail atmosphere is charged with an affectation of unconsciousness; not only is every transaction impersonal, it is mechanical; ere long it must become automatic. In many cases there is to be encountered a certain defiant attitude to the last degree unhappy in its effects on the manners involved—a certain self-assertion which begs the question, else unmooted, of social equality, with the result for the time being of the most unsocial relation probably existing among men. Perfect personal equality for the time being invariably exists between customer and tradesman in France; the man or woman who serves you is first of all a fellow-creature; a shop, to be sure, is not a *conversazione,* but if you are in a loquacious or inquisitive mood you will be deemed neither frivolous nor familiar—nor yet an inanimate obstacle to the flow of the most important as well as the most impetuous of the currents of life.

Certainly, in New York, we are too vain of our bustle to realize how mannerless and motiveless it is. The essence of life is movement, but so is the essence of epilepsy. Moreover the life of the New Yorker who chases street-cars, eats at a lunch counter, drinks what will "take hold" quickly at a bar he can quit instantly, reads only the head-lines of his newspaper, keeps abreast of the intellectual movement by inspecting the display of the Elevated Railway newsstands while he fumes at having to wait two minutes for his train, hastily buys his tardy ticket of sidewalk speculators, and leaves the theater as if it were on fire—the life of such a man is, notwithstanding all its futile activity, varied by long spaces of absolute mental stagnation, of moral coma. Not only is our hurry not decorous, not decent; it is not real activity, it is as little as possible like the animated existence of Paris, where the moral nature is kept in constant operation, intense or not as the case may be, in spite of the external and material tranquillity. Owing to this lack of a real, a rational activity, our individual civilization, which seems when successful a scramble, and when unlucky a *sauve qui peut,* is, morally as well as spectacularly, not ill described in so far as its external aspect is concerned by the epithet *flat.* Enervation seems to menace those whom hyperæsthesia spares.

" We go to Europe to become Americanized," says Emerson, but France Americanizes us less in this sense than any other country of Europe, and perhaps Emerson was not thinking so much of her democratic development into social order and efficiency as of the less American and more feudal European influences, which do indeed, while we are subject to them, intensify our affection for our own institutions, our confidence in our own outlook. One must admit that in France (which nowadays follows our ideal of liberty perhaps as closely as we do hers of equality and fraternity, and where consequently our political notions receive few shocks) not only is the life of the senses more agreeable than it is with us, but the mutual relations of men are more felicitous also. And alas! Americans who have savored these sweets cannot avail themselves of the implication contained in Emerson's further words—words which approach nearer to petulance than anything in his urbane and placid utterances—" those who prefer London or Paris to America may be spared to return to those capitals." " Il faut vivre, combattre, et finir avec les siens," says Doudan, and no law is more inexorable. The fruits of foreign gardens are, however delectable, enchanted for us; we may not touch them; and to pass our lives in covetous inspection of them is as barren a performance as may be imagined. For this reason the question " Should you like better to live here or abroad?" is as little practical as it is frequent. The empty life of the " foreign colonies " in Paris is its sufficient answer. Not only do most of us *have* to stay at home, but for everyone except the inconsiderable few who can better do abroad the work they have to do, and except those essentially un-American waifs who can contrive no work for themselves, life abroad is not only less profitable but less pleasant. The American endeavoring to acclimatize himself in Paris hardly needs to have cited to him the words of Epictetus: " Man, thou hast forgotten thine object; thy journey was not *to* this, but *through* this "—he is sure before long to become dismally persuaded of their truth. More speedily than elsewhere perhaps, he finds out in Paris the truth of Carlyle's assurance: " It is, after all, the one unhappiness of a man. That he cannot work; that he cannot get his destiny as a man fulfilled." For the work which insures the felicity of the French life of the senses and of French human relations he cannot share; and, thus, the question of the relative attractiveness of French and American life—of Paris and New York—becomes the idle and purely speculative question as to whether one would like to change his personal and national identity.

And this an American may permit himself the chauvinism of believing a less rational contradiction of instinct in himself than it would be in the case of anyone else. And for this reason: that in those elements of life which tend to the development and perfection of the individual soul in the work of fulfilling its mysterious destiny, American character and American conditions are especially rich. Bunyan's genius exhibits its characteristic felicity in giving the name of Hopeful to the successor of that Faithful who perished in the town of Vanity. It would be a mark of that loose complacency in which we are too often offenders, to associate the scene of Faithful's martyrdom with the Europe from which definitively we set out afresh a century ago; but it is impossible not to recognize that on our forward journey to the celestial country of national and individual success, our conspicuous inspiration and constant comforter is that hope whose cheering ministrations the "weary Titans" of Europe enjoy in far narrower measure. Living in the future has an indisputably tonic effect upon the moral sinews, and contributes an exhilaration to the spirit which no sense of attainment and achieved success can give. We are after all the true idealists of the world. Material as are the details of our preoccupation, our sub-consciousness is sustained by a general aspiration that is none the less heroic for being, perhaps, somewhat *naïf* as well. The times and moods when one's energy is excited, when something occurs in the continuous drama of life to bring sharply into relief its vivid interest and one's own intimate share therein, when nature seems infinitely more real than the societies she includes, when the missionary, the pioneer, the constructive spirit is aroused, are far more frequent with us than with other peoples. Our intense individualism happily modified by our equality, our constant, active, multiform struggle with the environment, do at least, as I said, produce *men;* and if we use the term in an esoteric sense we at least know its significance. Of our riches in this respect New York alone certainly gives no exaggerated idea—however it may otherwise epitomize and typify our national traits. A walk on Pennsylvania Avenue; a drive among the "homes" of Buffalo or Detroit—or a dozen other true centers of communal life which have a concrete impressiveness that for the most part only great capitals in Europe possess; a tour of college commencements in scores of spots consecrated to the exaltation of the permanent over the evanescent; contact in any wise with the prodigious amount of right feeling manifested in a hundred ways throughout a country whose prosperity stimulates generous impulse, or with the number of " good fellows " of large, shrewd, humorous views of life, critical perhaps rather than constructive, but at all events untouched by cynicism, perfectly competent and admirably confident, with a livelier interest in everything within their range of vision than can be felt by anyone mainly occupied with sensuous satisfaction, saved from boredom by a robust imperviousness, ready to begin life over again after every reverse with unenfeebled spirit, and finding, in the working out of their own personal salvation according to the gospel of necessity and opportunity, that joy which the pursuit of pleasure misses—experiences of every kind, in fine, that familiarize us with what is especially American in our civilization, are agreeable as no foreign experiences can be, because they are above all others animating and sustaining. Life in America has for everyone, in proportion to his seriousness, the zest that accompanies the " advance on Chaos and the Dark." Meantime, one's last word about the America emphasized by contrast with the organic and *solidaire* society of France, is that, for insuring order and efficiency to the lines of this advance, it would be difficult to conceive too gravely the utility of observing attentively the work in the modern world of the only other great nation that follows the democratic standard, and is perennially prepared to make sacrifices for ideas.

[From *French Traits,* by W. C. Brownell. Copyright, 1888, 1889, by Charles Scribner's Sons.]

THE TYRANNY OF THINGS

Edward Sandford Martin

A TRAVELER newly returned from the Pacific Ocean tells pleasant stories of the Patagonians. As the steamer he was in was passing through Magellan's Straits some natives came out to her in boats. They wore no clothes at all, though there was snow in the air. A baby that came along with them made some demonstration that displeased its mother, who took it by the foot, as Thetis took Achilles, and soused it over the side of the boat into the cold sea-water. When she pulled it in, it lay a moment whimpering in the bottom of the boat, and then curled up and went to sleep. The missionaries there have tried to teach the natives to wear clothes, and to sleep in huts; but, so far, the traveler says, with very limited success. The most shelter a Patagonian can endure is a little heap of rocks or a log to the windward of him; as for clothes, he despises them, and he is indifferent to ornament.

To many of us, groaning under the oppression of modern conveniences, it seems lamentably meddlesome to undermine the simplicity of such people, and enervate them with the luxuries of civilization. To be able to sleep out-o-doors, and go naked, and take sea-baths on wintry days with impunity, would seem a most alluring emancipation. No rent to pay, no tailor, no plumber, no newspaper to be read on pain of getting behind the times; no regularity in anything, not even meals; nothing to do except to find food, and no expense for undertakers or physicians, even if we fail; what a fine, untrammeled life it would be! It takes occasional contact with such people as the Patagonians to keep us in mind that civilization is the mere cultivation of our wants, and that the higher it is the more our necessities are multiplied, until, if we are rich enough, we get enervated by luxury, and the young men come in and carry us out.

We want so many, many things, it seems a pity that those simple Patagonians could not send missionaries to us to show us how to do without. The comforts of life, at the rate they are increasing, bid fair to bury us soon, as Tarpeia was buried under the shields of her friends the Sabines. Mr. Hamerton, in speaking of the increase of comfort in England, groans at the " trying strain of expense to which our extremely high standard of living subjects all except the rich." It makes each individual of us very costly to keep, and constantly tempts people to concentrate on the maintenance of fewer individuals means that would in simpler times be divided among many. " My grandfather," said a modern the other day, " left $200,000. He was considered a rich man in those days; but, dear me! he supported four or five families—all his needy relations and all my grandmother's." Think of an income of $10,000 a year being equal to such a strain, and providing suitably for a rich man's large family in the bargain! It wouldn't go so far now, and yet most of the reasonable necessaries of life cost less to-day than they did two generations ago. The difference is that we need so very many comforts that were not invented in our grandfather's time.

There is a hospital, in a city large enough to keep a large hospital busy, that is in straits for money. Its income from contributions last year was larger by nearly a third than its income ten years ago, but its expenses were nearly double its income. There were some satisfactory reasons for the discrepancy—the city had grown, the number of patients had increased, extraordinary repairs had been made—but at the bottom a very large expenditure seemed to be due to the struggle of the managers to keep the institution up to modern standards. The patients are better cared for than they used to be; the nurses are better taught and more skillful; " conveniences " have been greatly multiplied; the heating and cooking and laundry work is all done in the best manner with the most approved apparatus; the plumbing is as safe as sanitary engineering can make it; the appliances for antiseptic surgery are fit for a fight for life; there are detached buildings for contagious diseases, and an out-patient department, and the whole concern is administered with wisdom and economy. There is only one distressing circumstance about this excellent charity, and that is that its expenses exceed its income. And yet its managers have not been extravagant: they have only done what the enlightened experience of the day has considered to be necessary. If the hospital has to shut down and the patients must be turned out, at least the receiver will find a well-appointed institution of which the managers have no reason to be ashamed.

The trouble seems to be with very many of us, in contemporary private life as well as in institutions, that the nlightened experience of the day invents more necessaries han we can get the money to pay for. Our opulent friends e constantly demonstrating to us by example how indispensably convenient the modern necessaries are, and we keep ring them until we either exceed our incomes or miss higher concerns of life in the effort to maintain a complete outfit of its creature comforts.

And the saddest part of all is that it is in such great measure an American development. We Americans keep inventing new necessaries, and the people of the effete monarchies gradually adopt such of them as they can afford. When we go abroad we growl about the inconveniences of European life—the absence of gas in bedrooms, the scarcity and sluggishness of elevators, the primitive nature of the plumbing, and a long list of other things without which life seems to press unreasonably upon our endurance. Nevertheless, if the *res angustæ domi* get straiter than usual, we are always liable to send our families across the water to spend a season in the practice of economy in some land where it costs less to live.

Of course it all belongs to Progress, and no one is quite willing to have it stop, but it does a comfortable sufferer good to get his head out of his conveniences sometimes and complain.

There was a story in the newspapers the other day about a Massachusetts minister who resigned his charge because someone had given his parish a fine house, and his parishioners wanted him to live in it. His salary was too small, he said, to admit of his living in a big house, and he would not do it. He was even deaf to the proposal that he should share the proposed tenement with the sewing societies and clubs of his church, and when the matter came to a serious issue, he relinquished his charge and sought a new field of usefulness. The situation was an amusing instance of the embarrassment of riches. Let no one to whom restricted quarters may have grown irksome, and who covets larger dimensions of shelter, be too hasty in deciding that the minister was wrong. Did you ever see the house that Hawthorne lived in at Lenox? Did you ever see Emerson house at Concord? They are good houses for American to know and remember. They permitted thought.

A big house is one of the greediest cormorants which can light upon a little income. Backs may go threadbare and stomachs may worry along on indifferent filling, but a house *will* have things, though its occupants go without. It is rarely complete, and constantly tempts the imagination to flights in brick and dreams in lath and plaster. It develops annual thirsts for paint and wall-paper, at least, if not for marble and wood-carving. The plumbing in it must be kept in order on pain of death. Whatever price is put on coal, it has to be heated in winter; and if it is rural or suburban, the grass about it must be cut even though funerals in the family have to be put off for the mowing If the tenants are not rich enough to hire people to keep their house clean, they must do it themselves, for there is no excuse that will pass among housekeepers for a dirty house. The master of a house too big for him may expect to spend the leisure which might be made intellectually or spiritually profitable, in acquiring and putting into practice fag ends of the arts of the plumber, the bell-hanger, the locksmith, the gasfitter, and the carpenter. Presently he will know how to do everything that can be done in the house, except enjoy himself. He will learn about taxes, too, and water-rates, and how such abominations as sewers or new pavements are always liable to accrue at his expense. As for the mistress, she will be a slave to carpets and curtains, wall-paper, painters, and women who come in by the day to clean. She will be lucky if she gets a chance to say her prayers, and thrice and four times happy when she can read a book or visit with her friends. To live in a big house may be a luxury, provided that one has a full set of money and an enthusiastic housekeeper in one's family; but to scrimp in a big house is a miserable business. Yet such is human folly, that for a man to refuse to live in a house because it is too big for him, is such an exceptional exhibition of sense that it becomes the favorite paragraph of a day in the newspapers.

An ideal of earthly comfort, so common that every reader must have seen it, is to get a house so big that it is burdensome to maintain, and fill it up so full of jimcracks that it is a constant occupation to keep it in order. Then, when the expense of living in it is so great that you can't afford to go away and rest from the burden of it, the situation is complete and boarding-houses and cemeteries begin to yawn for you. How many Americans, do you suppose, out of the droves that flock annually to Europe, are running away from oppressive houses?

When nature undertakes to provide a house, it fits the occupant. Animals which build by instinct build only what they need, but man's building instinct, if it gets a chance to spread itself at all, is boundless, just as all his instincts are. For it is man's peculiarity that nature has filled him with impulses to do things, and left it to his discretion when to stop. She never tells him when he has finished. And perhaps we ought not to be surprised that in so many cases it happens that he doesn't know, but just goes ahead as long as the materials last.

If another *man* tries to oppress him, he understands that and is ready to fight to death and sacrifice all he has, rather than submit; but the tyranny of *things* is so subtle, so gradual in its approach, and comes so masked with seeming benefits, that it has him hopelessly bound before he suspects his fetters. He says from day to day, " I will add thus to my house;" " I will have one or two more horses;" " I will make a little greenhouse in my garden;" " I will allow myself the luxury of another hired man;" and so he goes on having things and imagining that he is richer for them. Presently he begins to realize that it is the things that own him. He has piled them up on his shoulders, and there they sit like Sindbad's Old Man and drive him; and it becomes a daily question whether he can keep his trembling legs or not.

All of which is not meant to prove that property has no real value, or to rebut Charles Lamb's scornful denial that enough is as good as a feast. It is not meant to apply to the rich, who can have things comfortably, if they are philosophical; but to us poor, who have constant need to remind ourselves that where the verbs *to have* and *to be* cannot both be completely inflected, the verb *to be* is the one that best repays concentration.

Perhaps we would not be so prone to swamp ourselves with luxuries and vain possessions that we cannot afford, if it were not for our deep-lying propensity to associate with people who are better off than we are. It is usually the sight of their appliances that upsets our little stock of sense, and lures us into an improvident competition.

There is a proverb of Solomon's which prophesies financial wreck or ultimate misfortune of some sort to people who make gifts to the rich. Though not expressly stated, it is somehow implied that the proverb is intended not as a warning to the rich themselves, who may doubtless exchange presents with impunity, but for persons whose incomes rank somewhere between "moderate circumstances" and destitution. That such persons should need to be warned not to spend their substance on the rich seems odd, but when Solomon was busied with precept he could usually be trusted not to waste either words or wisdom. Poor people *are* constantly spending themselves upon the rich, not only because they like them, but often from an instinctive conviction that such expenditure is well invested. I wonder sometimes whether this is true.

To associate with the rich seems pleasant and profitable. They are apt to be agreeable and well informed, and it is good to play with them and enjoy the usufruct of all their pleasant apparatus; but, of course, you can neither hope nor wish to get anything for nothing. Of the cost of the practice, the expenditure of time still seems to be the item that is most serious. It takes a great deal of time to cultivate the rich successfully. If they are working people their time is so much more valuable than yours, that when you visit with them it is apt to be your time that is sacrificed. If they are not working people it is worse yet. Their special outings, when they want your company, always come when you cannot get away from work except at some great sacrifice, which, under the stress of temptation, you are too apt to make. Their pleasuring is on so large a scale that you cannot make it fit your times or necessities. You can't go yachting for half a day, nor will fifty dollars take you far on the way to shoot big game in Manitoba. You simply cannot play with them when they play, because you cannot *reach;* and when they work you cannot play with them, because their time then is worth so much a minute that you cannot bear to waste it. And you cannot play with them when you are working yourself and they are inactively at leisure, because, cheap as your time is, you can't spare it.

Charming and likeable as they are, and good to know, it must be admitted that there is a superior convenience about associating most of the time with people who want to do about what we want to do at about the same time, and whose abilities to do what they wish approximate to ours. It is not so much a matter of persons as of times and means. You cannot make your opportunities concur with the opportunities of people whose incomes are ten times greater than yours. When you play together it is at a sacrifice, and one which *you* have to make. Solomon was right. To associate with very rich people involves sacrifices. You cannot even be rich yourself without expense, and you may just as well give over trying. Count it, then, among the costs of a considerable income that in enlarging the range of your sports it inevitably contracts the circle of those who will find it profitable to share them.

[From *Windfalls of Observation,* by Edward Sandford Martin. Copyright, 1893, by Charles Scribner's Sons.]

FREE TRADE VS. PROTECTION IN LITERATURE

Samuel McChord Crothers

In the old-fashioned text-book we used to be told that the branch of learning that was treated was at once an art and a science. Literature is much more than that. It is an art, a science, a profession, a trade, and an accident. The literature that is of lasting value is an accident. It is something that happens. After it has happened, the historical critics busy themselves in explaining it. But they are not able to predict the next stroke of genius.

Shelley defines poetry as the record of "the best and happiest moments of the best and happiest minds." When we are fortunate enough to happen in upon an author at one of these happy moments, then, as the country newspaper would say, "a very enjoyable time was had." After we have said all that can be said about art and craftsmanship, we put our hopes upon a happy chance. Literature cannot be standardized. We never know how the most painstaking work may turn out. The most that can be said of the literary life is what Sancho Panza said of the profession of knight-errantry: "There is something delightful in going about in expectation of accidents."

After a meeting in behalf of Social Justice, an eager, distraught young man met me, in the streets of Boston, and asked:

"You believe in the principle of equality?"

"Yes."

"Don't I then have just as much right to be a genius as Shakespeare had?"

"Yes."

"Then why ain't I?"

I had to confess that I didn't know.

It is with this chastened sense of our limitations that we meet for any organized attempt at the encouragement of literary productivity. Matthew Arnold's favorite bit of irreverence in which he seemed to find endless enjoyment was in twitting the unfortunate Bishop who had said that "something ought to be done" for the Holy Trinity. It was a business-like proposition that involved a spiritual incongruity.

A confusion of values is likely to take place when we try to "do something" for American Literature. It is an object that appeals to the uplifter who is anxious to "get results." But the difficulty is that if a piece of writing *is* literature, it does not need to be uplifted. If it is not literature, it is likely to be so heavy that you can't lift it. We have been told that a man by taking thought cannot add a cubit to his stature. It is certainly true that we cannot add many cubits to our literary stature. If we could we should all be giants.

When literary men discourse with one another about their art, they often seem to labor under a weight of responsibility which a friendly outsider would seek to lighten. They are under the impression that they have left undone many things which they ought to have done, and that the Public blames them for their manifold transgressions.

That Great American Novel ought to have been written long ago. There ought to be more local color and less imitation of European models. There ought to have been more plain speaking to demonstrate that we are not squeamish and are not tied to the apron strings of Mrs. Grundy. There ought to be a literary center and those who are at it ought to live up to it.

In all this it is assumed that contemporary writers can control the literary situation.

Let me comfort the over-strained consciences of the members of the writing fraternity. Your responsibility is not nearly so great as you imagine.

Literature differs from the other arts in the relation in which the producer stands to the consumer. Literature can never be made one of the protected industries. In the Drama the living actor has a complete monopoly. One might express a preference for Garrick or Booth, but if he goes to the theater he must take what is set before him. The monopoly of the singer is not quite so complete as it once was. But until canned music is improved, most people will prefer to get theirs fresh. In painting and in sculpture there is more or less competition with the work of other ages. Yet even here there is a measure of natural protection. The old masters may be admired, but they are expensive. The living artist can control a certain market of his own.

There is also a great opportunity for the artist and his friends to exert pressure. When you go to an exhibition of new paintings, you are not a free agent. You are aware that the artist or his friends may be in the vicinity to observe how First Citizen and Second Citizen enjoy the masterpiece. Conscious of this espionage, you endeavor to look pleased. You observe a picture which outrages your ideas of the possible. You mildly remark to a bystander that you have never seen anything like that before.

"Probably not," he replies, "it is not a picture of any outward scene, it represents the artist's state of mind."

"O," you reply, "I understand. He is making an exhibition of himself."

It is all so personal that you do not feel like carrying the investigation further. You take what is set before you and ask no questions.

But with a book the relation to the producer is altogether different. You go into your library and shut the door, and you have the same sense of intellectual freedom that you have when you go into the polling booth and mark your Australian ballot. You are a sovereign citizen. Nobody can know what you are reading unless you choose to tell. You snap your fingers at the critics. In the "tumultuous privacy" of print you enjoy what you find enjoyable, and let the rest go.

Your mind is a free port. There are no customs house officers to examine the cargoes that are unladen. The book which has just come from the press has no advantage over the book that is a century old. In the matter of legibility the old volume may be preferable, and its price is less. Whatever choice you make is in the face of the free competition of all the ages. Literature is the timeless art.

Clever writers who start fashions in the literary world should take account of this secrecy of the reader's position. It is easy enough to start a fashion, the difficulty is to get people to follow it. Few people will follow a fashion except when other people are looking at them. When they are alone they relapse into something which they enjoy and which they find comfortable.

The ultimate consumer of literature is therefore inclined to take a philosophical view of the contentions among literary people, about what seem to them the violent fluctuations of taste. These fashions come and go, but the quiet reader is undisturbed. There are enough good books already printed to last his life-time. Aware of this, he is not alarmed by the cries of the "calamity howlers" who predict a famine.

From a purely commercial viewpoint, this competition

with writers of all generations is disconcerting. But I do not see that anything can be done to prevent it. The principle of protection fails. Trades-unionism offers no remedy. What if all the living authors should join in a general strike! We tremble to think of the army of strike-breakers that would rush in from all centuries.

From the literary viewpoint, however, this free competition is very stimulating and even exciting. To hold our own under free trade conditions, we must not put all our thought on increasing the output. In order to meet the free competition to which we are exposed, we must improve the quality of our work. Perhaps that may be good for us.

DANTE AND THE BOWERY

Theodore Roosevelt

It is the conventional thing to praise Dante because he of set purpose "used the language of the market-place," so as to be understood of the common people; but we do not in practice either admire or understand a man who writes in the language of our own market-place. It must be the Florentine market-place of the thirteenth century—not Fulton Market of to-day. What infinite use Dante would have made of the Bowery! Of course, he could have done it only because not merely he himself, the great poet, but his audience also, would have accepted it as natural. The nineteenth century was more apt than the thirteenth to boast of itself as being the greatest of the centuries; but, save as regards purely material objects, ranging from locomotives to bank buildings, it did not wholly believe in its boasting. A nineteenth-century poet, when trying to illustrate some point he was making, obviously felt uncomfortable in mentioning nineteenth-century heroes if he also referred to those of classic times, lest he should be suspected of instituting comparisons between them. A thirteenth-century poet was not in the least troubled by any such misgivings, and quite simply illustrated his point by allusions to any character in history or romance, ancient or contemporary, that happened to occur to him.

Of all the poets of the nineteenth century, Walt Whitman was the only one who dared use the Bowery—that is, use anything that was striking and vividly typical of the humanity around him—as Dante used the ordinary humanity of his day; and even Whitman was not quite natural in doing so, for he always felt that he was defying the conventions and prejudices of his neighbors, and his self-consciousness made him a little defiant. Dante was not defiant of conventions: the conventions of his day did not forbid him to use human nature just as he saw it, no less than human nature as he read about it. The Bowery is one of the great highways of humanity, a highway of seething life, of varied interest, of fun, of work, of sordid and terrible tragedy; and it is haunted by demons as evil as any that stalk through the pages of the *Inferno*. But no man of Dante's art and with Dante's soul would write of it nowadays; and he would hardly be understood if he did. Whitman wrote of homely things and every-day men, and of their greatness, but his art was not equal to his power and his purpose; and, even as it was, he, the poet, by set intention, of the democracy, is not known to the people as widely as he should be known; and it is only the few—the men like Edward FitzGerald, John Burroughs, and W. E. Henley—who prize him as he ought to be prized.

Nowadays, at the outset of the twentieth century, cultivated people would ridicule the poet who illustrated fundamental truths, as Dante did six hundred years ago, by examples drawn alike from human nature as he saw it around him and from human nature as he read of it. I suppose that this must be partly because we are so self-conscious as always to read a comparison into any illustration, forgetting the fact that no comparison is implied between two men, in the sense of estimating their relative greatness or importance, when the career of each of them is chosen merely to illustrate some given quality that both possess. It is also probably due to the fact that an age in which the critical faculty is greatly developed often tends to develop a certain querulous inability to understand the fundamental truths which less critical ages accept as a matter of course. To such critics it seems improper, and indeed ludicrous, to illustrate human nature by examples chosen alike from the Brooklyn Navy Yard or Castle Garden and the Piræus, alike from Tammany and from the Roman mob organized by the foes or friends of Cæsar. To Dante such feeling itself would have been inexplicable.

Dante dealt with those tremendous qualities of the human soul which dwarf all differences in outward and visible form and station, and therefore he illustrated what he meant by any example that seemed to him apt. Only the great names of antiquity had been handed down, and so, when he spoke of pride or violence or flattery, and wished to illustrate his thesis by an appeal to the past, he could speak only of great and prominent characters; but in the present of his day most of the men he knew, or knew of, were naturally people of no permanent importance—just as is the case in the present of our own day. Yet the passions of these men were the same as those of the heroes of old, godlike or demoniac; and so he unhesitatingly used his contemporaries, or his immediate predecessors, to illustrate his points, without regard to their prominence or lack of prominence. He was not concerned with the differences in their fortunes and careers, with their heroic proportions or lack of such proportions; he was a mystic whose imagination soared so high and whose thoughts plumbed so deeply the far depths of our being that he was also quite simply a realist; for the eternal mysteries were ever before his mind, and, compared to them, the differences between the careers of the mighty masters of mankind and the careers of even very humble people seemed trivial. If we translate his comparisons into the terms of our day, we are apt to feel amused over this trait of his, until we go a little deeper and understand that we are ourselves to blame, because we have lost the faculty simply and naturally to recognize that the essential traits of humanity are shown alike by big men and by little men, in the lives that are now being lived and in those that are long ended.

Probably no two characters in Dante impress the ordinary reader more than Farinata and Capaneus: the man who raises himself waist-high from out his burning sepulcher, unshaken by torment, and the man who, with scornful disdain, refuses to brush from his body the falling flames; the great souls—magnanimous, Dante calls them—whom no torture, no disaster, no failure of the most absolute kind could force to yield or to bow before the dread powers that had mastered them. Dante has created these men, has made them permanent additions to the great figures of the world; they are imaginary only in the sense that Achilles and Ulysses are imaginary—that is, they are now as real as the figures of any men that ever lived. One of them was a mythical hero in a mythical feat, the other a second-rate faction leader in a faction-ridden Italian city of the thirteenth century, whose deeds have not the slightest importance aside from what Dante's mention gives. Yet the two men are mentioned as naturally as Alexander and Cæsar are mentioned. Evidently they are dwelt upon at length because Dante felt it his duty to express a peculiar horror for that fierce pride which could defy its overlord, while at the same time, and perhaps unwillingly, he could not conceal a certain shuddering admiration for the lofty courage on which this evil pride was based.

The point I wish to make is the simplicity with which Dante illustrated one of the principles on which he lays most stress, by the example of a man who was of consequence only in the history of the parochial politics of Florence. Farinata will now live forever as a symbol of the soul;

yet as an historical figure he is dwarfed beside any one of hundreds of the leaders in our own Revolution and Civil War. Tom Benton, of Missouri, and Jefferson Davis, of Mississippi, were opposed to one another with a bitterness which surpassed that which rived asunder Guelph from Ghibellin, or black Guelph from white Guelph. They played mighty parts in a tragedy more tremendous than any which any mediæval city ever witnessed or could have witnessed. Each possessed an iron will and undaunted courage, physical and moral; each led a life of varied interest and danger, and exercised a power not possible in the career of the Florentine. One, the champion of the Union, fought for his principles as unyieldingly as the other fought for what he deemed right in trying to break up the Union. Each was a colossal figure. Each, when the forces against which he fought overcame him—for in his latter years Benton saw the cause of disunion triumph in Missouri, just as Jefferson Davis lived to see the cause of union triumph in the Nation —fronted an adverse fate with the frowning defiance, the high heart, and the stubborn will which Dante has commemorated for all time in his hero who "held hell in great scorn." Yet a modern poet who endeavored to illustrate such a point by reference to Benton and Davis would be uncomfortably conscious that his audience would laugh at him. He would feel ill at ease, and therefore would convey the impression of being ill at ease, exactly as he would feel that he was posing, was forced and unnatural, if he referred to the deeds of the evil heroes of the Paris Commune as he would without hesitation refer to the many similar but smaller leaders of riots in the Roman forum.

Dante speaks of a couple of French troubadours, or of a local Sicilian poet, just as he speaks of Euripides; and quite properly, for they illustrate as well what he has to teach; but we of to-day could not possibly speak of a couple of recent French poets or German novelists in the same connection without having an uncomfortable feeling that we ought to defend ourselves from possible misapprehension; and therefore we could not speak of them naturally. When Dante wishes to assail those guilty of crimes of violence, he in one stanza speaks of the torments inflicted by divine justice on Attila (coupling him with Pyrrhus and Sextus Pompey—a sufficiently odd conjunction in itself, by the way), and in the next stanza mentions the names of a couple of local highwaymen who had made travel unsafe in particular neighborhoods. The two highwaymen in question were by no means as important as Jesse James and Billy the Kid; doubtless they were far less formidable fighting men, and their adventures were less striking and varied. Yet think of the way we should feel if a great poet should now arise who would incidentally illustrate the ferocity of the human heart by allusions both to the terrible Hunnish "scourge of God" and to the outlaws who in our own times defied justice in Missouri and New Mexico!

When Dante wishes to illustrate the fierce passions of the human heart, he may speak of Lycurgus, or of Saul; or he may speak of two local contemporary captains, victor or vanquished in obscure struggles between Guelph and Ghibellin; men like Jacopo del Cassero or Buonconte, whom he mentions as naturally as he does Cyrus or Rehoboam. He is entirely right! What one among our own writers, however, would be able simply and naturally to mention Ulrich Dahlgren, or Custer, or Morgan, or Raphael Semmes, or Marion, or Sumter, as illustrating the qualities shown by Hannibal, or Rameses, or William the Conqueror, or by Moses or Hercules? Yet the Guelph and Ghibellin captains of whom Dante speaks were in no way as important as these American soldiers of the second or third rank. Dante saw nothing incongruous in treating at length of the qualities of all of them; he was not thinking of comparing the genius of the unimportant local leader with the genius of the great sovereign conquerors of the past—he was thinking only of the qualities of courage and daring and of the awful horror of death; and when we deal with what is elemental in the human soul it matters but little whose soul we take. In the same way he mentions a couple of spendthrifts of Padua and Siena, who come to violent ends, just as in the preceding canto he had dwelt upon the tortures undergone by Dionysius and Simon de Montfort, guarded by Nessus and his fellow centaurs. For some reason he hated the spendthrifts in question as the Whigs of Revolutionary South Carolina and New York hated Tarleton, Kruger, Saint Leger, and De Lancey; and to him there was nothing incongruous in drawing a lesson from one couple of offenders more than from another. (It would, by the way, be outside my present purpose to speak of the rather puzzling manner in which Dante confounds his own hatreds with those of heaven, and, for instance, shows a vindictive enjoyment in putting his personal opponent Filippo Argenti in hell, for no clearly adequate reason.)

When he turns from those whom he is glad to see in hell toward those for whom he cares, he shows the same delightful power of penetrating through the externals into the essentials. Cato and Manfred illustrate his point no better than Belacqua, a contemporary Florentine maker of citherns. Alas! what poet to-day would dare to illustrate his argument by introducing Steinway in company with Cato and Manfred! Yet again, when examples of love are needed, he draws them from the wedding-feast at Cana, from the actions of Pylades and Orestes, and from the life of a kindly, honest comb-dealer of Siena who had just died. Could we now link together Peter Cooper and Pylades, without feeling a sense of incongruity? He couples Priscian with a politician of local note who had written an encyclopædia and a lawyer of distinction who had lectured at Bologna and Oxford; we could not now with such fine unconsciousness bring Evarts and one of the compilers of the *Encyclopædia Britannica* into a life comparison.

When Dante deals with the crimes which he most abhorred, simony and barratry, he flails offenders of his age who were of the same type as those who in our days flourish by political or commercial corruption; and he names his offenders, both those just dead and those still living, and puts them, popes and politicians alike, in hell. There have been trust magnates and politicians and editors and magazine-writers in our own country whose lives and deeds were no more edifying than those of the men who lie in the third and the fifth chasm of the eighth circle of the Inferno; yet for a poet to name those men would be condemned as an instance of shocking taste.

One age expresses itself naturally in a form that would be unnatural, and therefore undesirable, in another age. We do not express ourselves nowadays in epics at all; and we keep the emotions aroused in us by what is good or evil in the men of the present in a totally different compartment from that which holds our emotions concerning what was good or evil in the men of the past. An imitation of the letter of the times past, when the spirit has wholly altered, would be worse than useless; and the very qualities that help to make Dante's poem immortal would, if copied nowadays, make the copyist ridiculous. Nevertheless, it would be a good thing if we could, in some measure, achieve the mighty Florentine's high simplicity of soul, at least to the extent of recognizing in those around us the eternal qualities which we admire or condemn in the men who wrought good or evil at any stage in the world's previous history.

Dante's masterpiece is one of the supreme works of art that the ages have witnessed; but he would have been the last to wish that it should be treated only as a work of art, or worshiped only for art's sake, without reference to the dread lessons it teaches mankind.

[From *History as Literature and Other Essays,* by Theodore Roosevelt. Copyright, 1913, by Charles Scribner's Sons.]

THE REVOLT OF THE UNFIT

Nicholas Murray Butler

There are wars and rumors of wars in a portion of the territory occupied by the doctrine of organic evolution. All is not working smoothly and well and according to formula. It begins to appear that those men of science who, having derived the doctrine of organic evolution in its modern form from observations on earthworms, on climbing-plants, and on brightly colored birds, and who then straightway applied it blithely to man and his affairs, have made enemies of no small part of the human race.

It was all well enough to treat some earthworms, some climbing-plants, and some brightly colored birds as fit, and others as unfit, to survive; but when this distinction is extended over human beings and their economic, social, and political affairs, there is a general pricking-up of ears. The consciously fit look down on the resulting discussions with complacent scorn. The consciously unfit rage and roar loudly; while the unconsciously unfit bestir themselves mightily to overturn the whole theory upon which the distinction between fitness and unfitness rests. If any law of nature makes so absurd a distinction as that, then the offending and obnoxious law must be repealed, and that quickly.

The trouble appears to arise primarily from the fact that man does not like what may be termed his evolutionary poor relations. He is willing enough to read about earthworms and climbing-plants and brightly colored birds, but he does not want nature to be making leaps from any of these to him.

The earthworm, which, not being adapted to its surroundings, soon dies unhonored and unsung, passes peacefully out of life without either a coroner's inquest, an indictment for earthworm slaughter, a legislative proposal for the future protection of earthworms, or even a new society for the reform of the social and economic state of the earthworms that are left. Even the quasi-intelligent climbing-plant and the brightly colored bird, humanly vain, find an equally inconspicuous fate awaiting them. This is the way nature operates when unimpeded or unchallenged by the powerful manifestations of human revolt or human revenge. Of course if man understood the place assigned to him in nature by the doctrine of organic evolution as well as the earthworm, the climbing-plant, and the brightly colored bird understand theirs, he, too, like them, would submit to nature's processes and decrees without a protest. As a matter of logic, no doubt he ought to; but after all these centuries, it is still a far cry from logic to life.

In fact, man, unless he is consciously and admittedly fit, revolts against the implication of the doctrine of evolution, and objects both to being considered unfit to survive and succeed, and to being forced to accept the only fate which nature offers to those who are unfit for survival and success. Indeed, he manifests with amazing pertinacity what Schopenhauer used to call "the will to live," and considerations and arguments based on adaptability to environment have no weight with him. So much the worse for environment, he cries; and straightway sets out to prove it.

On the other hand, those humans who are classed by the doctrine of evolution as fit, exhibit a most disconcerting satisfaction with things as they are. The fit make no conscious struggle for existence. They do not have to. Being fit, they survive *ipso facto*. Thus does the doctrine of evolution, like a playful kitten, merrily pursue its tail with rapturous delight. The fit survive; those survive who are fit. Nothing could be more simple.

Those who are not adapted to the conditions that surround them, however, rebel against the fate of the earthworm and the climbing-plant and the brightly colored bird, and engage in a conscious struggle for existence and for success in that existence despite their inappropriate environment. Statutes can be repealed or amended; why not laws of nature as well? Those human beings who are unfit have, it must be admitted, one great, though perhaps temporary, advantage over the laws of nature; for the laws of nature have not yet been granted suffrage, and the organized unfit can always lead a large majority to the polls. So soon as knowledge of this fact becomes common property, the laws of nature will have a bad quarter of an hour in more countries than one.

The revolt of the unfit primarily takes the form of attempts to lessen and to limit competition, which is instinctively felt, and with reason, to be part of the struggle for existence and for success. The inequalities which nature makes, and without which the process of evolution could not go on, the unfit propose to smooth away and to wipe out by that magic fiat of collective human will called legislation. The great struggle between the gods of Olympus and the Titans, which the ancient sculptors so loved to picture, was child's play compared with the struggle between the laws of nature and the laws of man which the civilized world is apparently soon to be invited to witness. This struggle will bear a little examination, and it may be that the laws of nature, as the doctrine of evolution conceives and states them, will not have everything their own way.

Professor Huxley, whose orthodoxy as an evolutionist will hardly be questioned, made a suggestion of this kind in his Romanes lecture as long ago as 1893. He called attention then to the fact that there is a fallacy in the notion that because, on the whole, animals and plants have advanced in perfection of organization by means of the struggle for existence and the consequent survival of the fittest, therefore, men as social and ethical beings must depend upon the same process to help them to perfection. As Professor Huxley suggests, this fallacy doubtless has its origin in the ambiguity of the phrase "survival of the fittest." One jumps to the conclusion that fittest means best; whereas, of course, it has in it no moral element whatever. The doctrine of evolution uses the term fitness in a hard and stern sense. Nothing more is meant by it than a measure of adaptation to surrounding conditions. Into this conception of fitness there enters no element of beauty, no element of morality, no element of progress toward an ideal. Fitness is a cold fact ascertainable with almost mathematical certainty.

We now begin to catch sight of the real significance of this struggle between the laws of nature and the laws of man. From one point of view the struggle is hopeless from the start; from another it is full of promise. If it be true that man really proposes to halt the laws of nature by his legislation, then the struggle is hopeless. It is only a question of time when the laws of nature will have their way. If, on the other hand, the struggle between the laws of nature and the laws of man is in reality a mock struggle, and the supposed combat merely an exhibition of evolutionary boxing, then we may find a clew to what is really going on.

It might be worth while, for example, to follow up the suggestion that in looking back over the whole series of products of organic evolution, the real successes and permanences of life are to be found among those species that have been able to institute something like what we call a social system. Wherever an individual insists upon treating himself as an end in himself, and all other individuals as his actual or potential competitors or enemies, then the fate of the earthworm, the climbing-plant, and the brightly colored bird is sure to be his; for he has brought himself under the jurisdiction of one of nature's laws, and sooner or later he must succumb to that law of nature, and in the struggle for existence his place will be marked out for him by it with unerring precision. If, however, he has developed so far as to have risen to the lofty height of human sympathy, and thereby has learned to transcend his individuality and to make himself a member of a larger whole, he may then save himself from the extinction which follows inevitably upon proved unfitness in the individual struggle for existence.

So soon as the individual has something to give, there will be those who have something to give to him, and he elevates himself above this relentless law with its inexorable punishments for the unfit. At that point, when individuals begin to give each to the other, then their mutual co-operation and interdependence build human society, and participation in that society changes the whole character of the human struggle. Nevertheless, large numbers of human beings carry with them into social and political relations the traditions and instincts of the old individualistic struggle for existence, with the laws of organic evolution pointing grimly to their several destinies. These are not able to realize that moral elements, and what we call progress toward an end or ideal, are not found under the operation of the law of natural selection, but have to be discovered elsewhere and added to it. Beauty, morality, progress have other lurking-places than in the struggle for existence, and they have for their sponsors other laws than that of natural selection. You will read the pages of Darwin and of Herbert Spencer in vain for any indication of how the Parthenon was produced, how the Sistine Madonna, how the Ninth Symphony of Beethoven, how the *Divine Comedy,* or *Hamlet* or *Faust*. There are many mysteries left in the world, thank God, and these are some of them.

The escape of genius from the cloud-covered mountaintops of the unknown into human society has not yet been accounted for. Even Rousseau made a mistake. When he was writing the *Contrat social* it is recorded that his attention was favorably attracted by the island of Corsica. He, being engaged in the process of finding out how to repeal the laws of man by the laws of nature, spoke of Corsica as the one country in Europe that seemed to him capable of legislation. This led him to add: "I have a presentiment that some day this little island will astonish Europe." It was not long before Corsica did astonish Europe, but not by any capacity for legislation. As some clever person has said, it let loose Napoleon. We know nothing more of the origin and advent of genius than that.

Perhaps we should comprehend these things better were it not for the persistence of the superstition that human beings habitually think. There is no more persistent superstition than this. Linnæus helped it on to an undeserved permanence when he devised the name *Homo sapiens* for the highest species of the order primates. That was the quintessence of complimentary nomenclature. Of course human beings as such do not think. A real thinker is one of the rarest things in nature. He comes only at long intervals in human history, and when he does come, he is often astonishingly unwelcome. Indeed, he is sometimes speedily sent the way of the unfit and unprotesting earthworm. Emerson understood this, as he understood so many other of the deep things of life. For he wrote: "Beware when the great God lets loose a thinker on this planet. Then all things are at risk."

The plain fact is that man is not ruled by thinking. When man thinks he thinks, he usually merely feels; and his instincts and feelings are powerful precisely in proportion as they are irrational. Reason reveals the other side, and a knowledge of the other side is fatal to the driving power of a prejudice. Prejudices have their important uses, but it is well to try not to mix them up with principles.

The underlying principle in the widespread and ominous revolt of the unfit is that moral considerations must outweigh the mere blind struggle for existence in human affairs.

It is to this fact that we must hold fast if we would understand the world of to-day, and still more the world of to-morrow. The purpose of the revolt of the unfit is to substitute interdependence on a higher plane for the struggle for existence on a lower one. Who dares attempt to picture what will happen if this revolt shall not succeed?

These are problems full of fascination. In one form or another they will persist as long as humanity itself. There is only one way of getting rid of them, and that is so charmingly and wittily pointed out by Robert Louis Stevenson in his fable, "The Four Reformers," that I wish to quote it:

"Four reformers met under a bramble-bush. They were all agreed the world must be changed. 'We must abolish property,' said one.

"'We must abolish marriage,' said the second.

"'We must abolish God,' said the third.

"'I wish we could abolish work,' said the fourth.

"'Do not let us get beyond practical politics,' said the first. 'The first thing is to reduce men to a common level.'

"'The first thing,' said the second, 'is to give freedom to the sexes.'

"'The first thing,' said the third, 'is to find out how to do it.'

"'The first step,' said the first, 'is to abolish the Bible.'

"'The first thing,' said the second, 'is to abolish the laws.'

"'The first thing,' said the third, 'is to abolish mankind.'"

[From *Why Should We Change Our Form of Government,* by Nicholas Murray Butler. Copyright, 1912, by Charles Scribner's Sons.]

ON TRANSLATING THE ODES OF HORACE

W. P. Trent

In a letter written on August 21, 1703, to Robert Harley, afterward Earl of Oxford and Prime Minister, by Dr. George Hickes, the famous scholar and non-juror, there is a reference to " old Dr. Biram Eaton who has read Horace over, as they tell me, many hundred times, oftener, I fear, than he has read the Gospels." Dr. Biram Eaton has escaped an article in the *Dictionary of National Biography*, and, so far as I know, he has never been reckoned by Horatians among their patron saints. In view of the slur cast upon him by Dr. Hickes I should like to propose his canonization, but I should much prefer to lay a wager that he found time between his readings to try to turn some of the odes of his favorite writer into English verses, probably into couplets resembling those of Dryden. And I should also be willing to wager that before and after making each of his versions, he gave expression, in some form or other, to the proverbial statement that to attempt to translate Horace is to attempt the impossible.

Perhaps we owe to this proverbial impossibility the fact that the translator of Horace is always with us. A living antinomy, he writes a modest preface; then exclaiming in the words of his master, " *Nil mortalibus ardui est,*" he tries to scale very heaven in his folly, to rush blindly *per vetitum nefas*. But because he has loved much, therefore is much forgiven him. To love Horace and not attempt to translate him would be to flout that principle of altruism in which some modern thinkers have discovered, more poetically perhaps than philosophically, the motive force of civilization. " We love Horace, and hence we must try to set him forth in a way to make others love him," is what all translators, it would seem, say to themselves, consciously or unconsciously, when they decide to publish their respective renditions. . And who shall blame them? Where is the critic competent to judge their work, who has not himself listened to the Siren's song, if but for a moment in his youth, who has not a version of some ode of Horace hid away among his papers, the memory of which will doubtless forever prevent him from flinging a stone at any fellow-offender?

It is not only impossible to translate Horace adequately, but it is impossible to explain satisfactorily the causes of his unbounded popularity—a popularity illustrated by the fact that when that well-known group of American booklovers, the Bibliophile Society, were seeking to determine what great man of letters they would first honor by issuing one or more of his works in sumptuous form, they chose—not an author of their own day or nation or language—but a writer dead nearly two thousand years, of alien race and tongue, spokesman of a civilization remote and strange, the Horace of the immortal Odes. Yet admirers of Lucretius and of Catullus tell us very plainly and insistently that this Horace of the Odes is not a great poet. We listen respectfully to the charge and somehow we do not seem greatly to resent it; we merely read the Odes, if possible, more diligently and affectionately—not, it is true, in the splendid Bibliophile volumes, but in some well-worn pocket edition that has accompanied us on our journeys, or, like one I own, has helped us to while away the hours on a deer stand, through which the deer, as shy as the fawn with which the poet compared Chloë, simply would not run. If we own such a pocket volume, we leave our critical faculties in abeyance when Dante, in the *Inferno,* introduces Horace to us along with Homer and Ovid and Lucan; for do not our hearts tell us that in the truest sense of the phrase, he is worthy to walk with the greatest of this mediævally assorted company? We feel sure that Virgil must have loved him as a man; we have proof that Milton admired him as a poet. We deny to him " the grand manner," but we attribute to him every charm. When we seek to analyze this charm, we are left with the suspicion that, after we have pointed out many of its elements, such as humor, vivacity, kindliness, sententiousness, and the like, there are as many others, equally potent but more subtle, that escape us altogether. So we turn the hackneyed saying into " the charm is the man," and contentedly exchange analysis for enjoyment. And yet we are persuaded that no author is more worthy of the painstaking, detailed study characteristic of modern scholarship than is this same Epicurean poet, who so utterly defies analysis and would be the first, were he not but " dust and a shade," to smile at our ponderous erudition. We feel that the scholar who shall devote the best years of his life to studying the influence of Horace upon subsequent writers in the chief literatures and to collecting the tributes that have been paid to his genius by the great and worthy of all lands and ages, will deserve sincere benedictions. We conclude, in short, that that exquisite epithet, " the well-beloved," so inappropriately bestowed upon the worthless and flippant French King, belongs to Horace, and to Horace alone, *jure divino.*

But this praise of Horace and this defense of his translators fails to justify or explain the writing of this paper. An honest confession being good for the soul, I will confess that the remarks that follow were first employed to introduce some versions of selected Odes I was once rash enough to publish. It is not a good sportsman that shuts his eyes and bangs away with both barrels at a flock of birds, and I now doubt whether I was wise in trying to bring down readers, if not with my verse-barrel, at least with my prose-barrel. Being older, I use at present only one barrel at a time and, perhaps for the same reason, I am wont to try the prose-barrel. And fortunately I can apply to the comments I intend to make on Horatian translators the quotation I used in order to mollify irate readers of my own verse renderings. It came from a once popular, now forgotten poet, the Rev. John Pomfret, and it ran as follows:—" It will be to little purpose, the Author presumes, to offer any reasons why the following POEMS appear in public; for it is ten to one whether he gives the true, and if he does, it is much greater odds whether the gentle reader is so courteous as to believe him."

So much has been written on the methods of Horace's translators, and so much remains to be written, that it is hard to determine where to begin; but perhaps the preface of the late Professor Conington to his well-known translation of the Odes will furnish a proper point of departure. Few persons, whether translators or readers, are likely to object to Conington's first premise that the translator ought to aim at " some kind of metrical conformity to his original." To reproduce an original Sapphic or Alcaic stanza in blank verse, or in the couplets of Pope, is at once to repel the reader who knows Horace well, and to give the reader who is unacquainted with Latin lyric poetry a totally erroneous conception of the metrical and rhythmical methods of the poet. To render a compressed Latin verse by a diffuse English one is to do injustice, as Conington observes, to the sententiousness for which Horace is justly celebrated, although the English scholar, had he written after the appearance of Mr. Gladstone's attempt to render the Odes, might with propriety have added that the translator should not, in his avoidance of diffuseness, be seduced by the facility of the octosyllabic couplet. To translate Horace's odes into anything but quatrains, except on occasions, is also to offend the meticulous Horatian and to mislead any reader who seeks to know the poet through an English rendering. It would seem, however, that when Professor Conington insisted that an English measure once adopted for the Alcaic must be used for every ode in which Horace employed the stanza just named, he went far toward hampering the translator, who, despite his proneness to offend, has his rights. That such uniformity ought to be aimed at, and that it will, as a rule, be aimed at, is doubtless true; but there is an element of the problem with which Conington does not seem sufficiently to have reckoned.

This is rhyme, which he assumed to be necessary to a successful rendition of an ode of Horace. A particular stanza not employing rhyme may probably be used without resulting loss in translating every ode written in a special form. Yet this may not be the case with a stanza employing rhymes, if the translator aim, as he should, at a fairly, though not an awkwardly literal rendering of the language of his original. There will necessarily be coincidences of sound in a literal prose version of a Latin stanza that will suggest a definite and advantageous arrangement of rhymes for a poetical version. To adopt a certain English stanza in which to render a certain Latin stanza wherever it occurs, is to do away with this natural advantage, which presents itself oftener than might at first be supposed.

Concrete examples will serve to make my meaning clear. The third ode of the first book, the admirable "Sic te diva potens Cypri," is written in what is called the Second Asclepiad meter; so is the delightful ninth ode of the third book, the "Donec gratus eram." We will assume that for the first of these odes the translator has chosen a quatrain with alternating rhymes (a, b, a, b). Following Professor Conington's rule of uniformity, he must employ the same stanza for the second of the two odes, which, by the way, Conington himself did not do, for reasons which he gave at length. Now the fifth stanza of the "Donec gratus eram" runs as follows:—

> "Quid si prisca redit Venus
> Diductosque jugo cogit aëneo,
> Si flava excutitur Chloë
> Rejectaeque patet janua Lydiae?"

This may be rendered in prose:—

"What if the former Love return and join with brazen yoke the parted ones, if yellow-haired Chloë be shaken off, and the door stand open for rejected Lydia?"

If my memory does not deceive me, it was this stanza, and especially one word in its last verse, that determined the arrangement of rhymes in a version I attempted years ago, "Consule Planco." This verse seemed to run inevitably into

> "And open stand for Lydia the *door*."

It needed but a moment to detect in the first verse of the stanza a possible rhyme-word. The syllable *re* of *redit* furnished *more,* not the most apt of rhymes with *door,* but still sufficient, as things go with amateur translators, and with a perhaps pardonable tautology I wrote

> "What if the former Love once more
> Return—"

Two other rhymes were found with little difficulty in the *di* of *diductos* and in *excutitur,* which suggested *wide* and *cast aside,* and the whole stanza, omitting strictly metrical considerations, appeared, or rather might have appeared, for I have changed it slightly, as follows:—

> "What if the former Love once more
> Return and yoke the sweethearts parted wide,
> If fair-haired Chloë be cast aside,
> And open stand for Lydia the door?"

This stanza seemed to have the merit of almost complete literalness, since it omitted only two epithets, and I thought it had no unpardonable defects of rhythm and diction. So I took it as a model, and with little difficulty translated the entire ode—with what success I should not say and others need not inquire.

That rhymes and their position in the stanza are often determined for the translator by his original or else by a prose rendering of that original seems also to be shown by the following version of the closing ode of the first book (Carm. xxxviii)—the graceful "Persicos odi":—

> "I hate your Persian trappings, boy,
> Your linden-woven crowns annoy,
> Cease searching for the spot where blows
> The lingering rose.
>
> "To simple myrtle nothing add;
> The myrtle misbecomes, my lad,
> Nor thee nor me drinking my wine
> 'Neath close-grown vine."

Here "puer," boy, and "Displicent," displease or annoy, seem to determine, not merely the first rhyme, but the rhyme arrangement (a, a), and it needs but a glance at the close of the first stanza of the original to show that another word rhyming with "boy" would be hard to obtain. It follows that, if we are to have a quatrain, the third and fourth verses should probably be made to rhyme (b, b), and it is not difficult to comply with this requirement, or to cast the second stanza in the mold of the first. It is, alas! too true that no equivalent to "blows" will be found in Horace, that "Sedulus curo" has been unceremoniously thrown aside, that the poet does not specifically mention "wine" as the beverage he liked to drink in his rustic arbor. But a "rose," which Horace does mention, certainly "blows" or blooms very often in English verse; it is not too far-fetched to get "nothing add" and "lad" out of "nihil allabores" and "ministrum"; and "vine" ("vite") has suggested "wine" to many generations of poets. But it is rhyme suggestions and their influence upon the choice of stanzaic form that have occasioned this mild protest against Professor Conington's precepts of rigid stanzaic conformity. I am convinced, from the above examples and from many more, not only that uniformity of stanza is not to be strictly insisted upon when one is employing rhymes, but also that translators should search more diligently than they appear to do for the rhyme suggestions implicit in so many Horatian stanzas.

Upon other points it is easier to agree with Conington. For most of the odes the iambic movement natural to English is preferable, as Milton may be held to have perceived. He abandoned rhyme in his celebrated version of the "Quis multa gracilis" (i., v.), and hence he had an excellent opportunity to indulge in experiments in so-called logaœdic verse. But he clung to the iambic movement, and the fact is significant, although not to be pressed, since he gave us no other rendering of an entire ode. Here too, however, I must plead for a careful study of each ode by the would-be translator, for there seem to be cases in which it would be almost disastrous to attempt a version in iambics. Such a case is presented by the beautiful "Diffugere nives" (iv., vii.). The iambic renderings of Professor Conington and Sir Theodore Martin seem to stray far from the original movement—as far as the former's "'No 'scaping death' proclaims the year" does from the diction of Horace or of any other good poet. It is true that English dactyls are dangerous things, especially in translations, where the padding or packing which is natural to the measure when employed in English, is increased by the padding inevitably introduced into a translation from a synthetic into an analytic language. Yet the dactylic movement of the First Archilochian, in which the "Diffugere nives" is written, is hardly without great loss to be represented by any use of English iambics. It presents more difficulty than the introduction of something resembling the movement of dactylic hexameters proper into our blank verse.

When the translator makes up his mind to attempt a close approximation to the Horatian meter, it would seem that he should eschew the use of rhyme as likely to operate against that effect of likeness to the original which he is striving to secure. But, since the use of rhyme in lyric poetry appears, as Conington held, to be essential at present if the English version is to be acceptable as poetry, this close approximation can be desirable in a few special cases only. It will not do to dogmatize on such matters, but it may be safely said that no poet, not even Milton or Whitman, has yet accustomed the English or the American ear to the use of rhymeless verse in lyrical poetry. Here and there a successful rhymeless lyric, such as Collins's "Ode to Evening" and Tennyson's "Alcaics" on Milton, shows us that rhymeless stanzas may occasionally be used for lyric purposes with good effect; but thus far those translators of Horace who have made a practice of eschewing rhyme have failed, as a rule, like the first Lord Lytton,[1] to give us versions that

[1] Just as I am revising these comments, the two volumes of the Earl of Lytton's admirable biography of his grandfather find themselves on my table. As was to be expected, they contain several interesting references to Horace. "He is the model for popular lyrics, and certainly the greatest lyrist extant." Again—"Observe

charm. Yet charm is what the translator of Horace should chiefly endeavor to convey.

I am still more confident that Conington was right when he insisted that the English rendering should be confined "within the same number of lines as the Latin." He was surely right when he taxed Sir Theodore Martin, who so frequently violated this rule, with an exuberance that is totally at variance with the severity of the classics. Such exuberance is almost certain to result if the translator abandon the strict number of the lines into which the Roman poet compressed his thought. It results, too, from the use of stanzas of over four verses each. There is no other rule of translating that will so effectively insure a successful retention of the diction of the original as this of the line for line rendering, whenever such rendering is possible. And that the diction and the thought of the poet should be more closely followed than is usually the case, admits of no manner of doubt. We have already seen that a close scrutiny of the Latin will often suggest an almost literal rendering of the thought and diction. Such a rendering is more desired by the reader who is familiar with Horace than by the reader who is not, but it will be both pleasing and serviceable to the latter, if the quality of literalness be not too slavishly obtained. Metrical considerations and general smoothness ought, as a matter of course, to weigh with every translator, but surely they ought not to outweigh accurate rendering of diction and thought, especially the diction and thought of a poet so felicitous as Horace in his phrasing, and so just and happy in his observation of life.

In this connection I am not sure but that Conington went

how wonderfully he compresses and studies terseness, as if afraid to bore an impatient, idle audience; secondly, when he selects his picture, how it stands out—Cleopatra's flight, the speech of Regulus, the vision of Hades in the ode on his escape from the tree, &c."

too far when he recommended the Horatian translator to hold by the diction of our own Augustan period. That the Age of Pope corresponds in many ways with that of Horace is true enough, and the student of the poetry of the eighteenth century who cares at all for the poets he studies is almost sure to be an admirer of the "Roman bard" whom Pope imitated. But the diction of Horace does not strike one as stilted, while that of Pope often does; and for a translator of our own days to employ a diction that seems in any way stilted is fatal not merely to the popularity and hence to the present effectiveness of his work, but also, in all probability, to its intrinsic value. There is a good deal of the commonplace also in the poetry produced in the eighteenth century; but commonplace the translator of Horace can least afford to be. Horace himself may approach dangerously near the commonplace, yet he seems always to miss it by a dexterous and graceful turn. The translator, running after, will miss this turn sufficiently often, as it is; he cannot, therefore, afford to steep himself in a literature that has a tendency to the commonplace. But just as little can he afford to steep himself in the Romantic Poets from Shelley to Swinburne. A translation, whether from the Greek or the Latin, imbibing the luxuriance of imagination and phrasing characteristic of these modern poets, may satisfy a reader still in his intellectual teens, but the reader who makes use of a translation of Horace is likely to have passed out of that period of immaturity. It may be heretical, but I fancy that the translator of Horace who steeps himself in Keats or Tennyson, will be even less likely to give us the ideal rendering than the translator who steeps himself in Pope. Luxuriance and elegance may at times be more displeasing than excessive polish and point.

To mention the eighteenth century is to bring up the thought of Horatian paraphrases. A successful paraphrase is sometimes better as poetry than a good poetical translation, and it not infrequently conveys a juster idea of the spirit of Horace. It is almost needless to praise the work in this kind of Mr. Austin Dobson and of the late Eugene Field. But a paraphrase, however good, can never be entirely satisfying either to the reader that knows Horace or to the reader that desires to know him. Nor can a prose version be thoroughly satisfactory. What is wanted is not merely the drift of the poet's thought, but, as near as may be, what he actually sang. The paraphrase may sing, and the prose version may give us the thought in nearly equivalent words, which may carry along with them not a little of the poet's feeling; but neither answers all our requirements as well as a good rendering in verse may do—such a rendering, for example, as that which the late Goldwin Smith gave of the " Cœlo tonantem " (iii., v.)—yet there is surely room for all these forms of approach to a poet who is, paradoxically enough, at one and the same time, the most approachable and the most unapproachable of writers.

But one could write forever upon the topic of poetical translation in general, and of the translation of Horace's odes in particular. It is a subject about which people will differ to the end of time; a subject the principles of which will never be thoroughly exemplified in practice. Still, it always seems to fascinate those who discuss it, and they have a way of hoping that what they have said about it will not be without value to those who want to read about it. " Hope springs eternal in the human breast," said the poet who also wrote of his great master lines that have not been surpassed in their kind:—

> " Horace still charms with graceful negligence,
> And without method talks us into sense,
> Will like a friend familiarly convey,
> The truest notions in the easiest way."

DATE DUE